D1261363

LBJ and the Presidential Management of Foreign Relations

An Administrative History of the Johnson Presidency Series

EMMETTE S. REDFORD AND JAMES E. ANDERSON, EDITORS

LBJ and the Presidential Management of Foreign Relations

PAUL Y. HAMMOND

Foreword by
Emmette S. Redford and James E. Anderson

University of Texas Press   Austin

Requests for permission to reproduce material from this work
should be sent to Permissions, University of Texas Press, Box 7819,
Austin, TX 78713-7819.

∞ The paper used in this publication meets the minimum requirements of American National Standard for Information Sciences—
Permanence of Paper for Printed Library Materials, ANSI Z39.48–1984.

Library of Congress Cataloging-in-Publication Data

Hammond, Paul Y.
    LBJ and the presidential management of foreign relations / by
Paul Y. Hammond.—1st ed.
        p.   cm.—(An Administrative history of the Johnson
presidency series)
    Includes blibliographical references and index.
    ISBN 0-292-76536-3
        1. Johnson, Lyndon B. (Lyndon Baines), 1908–1973.   2. United
States—Foreign relations—1963–1969.   I. Title.   II. Series:
Administrative history of the Johnson presidency.
E847.2.H36   1992
973.923'092—dc20   92-13219
                                                          CIP

For Julia Claire Hammond and her cousins

Contents

Foreword

THIS IS THE NINTH in a series of publications designed to comprise an administrative history of the Johnson presidency. The series concentrates attention on the processes and problems in presidential management of the executive branch during the Johnson years.

Some of the studies in the series deal with the infrastructure of presidential management—the structures, personnel, and operating arrangements for executive decision making and policy administration. Included are Emmette S. Redford and Marlan Blissett, *Organizing the Executive Branch: The Johnson Presidency* (University of Chicago Press, 1981); Richard L. Schott and Dagmar Hamilton, *People, Positions, and Power: The Political Appointments of Lyndon B. Johnson* (University of Chicago Press, 1983); Emmette S. Redford and Richard E. McCulley, *White House Operations: The Johnson Presidency* (University of Texas Press, 1986); and David M. Welborn and Jesse Burkhead, *Intergovernmental Relations in the American Administrative State: The Johnson Presidency* (University of Texas Press, 1989). Another study examines the exercise of the executive function in the appointment of judges: Neil D. McFeeley, *Appointment of Judges: The Johnson Presidency* (University of Texas Press, 1987).

Other volumes in the series deal with the presidential management of policymaking and implementation processes in particular policy areas. In addition to the book on foreign policy, these include W. Henry Lambright, *Presidential Management of Science and Technology: The Johnson Presidency* (University of Texas Press, 1985); James E. Anderson and Jared E. Hazelton, *Managing Macroeconomic Policy: The Johnson Presidency* (University of Texas Press, 1986); and Harvey C. Mansfield, Sr., *Illustrations of Presidential Management: Johnson's Cost Reduction and Tax Increase Campaigns* (Lyndon B. Johnson School of Public Affairs, 1988).

Yet other studies are underway that focus on presidential management of the implementation of civil rights legislation, presidential management of the Vietnam War, and White House roles in economic regulation.

This series of studies has been financed by a grant from the National Endowment for the Humanities, with additional aid from the Lyndon Baines Johnson Foundation, the Hoblitzelle Foundation, and the Lyndon B. Johnson School of Public Affairs of the University of Texas at Austin.

The findings and conclusions in the various works in this series do not necessarily represent the view of any donor.

EMMETTE S. REDFORD
PROJECT DIRECTOR

JAMES E. ANDERSON
DEPUTY DIRECTOR

PREFACE. Where We Are Going: Presidential Management and the External Presidency

THIS BOOK IS ABOUT Lyndon B. Johnson's role as president in handling foreign policy. It views that role primarily in terms of his contacts with other U.S. officials through whom he worked and the processes he employed to decide upon policy and see through its implementation. It deals in this particular sense with the *presidential administration* of foreign relations, but it is not a conventional, descriptive administrative study. It is an exploratory venture. The ideas that it applies are unfinished. This brief chapter explains why and tells the reader what to expect.

It is now more than thirty years since Richard Neustadt broke new ground in his book *Presidential Power: The Politics of Leadership*.[1] Neustadt showed us that the presidency must be understood in terms of the wholeness of the president's role, the combination of constitutional and political powers and functions that the American presidency encompasses, a wholeness that is much greater than the sum of its parts.[2]

The implications of Neustadt's explanation of presidential leadership and action for the internal workings of the American political system are profound. They have influenced a generation of scholarship on the presidency and directly influenced at least one president. Their effect has been to enhance the general quality of scholarship on the presidency. This has been the case primarily with respect to the *internal* presidency. By this I mean the president's struggle to be master of the executive branch with the Congress and the public. Neustadt's thesis about presidential leadership and power has been less well understood and less applied with respect to American foreign relations and policy, when the president attends to the formation and implementation of policies dealing with foreign governments and other organizations external to the United States, which is the subject of this book. This neglect of the *external* presidency can be laid in part to the discrediting of the external presidency as a result of Lyndon Johnson's handling of Vietnam, but it also reflects difficulties with the employment of contemporary ideas about democratic leadership.

Students of the internal presidency have been able to proceed on the basis of a more widely accepted set of political values than students who address the external presidency. Nowhere is this problem better illustrated than with respect to Neustadt's own work. He himself expanded the foreign relations aspect of his own interests in *Alliance Politics*, an influential little volume which he published in 1970, but in doing so he did little to advance his earlier pioneering inquiry into presidential power and leadership. He virtually ignored the issue of the president's unique situation, which he had developed in *Presidential Power*. He pursued, instead, a less controversial theme which he had employed in that book—that of pluralistic government, a grouping of interests that contend and cooperate with one another. In this later work he attended to the impediments to cooperation at the expense of one of the central themes of *Presidential Power*, the implications of contention and conflict. Neustadt published a revised edition of *Presidential Power* in 1980 and another in 1990 which included new material. Neither broke new ground to explore the external presidency.[3]

Alliance Politics is a cautionary tale about the difficulties of bilateral cooperation between the United Kingdom and the United States. Its message comes through with increasing force as Neustadt spreads before the reader the obstacles to Anglo-American understanding which he found at the interface between officials in "Whitehall" and the "White House" and beyond. It leads to Neustadt's final point, that managing relations with other governments is very difficult to get right, which he makes with a revealing personal reference.

The pluralist concept of politics and even of government is of a marketplace of competing interests that distribute power and other political valuables. It has been a serviceable and popular justification for *internal* politics in the United States, including the functioning of the presidency. It has served to reconcile presidential power and action to internal democratic ends and procedures. One way it has reconciled them has been to show that the president is less powerful than he appears to be, a thesis which Neustadt adopted and employed to great advantage. Pluralism has not been as popular or successful in reconciling with democratic norms the presidency's employment of presidential power and action in *external* relations, not at least as Presidents Johnson and Nixon exercised power externally in the sixties and early seventies.

In the period that Neustadt's work spans—from the mid-fifties to the late sixties—the president's conduct of foreign relations came under serious attack. Neustadt experienced that attack directly and personally. When *Presidential Power* was first being widely read, at the beginning of the sixties during the Kennedy administration, Neustadt was a professor at Columbia University. At that time, the reaction of his academic colleagues to his extraordinary access to President Kennedy, to the extent that they knew about it, was similar to their reaction to other academics with access to the president. It was mostly favorable because its consequences seemed largely favorable. The new status which academics had attained in Washington boosted the status of universities.

At the end of the sixties the situation had changed dramatically. American university faculties, in a widespread change in attitudes, had become alienated from the presidency. As a senior professor at the Kennedy School of Government at Harvard, Neustadt himself would have encountered suspicion and hostility on the Harvard campus toward faculty members or anyone else who had been involved with the Johnson White House or was involved with the new Nixon administration.

Neustadt's *Alliance Politics* reflects this change of mood about the presidency. In it he analyzed two historical episodes involving crises in Anglo-American relations in which the American president's role was central. The first involved Eisenhower. It was the crisis in Anglo-American relations precipitated by Britain's participation with France and Israel in the Suez War against Egypt in 1956. The second involved Kennedy. It was the crisis generated by the cancellation of the development of the American airborne missile, Skybolt, which the British were counting on to deliver their nuclear weapons. Neustadt described the Anglo-American alliance as an exceptionally close, tightly knit relationship between two governments and governing societies bound with strong networks of personal friendship. Despite close relations between these two political communities, indeed, arising out of them, he found in both crises intricate misperceptions, misunderstandings, and misassessments by officials in each government of officials in the other which, in turn, produced serious missteps in their cooperative dealings. In both cases, on both sides of the Atlantic, government officials took actions which harmed their friends on the other side unintentionally and harmed their common interests.

The Suez and Skybolt cases provided an excellent opportunity for Neustadt to examine his thesis about holistic presidential power and the the uniqueness of the president's role, a thesis which had immediately become influential when he introduced it eight years earlier. He might have used these cases to push on and apply his thesis to the nurturing and protection of presidential power in dealings with allies. He did not. He focused mainly on the impediments to cooperation between the two governments without special reference to presidential power.

Eisenhower's diplomacy during the Suez crisis could have provided a solid vehicle for examining presidential power. Eisenhower had been the main foil, or negative model, for Neustadt's development in the 1950s of his ideas about the necessity for presidential leadership which required the president to exploit the assets of his office in the competitive struggle of American politics. Eisenhower, in Neustadt's view at the time, had usually not understood this rule. Neustadt could have employed the Suez case to take himself back to his first judgments about Eisenhower and therefore to the roots of his thesis about presidential power. But he did not.

Writing more than a decade later, Neustadt was positive in his appraisal of Eisenhower's behavior in the Suez case. In some respects he even anticipates the new appreciation of Eisenhower's presidency which occurred in revisionist writings in the eighties. (These are discussed briefly in Chapters 6 and 7.) The structured, directive style which Eisenhower employed in dealing with his Secretary of State as well as with others in the Suez case, and which he employed in conjunction with presidential restraint, now appealed to Neustadt. They had not when he wrote *Presidential Politics* in the late fifties, nor did they in 1963, when he testified before Senator Henry M. Jackson's Subcommittee on National Security Staffing and Operations of the Senate Committee on Government Operations.[4]

The conduct of the British and French, in secretly planning, in cooperation with Israel, to attack Egypt in order to recover control over the Suez Canal, and then in attacking it without consulting the United States, was intended to force Eisenhower's hand. Yet both governments depended heavily on the United States economically and militarily. If Eisenhower had simply acquiesced in their attack once it was underway, Britain and France would be setting the terms of American support for them. If, as they evidently hoped, he would go further and actively cooperate with their attack, the United States would be vulnerable to other embarrassing, hand-forcing, faits accomplis. He would have encouraged them and other American allies and client states to draw, or try to draw, the United States into other ventures which it would not have approved in advance. What would the British and French do next in the knowledge that the United States could be induced to go along? What would other powers do if they learned from the Suez War the lesson that they, too, could trap Washington into doing what they could not persuade Washington beforehand to do?

It was an embarrassing moment for all concerned. The formalities of NATO cooperation depicted it as an association of sovereign equals, but they were not all equal. There were small powers like Belgium and Denmark and medium powers like Britain and France, and then there was a superpower, or hegemon, the United States. Sometimes the hegemon got out in front, as it had with the Marshall Plan or the defense of Korea, declaring its intention and challenging other states to come along. In the case of the Marshall Plan, it was Western Europe and the Soviet Union that the United States as the hegemonic power had challenged. In the Korean case, it was the U.N. If NATO members were equal, then the British and French could likewise act and challenge. Suez was in this respect a moment of truth. Eisenhower would not go along. Had he gone along, American hegemony would have been transformed from an order setter for the North Atlantic Alliance into a license for smaller powers to trap the United States into doing their business on their terms, from a source of order to a source of chaos. The implications for presidential power would have been commensurately profound.

These were the issues at stake when Eisenhower forced London and Paris to back down from their attack. To explore these issues when Neustadt examined the Suez crisis at the end of the sixties would have been to push on into external relations the inquiry which he had begun ten years earlier in the nurturing and protection of presidential power.

Did Eisenhower, in standing down the British and French, understand these stakes for American power and for his presidency? The answer is very important. It is also not obvious, and Neustadt did not attempt to provide it. It would have required examining the harder side of Anglo-American relations where national interests were in virtual conflict. Suez posed an issue of alliance discipline which was embarrassing to explain yet essential to deal with from the standpoint of American interests. It posed as well as has any single incident in the postwar era the question of how unique was presidential power in international affairs. The Neustadt of *Presidential Politics* would have penetrated this thicket in order to explore the president's role as political leader in the face of political interest rivalry and pressures from below to entrap him. Ten years later the Neustadt of *Alliance Politics* did not.

Although it was less powerful for this purpose, the Skybolt case could also have served as a convenient vehicle for inquiring about the external dimensions of presidential power. It could have served Neustadt himself particularly well in that pursuit because he had special, direct knowledge about presidential power in this case. Kennedy had embraced Neustadt's ideas about the presidency at the beginning of his administration, even recommending *Presidential Politics* to Oval Office visitors. On the basis of the book, he drew Neustadt into a singular role in the White House staff. Neustadt learned the Skybolt story on an assignment from the president. No case writer has had better sponsorship or access! Later, when Neustadt lectured and then wrote about Skybolt, he had an opportunity to inquire into how a president who shared his views about presidential power actually employed it.

Skybolt could have served an inquiry about the differences in interest between the president and his staff as they dealt with the British. For instance, Neustadt described how Kennedy came to recognize what his subordinates were all too slow to recognize (or denied), that there was a serious conflict with the British over Skybolt, which he took it upon himself to resolve. This was a good start on the subject of Anglo-American conflict over Skybolt—actual conflict, not simply misunderstandings. It could have been approached by inquiring about *intentional* conflictive behavior on both sides. Had Neustadt been interested in the harder side, in addition to his interest in the unintended obstacles to cooperation, he could have gone on to probe the extent of dissembling and deception at the Cabinet level and lower in both countries.

These very issues were raised by a report that had been published by Henry Brandon, a distinguished British journalist assigned to Washington, whom Neustadt knew well. Brandon had reported that a Royal Air Force Group Captain assigned as liaison to the Pentagon was thoroughly informed about McNamara's plans to cancel Skybolt and kept his contacts in Whitehall informed about them.[5] Brandon's claim, whether true or not, raises at least two questions. One is whether British officials in London feigned ignorance or incomprehension or misperception to hide their foreknowledge of the impending cancellation of Skybolt, and therefore proceeded in bad faith to make their claim for compensation with respect to it. The second question is, if so, who was in on the deception? In particular, was the prime minister, Harold Macmillan, whom Kennedy compensated so generously for the Skybolt cancellation, in on it?

To raise such a question is to conjecture about whether the Anglo-American relationship was not more competitive, more manipulative, more guileful than Neustadt depicts it to have been. That conjecture, if true, supports the suspicion that Macmillan played

Kennedy for a fool at the Nassau Conference, a thought that occurred to some of Kennedy's subordinates. That possibility would not be incompatible with Neustadt's conception of Anglo-American relations, but it would require a fuller description of it. To have dealt with this harder side of a close bilateral relationship would have enabled Neustadt to put into sharper focus the presidential role in terms comparable to central themes in *Presidential Politics* which give greater weight to conflict in politics.

One objective of this book is to place "alliance politics" in the context of presidential leadership and power politics. Chapter 3 deals with an "alliance politics" relationship with India during the Johnson administration, a relationship that might have been handled in that chapter much as Neustadt dealt with Anglo-American relations, particularly with reference to the Skybolt affair. But it is not. It is treated quite differently. In Chapter 3, while the parallel interests and ongoing dealings of the Indo–United States bilateral relationship are acknowledged, the roots of conflict in the relationship are given serious attention and the utility of Johnson's hard stand with the Indians receives extended attention.

Writing *Alliance Politics* was an occasion for Neustadt to reflect on what he had learned about presidential politics on assignment for Kennedy. It was also an opportunity for him to go back to historical information about Eisenhower and examine more fully presidential leadership in the conduct of foreign relations during the crisis caused by the Suez War in 1956, with particular attention to the protection and enhancement of presidential power. In both cases he chose not to. The Neustadt of *Alliance Politics* avoided the harder side of Anglo-American relations in order to take up a task which he was not uniquely qualified to perform, to apply to Anglo-American relations a pluralist model that minimized the difference between the president and his own staff, and minimized the significance of presidential leadership. Neustadt directed his attention chiefly to the level below the presidency, which enabled him to do this. It must be said that he employed great skill in presenting what he observed, that relations at that level between two close allies are like relations between great federal agencies in Washington.[6] The big difference was that he did not pursue the hard questions that he had dealt with at length in *Presidential Power*, such as how presidents generated and managed conflicts to achieve their own ends.

Neustadt's *Alliance Politics* has been one of the more influential studies of American foreign relations of recent decades. Noting what he chose *not* to do in it can scarcely detract from its much-deserved reputation. Noting as I have what he chose not to do serves to indicate what happened on a larger landscape to attitudes about presidential leadership during the decade of the sixties. By 1970, when Neustadt wrote *Alliance Politics*, he was not alone in demonstrating a loss of confidence and therefore of interest in presidential leadership. The attack on the "imperial presidency" was well underway.

For his part, as mentioned earlier, Neustadt, in ending *Alliance Politics*, explained his attachment to foreign policy pluralism to the neglect of the power and politics of the external presidency. His assignment from Kennedy had been to look into why the Skybolt affair had caused so much trouble between the British and the Americans. It had resulted in a written report to Kennedy. Neustadt explains that when he sent it to Kennedy he also asked for an appointment with the president so that he could extend his report by conveying lessons learned, which he preferred not to write down, about the way the machinery of the U.S. government worked in relationship to that of an ally. Kennedy agreed, but the meeting never took place because of his death. "One of the things" Neustadt considered raising with Kennedy while he anticipated the meeting "lay outside of my assignment, to say nothing of my field of observation: I considered asking whether, in the light of our machine's performance on a British problem, he conceived that it could cope with South Vietnam's." Writing in 1970, Neustadt did not claim that he would have certainly raised it. "But it was a good question, better than I knew. It haunts me still."[7]

The present study was written during a period of returning acceptance of presidential power exercised in foreign relations. In practice, this trend is associated with Presidents Reagan and Bush. In Reagan's case it reflected his success as a popular politician and his sometimes surprising and not always wise or even constitutional exercise of presidential initiative in foreign affairs. In Bush's case it reflects his perceived success, or luck, in dealing with the Soviet Union and the Middle East. Serious reflection about the exercise of presidential power in foreign relations which credits its potential uses as well as its dangers has been notably scarce during the past decade. Two strands of scholarship have some potential for this purpose. One, in the field of international relations theory, deals with the issue of national power as it is manifest in the phenomenon of superpower leadership, specifically of American hegemony. This subject will be discussed in Chapter 7. The other deals with presidential power itself, in the person of President Eisenhower.

The revisionist literature on Eisenhower tells us that he was a better president than we thought. With respect to foreign relations, John Burke and Fred Greenstein explain that he was better because he took seriously the *structure* of the presidency, which is to say, the National Security Council and its elements in particular. He employed procedures which made use of this structural asset and which they claim enabled him to be more discriminating than some later presidents have been in choosing what to avoid and what to deal with as president and what to involve the nation in.[8]

The Eisenhower revisionists have identified but they have not examined diligently the central question of initiative-taking in foreign relations by the U.S. president as leader of the leading national power. That, I believe, is the challenge that Neustadt laid down for students of foreign relations, especially those students who are interested in the holistic presidency, which combines political leadership with management and administration. It is this challenge which this book seeks to clarify.

The most acute problem which this combination poses with respect to the presidency in foreign relations is in knowing with sufficient precision and reliability what the foreign or external effects of governmental action—and presidential action in particular—will be. We do not even know with any precision what attributes of presidential action promote what sorts of desirable outcomes in foreign relations. We know *something* about what kinds of presidential action promote what kinds of U.S. governmental outputs, although the lessons of Neustadt's *Alliance Politics* and related works on governmental processes strongly qualify our conclusions even about this matter, just as, with respect to internal policy, implementation is often full of surprises.[9] Reflecting this situation, the present study devotes most of its attention to examining presidential action (and inaction) in relationship to their consequences for foreign relations. Its major purpose is to develop explanations that link internal organizational processes with their external effects or consequences.

This book proceeds at two levels. Chapter 1 launches it as administrative history. On this level the goal is modest, to provide a brief general account of how the Johnson administration organized to make foreign policy and conduct foreign relations and to explore structural issues further in the particular cases that follow. Chapter 2 begins a more ambitious inquiry, to define the issues of the presidential control and management of foreign relations through the experience of the Johnson administration. It is on this second level that the issues of the president's political leadership and power are considered.

As administrative history, it must be said, no attempt has been made in this study to be comprehensively descriptive. Chapter 1 provides a brief description of personnel and structure. After that I turn to the main issues of description and explanation—the "how" and "why" of the Johnson administration's foreign policy process— by examining three subject areas. The first deals with foreign aid and relations with developing countries, which I address through a case study dealing with Johnson's handling of the Indian food crisis of 1965–1967. The second deals with U.S. military cooperation with Western Europe, which I address through a case study about the American proposal for a multilateral nuclear force for NATO, called the MLF. These may be considered case studies. They provide intensive descriptions of organizational processes at the level of presidential action. They then serve as the basis for generalizations and explanations which depend also on other information, mainly about Johnson's foreign policy. In this way, the study seeks to strengthen the empirical basis for theories about the presidential management of foreign policy in general and about Johnson's management of foreign policy in particular.

The third subject, which in certain respects is also treated as a case study, deals with Johnson's handling of American policy toward Vietnam. The subject itself may be regarded as much larger than the subjects covered by the other two cases, if size can in this respect be considered an objective fact. If so, the space devoted to it bears no relationship to its size. It is therefore even more conspicuously selective in what it deals with in order to achieve a descriptive intensity that can serve as the basis for confident observations. It focuses on Johnson's Vietnam decisions during the period from the presidential election of November 1964 through July 1965, ending with what amounted to a decision to commit the United States to a large-scale land war in Vietnam.

The reader should be aware of a progression in the employment of cases which occurs in this volume. Chapter 3 deals with the Indian case. The Indian case is composed of the most original historical work of the three case studies. To construct the Indian case I relied heavily on primary sources—documentation found primarily at the Johnson Library in Austin. This is not to say that I have been first in virgin territory. I have in fact made much use of previous work, particularly the excellent scholarship of James W. Bjorkland and of his mentors, Professors Lloyd I. Rudolph and Susanne H. Rudolph.

Chapters 4 and 5 deal with the MLF and Chapter 6 with Vietnam. I chose the MLF precisely because the territory was not virgin— because strong work, on which I knew I could rely, had already been done on it, mainly an excellent case study by John Steinbruner.[10] Here, the objective has been to push further in a quite different context the ideas developed in connection with the Indian case.

The "different context" is, of course, American relations with Western Europe, especially through the structure of NATO. In a sense, NATO is the parallel to Vietnam. Both are major components of Johnson's foreign policy. Viewed in these terms, the handling of the MLF proposal parallels with respect to Vietnam Johnson's November 1964 through July 1965 decisions. Both the MLF episode and these Vietnam decisions are revealing parts of larger foreign relations.

There is more observation and less description in the MLF chapters (4 and 5), and the ratio shifts further in the Vietnam chapter (Chapter 6). The Vietnam chapter takes advantage of the fine scholarship that is now available on this difficult subject.

The last chapter returns to broader themes about presidential power. Noting that some of the harsher judgments about Johnson's management of foreign relations have moderated over time, and arguing that some of the remaining criticisms deal with him as though he should have acted like a judicious clerk, I note that behind much criticism, and behind the moderating of it, stand differences about how presidents *should* behave, particularly differences which deal with how presidents use their power as president and the power of the United States as a superpower. In earlier chapters I have not hesitated to draw out observations about the exercise of presidential power. Here, by way of conclusion, is my final attempt to deal with the interrupted theme of Richard Neustadt's *Presidential Power*.

So much for these anticipations.

Acknowledgments

THIS BOOK IS ROOTED in the questions that I asked myself during the time it covers—the mid-1960s. The years since then until I began in earnest to write it may be regarded as a period of passive gestation and it should be no surprise, therefore, that I find it difficult to recall, identify, and acknowledge properly much of the assistance I received from colleagues during that period. One stands out, however: the late Wayne Wilcox. His observations about India's food policies came at a time when I was wrestling with reverse influence in U.S. military and economic assistance and held my attention to that phenomenon.

Three colleagues were directly helpful and supportive. James E. Anderson, I. M. Destler and Emmette Redford read the manuscript. They offered general guidance and saved me from specific errors. I did not always take their advice. When I did, the manuscript improved. Also, Lloyd I. and Susanne Hoeber Rudolph, at an early stage, generously shared the resources of their rich knowledge of Indian politics.

A long succession of research assistants helped me, sometimes with matters of substance and interpretation. They are: Cynthia Anasson-Waskiewicz, Michael Bryant, Cynthia H. Cohen, Hanna Freij, Theophilus Gemelus, Curt Gergely, Andrea Lewis, William Newmann, James Palmer, Dale Perry, Phillip Powlick, Gary W. Rogers, John Rogers, Vicki L. Rundquist, and Richard McCully. Enid J. Johnson, at the end, saw me through the final throes of word processing.

More generally, a supportive environment among my colleagues in the Graduate School of Public and International Affairs at the University of Pittsburgh helped me. But neither they nor the named persons above should share my responsibility for the shortcomings of this work. Those are mine alone.

PAUL Y. HAMMOND
PITTSBURGH, FEBRUARY, 1992

I. Johnson's Foreign Relations: Toward a Broader Inquiry

The Takeover Phase

LESS THAN TWO WEEKS after he succeeded the assassinated John F. Kennedy as president, Lyndon B. Johnson motored in late afternoon the four short blocks down New Hampshire Avenue from the White House to the Department of State, where he met with senior foreign affairs officials assembled in the large conference hall just off 23rd Street. He took with him Speaker of the House John W. McCormack, who was next in the line of succession to the presidency. McCormack was a frail seventy-one-year-old. In a warm, extemporaneous speech, Johnson described the Department of State as the "central force in the framing and execution" of foreign policy. "Often in the past," he said, the department's role "has been made difficult by misunderstanding and by intemperate criticism." He also spoke of his high respect for the Secretary of State, Dean Rusk. He told his audience that he recognized their need for the backing of their superior officers in order to do their jobs well and assured them that the "Department of State will get that kind of backing from me."[1]

While confining his remarks to generalities, Johnson conveyed a more pointed message to those who were aware of the way his predecessor had handled foreign relations. Kennedy, it is said, chose to be his own Secretary of State; that is why he picked Dean Rusk for that position. Johnson's remarks signaled that he intended to work through Rusk and leave foreign affairs to the State Department more than Kennedy had done.

New presidents often claim that they will cut the White House staff and rely more than did their predecessors on the statutory departments, primarily the Departments of State and Defense. That is what these departments ordinarily want to hear; it is also what the Congress wants to hear, for the White House staff is protected by executive privilege from congressional oversight.

In some but not all respects, Johnson followed his first reactions about how to run foreign affairs. He was scarcely innocent of the competitive world of the Washington bureaucracy. He had learned the game early in his years as a New Deal congressman from Texas.[2] He had built a network of contacts in the federal agencies, and he proved highly effective in exploiting it to the advantage of his Texas constituents. He refined this skill when he moved to the Senate in 1948. Perhaps this very experience, which was different from Kennedy's, at least in intensity and duration, had made him more respectful of organizational channels and of the resourcefulness of government officials. As president he was less inclined than Kennedy had been to skip echelons and deal with subordinates. He worked with agency heads and let them handle the subordinates. He also expected agency heads to cope with their own problems in the Congress,[3] despite his own well-recognized skills in that department. Johnson's style of managing foreign policy was shaped by these factors.

The Kennedy Legacy

Johnson was relatively cautious in his approach to Cabinet and sub-cabinet appointments.[4] In the foreign policy sector of the executive branch, as was common elsewhere, he decided to keep Kennedy's appointees in place and immediately came to depend heavily on McGeorge Bundy, Kennedy's National Security advisor, Robert S. McNamara, Kennedy's Secretary of Defense, and Rusk. This top team remained intact for thirty-nine months, when Bundy resigned to become president of the Ford Foundation. Walt Rostow, who succeeded him, stayed to the end. McNamara stayed until March 1968, to be succeeded by Clark Clifford, a prominent Washington lawyer, who had been a close advisor of Johnson's since the Truman administration. At the Treasury Department, Douglas Dillon remained as secretary until after the 1964 election. Henry Fowler, who replaced him, was also an old Washington friend of Johnson's.

At State, Johnson made two significant appointments at the sub-cabinet level, one early in his administration, one late. Within weeks of becoming president, Johnson had appointed Thomas Mann as Assistant Secretary of State for Inter-American Affairs. The press depicted Mann as a "Johnson man." He was not, in the usual political sense, but his appointment was important as a test case and a demonstration that Johnson meant to shape the loyalty of the Cabinet and subcabinet to his administration. Mann was a Texan, but not a crony from Texas. Like Johnson, he was skeptical about Kennedy's program for Latin America, the Alliance for Progress. He was a career foreign service officer who had served in the Eisenhower administration as an assistant secretary.

Mann's appointment enabled Johnson to set his stamp on both the substance of foreign policy and the method of administering it in a region where the Kennedy administration's own stamp was particularly conspicuous and different. Johnson would be cautious about trusting his own judgment and imposing his own views in the prime areas of foreign relations: Europe, national security, and monetary affairs. Relations with the less developed countries (LDCs), particularly with reference to matters of economic and political development, were another matter. Mann's appointment was the first indication of Johnson's confidence in dealing with the developing regions.

Kennedy had brought to office with him a large group of talented "in-and-outers" with interests in foreign relations and with varied experience. A disproportionate number of them had directed their attention to Latin America. They had generated the Alliance for Progress, which was an ambitious program for political and economic reform for that region. Despite Kennedy's conspicuous support of it, the Alliance was much troubled by late 1963. The main premise of the Alliance was that, with a modest or perhaps generous amount of U.S. development aid, accompanied by a considerable amount of political promotion, Latin American oligarchies would share their power and privileges with others in the expectation that orderly political change and economic prosperity would result. By Kennedy's death it was clear that the level of U.S. development aid would be modest and that Latin American regimes were doing little or nothing to fulfill their end of the bargain. Their political and economic elites remained as resistant to change as ever.

The Alliance for Progress was also in trouble in the way it was run in Washington. At the time of Kennedy's death, responsibility for Latin American policy was divided among three officials. One was the Assistant Secretary of State for Inter-American Affairs, Edwin M. Martin, who was the most obvious line official to carry that responsibility. The second was Richard Goodwin, a Kennedy speech writer and presidential assistant whose access to the president undercut the assistant secretary's authority. The third was Theodore Moscoso, the deputy director of the Agency for International Development (AID), who also had direct access to Kennedy. In addition, several White House staff members, including the historian Arthur Schlesinger, Jr., and an outside advisor, Adolph A. Berle, who had pioneered a similar program for Latin America in the 1930s, dealt directly with Kennedy on Latin American affairs.

Johnson appointed Mann both regional assistant secretary and regional deputy director at AID. In doing so, he expected Mann to end this chaos. He also expected him to set a different course for regional policy. Johnson was generally more optimistic about economic and political development. His enthusiasm for the Mekong Delta plan for Vietnam, and for Ayub Khan's successful economic programs in Pakistan after 1958, indicates this optimism. It was not the general idea that economic development drives political development which aroused his skepticism, but the particular application of this tenet in Latin America. In turning to Mann, he was turning to more reliance on the private sector—on "trade not aid," to recall an aphorism that summarized this shift in the Eisenhower administration, when Mann had formed his views on the subject. By turning to Mann, above all, Johnson had set his stamp on Latin American policy, tested Rusk's willingness to accept this shift (Rusk passed the test), and tidied up an administrative mess that Kennedy had left him.

Mann's appointment was Johnson's early significant subcabinet appointment. His appointment of Nicholas deB. Katzenbach as Under Secretary of State in October 1966 was his later one. Mann was a professional foreign service officer whose skepticism about the Alliance and conservative views about Latin American development matched Johnson's. Katzenbach was an equivalent appointment at the administrative level in the Department of State.

Katzenbach's career in the federal government and in the Johnson administration began in the Justice Department, where he was closely associated with Bobby Kennedy. After watching him carefully, Johnson appointed him Attorney General in January 1965. Twenty-one months later he moved Katzenbach to the Department of State to replace George Ball as under secretary. Katzenbach had been educated at Exeter, Princeton, Oxford, and the Yale Law School. Placing him in the chief administrative post in the Department of State was much like picking Mann for the regional assistant secretary post. Johnson chose him because his general credentials could scarcely be challenged by the Eastern Establishment, to whom Johnson deferred on the core foreign policies. Yet Katzenbach was a newcomer to foreign affairs—Johnson's newcomer.

State and Defense Compared

The State and Defense Department teams which Johnson inherited from Kennedy were wholly different from one another. At State, Rusk had not picked his own team. In fact, Kennedy picked Rusk only after choosing Under Secretary Chester Bowles, U.N. Ambassador Adlai Stevenson, and Assistant Secretary for African Affairs G. Mennan Williams.[5] Teamwork problems arose immediately in State, requiring a painful purge in November 1961, and they continued, to Kennedy's evident puzzlement. Charles E. Bohlen, the Soviet expert, reports Kennedy's reaction at the beginning of the Cuban missile crisis: "He seemed to be irritated that the State Department had not come up with the answers to questions he had asked about Cuba and the missile crisis. 'Chip,' he exploded, 'what is wrong with that God-damned department of yours? I never can get a quick answer no matter what question I put to them.' "

Bohlen gave him a conventional answer, and then added: "In regard to the department as a whole, the fault is yours." At Defense, McNamara, before agreeing to become secretary, drew a clear commitment from Kennedy that he would be able to name his own subordinates.[6] Moreover, McNamara had quickly proved to be extraordinarily effective, and Kennedy was as a result content to deal with the Defense Department, including the Joint Chiefs of Staff, largely through him. In this respect there could scarcely have been a starker contrast with the Department of State.

The small but influential International Security Affairs office (ISA) in OSD (the Office of the Secretary of Defense) was headed at first by Paul Nitze, and later by John T. McNaughton. It had none of the depth in staff expertise found in the regional office of the Department of State. In one respect, however, this proved to be an advantage. ISA could be more responsive than State because it was a small, single team. Kennedy and his White House staff found State guidance unresponsive or, more often, hopelessly waffled.[7] Both maladies could be attributed routinely to the effects of clearing policy through a large, complex bureaucratic apparatus, whether or not its political managers were a coherent team. Defense had the advantage in size, team coherence, and latitude of decision—at least while foreign policy issues did not endanger the core interests of the armed services and arouse them to demand more voice in OSD's foreign policy positions. It was Vietnam which eventually changed this situation, but meanwhile, ISA's reputation for responsiveness had become firmly fixed by the time of Kennedy's death.

Rusk at State

Rusk had been handicapped in dealing with Kennedy by his style of presiding over the Department of State. Kennedy, in dealing with State, was an irreverent outsider, at first friendly and demanding, but increasingly impatient. Rusk acted like a friendly insider, respectful of the professionals, and supportive of them. He held a firmly fixed view, which clashed with Kennedy's, about how the Secretary of State should deal with the president. He had gained experience while serving under George Marshall and Dean Acheson during the Truman administration. In dealing with the Department of State, Kennedy was inclined to skip echelons and to work around the secretary. He intended to be, and in a sense was, his own Secretary of State. His behavior evidently reflected also a degree of disappointment in Rusk. Rusk had told Kennedy that he could not stay longer than four years.[8]

This led to the rumor—the sort of rumor that has its own reality—that Kennedy would replace Rusk after the 1964 election. Johnson trusted Rusk. This situation remained largely unaltered throughout Johnson's presidency. Both were Southerners from poor families, and both virtually the same age. (Johnson was fifty-six in 1964, Rusk, fifty-five.) Rusk had lost ground with Kennedy over his strong belief that the Secretary of State should advise the president in private; Kennedy preferred to watch his advisors argue out an issue among themselves. He accorded Rusk no special status as Secretary of State. Yet Rusk tried to claim it and the result was an impasse. He would often sit "Buddha-like," sometimes barely containing his irritation at what he saw as the intervention of amateurs in the business of the Department of State.[9] He was saving his own advice for airing in private sessions with the president. Patently, his operating style fit into Johnson's White House better than it did into Kennedy's. Johnson preferred policy discussions to be more managed than Kennedy did. Meetings with the president were for when the discussion was over, to record the prevailing view, much as a Senate vote recorded the votes that he had already counted.

The National Security Council Staff

Presidents are free to organize the White House staff as they choose.[10] A common pattern for handling external affairs is to appoint a Special Assistant for National Security Affairs (or some variant on that title) and assign external matters and the necessary staff to him or her. This pattern originated as an arrangement for providing supporting staff for the National Security Council (NSC), which is a supercabinet, or special subcommittee of the Cabinet, and the staff of the special assistant has usually been called the NSC staff, or more recently, simply (and quite incorrectly) the NSC. Under Johnson, the NSC staff remained small, even counting co-opted Department of State officers like Henry Owen, who did not show on the White House books. From time to time, other members of the Johnson staff got into foreign policy matters, particularly (but not always) when they cut across domestic politics; but the division of labor was distinct and its application remained relatively uncontested.[11]

Kennedy had deliberately reduced the role of the NSC as a Cabinet committee. Eisenhower had built two structures that Kennedy "rubbed out," first, the Operations Coordination Board (OCB), which was designed to monitor the implementation of NSC-based presidential decisions. The more important Planning Board, a replica of the NSC composed of second-level departmental representatives (under secretaries or assistant secretaries) which was the main working committee for the NSC, Kennedy allowed to wither. One effect of this change increased the weight of the NSC staff as a presidential tool. Johnson made greater use of NSC meetings themselves than had Kennedy, but he did not rebuild the working committee structure. Cabinet meetings, as Richard Fenno demonstrated, are not a very effective forum for providing a president with information and advice from the principal officers of his administration.[12] The same factors affect the NSC: its members would prefer to deal with him one-on-one in matters of any importance to them. Kennedy virtually wrote it off for that reason. Eisenhower's critics saw him use the NSC out of a naive faith in formal staffing processes. Fred Greenstein argues that he employed it skillfully, exploiting the considerable uses of the formal organization and reducing the drawbacks by backing up the formal process with informal procedures—primarily, an Oval Office caucus—to insure the utility of NSC formalities.[13]

If Eisenhower's military service had taught him how to shape the use of formal organizations to his own purposes, Johnson's service in the Senate—particularly the Senate lobbies—taught him parallel skills. He employed the NSC in at least three ways that paralleled Eisenhower's use of it. One was to explore issues well ahead of any pressure for an immediate policy decision.[14] Eisenhower's equivalent use of it was in discussions about planning and general policy documents, discussions and documents that his critics considered of little or no value.[15] A second was simply to brief its members, not consult them. Accounts of Eisenhower's NSC meetings clearly indicate that this was sometimes their function.[16] A third was a legitimizing function, to record the (preferably unanimous) agreement of his advisors to a course of action upon which he had decided. Eisenhower's equivalent use was to conduct a discussion in the NSC that would proceed toward a conclusion already agreed upon in the Oval Office. There were differences, of course. Johnson was somewhat less comfortable with divergent views expressed in the large, formal NSC meetings than was Eisenhower and less inclined to be seen to make a decision on the spot. Both wanted to control the outcome. Eisenhower's personal style in accomplishing control left him open to the charge that he relied too much on administrative formalities where political, or at least high policy, issues were involved. Johnson's left him open to the charge that he was overly manipulative, that his advisory process was a sham. This impression about Johnson and his ways, undoubtedly in part true, became a special problem when his advisory process became the subject of intensive critical examination, as indeed it still is, due largely to the failure of Johnson's Vietnam policy. But "sham" exaggerates the uniqueness as well as the artifice of Johnson's NSC advisory deliberations.

Johnson's administrative style reflected his years in the House and Senate, particularly his experience in the Senate leadership. In the Congress, he was used to dealing with large volumes of paper flow. He adapted quickly to a similar feature of the presidency. In the Congress he also concerned himself with much detail about legislation and constituency interests. He was fascinated by detail, good at absorbing it, and skillful in employing it for his own purposes. In the White House he remained a detail man,[17] but his penchant for detail had quite different implications there, as we shall see. In the case of the Indian grain shortage, which is covered in Chapter 3, his detailed knowledge about the status of American grain shipments to India and of the distribution of grain within India bolstered his resolve to stick to his policy of limiting grain shipments against pressures to ship more grain that came from both inside and outside his government. In Vietnam, very likely it contributed to his deep involvement with military operations, an inclination he could not have indulged in the Senate or House with the same consequences. It may in part account for his decision to send troops into the Dominican Republic in 1964.[18]

Johnson, while more inclined than Kennedy to emulate Eisenhower in the way he handled national security matters, made less use of the NSC than Eisenhower had. Several explanations for this fact can be advanced. One, already mentioned, was his fascination with detail, which sometimes led him to ignore or elude knowledgeable advice. A second had to do with his skills in handling the bureaucracy. He was extraordinarily good in obtaining information through normal channels and in controlling his subordinates, and he made good use of these talents. He was less conspicuous than Kennedy in employing tactics to get information from extraordinary sources of information in order to avoid capture by his subordinates because of these very talents. It is an unresolved question whether he was more of a captive of his staff than was Kennedy, but no doubt he appeared to be more of a captive than Kennedy did when the two were judged by the same procedural standards.

"Johnson certainly downgraded the NSC as an advisory body," David C. Humphrey has written, "mainly for reasons that have motivated other presidents to do the same."[19] He used a variety of other means to seek advice. In the Senate he had sought out notables whom he trusted, and he extended this habit in the White House. There were Washingtonians like Clark Clifford, Dean Acheson, and Abe Fortas whom he saw regularly, and his reach went well beyond Washington. For instance, his staff had standing instructions that the president would see the English writer Barbara Ward whenever she was in town. He saw congressmen and senators alone, and in groups, and more often telephoned them and took calls from them. Johnson employed the telephone aggressively to extend his access to people outside the White House and outside Washington.

In early February 1964, the so-called Tuesday lunches began when Johnson met privately with Rusk, McNamara, and Bundy at the White House. Over the nearly five years that followed, the Tuesday lunch would meet more than twice the seventy-five times the NSC met.[20] During the first year, it was discontinued for a few months during and after the presidential election; shorter recesses occurred when Johnson was in Texas and Congress was not in session. For Johnson, it was similar to the Tuesday luncheon meetings of the Senate Democratic Policy Committee and sometimes followed the rhythms of the Senate. It remained small. During the first years the foursome were the core, with others invited with Johnson's specific approval for specific purposes. Bill Moyers (later, George Christian), the White House press officer, became a regular member in 1966. In 1967 the director of Central Intelligence, Richard Helms, and the chairman of the Joint Chiefs of Staff, General Earle Wheeler, began to attend regularly. Except for brief periods when Joseph Califano or Tom Johnson sat in to take notes, Bundy (later, Rostow) did the notetaking.

The Tuesday lunch was deceptively informal. The NSC and the Cabinet, with all their staffing formalities, provided the many officials who were uninvited the opportunity to prepare staff papers and the impression (sometimes illusory) that their views had been "heard." A properly staffed Cabinet-level meeting has an agenda, which is circulated to participants in advance so that they can come prepared to the meeting. It also has a follow-up staffing procedure that informs at least the immediate subordinates of members present about what happened. The Tuesday lunch gave the impression of no agenda and no procedure for follow-up. In fact, it operated with a frugal support system: There was an agenda, approved by Johnson, and the National Security advisor (Bundy, later Rostow) took notes. The notes were held closely and most of the follow-up was oral. Much care for security evidently paid off. Rostow claimed no knowledge of any leaks.[21] As might be expected, participants were more inclined to like it and senior officials who were excluded from its small circle were not. William P. Bundy, who served at the beginning of the Johnson administration as Assistant Secretary of Defense for International Security Affairs and later as Assistant Secretary of State for East Asian and Pacific Affairs, was one of the latter. He considered the Tuesday lunch "an abomination . . . because it was *so* unstructured, so without an opportunity to know what might be discussed. . . . There was no preparation. And there was almost no read-out."[22]

After the Soviet Union's coup in launching the first space satellite, *Sputnik*, in 1956 made American foreign policy publics skeptical about his military space program, Eisenhower was to some extent protected by his conspicuous reliance upon NSC formalities from appearing to be isolated and unaware. At least within the foreign policy agencies, the prevailing view was that the system did not cut them off from the president. As alienation over Johnson's Vietnam policies grew inside and outside the government, Johnson's use of the Tuesday lunch as the president's primary working committee for foreign policy became the basis of claims that he was isolated, that he had cut himself off, that he had confined himself to a small group of men with similar views.[23] Rostow makes a persuasive but not overwhelming case that Johnson exposed himself to a variety of viewpoints, although *his own behavior* was a major source of criticism in this respect. More recent scholarship confirms this claim.[24] Johnson's problem was not literal isolation from other viewpoints. This subject will be discussed further in Chapter 6. Johnson was no prisoner of his staff, but the Tuesday lunch failed to do what Eisenhower's NSC formalities did, demonstrate that he was not a prisoner of a narrow group of advisors.

Any National Security advisor must define his own role within boundaries set by the president. Bundy's role as National Security advisor to Kennedy, and then to Johnson, was, in Alexander George's useful term, that of a "custodian-manager."[25] He worked to see that the president learned the views of pertinent advisors and, when it was important, to generate and assure the presentation of other knowledgeable views.

In the present study, the way Bundy prepared the ground for Johnson's back-off from his commitment to the MLF is the clearest example of the initiative Bundy was prepared to take as custodian-manager to see that Johnson's advisory functions were performed for him. Six months before the back-off, he brought in Richard Neustadt in an effort to set up credible alternative advice on the MLF. No available evidence indicates that either Bundy or Neustadt had a clear view then what the alternative would be to the agenda of the MLF promoters. The two evidently agreed mainly that something should be done to protect Johnson's options. In early December, the payoff from this initiative came when Bundy presented Johnson with a serious alternative to his support for the MLF.

Bundy's behavior with respect to Vietnam is less clearly that of a "custodian-manager," as will be apparent in Chapter 6 when we discuss Johnson's decisions in late 1964 and up to mid-1965. The most obvious interpretation of Bundy's behavior, and the one most commonly taken, is that he became a hawk and pushed Johnson in the direction of escalation. An alternative interpretation is that Bundy and McNamara became decision-forcers, intent upon getting Johnson to act in the face of a deteriorating situation which he was ignoring while he concentrated on other matters—at first, on the election of 1964, then again on his domestic program. This interpretation squares with McNamara's and Bundy's later manifest opposition to Johnson's war policy. Getting the president to pay attention to problems in good time is the business of his advisors. They often play the role of action-forcers. There was something of the action-forcer in Bundy's role in the MLF decisions and the role of Bundy and later, Walt Rostow, his successor, in Johnson's dealings with the Indian grain shortage.

Rostow, in the way he handled the views of others, generated less confidence than Bundy had among Johnson's advisors that the president was exposed to a wide range of views. There was an objective basis for this difference. Rostow acted more persistently as a policy advocate when he spoke and wrote than did Bundy, and sometimes he cut persons or agencies out of the president's advisory process. There was also a subjective basis for it: the growing frustrations within the Johnson administration over Vietnam during the thirty-four months that Rostow served in the advisory post. He was, for his own part, more aware than were his critics of the range of Johnson's exposure to other sources—to the media, to outside advisors, to Johnson's night reading, which was voracious and burdensome.[26] Rostow's clearest departure from Bundy's custodial style was in failing to make the sort of elaborate effort to generate alternative channels of information and advice.

Johnson could be misled. But he was highly sensitive to the question of capture. For instance, in June 1967, during the Arab-Israeli Six Day War, he brought in Bundy, who was now president of the Ford Foundation, as a part-time advisor to head a committee on a long-term Middle East peace settlement, a maneuver that displaced Walt Rostow as Johnson's White House advisor on that subject. Evidently he considered Rostow a partisan on that subject and wanted to assure himself an independent viewpoint on it. Earlier, he had drawn all matters involving Israel that were being handled in the Middle East regional bureau of the State Department and the International Security Affairs division in the Pentagon (the Pentagon's "Little State Department") under close White House supervision. Bundy's committee was further to offset what Johnson considered to be the pro-Israel viewpoint of the Under Secretary of State, Eugene Rostow, who was Walt Rostow's brother. One should not, in noting this fact, attribute more to it than the immediate considerations governing it. There is no evidence that Johnson's confidence in either of the Rostow brothers had otherwise diminished. Both were exceptionally well qualified foreign policy officials who continued to enjoy his confidence. Johnson's use of the Bundy committee in this way was Johnson at his best and worst—prudent and manipulative.

In certain aspects it was easier for a National Security advisor to act as custodian-manager to Johnson than to Kennedy. Kennedy worked conspicuously at limiting (but not of course eliminating) the control that anyone exercised over his information channels. The rationale for this behavior applied the Schlesinger-Neustadt conception of competitive sources of information. According to Schlesinger, Kennedy "mentioned to me many times the account of Roosevelt's fluid administrative methods in the last section of [my book] *The Coming of the New Deal*."[27] His habit of permitting his immediate staff easy access to himself was as much driven by his personality as by this consideration, but it did serve Kennedy's purpose of escaping the fate of becoming a "prisoner in the White House." Kennedy's worry over this fate reflected his assessment of Eisenhower, an assessment formed before Kennedy read or sought the advice of Neustadt, who shared it. Fred Greenstein has made a powerful if slightly exaggerated case that Neustadt and Kennedy were wrong. But Greenstein does not show that Kennedy was wrong in adopting the Schlesinger-Neustadt model. On the contrary, by showing us an Eisenhower with highly developed skills at managing large-scale organizations in a deeply political environment, he demonstrates at best that his "hiding hand" model is appropriate to the highly experienced executive. By elimination, he leaves the Schlesinger-Neustadt model to amateur executives like Kennedy and Johnson. The fact that the Schlesinger-Neustadt model was built on Roosevelt, who is supposed to be the consummate political executive, gives only momentary challenge to this theory. Roosevelt, as a major innovator in the presidency, had fewer choices about his management style than, thanks to him, his successors have had.[28] Kennedy's avoidance of orderly staffing practices—for instance, as often reported, sometimes making direct contact with middle-level officials in the State Department and CIA (rarely in the Department of Defense)—complicated Bundy's task of providing him with balanced coverage of national security issues. Johnson followed more orderly procedures in dealing both with his White House staff and with federal agencies, a practice that placed Bundy and Rostow more advantageously as traffic managers of what Johnson read about foreign affairs than Bundy had exercised over Kennedy's reading. But they gained virtually no control over Johnson's telephoning. Moreover, such control as they exercised over Johnson's foreign policy traffic was partially offset by Johnson's more manipulative treatment of his advisors and assistants, including his National Security advisor.

The question about Johnson's handling of inside advice is complex. It is quite clear that his very considerable interpersonal skills included forms of social intimidation which he employed selectively but often. The "Johnson treatment" was better adapted to the lobbies of Congress, where he served before 1961, than to the meeting rooms of the White House. If we are to rank presidents on personal intimidation, Johnson stands apart among modern presidents. Although in this respect his personal style was conspicuous, its effect on the presidential advisory process can be exaggerated. No doubt in employing it Johnson shaped the advice that came to him. But that itself did not make him unique among presidents. The question here, as with other aspects of Johnson's advisory process, comes down mainly to what is normal, what is reasonable to expect.

The Setting: Johnson and the World

Johnson had been a close observer of the postwar development of U.S. foreign policy and, increasingly, a participant in it. He came to the presidency in 1963 after eleven years in the House of Representatives, twelve in the Senate, and more than two as vice president. In the Senate, he served on the Foreign Relations and Armed Services committees and beginning in 1953, as Senate majority leader. In the latter role he had cooperated with a Republican administration in defense and foreign relations. Throughout his Senate service, he was identified with America's postwar alliance system. He was not unique in his cooperation with the White House, even across party lines. But his years of cooperation may have predisposed him as president to be deferential about the main elements of the alliance system once he became president.

To be the agenda-setter equates with skills at political entrepreneurship. To a remarkable degree, Lyndon Johnson as president was a political entrepreneur in domestic politics. He looked for and seized opportunities for policy innovation. He looked for constituencies whose needs he could meet. In foreign relations, Johnson's behavior was quite different. He denied himself at the outset large programmatic initiatives that would win him the high ground. He preferred to concentrate on domestic policy initiatives. The foreign policy agenda was already set, with issues largely defined and solutions largely fashioned in many areas. This was particularly the case with respect to Europe.

The core of the American security system was NATO, the North Atlantic Treaty Organization, and the alliance with Western Europe. This European priority was deeply rooted. It reflected the same priority that had been laid down in the Army General Staff's Plan Orange in the thirties, which had provided the rationale for the major strategic military decisions of the United States in World War II. It is a principal tenet of strategy to fix on the central objective. Plan Orange stated that, beyond the United States, Western Europe's security came first. The same view prevailed when George C. Marshall, the senior military leader during World War II and, later, Secretary of State during a critical period, launched the Marshall Plan to save Western Europe from economic and political collapse.

For the United States, NATO institutionalized the Europe-first priority. It committed the United States to the defense of Western Europe not only in terms of a formal treaty obligation (i.e., the stated American commitment to come to the defense of Western Europe), but also by entangling American military forces with Europe's. American soldiers and airmen were stationed permanently in Western Europe; the senior military leader of NATO was an American officer; the largest single task that justified annual U.S. defense budgets was the defense of Western Europe. When Johnson became president, Western Europe was the center of gravity of the American security system and it remained so throughout his presidency. As had been the case during the Truman administration, however, a land war in Asia drew the largest portion of American military resources, draining American forces in Europe and depleting NATO reserves in the United States. In the middle of the Korean War agony, General Omar Bradley, the chairman of the Joint Chiefs of Staff, had characterized that war as "the wrong war at the wrong place, at the wrong time, and with the wrong enemy," a view that many Europeans supported. General Bradley's remark could have served to express frustrations in Europe and in Washington about the Vietnam War as well. The priority was Europe. Why then was the United States pinned down in Asia?

Two issues regarding Europe in particular were pending at the time Johnson became president, trade liberalization and the multilateral nuclear force. Congress had enacted a Trade Expansion Act in 1962 that gave the president powerful bargaining tools to negotiate the mutual reduction of trade barriers with Europe's Common Market. Negotiations were delayed when the French president, de Gaulle, vetoed Britain's membership in the Common Market. The so-called "Kennedy Round" negotiations actually began in 1964. They were completed in mid-1967, after a dramatic last-minute crisis, against a deadline imposed by the act. They achieved major results in trade liberalization.

The Kennedy Round was protracted and technical. It required a coordinated negotiating position for the whole of the U.S. government. In the scheme of things, no federal department was the lead agency. Kennedy had appointed and Johnson retained Christian A. Herter as his special representative for trade negotiations. Herter (later succeeded by William Roth) handled the coordination task. From the beginning, Bundy and his staff played a back-stopping role to the negotiations. The route to the president, whose continuing support in any case was critical, lay through Bundy. While the trade negotiations dragged on, more urgent trade-related monetary issues arose that posed similar problems of coordination. They were the province only in part of the Treasury Department. Usually they were also the province of State or the Commerce Department or Defense or the Office of Management and Budget (OMB), or all of them. The balance of payments, which had been favorable for years, had become adverse in the late fifties, draining gold from the United States. Continuing deficits contracted offshore dollar debts, and therefore the international supply of money, since the dollar was the principal reserve currency for the rest of the world. It was an awkward situation requiring several measures to remedy it. During Kennedy's administration, Bonn agreed to help by offsetting the drain on the dollar incurred by American forces in Germany. As the deficit persisted into the Johnson administration, these arrangements were adjusted and extended.

At the same time, negotiations proceeded with the Western Europeans to establish Special Drawing Rights (SDRs) as another form of international currency, and Johnson seized opportunities to protect American gold deposits and weaken their link to the dollar by establishing a "two-tier" system. These moves did not occur in isolation from other developments in Western Europe and in American policy. Secretary of Defense McNamara, fearing that worries about the dollar drain from American military forces in Europe would force the withdrawal of American troops, launched an aggressive arms sales campaign in Europe to earn dollars with American-manufactured military equipment. On all monetary and trade matters, President de Gaulle of France posed special problems. He complicated the Kennedy Round, obstructed the SDR negotiations, and actively spoiled American efforts to protect the gold standard. The Germans and British were more cooperative, but posed their own problems. The German economic miracle, after nearly twenty years of boom, had come to an end; Ludwig Erhard, the German Chancellor, lost an election in 1966 at the very time when Washington was seeking more concessions. The Labour Government in Great Britain, accepting the implications of slow economic growth, devalued the pound in 1967.

McNamara started his arms sales campaign by simply assigning the task to an energetic civil servant, Henry Kuss. These other moves all required cross-agency coordination based on Johnson's foreknowledge and acquiescence. Reflecting Bundy's style of "custodial-manager" staffing,[29] the practice developed of special interdepartmental committees or "command groups,"[30] usually at the assistant secretary level, linked to the president through Francis Bator, the Deputy Special Assistant for National Security Affairs, who had succeeded Kennedy's appointee, Carl Kaysen, in 1965, and was himself succeeded in 1967 by Edward Fried. The so-called Deming Group, named after Frederick L. Deming, the Under Secretary of the Treasury for Monetary Affairs, was one of these. It dealt with a series of monetary issues. Another one supported Ambassador Roth through the final weeks of the Kennedy Round.

The command groups for which Bator and Fried provided custodial support dealt with trade and monetary policy. They seem to have been regarded by most who were in a position to judge them as relatively successful. It is therefore instructive to note what they accomplished and how they worked.

The Eisenhower administration had attempted to gain popular support for a more liberal trade policy, and the effort backfired. For every voter who was aroused to support trade liberalization, more than one was aroused to oppose it. The Kennedy administration, knowing what had happened, could scarcely take trade reform into the black world of deniable government operations, but it could, and did, back away from a contest to popularize liberal trade policy which would pit it against popular protectionist forces.[31] The Johnson administration followed the same course. The command groups were well suited to this tactic because they handled coalition building within the government just about as discreetly as it could be handled—very close to the president, where he could keep his eye on it and lend his weight to it, but inconspicuous (sometimes the very existence of command groups was unknown beyond a narrow circle in the government). It also suited Johnson's personal style of closely held deliberative procedures.

The command groups reconciled bureaucratic interests by using two distinct techniques, White House co-optation and secrecy. They were run in such a way as to avoid their becoming forums in which representatives of agencies hammered out compromises among entrenched agency positions. Participants were there to do the president's business, not to "stand where they sat." Once a presidential position was formed, their job was to gain the necessary support within their own agency. With secrecy maintained, the selling job could be limited mainly to the top officials of the agencies involved, whose perspective, in the absence of contrary positions, could be presidential. There was no coalition-building; no painful and slow clearance procedures followed. Two facts clearly demonstrate that this remarkable description was fairly accurate. One was that the trade negotiator, William Roth, worked without benefit of a painfully forged set of negotiating instructions, the preparation of which could have served to arouse and involve a host of potential players. The other was that, when Congress passed a resolution intended to provide guidance for (and significantly constrain) Roth, he proceeded to ignore it successfully. Roth simply proceeded with his negotiations, closely monitored by Johnson, and in the end, Congress ratified the results, ignoring its own resolution. The procedures of the command groups were developed to avoid arousing factional inter-

ests inside and outside the government and to escape interdepartmental conflict. This is an important point; equally important is
that they largely succeeded.

The White House–based trade and monetary policy command
groups formulated policy and followed up on it. If these groups could
be compared with any other mechanism, it would be the Planning
Board, the subcabinet or working-level version of the NSC that anchored much of the work of the NSC during the Eisenhower administration, together with the defunct OCB of the Eisenhower administration. The most distinctive feature of these command groups was
their relationship to politics. They worked under Johnson's watchful
eye and active control. No doubt there were at least two reasons for
this, each political in a different way. First, trade policy negotiations—the Kennedy Round negotiations were completed in mid-
May 1967—affected all sorts of domestic economic interests in the
United States. Johnson took very seriously these interests and their
implications not only for trade legislation itself, but also for his own
legislative program. Second, these matters were handled in the White
House at the NSC staff or subcabinet level.[32] They usually did not
involve the Cabinet—indeed, they circumvented it. Without the
mechanism of the command groups, the president could expect to
be confronted by established departmental positions in the Cabinet,
something which he liked to avoid.

Command groups were a successful method of dealing with the
president's stakes in trade and monetary policy. The success provided an appealing model for other policy areas where the conditions for similar successes usually did not exist. The staffing procedure was designed not to array before Johnson a set of options, but
rather to provide him with a discreetly engineered position that no
agency would oppose, one that could be employed in international
negotiations with confidence that dissent would not occur, because
of the process by which it had been reached. These command groups
were in an important respect akin to what Eisenhower intended to
achieve by the formality of his NSC structure. Regular meetings of
the Planning Board and the NSC itself were intended to establish
working relationships that would enable these staffs to function
smoothly in a crisis. More significantly, they were intended to draw
participants into a presidential outlook, much like Johnson's command groups.

Johnson did not involve the Secretary of the Treasury regularly as
a participant in foreign policy discussions, as he did the Secretary of
Defense, a practice that was less worthy of notice in the sixties than
it came to be in the eighties. He did not come to rely on his National

Security advisor to a degree that undermined the authority of his Secretary of State as did Nixon[33] or Carter.[34]

Skeptical Deference in Foreign Economic and Military Policy toward Europe

Trade and monetary policy required dealing mainly with the Western European governments and, increasingly, Japan. Policy regarding the major developed economies engaged senior people in State, the monetary and international experts in Treasury, and the foreign trade experts at Commerce. Such matters as the balance of payments problems created by the presence of American forces in Europe also engaged the Secretary of Defense. Johnson was a close observer, a critical supervisor, of how these matters were handled. His approach to them can be appropriately called skeptically *deferential*, although at some risk of misunderstanding. He would monitor and instruct, challenge and test. His effect on the outcome in some cases was, it has been claimed,[35] considerable. There seems to be little reason to challenge this observation. But in the end, his choices were to reject or acquiesce, and he acquiesced.[36]

Johnson also followed this style with respect to major defense policies and to Europe. These two policy areas heavily overlapped. Extending the benefits of deterrence to NATO countries was a major function performed by U.S. strategic nuclear forces. The three armed services were likewise heavily engaged in meeting U.S. conventional force commitments to NATO. Major diplomatic issues involving Western Europe rarely failed to involve either trade or monetary factors of a military security dimension, or both.

The normalities of deferential presidential decision making with respect to Europe were well established by the time Johnson became president, particularly with respect to European security policy. There was no need to improvise the likes of command groups to deal with European security. On the State Department side, as was common, the senior officers of the department, career and political, were mainly involved with Europe. Johnson's predecessors—Kennedy, with exceptional self-confidence, and Eisenhower, with exceptional experience in Europe—could comfortably stand down this array of talent and conviction. Johnson, however, lacked the basis for a comparable attitude toward European diplomacy. Until his skepticism was aroused, he was deferential about European-related foreign policy.

Johnson felt more confident about his grasp of defense policy issues, but he also displayed a certain deference in this area as well. This posture was rooted in his legislative experience and the extraordinary leadership of Robert S. McNamara, the Secretary of Defense whom Johnson inherited from Kennedy at the height of his commanding domination in the Department of Defense. As already noted, Johnson kept McNamara in that office until his own final year in the presidency. Coming from an experienced legislative leader, Johnson's deference was scarcely sentimental confidence; rather, it recognized the several roles that military leaders play in the political process, their symbolic and authoritative roles as well as their administrative and technical roles. The military can be managed, but not by airing or responding to their every concern; they need to be managed with critical oversight, which means by watching carefully their handling of programs, missions, resource questions, and force designs and deployments. McNamara, by the time Johnson became president, had established a reputation—among others, with Johnson—that he performed this role well. Aided by a strong team of civilians, he was an aggressive supervisor of the Department of Defense. His active management style enabled Johnson to be a more passive critical supervisor of the Defense Department, depending on McNamara until the scale of his own engagement with the military in Vietnam drew him into a more direct and active supervisory role for himself. Even then, McNamara remained the principal presidential agent for defense policies, including Vietnam, until Johnson replaced him with Clark Clifford. Clifford, it turned out, although by reputation a hawk, proved to be wholly lacking in deference to the military, at least with respect to the Vietnam war effort. He became the leading proponent in the Johnson administration of unilateral withdrawal.

The Third World: Alternatives to Critical Deference

Europe was the central concern of State and Defense, and of the international bureaus in Treasury and Commerce. AID and Agriculture directed their attention more to the developing world. The Far East regional bureau in State was involved with the president and the military because of Vietnam. The regional bureau for the Middle East and South Asia drew his attention for another reason, Israel. Johnson watched Israeli policy closely and denied as many players in the government as possible access to it, an arrangement that affected the way both the international security affairs office in Defense and the regional desk in State handled their ordinary business in the Middle East. When the Arab-Israeli War broke out in 1967, the White House had already positioned itself to manage closely the American role in managing the crisis.

The African regional bureau remained a peripheral interest of the White House, and therefore enjoyed a considerable autonomy except when it became necessary for Johnson to respond to crises, as was the case in the Congo in July 1967, when he sent three C-130 transport aircraft to aid the government of Colonel Joseph Mobutu. He asked G. Mennan Williams, the Assistant Secretary of State for African Affairs, whom he had inherited from Kennedy, to come up with some sort of large African initiative. Johnson seemed to want for Africa something like the Mekong Valley development project for Vietnam, which had caught his imagination, or the Lilienthal plan for the Middle East.[37] These were huge water and energy projects that supposedly would satisfy enough aspirations in a region to permit resolving major regional conflicts, even the conflicts between Hanoi and Saigon and between Israel and its neighbors. In conception, they combined the New Deal's TVA project and the Marshall Plan. With a similar prospect in mind for Africa, Johnson delivered a speech on African regionalism in May 1966 and assigned Edward Korry, his ambassador to Ethiopia, to study and propose. Korry's report was disappointing. No grand vision developed for Africa. It remained peripheral to Johnson, a place for reactions, not programmatic action, certainly not the grand projects that appealed to him.

For Latin America, Johnson's problem was not to discover and promote a big idea, but to cope with the one that Kennedy had propagated, the Alliance for Progress. His efforts to bring it under control have already been sketched. He made the best of what survived from Kennedy's grand design for Latin America with his own conference at Punte del Este—the same place where Kennedy had promoted the Alliance. For Johnson, Punte del Este was the place to launch a more modest regional scheme that kept regional cooperation alive and did not depend as heavily on American economic concessions.

Johnson's Latin American policy proceeded in two modes. One was programmatic and multilateral and attempted to set the agenda and define the terms of success. The other was bilateral, even unilateral, ad hoc and responsive. His adaptation of the Alliance for Progress was largely in the first mode. His reaction to regime crises in Brazil and the Dominican Republic[38] was in the second mode. As awkward as it was for Johnson to have to cut down the unrealistic expectations that accompanied the Alliance in both Latin America and Washington, the reactive mode was more awkward.

In March 1964, Brazil's civilian regime under President João Goulart fell to a military coup. The army abandoned long-observed standards of constitutional restraint to establish what it presented as a caretaker government and to initiate a well-planned program of social, economic, administrative, and political reforms. At the time, Goulart had been moving rapidly toward a left-wing coup.[39] The army stayed to rule for twenty years, permanently altering the complexion of Brazilian politics—and, incidentally, the army. Although we have the benefit of hindsight, it does not permit us to compare the benefits and drawbacks of Brazil's military rule since 1964 with what might have happened without it.

Critics claim that the United States instigated or encouraged the military coup. That is unlikely.[40] American assistance to the Brazilian military over forty previous years had doubtless influenced the Brazilian military officers to see themselves as a professional elite, a guardian class, a view that under most circumstances would lead them to avoid direct involvement in politics—among other reasons, to preserve the integrity of the armed forces. In more recent years, the American war colleges had tended to broaden their curricula so as to educate American officers in the larger issues of government, and the Brazilian military had followed suit, drawing civilian officials as well as military officers into these studies. The major American error was in failing to perceive what happened to American military professionalism when it was exported in this manner. The problem became exacerbated when the Kennedy administration promoted a "civic action" role and a "counterinsurgency" mission for the military in Latin America.

As the coup took shape, Ambassador Lincoln Gordon, who had been a principal architect of the Alliance for Progress, called for standby naval forces. The American options, as it appeared to the Johnson administration, were to discourage the coup and prolong the time of chaos before the coup succeeded, or endorse it and reduce the chaos and disorder. It was a familiar dilemma for a hegemonic power. Gordon's recommendations were accepted. Several accounts to the contrary, it is unlikely that the United States could have prevented the military coup. The Brazilian army was by then a mature military institution. As its leaders planned the coup, they pointedly separated themselves from its American contacts.[41]

Four years later, after close cooperation between the United States and Brazil's military leaders, during which time Brazil's major adverse economic trends were reversed, another ambassador, John Tuthill, distanced the United States from the regime in Rio as evidence mounted of growing political repression. Gordon's call in 1964 could, in retrospect, be seen as that of an experienced economic development official favoring the group that promised rational economic decisions.

Rusk and Johnson had timely reports from Gordon and time to decide deliberately how to respond. Johnson's role in the Brazilian coup was to be informed and to acquiesce. It was reactive. To describe it thus is not to ignore the programmatic component of U.S. policies in Brazil. But American foreign aid programs were a normal condition. It was the extraordinary condition of a regime challenge that drew the attention of and required a decision from the president.

The intervention in the Dominican Republic, which occurred a year later, just as Johnson was beginning to face up to his most fateful decisions about Vietnam, was the most conspicuously embarrassing of Johnson's reactive policies in Latin America. In April 1965, the regime in Santo Domingo disintegrated. When the American ambassador appealed for military intervention to save American lives, Johnson sent troops. A day later, advised by intelligence sources— mainly from the FBI[42]—that the contest was between generals and communists, he sent more troops, having been convinced that otherwise there would be a communist takeover. He acted in too much haste. Although evidently none of his advisors dissented from his decision, they were divided. Johnson may have been manipulated to act in haste—perhaps by the embassy, perhaps by the FBI. More likely he was responding to clumsy intelligence reports which alarmed him with the prospect that if he did not act he would be responsible for another Cuba—another embarrassing communist takeover in the Caribbean.

Once Johnson decided on intervention, he acted quickly, without consulting his allies. Having acted, he turned to the Organization of American States for diplomatic support, and then for a means to extricate American forces. He asked the OAS to establish an inter-American military force to restore order and replace U.S. forces in the country. The intervention touched a raw nerve throughout Latin America. The OAS, which had at first been ignored, and then was incapable of prompt action, proved remarkably cooperative, under the circumstances, in sponsoring the political reconciliation and the supervisory forces that facilitated an American withdrawal.

Dealing with the Soviet Bloc

These developments took place while Johnson increased U.S. forces defending South Vietnam and therefore in a war with North Vietnam. North Vietnam was governed by an anti-colonial communist regime which looked to China and to the Soviet Union for support in its struggle against the United States to gain control over all of Vietnam. For the United States, the Soviet factor hung over the Vietnam War. It dominated the aircraft bombing campaigns and prevented the blockading of North Vietnamese harbors, which would have cut Soviet supply lines. For their part the Soviets avoided a direct confrontation with the United States. When Johnson met the Soviet premier, Alexei Kosygin, at Glassboro in 1967, the Soviets demanded that the United States withdraw its forces from South Vietnam in order to improve relations and thaw the chill that had developed due to the escalation of American bombing. Despite these disappointments, the two governments cooperated to achieve modest objectives in nuclear diplomacy. They agreed on a draft treaty to prohibit the proliferation of nuclear weapons to medium and small powers and had made some progress on the terms of a strategic arms agreement before the effort was abandoned in August 1968 when the Soviet suppression of Czechoslovakia made it impossible for the United States to proceed.

Similarly, the two superpowers were able at first to cooperate in Laos and to moderate their competition in the Middle East. Their limited Middle East cooperation was challenged in 1967 when Nasser ordered his troops into the Sinai desert and expelled the United Nations peace-keeping forces there. Neither Johnson nor Israel was alarmed by this, but when Nasser closed the Straits of Tiran, Israel responded with a preemptive attack, which devastated the combined forces of Egypt, Jordan, and Syria, and Johnson attempted joint action with the Soviets, the British, and the French to diffuse tension in the area. For their part the Soviets stood by and watched while their allies, Egypt and Syria, went down in defeat. In fact, the Soviets did not replenish Egyptian and Syrian armaments until two weeks after the war had ended. Both superpowers showed that they were not interested in a direct confrontation as a result of local conflicts.[43]

The Cuban missile crisis, which occurred during October 1962, had demonstrated the urgent need for better crisis management between the superpowers and led to the establishment of the "hotline" linking Washington and Moscow. The Limited Test Ban Treaty of 1963 also followed, as did the expansion of consular facilities in both countries. Johnson, upon becoming president, immediately picked up on another cooperative venture with the Soviet Union, the Non-Proliferation Treaty, which was finished at the end of 1966.

Khrushchev, the venturesome Soviet General Secretary, was displaced by his politburo associates in October 1964. Hopeful about the new leadership in the Kremlin, Johnson appointed a blue-ribbon commission to expand trade with the Soviet Union. Predictably, it reported that the "time is ripe to make more active use of trade arrangements as political instruments in relations with Communist countries."[44] Johnson, in October 1966, announced his aim "to heal the wound in Europe which now cuts East from West and brother from brother." He went on: "We do not intend to let our differences on Vietnam or elsewhere prevent us from exploring all opportunities."[45] However, when the Soviets failed to help the United States wind down the Vietnam War, the Congress refused to relax trade restrictions, and the Johnson administration tightened trade controls against the Soviets. Western European allies and the Japanese, who had little sympathy for the United States on this matter, took up the slack.[46]

The United States protested the Soviet invasion of Czechoslovakia at the United Nations, but Johnson did not seriously consider direct aid to the Czech reformers. In this his reaction paralleled Eisenhower's when Russian troops suppressed Hungary in 1956. Leonid Brezhnev, the Soviet premier, correctly calculated that the risks of war with the West were negligible.[47] The Soviets were well aware of the limitations of American ability to exert change in Eastern Europe.

Vietnam and Domestic Politics

When Johnson became president, South Vietnam urgently needed a stable government capable of dealing with a growing insurgency that was supported by North Vietnam. Three weeks before Kennedy's death a military junta had toppled the regime of Ngo Dinh Diem that had ruled with American sponsorship and increasing material support since South Vietnam was created in 1954. The Kennedy administration, impatient with his corruption, repressiveness, and unpopularity, and particularly with his unwillingness to heed U.S. advice,[48] had let Diem fall. The military officers of the new government were ill-prepared to rule and unable to prevent their own displacement by military coup. During his first year, Johnson's narrow options in South Vietnam revolved around stabilizing the shifting alliances among the military in Saigon and providing enough help to keep the insurgents at bay—but not enough to provoke Hanoi to escalate, a prospect that Johnson's advisors feared would topple the wobbly new regime in Saigon.[49] These objectives were severely constrained by Johnson's resolve to direct the first efforts of his administration to a domestic legislative program and to keep Vietnam quiet through the presidential election of 1964, which he did.

With the election behind him, with the regime in Saigon weak and unstable with evidence of growing insurgent strength, Johnson raised the American commitment in a series of steps during the first half of 1965. In February he increased military assistance to Saigon in an effort to expand and strengthen the South Vietnamese army, and he ordered the bombing of targets in North Vietnam. These measures failed; the threat to Saigon continued to grow. With North Vietnamese regulars now the major form of aid to the insurgency from North Vietnam, Johnson decided upon a buildup of American ground forces. In May 1965, American troops in Vietnam numbered 35,000. By the end of the year there were more than 180,000; by the end of 1966, 380,000. They increased another 100,000 in 1967 and 60,000 more in 1968.

The scale of the American involvement, the fact that American forces became the main fighting elements in the war, robbed the South Vietnamese armed forces of incentives to fight effectively. Their performance ceased to be vital. Similarly, the American presence, particularly military and economic assistance, benefited the regime. Its special interest lay in keeping the Americans involved. In this situation, Hanoi obliged its rivals in Saigon. Its resolve to fight on until the South Vietnamese regime was defeated—at least the observable signs of that resolve—remained strong until Saigon fell in 1975.

The American bombing of North Vietnam, which began in early March 1965, split the Democratic Party. Fifteen Democratic senators signed an appeal to Johnson to stop the bombing. A similar protest came from Democrats in the House of Representatives. This was only the beginning. Many senators believed that Johnson had broken trust with them. As the war escalated, it became a common view that Johnson had dissembled with the Senate in August 1964 in order to win Senate approval of the Gulf of Tonkin resolution. By 1966 Johnson had lost much of his strength in the Congress— among the persons he knew best how to handle. He also had lost public support. The civil rights movement combined with the antiwar movement, and he could satisfy neither. Johnson coped with his antiwar critics by agreeing to bombing pauses and by offering to negotiate, but he was unable to satisfy or placate his critics with such tactics. They had become suspicious of him from his early tactics of keeping the war inconspicuous.

In February 1968, the Tet Offensive brought questions about the progress of the war and the antiwar criticism into sharp focus. The Viet Cong took heavy casualties in their attacks on urban centers in the South. But the strength of the attacks discredited administration claims about military progress and therefore about a diminishing threat. The Johnson administration lost a critical amount of domestic political support over Tet. His Gallup poll approval ratings indicate this shift. The rating had stood at 80 percent in early 1964. In March 1968, after a long fall, it reached 36 percent. His rating on the handling of the war fell even lower, to 26 percent.

In the growing crisis over Vietnam, Johnson denied his critics outside the executive branch any rallying points within his administration. Field commanders are particularly attractive potential rallying points for critics of a war or its prosecution. This fact puts the president into a special predicament as he exercises his role as commander-in-chief to deal with his major field commanders. The most notable examples of this predicament of presidents come from the nineteenth century—the Civil War and Teddy Roosevelt in the Spanish-American War. Douglas MacArthur, during the Korean War, had proved a political embarrassment to President Truman, as his father had to President Taft during the pacification of the Philippine Islands.[50] General Westmoreland, the commander of Vietnam military operations from 1963 until 1968, was an obvious prospect. But he was not inclined to ask for resources that the administration would not give him, and so avoided dissent. Robert McNamara, the Secretary of Defense, had become a skeptic, but he left the Johnson administration quietly in 1967. No one with the credibility of an insider broke publicly with Johnson. This was a notable case of the dog not barking which has gone largely unremarked.

Tet nonetheless hardened the dove-hawk split within the government. What was more ominous for Johnson's goal of executive-branch consensus, it opened a distinct civilian-military split that had been scarcely visible before. General Westmoreland, urged on and supported by the Joint Chiefs of Staff, now called for another 200,000 troops. Johnson consulted a prestigious group of nine former presidential advisors who recommended against further escalation of the war and favored greater efforts to negotiate a settlement. One of them, Clark Clifford, became Secretary of Defense in March 1968. Clifford, although generally hawkish, and known to be so, had, in July 1965, urged Johnson not to escalate the American involvement in Vietnam and to find a way out.[51] Johnson would scarcely have forgotten this advice when he appointed Clifford Secretary of Defense. At the very least, Johnson expected Clifford to reassess Vietnam policy. Possibly he anticipated that Clifford would press for winding down the war. In the event, he quickly became the leading skeptic. The prevailing view has been that he was co-opted as a skeptic by the civilian officials whom McNamara had left behind in OSD, and that Johnson was taken utterly by surprise by this development.

Johnson announced at the end of March that he was withdrawing from the presidential election. This act should have raised the credibility of his threats against North Vietnam because it eliminated Johnson's incentive to anticipate the election returns. He attempted to take advantage of this reinforced credibility to coerce Hanoi into a settlement favorable to Saigon's interests, but with little effect. The most common interpretation of Johnson's withdrawal was that the war had defeated him politically. The war remained stalemated for the rest of his term.

Reorganization Moves in State and Defense

During his presidency, Johnson took two major initiatives in the general management of foreign relations that reflected a concern about proceeding on the basis of an overall perspective. One was to extend relatively successfully the Program, Planning and Budgeting System (PPBS) that McNamara had imposed on the Department of Defense to the foreign relations agencies, along with all other agencies of the federal government. The other was to adopt the Taylor report. Johnson had commissioned General Maxwell D. Taylor in 1965 to study and recommend how better to coordinate all counterinsurgency activities in the federal government. At the time, Taylor was fresh from serving as ambassador to South Vietnam, where the American military and economic efforts were still visualized as directed against insurgency. When he reported, Taylor recommended a strengthening of the machinery of interdepartmental coordination of all foreign relations activities, rather than just those involving counterinsurgency, and promoted the placement of foreign relations coordinating mechanisms squarely in the Department of State. Johnson adopted Taylor's recommendations and issued them as National Security Action Memorandum (NSAM) 341 in March 1966.

NSAM 341 established the "SIG/IRG" system, a three-tiered arrangement for coordinating foreign policy in Washington. The SIG, at the top, was a Senior Interdepartmental Group that was to meet under the direction of the Under Secretary of State. Its task was comparable to that of the National Security Council, which at the time was little used and regarded as too large to be used by the president "as a forum for deciding major overseas matters."[52] The middle tier was composed of five Interdepartmental Regional Groups (IRGs), chaired by the Assistant Secretaries of State for each major region—Africa, Latin America, East Asia and Pacific, Europe, and Near East and South Asia. These groups were to coordinate foreign policy government-wide at the regional bureau level. The third tier was composed of country directors. They were to have the authority to coordinate country programs government-wide, authority that country desk officers clearly lacked.

At the time that the SIG/IRG system was imposed top-down on the executive branch, it was already percolating with organizational reform initiatives. One of them was Johnson's own effort to extend PPBS, under the direction of the Bureau of the Budget, to the Department of State, AID, and other foreign affairs agencies. Another initiative had begun within the Department of State and was already in an advanced stage. It was the Comprehensive Country Programming System (CCPS). PPBS for the foreign affairs community became a competitor with the CCPS. The two management systems had in common a commitment to programming concepts that sought to specify inputs and measure outputs. They differed about where they located oversight and control. CCPS was conceived as a system for managing from the Department of State the resources of all agencies devoted to foreign relations. PPBS immediately became a tool for resource management and accountability under the watchful eye of the Bureau of the Budget. CCPS had not won full support from Rusk when it had to face the Bureau of the Budget as a rival, and it lost the main battle. After a showdown in March 1966, CCPS became a planning aid for secondary regions, primarily Latin America, where its success was limited.

The Department of State's experience with both forms of program planning and analysis was disappointing. PPBS worked in the Department of Defense, to the extent that it did, because of two conditions lacking in its application to the Department of State. First, its designers in Defense were able to draw upon a rich base of knowledge and analytical techniques developed through years of pertinent research in the aerospace research firms—e.g., research that had developed sophisticated cost estimating techniques. Second, in Defense, expressing programs as agency capabilities or outputs was considered adequate. The strategic forces program, for instance, dealt in force capabilities. It was not considered a serious failing that program analysis in the Defense Department failed to measure the strategic forces' deterrent *effect*. But similar omissions were less excusable in dealing with the activities of the Department of State, where goals were not met until influence had actually occurred. Program evaluation in State had to deal with the *effects* of the State Department (and other agency) programs, and that proved very difficult to do.

Both the CCP and the PPB systems expressed output goals most precisely in terms of unilateral U.S. government activities, such as foreign aid transfers. They stated outputs less precisely as the goals of joint U.S.–host government activities, and then only on the assumption that those host government programs which the U.S. government supported were autonomous of other host government activities, which was rarely the case. It was not uncommon in staff work for the CCP and PPB systems also to describe preferred host government behavior as an intended output or effect of U.S. activities, but such statements were rarely linked by an explicit analysis to those activities. Yet such a linkage was a vital principle of both systems. Both were thus fatally weak in their analysis. Their statements about the preferred behavior of the host government stood as unsubstantiated wishes in the planning documents, and the causal connection between U.S. actions and host government actions usually remained unsubstantiated.

The country program for Brazil, for instance, could state that, during FY 1968, AID would provide the services of American police experts to train Brazilian state police. But it had no way of predicting or evaluating the impact of the actual training. It happened that the experts actually employed were retired New Jersey state police who were neither in a position to observe nor competent to evaluate anything except the immediate technical effect, or classroom performance, so to speak, of their training of Brazilian police. From the standpoint of U.S. policy, this was actually inconsequential. What should have been considered consequential, the effects of that training on Brazilian police work, no one in the AID mission or embassy staff in Brazil, much less in Washington at AID or State, had the capacity to deal with. This was a nontrivial matter. The commander of the state police in each of Brazil's states at that time was a professional military officer appointed by the military junta that ruled from Rio and Brasilia. AID and State could not tell (although of course they could speculate) whether the effect of American training was to reduce or increase the use of off-duty murder squads, which was a growing problem at that time, or whether the American training served to induce the Brazilian state police to act more professionally and less illegally.

To assess such effects of a police training program required some understanding of the social and institutional context in which it occurred. AID and embassy personnel had some background for such understanding, but not much, and very little incentive to employ their limited backgrounds for a critical evaluation of such a program. Normal program justification was based on the assumption that some American training was better than no training at all. The program was also justified by the common assumption among U.S. officials that the recipient government, in this case the Brazilian government, would not supply the training itself. The correctness of that judgment was critical for determining the value of American technical and economic assistance. If it were not correct, American assistance made little difference. The Brazilian state police were actually getting more training because AID had supplied it. The Brazilian government would have provided the training itself if the Americans had not.

Such American assistance programs operated on the margin of host government priorities. Presumably, if the Brazilian government had given a higher priority to training its state police, it would have found a way to do the job itself. In this respect, the technical, economic, and military assistance programs of the United States aimed to alter the priorities of recipient governments, but realistically, only marginally.

Viewed in this light, it should be clear that a rigorous program planning system, to be successful, would have to cope with the issues this illustration about Brazil reveals. Neither CCPS nor PPBS succeeded in giving operational meaning to the actual impact and influence of U.S. foreign policy programs. Bureaucratic tactics and constraints on innovation offer sufficient explanations for this failure to carry through with the necessary analysis, but a more fundamental explanation should be noted. For U.S. officials to evaluate foreign policy programs which were intended to change the political behavior of recipient governments, not simply achieve technical or administrative changes, a consensus was required that did not exist in Washington about how to determine the political effects of assistance programs, and therefore about how to deal with other governments as recipients of such programs.

So much for these programming systems. The SIG/IRG mechanism did not suffer from the same weaknesses, but it, too, was flawed. It lacked the top-level support that was critical to its success. It served as little more than a means for interdepartmental communication and compromise. Dean Rusk did not assert his access as Secretary of State to the president to provide positive guidance for the SIG. (As a matter of principle, he declined to relay downward much of what he and Johnson had discussed.) Lacking special guidance, the State Department chairmen of the SIG and the IRGs had little if any advantage in dealing with group members from other agencies, and with other members who had access to the president. The chairmen lacked the special status needed for guiding the coordination process.

Generating and employing influence to achieve such effects as were illustrated in the Brazilian example above may be considered the core function of the Department of State. At no time since World War II have expectations been higher than during the mid-sixties that this core function could be rationalized. The program management schemes, CCPS and PPBS, were ambitious efforts at such rationalization that failed. Had they worked, they would have assured the Department of State ascendancy in foreign policy. Similarly, the SIG/IRG system, had it been successfully implemented, would have established the Department of State as the undisputed locus of coordinating authority in foreign relations. But it also failed. The control of foreign relations remained during the Johnson administration, as it has almost invariably been in the modern era of the presidency, strongly influenced by the president's behavior and never the exclusive preserve of the Department of State.

Presidential Involvement: Comparison and Contrast

As already noted, in two important areas Johnson became persistently involved in foreign affairs in different ways, one dealing with the trade and monetary sector of foreign relations where his involvement was discreet, the other with military operations, or more precisely, Vietnam, where his involvement became an increasing preoccupation and an embarrassment to him. In both areas his objective was to minimize political engagement; in one he succeeded, in the other he failed. Johnson also inserted himself into other particular events, often quite unpredictably, such as the Dominican crisis, but these two exceptions stand out because of the extended time over which he was involved in them. Both have been referred to previously. Here it will be useful to summarize.

Trade negotiations, which are a major instrument of American foreign policy, are the responsibility of the U.S. Trade Representative (USTR), who reports directly to the president, not the Secretary of State or the Secretary of the Treasury. This arrangement was imposed by Congress in the course of passing the Trade Expansion Act of 1962 and reflected a judgment that the Department of State, where responsibility for these negotiations had previously been located, had "misused its position as a coordinator and negotiator."[53] Doubtless this judgment reflected protectionist concerns.[54] In practice, the State Department, perhaps because it is in charge of maintaining relations with other governments, perhaps because it has been less closely linked to constituency interests than the Departments of Commerce, Labor, and Agriculture, has been less attentive than they to protectionist concerns. In this, it is not alone among foreign ministries. To this day, the U.S. government has not integrated the handling of trade negotiations with the other elements of foreign relations—military, diplomatic, political, even with economic and military assistance, which depends upon trade surpluses.

International monetary policy, which is largely the domain of the Treasury Department, has, since the Johnson administration, increasingly come into a common orbit with military, diplomatic, and political elements in the formation and conduct of foreign policy. But it has come slowly, reflecting the fact that its effectiveness is heavily dependent upon multilateral cooperation. During the Johnson administration it remained largely a matter to be handled by special arrangements. Trade was a different matter. It was a familiar if dangerous minefield, recognized as such by Congress and by Johnson. International monetary policy was newer territory also recognized for its political dangers. Johnson wanted it handled nearby, where he could watch it, which he did.[55]

The Johnson administration was actually a transition period with respect to both the prominence of Treasury Department–related foreign policy matters and the way they were handled in the White House and at the Cabinet level. The U.S. trade balance had shifted into chronic deficit in the early sixties, a situation that would gradually force international monetary policy into a more central position in foreign relations and the Secretary of the Treasury into a more prominent role in the formation of foreign policy. During the Johnson administration monetary policy was handled separately through subcabinet coordinating committees, or groups, which were ad hoc (but sometimes highly durable) interdepartmental committees run by an international economist—first, Francis Bator and then Edward Fried—in the office of the National Security advisor, operating quite separately.

The other exception was Johnson's direct dealings with the Joint Chiefs of Staff, and down the chains of military command, his attention to what he considered to be the policy-relevant and politically sensitive details of the Vietnam War. It was an interest somewhat like his interest in the details of his domestic programs. Like the U.S. Trade Representative, at that time (indeed, until 1986), all members of the JCS had, by law, a right of access to the president. It is true that the president cannot be forced to listen to anyone. But the fact that the chiefs had a statutory right to see him assured that his neglect of them would arm his critics.

Johnson was inclined at the outset of his administration, and indeed throughout it, to deal through the Secretary of Defense with his military chiefs on most matters much as Kennedy had done. This arrangement was reflected in the fact that no military chiefs at first attended the Tuesday lunch, an informal meeting that Johnson held fairly regularly beginning as early as February 1964. As the American military involvement in Vietnam expanded, Johnson became more interested in its details. He began dealing directly with the chiefs, with General Westmoreland, and with the embassy in Saigon, eventually on a daily basis. Yet it was not until late 1967 that General Earle Wheeler, the chairman of the Joint Chiefs of Staff, attended the Tuesday lunches regularly.[56] This was remarkably late, considering how much contact Johnson had with the military. The lateness attests to the value he placed in the Tuesday lunch as a small meeting with civilian advisors on foreign affairs.

Johnson's direct involvement with the military was the least surprising development of the Vietnam War. Inevitably, however, it altered his relationship with his Secretary of Defense, Robert McNamara, and McNamara's relationship with the military establishment. McNamara was a positive force in shifting the Defense Department's attention to Vietnam in 1964 and 1965, but the shift weakened, and eventually broke, his domination over defense-related policy issues—budgets, weapons acquisition decisions, force posture. He lost his domination as he accommodated himself to the demands of the war and to the greater weight accorded the chiefs' opinions because they were spokesmen for the commanders of military operations.

Conclusion: Toward a Broader Inquiry

The United States government was, during the Johnson administration in the mid-sixties as it is today, a large, pluralistic government, accessible in most of its foreign policy elements to congressional oversight, to press coverage, and to foreign and domestic interest representation. The Johnson administration began, during the Thanksgiving holiday of 1963, with a broad consensus about the basic conditions for administering foreign relations, about the role of the president, about the instruments that the United States would employ in foreign relations, about the ends for which they would be employed. It ended with all of these things under challenge. Since its ending in early 1969, moreover, the consensus has made other shifts. One cannot evaluate administrative practices without reference to norms, and the relevant norms have been in flux. This book as a consequence not only examines the Johnson administration's management of foreign relations, but attempts to advance our general knowledge about presidential decision making and foreign policy management. The next chapter will lay out the framework for that broader inquiry.

2. The Larger Vision of Foreign Policy Management

The Foreign Policy Function and the Infrastructure

FOREIGN POLICY MEDIATES a state's relations with the external world. The way governments go about this mediation has implications for how the apparatus of their foreign relations should be structured and managed. They may go about it reactively, adapting to changes in the external environment. They may, if they have the resources, take the initiative, modifying or reshaping external conditions through extended programs and temporary "campaigns." They may follow a mixed strategy, both reacting and initiating. Whichever mediating strategy they employ, they may implement their strategies either coherently and deliberately, having employed some coordinating and planning mechanisms, or disjointedly, without central clearance and coordination. Whatever posture they take toward the external world, whether by choice or default, has important implications—which they may or may not perceive—for the way they organize the administration of their foreign relations.

Small powers must be mostly reactive. They must accept the fate of their smallness. Rarely do they have the resources to change the external environment very much. This was the situation in which the United States found itself as a new state at the end of the eighteenth century. But the situation had changed radically by the end of World War II. By then, the United States was the preeminent world power. It could and did modify external political, economic, and military conditions substantially. If it lacked skill in diplomacy or foresight in political analysis, these were less important because of the scale of its foreign policy enterprises (or programs). The U.S. became the manipulator of fate, the hegemon. In Dorwin Cartwright's terms, it influenced through ecological control.[1] Bargaining theory permits a different view of fate manipulation by substituting for the question, "How do we achieve our [bargaining] objectives?" the question, "Who benefits?" Game theory, by recognizing the possibility of creating win/win situations, permits a distinctly benevolent meaning to fate manipulation. The concept of fate manipulation is still usefully employed in analyses of goal-oriented national foreign policy programs, however, because such analyses must deal with program objectives and means. A parallel approach can be found in the international relations theory on hegemony.[2] Foreign policy anticipated the need for collective security, for strengthening allies and clients, for transforming economies, and for altering regional and local power balances. The United States rearmed itself, bolstered the economies and regimes of many allies and client states, entered into alliances, and sought cooperative relations with adversaries. While accomplishing these things, American officials and observers carried on a lively public dialogue about how the government should be organized to do these things. At the time of Johnson's takeover of the presidency, the most recent formal study available, *Personnel for the New Diplomacy*,[3] took account of the changing external conditions which American diplomacy needed to address and identified the changing options available to the United States. But it defined its own concern to be largely the same as that of the Foreign Service Act of 1946:[4] What safe measures could be taken to preserve and enhance the role of the Department of State? The public dialogue covered more ground, but with a thinner layer of analysis. It relied on conventional norms of organizational performance.[5]

In the present study it will be helpful to be more encompassing in our analysis, and to that end, we will refer to the *infrastructure* of foreign policy. Infrastructure means the governmental apparatus and procedures that handle foreign policy formation and that implement policy. The governmental apparatus is taken to mean the internal networks of the governmental process. It also refers to the networks of established, ongoing, if modulating, bilateral and multilateral relations that carry the burdens of implementation. Infrastructure extends these networks to include external networks as well. The term, as used here, extends the meaning in organization theory of standard operating procedures (SOPs)[6] to include these ongoing relations. Infrastructure includes not only organizational processes but also political processes. With reference to both, it includes descriptions of their outcomes. It includes outcomes because they are the objective of much that happens in organizational processes and because knowledgeable players often successfully predict them.

The infrastructure is composed of organizational and political regularities. It can be said to perform functions as these regularities are recognized and anticipated, and as this knowledge is employed to

achieve policy objectives. Players who recognize which aspects of
the game serve their common purposes, which aspects serve only
their own or someone else's purposes, and which are generally neutral or hostile in the benefits that they confer on particular players,
will play better than those who miss these distinctions. Sorting out
interests facilitates cooperation, a theme that has come strongly to
prominence recently in theories about international cooperation.[7]

The chief rationale for American foreign policy in the postwar era
was the containment of the Soviet Union. Containment was associated with a theory of coexistence in a bipolar world in which the
United States and the USSR could live without defeating each other.
The theory included the goal of a longer-term transformation of the
Soviet Union into a less threatening state with more democratic
values than the Stalinist Russia of 1946. Chapter 7 of this book will
discuss whether or not that era is now over, and if the experience of
the Johnson administration can instruct the U.S. on what steps it
should take next in its policy toward the old Soviet region.

Policy innovations in the United States have rarely been attributable to one person,[8] and containment is no exception. Yet to a
unique degree its articulation as a foreign policy doctrine (which we
might consider the first stage of policy innovation) can be attributed
to George Kennan.[9] As the highest ranking foreign service officer
(Minister Counselor) stationed in Moscow at the end of World War II,
he originally stated it in a series of five telegrams to the Department
of State at a critical time in 1946. The telegrams were widely circulated in the government. Kennan published their substance a year
later in the prestigious quarterly *Foreign Affairs* under the pseud-
onym "Mr. X."[10]

Kennan's own reaction to what later happened to his theory of
containment demonstrates the significance of what may be termed
the infrastructure of foreign relations. Kennan has explained that he
thought of the telegrams and the "Mr. X" article as stating principles, not a doctrine.[11] He had not intended the containment of Soviet power to mean "containment by military means of a military
threat, but the political containment of a political threat."[12] Accordingly, he had serious if qualified misgivings about NATO. As he explained these misgivings twenty years later, he seems to have been
as much troubled by what he correctly anticipated would become
one of NATO's main functions, to reassure Western Europeans that
the United States would not abandon them to the influence of Soviet power, as he was over its military character.[13] He objected to
NATO because of the prospect that it would divide Germany and
Europe permanently, rather than permitting the status of Western

Europe to remain subject to negotiation.[14] He wanted to preserve the flexibility of foreign policy against the effects of reducing it to what I have called the normal processes of governmental activities. Containment was to be achieved through diplomatic manipulation, not through alliances that entangled and constrained, producing ponderous and disjointed administrative processes in the U.S. government. As Kennan came to state it later, *his* road was not taken. Ten years after publication of his article, he described what he saw as the consequences: "The present system is based, throughout, on what appears to be a conscious striving for maximum fragmentation and diffusion of power."[15]

It is difficult to know (and of no great moment here) how much Kennan ever conceived of his preferences to be practical, for they matched more of a nineteenth-century model of diplomacy conducted by a powerful prime minister in charge of a relatively small, unitary government.[16] He was scarcely unaware of the forces that led down a different road and doomed his vision of directive diplomacy, but he chose to keep it alive as best he could. His view of a preferred mode of foreign policymaking sharpens the outline of what the Johnson administration had to deal with in the mid-sixties: Viewed from the White House, the infrastructure of American foreign policy required constant tending to assure the congressional and public bases of its support. There were normal procedures for doing this tending, but they could not be taken for granted. How much tending was required? Too much, Kennan feared.

Kennan's view of a directively led, maneuverable foreign relations reflected an acute sense of the limits of American power and the fragility of its steering mechanisms. "We are great and strong," he told a National War College audience in December 1948, "but we are not great enough nor strong enough to conquer or to change or to hold in subjugation by ourselves all . . . hostile or irresponsible forces."[17] The road taken followed the convictions of Keynesian expansionists, not those of Kennan: The U.S. economy could carry whatever burdens were necessary to meet the requirements of American security.[18] A similar view prevailed in the Kennedy and Johnson administrations. "We are the richest nation in the history of the world," Lyndon Johnson declared in July 1964. "We can afford to spend whatever is needed to keep this country safe and to keep our freedom secure. And we shall do just that."[19]

For Kennan and other traditional diplomatists, maintaining a steering capacity for the American president required minimizing dependence on other players within the U.S. and other involved governments. This meant limiting the influence of U.S. congressional leaders, agency chiefs, the military services and their chiefs, while controlling economic and other interests. Kennan, assigned to chair an international working group that drafted the North Atlantic Treaty, was present when the Allies began constructing the complex fabric of procedures that comprised and was associated with NATO. "I disliked," he recalled, "being placed in the position of spokesman for the views of unnamed figures in the legislative branch of our government." After the U.S. Undersecretary of State, Robert Lovett, dismissed a suggestion by a European representative because he believed that it would be unacceptable to the Senate, Kennan could not help but wish, though, that one of our European friends had stood up at that point and said: "Mr. Lovett, if you and your colleagues in the State Department cannot speak responsibly for American policy in this matter, will you kindly introduce us to the people who can?" Added Kennan: *"Our European friends had a right, it seemed to me, to deal with someone who had some latitude of decision, whose reflections and appreciations were relevant to the process of decision, and with whom it therefore paid to engage in rational discussion and argument."*[20]

Kennan's viewpoint reflected an age of smaller states with more compact political systems, and it was simply wrong. Europeans had no right to expect the United States government to behave as though it were a unitary actor, and therefore no right to expect a simple answer to the question "Who is in charge here?" They had no more right than the United States had a right, as Americans have often claimed, to deal with a united Europe. Kennan, of course, was speaking to some extent normatively at a time when Western Europeans were confronting an extraordinary challenge from the United States, in the form of the Marshall Plan, to take responsibility for setting and attaining region-wide goals. He would have preferred that the United States behave differently, much as the United States was demanding that Europeans behave differently.

But the broader experience of the United States in the postwar era has been with a diplomacy of constrained national players. The United States still does not, as a practical matter, have the right to expect Western Europeans, or other countries, to ignore domestic political pressures when addressing foreign affairs issues, and American officials openly make use of the same procedure as a reason for not submitting to foreign pressures. Such claims are the substance of the complex political games which have, in the postwar era, shaped the management of American foreign relations.

It is a nostrum that foreign policy has become increasingly tied up with domestic politics.[21] Foreign policy is always tied up with domestic politics, at some times more than at other times. Furthermore, foreign policy in the United States, in addition to involving the State Department or the president at the very least, involves the military establishment and the Treasury Department. The idea that governments, for the sake of rationality, should conduct foreign relations as though they were single persons, like the idea that business organizations, when acting rationally, act as though they are unitary persons, is still appealing if largely illusory. Only in one important respect does this idea have deadly substance: The presumption of unitary national decision making remains the accepted premise of American and (now) Russian requirements for nuclear deterrence and for the control of nuclear warfare (for those who believe the latter is possible).

The international system is not composed of states which behave the way firms are assumed to behave in classic economic theory. Unitary national actors in foreign relations is not an accurate description of reality. By the same token, norms of conduct that confine themselves to the premise of states as unitary actors factor out the most dangerous and promising of foreign policy games, the games that complex, multi-tiered actors play with one another. The route chosen by the United States for conducting its foreign relations in the modern era required it to come to terms with this complexity. It did so sometimes brilliantly, sometimes well, sometimes poorly, and sometimes tragically. This observation is the point of departure for the chapters that follow. They seek to illuminate how this complexity figured into the establishment, and particularly the implementation, of foreign policy. It is an assumption of this study that major players, including presidents, have often sought to employ the complexity of multiple-actor, multi-tiered foreign policymaking to their advantage and have sometimes been successful in doing so.

Kennan, it must be said, wanted a simpler game. He preferred to bank on statesmen. He wanted them to have "latitude of decision," to be able to maneuver out of catastrophe. He believed such arrangements were the better way, that domestic pressures are often the cause of wars, and that statesmen with sufficient latitude could prevent them.[22] To state these premises this plainly is to reveal their weakness, or at any rate their obsolescence, in the mid-twentieth century. Domestic pressures can constrain as well as compel warmaking, and statesmen with "latitude of decision" do not always choose wisely between war and peace. Statesmen could lead nations into catastrophe as well as enable them to escape it. Domestic forces can push nations over the brink, and can also restrain them. Kennan, it appears, worried about the former problem, but worried more about the dangers of the constraining force of government itself, of foreign policy bureaucratized. He recognized what was happening to American foreign policy and did not like it. He feared for it because too many government officials were becoming involved and influencing it. From the early 1950s onward, foreign policy became a matter of government programs and constraining alliances, as well as presidential leadership.

Secrecy, Dispatch, and Other Heroic Virtues

Johnson's presidency began at the high mark of support for presidential power in foreign relations. Officials and the attentive public expected the president to lead, and the virtues of secrecy and dispatch were rarely challenged in principle, while in practice they were often compromised. Not only liberal Democrats who revered the record of Franklin D. Roosevelt, but Republican leaders as well, had come to depend upon the president's playing of the heroic role as head of state in foreign relations. According to the heroic concept, the president was expected to direct foreign relations, to mobilize the necessary public and governmental support for it, and to function with almost unlimited formal authority in foreign affairs. The Bricker Amendment, a concoction of the early fifties, attempted to narrow the president's broad powers by requiring that executive agreements be ratified by the Senate. It challenged this concept of the president as heroic leader. After congressional support for the amendment faded in 1956, the heroic vision of the presidency stood unchallenged until Senators J. William Fulbright, Mike Mansfield, and Wayne Morse questioned Johnson over Vietnam in 1965.

By the time Lyndon Johnson became president in 1963, one could identify two distinct forces working to shape the administration of U.S. foreign relations which are still visible today. One force was the heroic role the presidency conspicuously played in foreign relations. The other was the largely unacknowledged influence that ordinary administration came to play in the postwar record of American hegemony. Both forces can be identified through commonplace observations about the U.S. government at work, yet the effect of these two forces on the conduct of foreign relations is not yet well understood.

The president as heroic leader in foreign relations, as is commonly recognized, is built into the Constitution, but it has two faces. It was John Jay who described one of them in an essay in *The Federalist* papers in 1787. Jay claimed the elemental qualities of *secrecy* and *dis-*

patch as the primary requirements for the conduct of foreign relations, justifying constitutional provisions restricting treaty-making to the president and the Senate. In this role the Senate was expected to act as a sort of privy council, advising the president. The House of Representatives was not to have a similar role. Jay's justification for such restricted participation in foreign relations showed a certain tact in the face of republican sentiments. "The Constitution," he wrote, "provides that our negotiations for treaties shall have every advantage which can be derived from talents, information, integrity, and deliberate investigations, on the one hand, and from secrecy and dispatch on the other."[23] Treaty-making was to be a business for a small segment of the governing elite. Its role was to "advise" the president and "consent" to his decisions. Jay, much like 1960s' nuclear strategists who crafted doctrines of flexible response, wanted the president, as head of state, to have a maximum range of choice. Jay believed that the United States, as a small power in the late eighteenth century, needed maximum maneuverability in its foreign relations in order to survive in an international system where it was one of the weaker states. By the mid-twentieth century, however, these conditions had changed. The United States had become the preeminent world power and its relationship to other world powers was reversed. Now, the United States encountered states that were relatively much weaker than itself. In the postwar era secrecy, dispatch, and executive energy scarcely lost their value to the United States as a great power, but other requirements grew to rival these older ones. The new requirements were those that had been associated more with Alexander Hamilton than Jay—with the management and direction of national assets rather than with diplomatic maneuver. This is the second face of the heroic executive in foreign relations. At first, in the Constitutional Convention, Hamilton had strongly supported the equivalent of a monarchy. His *Federalist* essays, reflecting the compromises of the convention, were more modest, but still advocated a strong chief executive. He attacked the lack of executive authority in the Articles of Confederation and argued for a strong administrative officer or executive in terms still appealing to some public administration reformers. It fell to Jay, who had more experience in foreign affairs, to defend the president's constitutional powers in what he usually called negotiations. In the late twentieth century, we would more broadly define this as diplomacy and foreign relations.

Foreign policy, beginning with the Marshall Plan in 1946, became a relatively large-scale, visible enterprise, whether viewed in comparison with other activities of the national government or in comparison with foreign policy enterprises of other governments. It was now Hamilton's vision of the virtues of executive power, not Jay's, which became relevant. With respect to foreign relations, this scale factor turned foreign policy as an internal task of administration into a complex business of winning support and managing a diverse set of military and economic activities. Externally, the size of the resources and the variety of the instruments that the government in Washington could employ extended the range of options open to the president and altered executive behavior. Where Jay had seen maneuverability as essential, other qualities such as building coalitions of support, managing administrative rivalries, monitoring, controlling, and adjusting implementation—were now needed. George C. Marshall, the general whose war plans had prevailed in World War II, employed his special mix of talents as strong executive leader as U.S. Secretary of State during the critical years 1947–1948. Marshall was, quite literally, the role model of Kennedy's and Johnson's Secretary of State, Dean Rusk. Such a grand vision as the Marshall Plan, and the programs that followed, required a knowledgeable and supportive Congress and a sympathetic and supportive executive branch to act reliably to inspire confidence in allies, clients, and adversaries.

Confidence could originate in the statesman with "latitude of decision." The statesman who could back up promises with the appropriate action inspired confidence. But latitude of decision could undermine as well as inspire confidence, for it could be employed to evade as well as to meet commitments. What could be delivered at the will of the statesman could be withheld as well. The confidence of America's allies and clients depended upon their knowledge that the United States could not do certain things as well as their knowledge of what it could do. The United States inspired confidence through its entanglements, by normalizing its participation in alliances, aid programs, and treaty commitments, and by turning the activities associated with its foreign participation into the commonplace, routine activities of government. In this respect, American foreign relations, even important foreign relations, became routine.

Quite apart from this will or resolve of statesman are the military, diplomatic, foreign economic, informational, cultural, and intelligence functions and programs which form the governmental apparatus of foreign relations. One could scarcely conceive of a foreign policy without each of the elements of this apparatus in at least some rudimentary form. The apparatus provides the means of implementing policy, for giving it substance, for turning intentions and declarations into concrete actions and programs.

The behavior of this apparatus became relatively predictable. It was the result of elaborately constrained bureaucratic and political forces[24] in a big, complex, pluralistic government. The fact that the workings and outcomes of these programs were relatively predictable turned the United States into a reliable foreign policy player—a player whose behavior could be counted upon because it could not easily be changed. This was a form of reliability not available to the foreign policy leader with a broad latitude of decision.

It was hardly surprising that foreign policy management, as normally conceived, involved acquiring and efficiently employing the required resources and coordinating related government actions— the Hamiltonian tasks. But it also involved exploiting the advantages that could be found in the fact that in certain respects the United States acted like a *coalition* of internal interests, not a person. The government could not fully coordinate its official statements and actions toward other governments. Its choices were often constrained visibly, and therefore credibly, by relatively independent groups and actors, such as congressional leaders, military officers, and prestigious private groups. The U.S. government, in dealing with other governments, operated with its latitude of choice visibly limited by the lively chaos characterizing its normal decision and implementation processes and by its dependence on internal political support. In the conduct of foreign policy the limits as well as the extent of options was something to exploit. One could not credibly promise or threaten without a latitude of choice, of course. That was the value of latitude. But the visible limits on latitude could also be valuable, for they could set limits on the foreign policy agenda and on the expectations of allies, clients, and adversaries. Foreign policy can be defined as an agenda of policies; it can also be defined as managing the range and limits of choice upon which any feasible agenda of substantive policies depends.

This task—the shaping of choices—requires an energetic, effective chief executive, but also, in the same person, a chief diplomat who can employ administrative skills with one eye on domestic political costs and the other on influencing other governments. The problem with the modern Hamiltonian vision of presidential foreign policy leadership is its requirement for action without specifying how action will produce the desired capacities for influencing or bargaining with other governments. Influence and bargaining are highly complex processes for executive leadership when it must cope with the internal and external networks of foreign relations.

Actual practice has generated a better way, one that has accommodated to the complexities arising when governments deal with one another at several levels. The decisional latitude—the limits of foreign policy choice defined by the situation—depends upon the assets available to the president and the president's agents. The decisions they make depend upon how well they can array, manage, and apply their assets. A major concern of this volume is to observe what foreign policy assets are actually available to the president and his agents, as well as to understand how these assets are and can be employed.

The President as Heroic Leader by Agreement

Looking back from the vantage point of more than twenty years after the era of Lyndon B. Johnson's presidency, one is struck by the difference in the kind of presidential behavior which is acceptable and preferred in today's world. After World War II, until Johnson's presidency, foreign affairs often seemed to offer presidents the opportunity frequently denied them in domestic legislative affairs to prevail. "In the realm of foreign policy," Aaron Wildavsky could write in 1966, with only some exaggeration, "there has not been a single major issue on which presidents, when they were serious and determined, have failed."[25] The important qualifier in this statement, however, was just how "serious and determined" presidents were to prevail in foreign affairs. Lyndon Johnson did not prevail with respect to Vietnam; and by the time American involvement in Vietnam ended, the disappointments over the role both he and his successor, Richard Nixon, played in conducting the war had weakened presidential authority in foreign relations. This weakening had strong implications for the way the U.S. government worked.[26] The limits set upon executive action were limits imposed by a Congress that had lost confidence in the president and was concerned about the reckless use of presidential power, but they were not intended to control the agenda with other states.

The acceptance of the heroic presidency was not simply a matter of acknowledging the status or power of the president as head of state. In the postwar era, through at least the first years of the Johnson presidency, the president's associates, and even most of his adversaries, agreed that exceptional dependence on the presidency was necessary in order to make sure the foreign policy apparatus of the government worked well. Two examples illustrate this point, one involving Truman, one, Eisenhower. The first originates with Neustadt, whose influential work helped clarify the function of the heroic presidency during the Kennedy and Johnson administrations.

Neustadt recounts an episode in December 1950, "at the wrenching turn of the Korean War" when he worked for Charles S. Murphy, the president's special counsel in Truman's White House staff. A White House usher found a document mistakenly left behind by Sen. Robert A. Taft, the Senate minority leader, after a meeting with Truman. Written by a Senate staffer, it advised the Republican leadership to avoid endorsing the administration's future conduct of the war. If the war were to go badly, the note stated, the Republicans would be free to accuse Truman of treason. For Neustadt, the point of the episode was propriety: Murphy, rejecting the advice of his assistants (including Neustadt) to leak the forgotten document to the press for immediate partisan advantage, returned it promptly to Taft.[27]

The anecdote serves a different purpose here: to indicate where the president stands in relationship to congressional leaders in his handling of foreign policy crises. In their own view, these leaders could not compete with or displace the president in crisis handling. They did not try. They could, however, watch and wait. They hoped, we may assume, that the president would succeed. But if he failed, they expected to gain partisan advantage from this failure. In any event, Truman's opponents in the Senate acknowledged that the presidency was the center of action in foreign relations; and Murphy, as Truman's man, while recognizing their hostile intent, accepted it as normal. Unlike his young aides, he had already come to terms with it. His returning of the forgotten document without exploiting it to partisan advantage is indicative of this. Murphy recognized that, as partisan as Sen. Taft intended to be, he could become still more partisan or be displaced by still worse partisans. In this sense, Murphy's handling of Taft's document was pragmatic. Murphy recognized that Truman and Taft *had a common interest not only in controlling the escalation of partisanship, but also in letting the president take the lead.* These common interests, perceived by an experienced presidential assistant, helped to define a norm upon which this study depends.

The second example of the president's irreducible role in foreign relations was the erosion of public confidence in President Eisenhower after the launching of *Sputnik,* the Soviet space triumph of 1957. Eisenhower was a popular and revered leader. Nowhere did his prestige stand higher than as a foreign policy leader.[28] At first out of conviction, and later, for reasons of health, he chose to limit his direct involvement in foreign and security affairs, therefore limiting his exploitation of the heroic foreign policy leadership role. *Sputnik* was an extraordinary public relations coup, because its impact on public opinion was worldwide. It mistakenly convinced many atten-

tive people in the United States and around the world that the Soviets were ahead of the United States in space and probably in other
areas of high technology. The public response in the United States
to this probability included a measurable loss of confidence in Eisenhower.[29] In the Congress, Republicans and Democrats faulted him
for not taking a stronger lead in national security policy.[30] The public reaction to *Sputnik,* due in part to Eisenhower's purposeful avoidance of the heroic presidential role, demonstrated how presidents
could expose themselves to domestic political risks.

Legislative relations were a significant element in both of these
cases. Lyndon Johnson was in the Senate when both occurred. He
played a major role in the congressional reaction to *Sputnik,* although he was not as partisan as Stuart Symington and John F. Kennedy, other Democratic senators with presidential aspirations at the
time. Anyone as close to these events as Johnson would very likely
have concluded that presidents risk losing the advantages of their
superior playing position if they fail to adapt to changing political
attitudes, or moods, toward national security issues. One could have
also concluded that shifts in public mood outpace changes in a president's public record.

These two episodes exemplify the behavior expected of a presidency not only by the president himself, but also by other major
actors in the government. The foreign policy process depends upon
a strong presidency even while elements of the foreign policy system challenge and resist presidential actions.

In the constitutional game, Neustadt told us, players who share
functions contend for power.[31] The foreign policy game, as it is
played in Washington, is certainly more complex than that. For one
thing, the incentives to win are perverse. The person who wins becomes accountable. In foreign relations rarely does anyone but the
president want to win, and sometimes even the president does not.[32]
Usually the president is expected and allowed to win. The other con-
tenders among the public, Congress, and in the executive branch let
the president win,[33] but not necessarily on his own terms.

The Presidency Constrained and Reinforced

Since mid-century, the president's role has been associated with an
assertive involvement wherever possible with foreign policy—the
essence of the heroic role. It has also, however, sometimes reflected
a quite different vision of American power constrained by foreign
entanglements, and therefore constrained by design. This alternative vision belongs to the American internationalists who seek a

government, and therefore a presidency, predisposed to support allies and maintain an active role in international affairs. The president's aim in this constrained role is to pursue stability and safety in international relations through bilateral and multilateral ties that bind, commit, and institutionalize. At the same time, these ties will reduce options for the government and therefore the presidency. A constrained government and presidency can, in turn, offer reassurance to allies and clients that the United States would maintain its commitments to them.[34]

For the American internationalist, the United States provides reassurance not only by declaring intentions in treaties and other pronouncements, but by taking concrete measures to implement commitments and close off other choices—for instance, by investing in common defenses at the expense of independent military capabilities. The late Robert Osgood, in his authoritative study of NATO three decades ago, noted its evolution "from a simple guaranty pact to a semi-integrated military organization [that] has been marked by the progressive entanglement of the United States in the military and political policies of Western Europe."[35]

U.S. involvement in NATO is just one example of the self-constraints accepted by the government in order to reassure allies. As commonly perceived on both sides of the Atlantic, the principal danger was (and in Europe, with certain adaptations, still is) an isolationist America, drawn by the demands of domestic politics away from its international obligations. According to the internationalist outlook, to avoid this eventuality, the U.S. government became involved in a network of treaties and alliances, in the partially integrated military organization of NATO in Europe, in similar if lesser forms of integration and entanglement in other regions, in military and economic aid programs.

The presidency was not the primary target of those who wanted to entangle the United States with the fate of other governments. Nevertheless, successive presidents have found their options necessarily reduced. The developments that stabilized political, military, and economic relations did so at the expense of functional, but not formal, national independence.

To understand the import of these developments, it is necessary to take account of them in their broadest meaning. The present study builds on these general patterns or normalities in the governmental process in three ways. First, it takes the meaning of governmental processes broadly to include customs and practices.[36] Second, American foreign policy is considered to be an extended activity of the governmental process, extended to include links with other governments and nongovernmental entities. Third, skilled players are recognized as being generally aware of the impact that foreign relations and internal politics can have on policymaking. They recognize the normalities of foreign policy processes, anticipate how players' actions relate to one another given these normalities, and try to apply this knowledge to achieve their ends. This knowledge and skill are valuable competitive assets.

We have already noted that the broad normalities of foreign relations alluded to above can be taken as the infrastructure of foreign policy. The foreign policy elements of the U.S. government must appear to the observer in two contradictory aspects. One is systematically dynamic. The other is inefficient and chaotic. By now it should be clear that both miss the same vital point, that the foreign policy sector is actually a resilient and open system of loosely coupled agencies, programs, operations, and personalities. Furthermore, it has at least a certain minimal political efficiency to it. That is to say, the infrastructure of normal procedures[37] tends to minimize the political costs of performing and maintaining foreign policy by relying on common perceptions and expectations within and across governments. That is its most fundamental, if least recognized, utility.

The U.S. government, we also noted earlier, is a reliable actor in foreign relations to the extent that its behavior can be predicted. In a phrase popularized by the bureaucratic politics literature, people and organizations can be counted on to "do their thing." The statement has no value unless "their thing" can be defined. Information about U.S. behavior in foreign relations has been readily available. It is often claimed that U.S. behavior, however, is not convergent or patterned, or at least actually purposeful, that it is unpredictable, even random. Nothing is further from the truth: The broad patterns of U.S. behavior in foreign relations have been quite clear. To be sure, the complaints about unpredictability are valid, but they apply to exceptional though often important behavior.

The problem for the analyst of foreign policy is how to sort out the normal functioning of the foreign policy process, which has strong patterns to it, from the abnormal and exceptional. The relationship between the "doing their thing" patterns of ordinary foreign policy behavior and the exceptional behavior of the U.S. government associated with political leadership is an important dialectic of U.S. foreign policy with respect to foreign aid programs in the sixties, to the operation of NATO, and to the projection of foreign military power in the Third World. These three subjects will be examined in greater detail, respectively, in Chapters 3 (on foreign aid),

4 and 5 (on Europe and NATO), and 6 (which deals with Vietnam). Patterns in the handling of relations with particular countries will also be observed in these chapters.

The Hero and the Infrastructure

The U.S. built a network of regularly performed actions and operations around the diplomatic activities of the late forties and fifties. This network building occurred primarily in the areas of foreign economic and military aid, information and propaganda activities, intelligence collection, and clandestine operations. Tended and sustained, these activities became institutionalized; performing them became the sustaining mission and the regular task of government agencies. The relatively stable procedures in the legislative and executive branches—administrative clearance and coordination, legislative authorization, appropriation, direction, and oversight—contributed to this routinization. These institutionalized activities served to define, implement, maintain, and normalize American foreign policy. At the same time, they reflect the widely shared expectation that the president would provide an extraordinary degree of leadership in foreign policy, performing what I have previously called his heroic role.

The central characteristic of these procedures has been their impact in turns on presidential power.[38] These elements of infrastructure may be considered instruments of presidential power when they support the ability to choose. But they can also have an opposite effect by denying the president choices. Such denial need not affect presidential power adversely. It may protect the executive from involvement in events and decisions preferably left to others, or to no one.

Regimes and Alliances

NATO is a major component of the American foreign policy infrastructure, the primary case of an institutionalized military alliance in the twentieth century. It can serve here to demonstrate the inclusiveness intended for the *infrastructure.*

NATO may be considered a *regime,* to employ a descriptive term that has enjoyed a vogue in writings about international relations, yet has remained strangely unused for this purpose.[39] The regime of the Atlantic economic-military alliance was founded, on the American side, by the Truman administration in cooperation with a bipartisan coalition of congressional leaders during the late forties. It was immediately noticed that the U.S. commitment to the Marshall Plan for the economic recovery of Europe, and to NATO for the rearmament of Western Europe, burdened the governmental process in Washington. These programs required annual legislative authorizations and appropriations and permanent agencies within the executive branch to run them. They required more of a role for the Congress than had been the case when foreign relations was largely a matter of traditional diplomacy. They also required new normalities in bipartisan executive-legislative cooperation. The program developed constituencies in the Congress, where members had voting records to defend, and in the executive branch, where presidential administrations inherited them, and where agencies held stakes in the administration of these programs. Private interests also became constituencies with stakes. Among them were the U.S. shipping industry, U.S. farmers, and U.S. manufacturers.[40]

For the United States in the sixties, the Central Treaty Organization (CENTO) and the Southeast Asia Treaty Organization (SEATO), in which the U.S. participated, were, as organized military alliances, serious formalities, but little more than that. Neither of them had integrated military or political organizations comparable to NATO's military and political headquarters.

The U.S. military apparatus and force deployments in Europe have been a regular, renewable, routinized part of American foreign relations. They require annual appropriations, which are carried in the annual Defense Department budget. Those legislative procedures are by no means utterly routine, but they are a regularly recurrent, highly structured way to deal with this commitment. The American ground, air, and sea forces assigned to Europe, the Mediterranean, and the Atlantic are dedicated to employment under NATO command and in NATO missions in case of NATO emergency, but they have been used for other purposes, as they were in Operation Desert Storm in the Persian Gulf in 1991. Their configuration, training, and exercising have been devoted to preparing them for their NATO mission. The existence of NATO, the U.S. leadership of it and commitment to it, have justified the continued stationing of U.S. forces in Europe, which, in turn, has strengthened the routinization of the U.S. commitment to NATO. Much the same can be said about the stationing of American troops in Korea. U.S. troops and the U.S. military command in Korea have been comparable in the sense that they have involved the routinizing of the American security commitment to Korea.

Other aspects of the infrastructure are revealed in U.S. relations with Asia and in trade policy. American commitments in Asia have changed substantially since reaching a high point during the Johnson administration. At that time, Johnson was attempting to win the war against the insurgency in South Vietnam and the regime in North Vietnam. These changes draw attention to John Jay's model of the executive who adapts and copes in a world he cannot dominate. When one forms and implements foreign policy under the pressure of events, one might be expected to focus on the variable margins of foreign relations and on ways of responding to immediate developments, to act pragmatically, even opportunistically. In fact, it has been Hamilton's executive, not Jay's, which has mattered the most, an executive with the qualities of the administrative chief, not those of the chief diplomat. As the postwar infrastructure was developed, the qualities of maneuverability and dispatch no longer applied. Instead, the requirement was for reliability and a steady commitment to programs.

Viewed in this light, aggressive, efficient diplomacy was not commonly accepted either in Washington or by the friendly trading partners of the U.S. government as a major goal for American foreign policy. Facility at bargaining with other governments to extract the maximum concessions on the assumption that the stakes were zero-sum did not fit the formative postwar condition. A more cooperative diplomatic game emerged for dealing with friendly powers. As a result of American optimism about free trade as a common interest of states, and American success as an alliance builder and economic power after the war, the United States was able to define its relations with friendly powers in terms of strong win/win or positive sum game relationships.

Free trade optimism was reinforced by an American condition that is now more clearly viewed from the experience of Japan's economic successes of the seventies and eighties. In the first two decades of the postwar era U.S. policies and U.S. negotiating positions were often underpinned by an export posture that subsidized American exports. Given the resolve of the Truman administration to aid Europe economically under the Marshall Plan, a certain kind of political logic, or expediency, dictated that it yield to domestic economic interests and require European states to buy American domestic products, even including American tobacco, with some of the Marshall Plan dollar credits. These required purchases were, by themselves, of little help in achieving the goals of the Marshall Plan, but they did assure the passage of the legislation that made other credits also available.

Given their interest in extending the policy instrument of foreign aid to the developing world, policymakers found similar ways to win steady support by vesting interests in foreign aid, not the least being Public Law 480 (PL 480), which provided the United States a convenient way to dispose of its surplus agricultural production. PL 480 had the particular feature of providing surplus American products at prices payable in local (nonconvertible) currencies. Recipient states, including in particular India, expected that these debts would eventually be forgiven or turned over to their own governments, as they in fact were. Positive sum optimism was thus reinforced with what we might call export optimism, and by favorable economic conditions. The U.S. economy could grow at a pace that moderated distributional politics while the fruits of the growth were "dumped" abroad. It is this combination of rapid growth and "dumping" (more judiciously, "export-oriented growth") that the Japanese have employed as a national economic strategy to such advantage in the more recent decades.

But we miss the vision of the years of positive-sum optimism combined with growth-and-dumping if we see them as nothing more than an open style of friendly relations. Compared with its application by Japan, growth-and-dumping had little vision to it with reference to the development of the American economy, but it did have a vision—a strategic vision—of foreign policy goals for the United States.

Treaties and other declaratory undertakings constrain national and presidential options by design. Even more tangible constraints grow out of actions directed to change objective facts, such as the capacity of South Korea to defend itself, of Egypt to govern itself, of India to feed its people, of Latin American countries to develop democratically. The stationing of American troops in Korea, the assisting of Brazil in the late fifties to develop a national war college (a project that, in the view of many, backfired in 1964, during the Johnson administration, when the Brazilian army took over the government), and the food and technical aid programs that formed in the fifties and early sixties, to say nothing of the famine relief program for India of the Johnson administration, are examples of constraining actions intended to alter objective conditions. They were commitments of the United States which took the form of programs not readily altered by a president. They generated networks of obligations and discreet opportunities to effect modest, incremental change which, sometimes, accumulated to become extensive change.

President Johnson occasionally referred to the burden on him of gaining congressional support for foreign policy measures, such as foreign economic aid, or the maintenance of forces in Europe or

Korea. Sometimes the burdensome task was to amend long-standing legislation or resist amendments; sometimes it was to win the votes needed for annual appropriations for foreign aid. It has often been noted that these procedures require the Congress to share political responsibility with the president. They also provide other benefits. The principal benefit is a normal procedure for adjusting and renewing the commitment of the U.S. government to its allies and foreign programs. These normal procedures, in turn, provide stability and continuity in foreign relations. The fact that these procedures became repetitive, that they are part of the routine of the Congress and the president, has provided reassurance in Washington and in the capitals of America's allies, clients, and antagonists. They have also been a continuing source of misunderstanding.[41]

While we need to be as clear as possible in the present study about these useful effects of normal foreign policy processes, we need also to acknowledge that they in fact can have perverse effects. A predictable infrastructure, one that involves patterns of institutional, noncontingent outcomes, robs its participants of influence by denying them leverage. It also facilitates the discreet exercise of influence over other governments at the technical level, where the give and take of functional cooperation is part of what becomes routine. Yet it can also result in the loss of influence over other players and other governments.

It is in this light that the Mansfield and Nunn resolutions and amendments are additionally instructive. Sen. Mansfield, by threatening legislative action unless Western Europeans carried more of the NATO burden, played a definite role in U.S. relations with Western Europe from 1966 until 1975, and Sen. Nunn has played a similar role more recently by reviving the Mansfield amendment device, by attempting to withdraw American troops from NATO unless more of the burden of defense was carried by Europeans. These legislative devices posed the threat that the United States would interrupt the routines of its support for NATO unless European members of NATO agreed to "free ride" less.[42] The independent acts of one congressional leader reduced the predictability of normal U.S. governmental processes and raised the prospect that the administration could, with less effort than had been previously supposed, take up the withdrawal option. The uncertainty of this situation strengthened the influence of the U.S. government with the European members of NATO. It induced them to pay closer heed to the sentiments behind the Mansfield and later the Nunn initiatives.

I. M. Destler argued that "to treat U.S. foreign policy primarily as the direct outcome of *decisions made by the President* is to distort the process considerably."[43] Foreign policy is generated by other forms of executive action besides the conspicuous "decisions" of the president that attract the attention of outside observers. One form is "to be ridden herd on," a phrase which he quotes from George Kennan. Another is captured by Graham Allison's phrase, the "management of piecemeal streams of decisions."[44] He worried about centralization: "What will happen on matters that cannot get 'the magistrate's attention?' " he asked, employing Alexander L. George's term. Here, indeed, is the problem. If foreign relations is in a class by itself among the issue areas of the federal government, it is because the president figures so centrally; and even if it is not in a class by itself, we must account for the president's significant role. At the same time, we must take account of the infrastructure, which, as noted, serves to enhance and inhibit the president in playing his heroic role.

It is the relationship between the hero and the clerks—the president and his immediate agents, on the one hand, and the keepers of the infrastructure on the other—that we must attend to in the chapters that follow. Three aspects of the hero-clerks relationship deserve brief further explanation here. First, the standards of synoptic rationality[45] would hold that foreign policy decision makers must anticipate the extended effects of foreign policy actions. Viewed in this light, the question of presidential performance, and indeed of the performance of the president's subordinates, comes down to how well they understand the workings of the infrastructure.

Second, we should question how much interest conflict can be expected in the multi-level games of foreign relations, i.e., how much conflict can be expected within one's own government, within other governments, and between governments, crosswise, linking different groups at the second and third levels. Understanding the relationships between internal and external games is vital. Even for knowledgeable bureaucratic political analysts the "model 1" norm is appealing: We *ought* to be able to speak with one voice and deliver on our threats and promises, and we *ought* as George Kennan said to be able to hold other governments accountable for what they agree to do, providing penalties and incentives for them of appropriate size at minimum cost to ourselves. The necessary inquiry begins when we recognize that these "oughts" are not necessities, but preferences that cannot be wholly achieved.

Third, even though states can be taken as unitary actors, at least for the purpose of holding them accountable and as a way of doing business with them—whether it is with respect to human rights, or arms control, or loans, or whatever—their options are limited for better and for worse by internal politics. As noted earlier, Kennan, at the beginning of the postwar era, was troubled particularly by this prospect—or by the fact that the president's spokesmen seemed to accept it as an unavoidable condition. The reaction in the late eighties to the extraordinary initiatives of the last Soviet leader, Mikhail Gorbachev, illustrates the ambivalent values of this constraint. His initiatives are seen to have been driven by internal factors, primarily economic but also political. These facts, to the extent that they are recognized, are a source of confidence because they explain Gorbachev and provide reassurance about the course he pursued. At the same time, they were a source of doubt about him. Would he be able to reduce the Soviet Union's foreign commitments and the risks involved in its relations with its adversaries? Would he be able to carry out economic reform? In its simplest form the doubt was expressed in Western Europe and the United States with two questions: "Can Gorbachev deliver?" and "How long will he last?" We now ask these questions about his successors.

Conclusion

Still a major component in the conduct of American foreign relations, despite the War Powers Act of 1973, and even after the executive-congressional contest over Nicaragua in the eighties, remains the protection of presidential authority and choice. This protection has had a special meaning in nuclear strategy. The original intent of "flexible response," as conceived at the end of the Eisenhower administration, and still its dominant meaning in the U.S. government at the end of the 1980s, was to protect presidential choice, i.e., to provide the president with a range of nuclear options at all times that would permit him to minimize nuclear danger. The president was not to be trapped by limited nuclear choices. Properly designed nuclear force postures and doctrines were supposed to provide the president with a suitable range of choice—suitable, that is, to the *president;* adequate systems of communication and operational plans were supposed to assure the effective authority to control and implement executive choices in a dangerous environment.

These requirements provided the starkest example of what is meant by heroic presidential action. In fact, flexible response was compromised not only because nuclear operations impose severe demands on command and control, but also because allies needed reassurance. Allies wanted to know, or believe, what Americans are often willing to tell them, that the president's choices are so constrained as to prevent his making any decision to opt out of their defense. A great variety of schemes have been devised since the early fifties, and were still being devised when the Cold War ended, to assure that this was the case. One such scheme, the Multilateral Force (MLF), is the focus of Chapters 4 and 5.

But foreign policy involves entangling alliances, economic, political, and military options foregone by design; actual and potential congressional action which limits executive choices; patterns of executive-congressional interactions; and patterns of executive-public interactions. All of these may constrain the exercise of executive choice. But this is to put the matter negatively when more is involved. Foreign relations, from the standpoint of a major power with allies, clients, and adversaries, which has been the usual American situation in the postwar era, involves the generation of options and the building of relationships of trust and fear—which is to say, the basis in credibility of friendly and hostile influence. For the existentialist (if not the pragmatist, the incrementalist, and the muddler), foreign policy is a stream of decisions, choices, and actions.

For the prudent investor, policymaking ought to be a stream of investment decisions about the productive employment of assets which will enlarge, discriminatingly, the range of choice and the capacity to influence. Foreign policy is viewed from this perspective in the present study. The four chapters that follow examine these relationships. With respect to influence, they consider how the internal games of governance relate to external games of influence.

This chapter has indicated that, with respect to the formation and implementation of foreign policy, there can be among individuals and groups a significant variation in performance. The Johnson administration's handling of selected foreign policies will serve as a means of examining these performance variants. Chapter 3 is a case study with commentary of Johnson's dealings with India during the grain famine of 1965–1967. The subject was selected because it marks the outer limits of Johnson's domination in foreign policy formation and execution. Chapters 4 and 5, likewise case studies with commentary, cover an important strand of U.S. relations with Western Europe during the Johnson administration, his policy toward the proposal to establish the so-called Multilateral Force (MLF). But the MLF case is scarcely similar to the Indian grain case as an example of dominating presidential control over policy; in fact, it is quite the contrary. Chapter 3 is fairly strongly interpretive as the conventions of case studies go; Chapters 4 and 5 are even more so. Chapter 6 deals with Vietnam. Only in a loose sense does it qualify as a case study. It is less descriptive and includes even more elements of commentary and interpretation regarding the workings of organizational processes.

If there are any grounds for ordering these chapters chronologically, it would be to put the chapter on India last. The author has chosen to present the Indian case first because its illustration of presidential domination over policy serves the development of the main ideas presented in this book.

The last chapter, 7, deals with generalizations about Johnson's foreign policy management record and observations about the general problems of presidential management of foreign policy. It builds on the issues laid down in Chapter 1 and the present chapter.

3. The Indian Famine and Presidential Leverage

ON A MILD SATURDAY MORNING in early November 1965, Lyndon Johnson telephoned Orville L. Freeman, his Secretary of Agriculture. He told Freeman that India's ambassador, B. K. Nehru, was sitting in the White House Rose Garden with him. Would Freeman come over? After Freeman arrived and greeted the president and Nehru, the ambassador turned to Johnson and asked, "What must we do?"[1]

The question was about the resumption of food shipments and economic aid to India. Johnson had suspended all aid to India (and Pakistan) two months earlier, after a three-week "war" had flared between the two countries over Kashmir. The suspension of food shipments came at a particularly difficult time for India. By the early sixties, the Indian government had become heavily dependent on American surplus wheat production. Well in advance of the June 1965 expiration of the agreement made a year earlier, the Indian government had asked the Americans for a two-year renewal. Indian officials expected a routine annual renewal of commitments. The logistics of handling so much grain required planning months in advance. But in April 1965, Johnson acted to prevent a routine renewal. Much to their dismay, Indian government officials found that, when their agreements with the Americans ran out at the end of June, the grain they needed was authorized by the president himself. By the time of the Rose Garden visit, Johnson had been refusing to authorize further shipments for several weeks.

No doubt India's grain shortage could be attributed to bad luck with the weather. The monsoon had failed to provide needed rain that year, and domestic grain production was a disaster. But prudence would have dictated that the Indian government maintain reserves against that contingency. India's desperate situation was the result of a long-term gamble not only that the United States would remain a reliable supplier of grain at a negligible price, but that it could be counted on to cope with the contingency of a national crop failure. India's grain reserves, by design, were in Kansas.[2]

By September 1965, New Delhi and Washington both knew that India faced famine. India depended upon a supply pipeline that extended back to the American Midwest. Johnson's cutoff assured that the flow of American grain would soon dry up. It instantly raised fears of disruption and famine. By November, these fears had grown acute.

Johnson answered the question that Ambassador Nehru put to him in the Rose Garden by stating that Freeman would be seeing India's Food and Agriculture Minister, Chidambaram Subramaniam, in Rome in three weeks at a Food and Agriculture Organization (FAO) conference. They should agree in Rome on specific measures to further strengthen India's food production as a precondition for resuming American aid. Johnson said that both men knew what needed to be done. Johnson had talked at length with Freeman about India's continuing dependency on U.S. grain in the early months of the Johnson administration, and the dialogue had continued thereafter. Johnson was concerned about India's lack of progress in solving the problem of dependency on American food imports. The outlook in the Department of Agriculture, where it was recognized (as the Indians knew) that American grain surpluses had to be disposed of, was that agricultural reforms that would make rural India more prosperous would substantially raise the demand for food in India. At any rate, agricultural reform in India, according to a prevailing view in the Department, would not have to come at the expense of American agricultural interests.

But the Johnson-Freeman dialogue had been interrupted in these recent weeks. Since Johnson had taken his initiatives with respect to grain for India, to take control and stop the shipments, he had refused to discuss the matter with Freeman—until the Rose Garden visit.[3]

Freeman and Subramaniam met as planned in Rome on November 25 and signed a secret agreement that set the rules for the Americans to supplement Indian grain supplies until the crisis was over. It dealt with what India would do immediately and over the months that followed to increase its food production. Indian officials had often declared their intention to achieve self-sufficiency in food production; the Rome Agreement stated the intention yet again, but went on to state how it would carry out the intention in terms of observable actions to be taken by the government of India. It stated these actions precisely enough that the Rome Agreement could serve as a working contract, so to speak, between Washington and

New Delhi. The terms of the Rome Agreement made it possible for the Indian government to know what it had to do to keep the grain shipments coming from the United States and made it possible for U.S. officials to monitor India's food policies and determine whether India was living up to its end of the bargain. This arrangement remained in effect over the critical year that followed and, after an interruption, until the food emergency was over. The existence and enforcement of what amounted to an enforceable contract are what made the Indian grain shortage, or rather, the Johnson administration's response to it, an extraordinary event of foreign policy management.

Johnson's handling of the Indian food shortage case is an extreme example of presidential initiative overriding routine policies in bilateral relationships that are predominantly friendly. It will serve to identify major questions about foreign policy management in the Johnson administration and more generally. For the sake of clarity the main points of this chapter can be summarized as follows:

* Johnson intervened in the handling of PL 480 grain shipments to India. He took direct control over these shipments, which he approved only month-by-month. He used this control over the supply of American grain to India to force the government of India to carry its reforms of agricultural production further than it would have taken them otherwise. His aim in increasing Indian grain production was to free India from dependency on U.S. grain imports. The Indian government had committed itself publicly to such reform, but had not effected the changes it claimed to be making. Very few Indian officials were firmly committed to agricultural reform. Others were committed only in principle and still others were either indifferent or hostile to it. In addition, the government was unable to act decisively about anything other than consensus-precipitating threats like the Chinese invasion of 1962. The famine had not produced the strong consensus in the Indian government necessary for a grand-scale reform of India's agricultural policy, in part because knowledgeable Indians expected the United States to solve their food problem.
* Washington and New Delhi had become accustomed to dealing with one another so as to minimize conflicts over policy, administration, and domestic political complications on both sides. Johnson, as an experienced American legislator, knew something about these practices. When he chose to intervene, circumstances were favorable in both Washington and New

Delhi for his intervention to be effective. On the American side, two factors made effective action possible once India's demands for enormous quantities of U.S. grain were known. First, U.S. grain surpluses, after many years at high levels, were shrinking. Second, responding to this change, and what it perceived to be its constituency's interests, the Department of Agriculture (USDA) was seeking a larger role in foreign relations, mainly to promote grain exports on cash and credit terms. These factors made it possible to consider stopping the shipment of grain to India and to seek an enforceable performance contract with the Indian government. On the Indian side, the appointment of a Minister of Food and Agriculture who was interested in major changes in India's food production policies and willing to employ American demands for change as a part of his own strategy for change established a point of influence for the United States.

* President Johnson's application of leverage against India demonstrates general relationships in the execution of foreign policy in any administration, particularly two: (1) the critical relationship between normal processes of foreign policy administration and directive policy, and (2) the relationship between both modes of foreign policy implementation and the employment of influence.

These points will now be explained in greater detail.

Making Foreign Aid a Habit

National economic development quickly evolved in the late forties into a major objective of American foreign policy. It was first pursued in Western Europe, where the immediate problem was recovery from war disruption and damage. Then it was applied to countries in other parts of the world, where the problem was usually defined as "underdevelopment." Economic development proved to be an elusive goal. By the Johnson era, this fact was quite clear, yet economic development remained a widely accepted objective of U.S. policy. It was a reflection of American ideas of progress more than of realities in the Third World.[4] It had also proved to be too narrow a concept. The central feature of an American aid program was a bargain that the United States would provide some economic and technical benefits on condition that the recipient country would take certain actions. These actions, it was supposed, would, in combination with the American benefits, generate economic development.

Western European economic recovery occurred more or less according to plan. Rarely, if ever, however, did actual results meet the expectations voiced in Washington during the early and mid-fifties about economic development outside of Europe, in the developing, pre-industrialized economies. Among the recognized causes of failure, one important element was the difficulty of getting recipient governments to deliver on their own promises. Two usually insurmountable obstacles prevented delivery. The first was their own manifest incapacity to act. This was a common characteristic of most governments. The second was the difficulty of measuring performance, which usually made it impossible for the United States to hold a recipient government to its promises even when it might be capable of meeting them.

Commodity aid to India—mainly surplus American grain—had been an important component of India's agricultural policies during the 1950s and early 1960s. Throughout the 1950s, U.S. economic aid officials, more planners and program implementors than bargainers, made the American export of grain to India under the surplus disposal statute PL 480 as predictable and routine as possible. India's national leaders were devoted to central economic planning of sorts. They had built their economic policies around five-year national economic plans. To accommodate this practice, as well as to reduce the "transaction costs" incurred in Washington by annual reviews in Congress of foreign aid projects, the Eisenhower administration had constructed a five-year commodity aid plan for India in the late 1950s. The Kennedy administration at first adopted even more enthusiastically than had its predecessor the idea of such long-range commitments, building this feature into its own major foreign aid initiative, the Alliance for Progress, a program—more accurately, a campaign—for economic and social development in Latin America.[5]

By 1965, American economic aid to India had been provided on a continuing basis for nearly fifteen years. The American AID officials in New Delhi and Washington were thoroughly familiar with the constraints on India's economic performance. They knew their Indian colleagues and the problems these officials faced. The Indians they dealt with likewise knew the problems of their U.S. counterparts. As the annual cycle of planning, negotiations, and legislative action (authorizations and appropriations) occurred year after year, a degree of mutual trust and tolerance developed among professional civil servants that amounted to a form of administrative integration across governments.

The Americans were sufficiently trustful to defend Indian performance, within the executive branch and in Congress, as the best that could be expected. The patience thus demonstrated by American program officers reassured Indian officials so much that they let their own grain reserves dwindle until India was dependent in the short term on the reserves "in Kansas."[6] Within each group, knowledge and norms shared with the other served to reassure, maintain confidence, and influence on a day-to-day basis while limiting expectations on each side about substantial change. The result was a relatively smooth working-level relationship between the two governments.

To be sure, stresses from above, from professional and appointive officials, and from the legislative chambers often disturbed this relationship. Both in the U.S. Congress and the Indian parliament questions about performance and influence in connection with U.S. foreign aid were raised. Information supplied by government spokesmen was greeted skeptically in Washington and New Delhi alike. But executive officials and legislators in both capitals had a stake in the smooth functioning of the aid program. It was, indeed, a symbiotic relationship, based on need on both sides: the Indians needing grain, the Americans needing to get rid of it. The two national groups of working-level administrators muddled through together, cooperating in the face of a complementary interest to make it easier for each to cope with its own bureaucratic difficulties.

Among the difficulties were the normal preferences of politicians, including Johnson, to avoid political trouble over foreign aid. It was not surprising, therefore, that the modalities of technical and economic (and after 1962, military) assistance to India fit minimax strategies: They gave heavy weight to avoiding errors and much less weight to achieving output or performance goals when such goals entailed risks to the foreign aid programs and their managers. "Best effort"[7] was a relatively riskless performance standard. It could not serve to prove that those American officials who were associated with Indian aid had failed or even erred.

American help with India's economic development plans reflected an American perception that the United States had an interest in their success. It also reflected the favorable opinion of many in the United States toward India's government. American critics of India rarely attacked it for being undemocratic—a common complaint in that period about many governments that Washington aided, such as Brazil, Peru, Pakistan, Iran, South Korea, Thailand, and Vietnam. India, to be sure, was sometimes attacked for being leftist or socialist. But the latter objection had weakened. President Kennedy shifted American foreign relations toward the democratic left. This shift favored India and strengthened its position vis-à-vis the United States. Kennedy's sending of Chester Bowles to India as ambassador in 1963 furthered this trend. Bowles was an enthusiastic advocate for India.

By the early 1960s, in Congress and within the executive branch as well, the idea of a long-term aid program had come under question. Where the Indian government had been able to obtain five-year commitments in the 1950s, now it could expect only two- or one-year commitments. Faced with delay and growing resistance in Congress, in 1964 the Johnson administration negotiated a one-year agreement which ended in June 1965. As that end approached, Johnson took the action cited previously. He vetoed the normal "roll-over" of commodity aid to India, a temporary extension that was designed to keep the grain flowing until Congress acted. When the agreement actually ended, commodity shipments continued moving on month-by-month presidential authorizations.

This practice of the U.S. president deciding, month-by-month, whether more American grain would be shipped to India was in effect by November 1965, when Johnson and Freeman met with Nehru, and in late November, when Freeman met with Subramaniam in Rome. It continued until March 1966, when Johnson loosened his grip on food shipments during a state visit of Prime Minister Gandhi to Washington. It was reimposed later that year, in August, and maintained until the grain crisis was over in 1968.

Johnson's involvement in Indian food aid was direct and decisive. His intervention abruptly altered a relatively stable linkage between two governmental bureaucracies. The changed relationship served, in turn, to support efforts already underway within the Indian government to change India's agricultural policies and to assure that they went further than they were otherwise likely to go. His intervention became a collaboration with a faction of Indian officials, lead by Subramaniam, who were, in effect, hard-line green revolutionists, who were willing to have their arms twisted by the American president, but who, to preserve their own credibility at home while advocating reform, complained about the arm twisting. Johnson's expressed motives assured that India made the maximum possible effort for agricultural reform and enlisted other governments in the effort, and preserved his credibility with the U.S. Congress; he was determined to demonstrate that he was not, as he would have put it, a "rat-hole" man. Johnson's critics have claimed that he acted out of personal pique with India's prime minister, Indira Gandhi, and to pressure her government to support his Vietnam policy. Further, they have argued that his efforts were in vain—that India was already carrying out the reforms he demanded; still further, that his demands were counterproductive because they punished America's

Indian friends. These critics are wrong. Johnson intervened largely to force India to reform its food policy, and he was largely successful in his intervention. In his memoirs Johnson does not give his interventions credit for India's self-help achievements, but Freeman does in his memoirs.[8] These claims are not wide of the mark, as further evidence will show.

The First Period of the Short Tether

India was not the most important issue in early 1965 for the Johnson administration. With a stunning electoral triumph in the presidential election of 1964, Johnson was pressing forward with his domestic programs, while European economic and security issues occupied the Department of State, the Department of Defense, and NSC officials. In midyear, as the annual rollover of foreign aid commitments approached, aid to India ranked high among aid programs. Yet the rollover question was handled routinely until Johnson, on his own initiative, vetoed it. When he did, there was only a hint of famine-sized grain shortages. But the failure of the harvest was soon confirmed. In the first months of 1965, as Indian officials sought to assure a smooth rollover of the commodity aid program for India, they had little success in competing with more urgent issues. But its urgency changed for Johnson when India, now desperate, turned almost exclusively to the United States for succor.

Several circumstances made Johnson's intervention in the commodity aid program for India promising in the prospect of its making a difference in India's agricultural policies:

1. The USDA had become a competitor to AID and the Department of State, a knowledgeable rival within the U.S. government to which Johnson could turn in seeking to change the way the U.S. government handled commodity aid.
2. Johnson and Freeman (the secretary, USDA) judged that India now had in place a food minister who was competent enough to deal with their demands for change in India's food policies.
3. The PL 480 agreement with India had expired. A new one needed to be negotiated.
4. Congress was visibly restive about existing arrangements and about India's performance under them.
5. The World Bank, which provided parallel aid to India, also had a parallel interest in inducing change in its long-standing aid policies in India.

The fourth of these circumstances, the restiveness of Congress, was scarcely new, but for a president usually able to dominate the legislative calendar, it was not simply a minor inconvenience for Johnson that Congress delayed passage of foreign aid legislation until exceptionally late in the 1965 legislative season. It was a downright embarrassment. Johnson had given his domestic agenda highest priority in Congress. A delay in Congress with foreign aid affected the momentum of his domestic legislative agenda, and for this reason Johnson was manifestly sensitive about Congress's skepticism regarding foreign aid. One could add, therefore, a sixth condition:

6. When Johnson acted to address the issues that troubled the Congress over foreign aid, his credibility in Washington, and presumably in New Delhi, was relatively high.

Freeman and the USDA: Setting the Internal Stage for Change

Perhaps the most critical requirement for Johnson's initiative was the availability of a well-developed idea about what to do and how to do it. The actual origins of the idea are dim. It became "available" when Freeman seized it and made it a major element in his effort to win a stronger role in foreign affairs for the Department of Agriculture.

American grain surpluses peaked in 1960, just before Freeman became Kennedy's Secretary of Agriculture. The USDA remained for several more years a major supplier of American grain to needy foreign governments,[9] but surpluses were declining and the USDA began to search for another role. Freeman, as Kennedy's Secretary of Agriculture, had staked out a positive mission for the USDA: to promote American food surpluses as a cash crop. He looked to a near future in which the U.S. balance of payment account deficits—by the early 1960s, these deficits were persistent—would be offset in part by the hard currency earnings of American food exports. It was an innovative objective, one that attempted to anticipate rather than wait and react to problems associated with world food markets, to recast agricultural policy from surplus disposal at the taxpayer's expense to a source of revenue (as well as foreign exchange), and to gain a player's role in economic foreign policy for the secretary and the department.

Freeman formed distinct friendships with both Kennedy and Johnson.[10] Both were impressed with his political savvy and his capacity to work through problems with the Congress and think in terms of the president's needs, despite the fact that his own political base in Washington was an agency historically held captive by a major if diminishing clientele group. Freeman, in turn, was adept at packaging and brokering policy ideas that he found in the USDA.

The attractions of Freeman's idea to export American farm products for cash grew with the mounting concern in Washington over the trade deficit. Johnson and his advisors feared growing pressures to withdraw American troops from Europe and other adverse reactions to the deficit. Robert McNamara, the Secretary of Defense, with Johnson's encouragement, had permitted the aggressive promotion of foreign arms sales, particularly in Europe, to assure that American troops could be kept there, and Johnson himself became involved in offset negotiations with the Federal Republic of Germany directed to this purpose.

Freeman, with strong support in his agency, had assumed the role of an innovator in agricultural policy. He was an agency head advocating a distinct plan to address a major national political problem of particular concern to the president. Reputedly, Freeman nourished presidential ambitions. The plan to sell grain for hard currency would give him and his department more bureaucratic territory in the prestigious domain of foreign relations. Freeman's bid for a role in foreign relations may have gained additional support in Johnson's eyes from Johnson's quarrel with Sen. Fulbright, who was chairman of the Senate Foreign Relations Committee.[11] PL 480 remained the unchallenged domain of the Senate Agriculture Committee. The more of a role that the USDA could assume in foreign relations, the less dependent it was on Fulbright, because USDA actions would not come within the purview of the Foreign Relations Committee.

But expanding the USDA's role in foreign relations challenged the established positions of the Department of State and the new foreign aid organization, the Agency for International Development (AID). USDA spokesmen argued that "only agricultural experts could really specify a less developed country's agricultural needs,"[12] that the State Department was too concerned with diplomacy and AID with industrial development. Amendments to PL 480 in 1964 and 1965 extended the powers of the Secretary of Agriculture over counterpart funds, and in 1966 an agreement with AID extended USDA's "role in planning, implementing, and evaluating technical assistance overseas."[13]

These laws provided Johnson with an alternative to established, patterned ways of handling foreign assistance. They reflected the importance to Congress, which Johnson keenly sensed, of the lack of demonstrable positive effects in aiding recipient countries. By expanding its mission, the USDA challenged the cautious positions assumed in AID and State, where experience had worn down expectations about what economic and commodity assistance should be able to accomplish. The "best possible effort" was the most common performance standard applied to economic assistance for India, as well as for other countries.[14] USDA's chief officials, with Freeman in the lead, insisted that aid recipient governments could be held accountable for achieving development goals. Freeman advocated tying commodity aid to performance.[15]

The USDA's bid offered an opportunity for a change in policy, an alternative to the status quo in foreign aid which protected ongoing programs and bilateral relationships, a status quo that was reinforced by the behavior of the Department of State. State tended to treat economic and military assistance programs with a certain complacency because these programs provided it with resources for achieving foreign policy objectives that did not count against its own budget.

Searching for the Key to Performance

Johnson, in his efforts to cope with congressional opposition, was the inheritor of a new mood of skepticism which followed from the disappointments over reforming foreign aid in the early sixties, particularly after the high expectations generated in the Kennedy administration's promotion of the Alliance for Progress.

Earlier, Walt Rostow, in a widely read and thoughtful tract published in time for use by the new Kennedy administration, had advocated (1) the multilateralization of economic assistance and (2) the adoption of political (as distinguished from economic) development objectives, (3) with assistance provided on the basis of measurable performance.[16] All three points were elements of a growing consensus among development experts in the universities and the government, including congressmen and their staffs. The experience with economic assistance during the fifties had demonstrated that economic development could not be isolated from the broader phenomenon of political development, although it could hardly be said that the relationship between the two was well understood or that there was much agreement about it.[17] According to the conventional wisdom of the time, economic aid donors needed to be multinational agencies. That experience had also shown that aid-recipient countries often found it difficult for political reasons to be seen accepting advice from another government. It was not a matter of conventional wisdom, although it was equally obvious, that conditional grants needed to be based on performance standards which would be sufficiently precise for effective enforcement. These two requirements were often in conflict with each other.

Within the U.S. government, strong voices advocating the multilateralization of aid could be found in the Treasury Department, where a concern about holding recipients to performance standards was growing. This view converged with a rising conviction among multilateral agencies that they ought to insist on performance. The Indian consortium, a group sponsored by the World Bank, was one of these. By March 1965, Robert Komer, the chief Asian expert on the NSC staff, reported to Johnson that "the other consortium donors agree that we should use our future pledges as a lever to get better economic performance."[18]

The Indian government had been highly effective in protecting itself from leverage employed by donors through foreign aid. Its first line of defense was the "steel frame" of a skilled civil service. First, Indians had become skilled "in dealing with Western agencies and functioning in the complex milieu of international institutions."[19] With a large, well-educated, and experienced civil service, India had a distinct competitive advantage over many of the newly created states. Indian officials had moved into central positions in these international agencies. They were attracted to such jobs and to jobs with western national agencies.[20]

Second, the Indian government had adopted and refined tactics for handling the international milieu, particularly development assistance. One of several tactics was to "keep its foreign aid bargaining dispersed." In a dispersed milieu, India could "occasionally . . . play off one benefactor against another," and in any case, maximize the autonomy of Indian development planning.[21]

Third, India's relatively strong central planning institutions provided effective protection against the efforts of foreign governments and international agencies to set priorities for India in the course of providing development assistance. John P. Lewis draws upon his own experience as an American foreign assistance official to describe how India's officials "by-pass any effective United States direction of indigenous development activity." The procedure has been for the Indian government to ". . . present to the United States authorities a long list, drawn from the next phases of its development plan, of projects requiring local financing and to say, in effect, 'These things are going to be done anyway. Which ones would you like to finance?' "[22]

Sometimes the United States "secured modifications in selected projects and occasionally [it] persuaded India to accept alternatives to those on the list," but it did not exercise "any major initiative as to project choice."[23]

The second line of defense—a much deeper defense—was the internal structure of India's political system. The United States had to deal with "the Centre"—i.e., the national government of India. But the Centre, in turn, had to reckon with a vast empire of states governed not only by the "steel frame" of the civil service, but also by the Congress Party, which was a federation of state parties. The implications of this important political fact for dealing with the United States can be seen in the way the Centre handled its first succession crisis, when Lal Bahadur Shastri became the head of the government upon the death of Jawaharlal Nehru in 1964.

Shastri postponed some industrialization projects and gave more priority to agriculture as part of his effort to stabilize his political support. These acts pleased those American officials—Bowles among them—who judged them a significant change in policy. Bowles had been encouraging India to shift its economic development priorities in the direction of food production, and the shift seemed to be an acquiescent response. But such a shift could have been superficial, insufficient, or simply unsuccessful. It could have been a gesture to please some political groups or accommodate a passing mood; it could have even been a serious undertaking which failed, the unrealized intention of a government carried along by events beyond its own control. This last possibility is not just speculation. Later, a common interpretation of the Congress Party setback in the national elections of 1967 was that the government had failed to achieve the results it claimed to seek with its economic reforms.[24] If this assessment is true, Johnson's short tether may have contributed to the shortfall in certain respects, but other factors were more prominent. For one, at a critical time for economic planning Shastri weakened central planning by turning to the villages for political support. He was coping with a fundamental regime problem of succession, and not responding to Bowles's persuasions. The latter were a mere whisper in the noise of India's domestic politics. Shastri was concerned with political survival, not Bowles's logic.

As remarked earlier, Freeman visited New Delhi in late April 1964, shortly after Shastri took these measures favoring agricultural interests. Shastri's concessions to rural interests had not actually been implemented by then, but he had taken another action that proved to be more important. He had appointed Subramaniam as Minister of Food and Agriculture. Talking with Indian officials, Freeman advocated the adoption of "capitalist" market measures (higher prices paid food producers, private farm businesses along with existing government and cooperative agencies) and modern technological measures (mainly fertilizers, but also improved seed and insecticides). Freeman's advice was ignored in New Delhi for economic reasons with which AID officials sympathized. It would prove harmful to two common goals of industry-centered economic development, the conservation of foreign exchange and import substitution.[25] It was Freeman's view, probably shared by Johnson, that the Indian government rejected his advice because of what he called "Fabian socialist" prejudices.

Freeman was impressed with India's new food minister. But he concluded that, despite the claim of Shastri's government that food production goals had been set to render India self-sufficient, the government was not carrying out this intention. Freeman had tried to persuade Indian officials to pursue self-help goals and had encountered a particularly effective form of self-protection. The Indian food minister, Swaran Singh,[26] agreed to self-help. He did not, however, agree to make the kind of changes in India's agricultural policies that Freeman advocated to achieve self-help. Bowles reported later that what Freeman advocated was being done.[27] The differences between Bowles and his embassy staff, on the one hand, and Washington, on the other, became evident with this report. But Singh was soon replaced in a cabinet shuffle by Subramaniam, who immediately expressed interest in actually pursuing self-help and the particular prospects of linking it to American aid.[28] The situation in India had now changed critically. From Freeman's standpoint, Subramaniam was willing but not yet able to act. Viewed in these terms, the cutoff had the potential of drawing the attention and focusing the purposes of an otherwise distracted Indian government. For Bowles, the cutoff was wholly unjustified and in fact counterproductive.

Johnson Begins to Move

In April 1965, Bundy's staff presented Johnson with a request for two large-scale continuance items, first, a "substantial advance out of next year's money to the Indian Consortium." Second, "AID would like to make a $100 million advance along these lines shortly" also. The request was part of the normal procedures often followed to assure that economic aid programs would continue from one fiscal year to the next. Without warning, Johnson responded "no." His explanation was brief if disingenuous: "because I'm afraid we may have no for[eign] aid bill."[29] He immediately went further, establishing procedures that required his specific approval for larger program loans, AID programs, PL 480 commodity shipments, and the Indian (and Pakistani) consortium loans.[30]

A week earlier, Johnson had asked Komer for a brief on U.S.-Indian relations. By then, tensions were rising between India and Pakistan along their southwestern border in the Rann of Kutch, as indicated by reciprocal troop deployments there. This development was immediately embarrassing to the Johnson administration because the U.S. government had been supplying both sides with arms (Pakistan since 1954 and India since 1962, following the Chinese incursion in Assam). Johnson claimed to be worried about adverse shifts in congressional moods when he first began to draw in the reins on aid renewals for India. Maybe he was not, but these military tensions would surely have become a factor for him at least by the end of June.

Johnson did not explain himself to the Bundy staff.[31] At first, they thought it would be a brief delay. Komer cabled Bowles to assure his government contacts in New Delhi that Washington recognized their needs, and at the same time, advised Johnson to conclude another one-year agreement in order to keep the grain pipeline to India full.[32] Komer had missed the seriousness of Johnson's intervention.

For many months Bundy and Komer knew little more than that Johnson was withholding or delaying his approval of foreign aid measures (money and commodity authorizations), and that his stated reason was his concern about congressional support. Nevertheless, Johnson's "no" was immediately translated into a "hold order" for PL 480 shipments.[33] The short tether or leash had been put into place.

Johnson's intervention was of the sort that produced mind-focusing, action-forcing deadlines. It took the AID associate director, John Gaud, a month to conclude that more was involved than a deadline exercise and tell his Indian contacts that the duration of the agreement was in question. The Indians had pressed well in advance for a two-year commitment; by May they were visibly nervous about the delay.[34]

These were the circumstances under which Johnson asked for a "quiet new look" at the whole foreign aid program. Two officials conducted it, the AID director, David Bell, and Thomas Mann, now the Under Secretary of State. The Bell-Mann report took a modestly critical position about foreign aid and recommended a one-year extension of the four-year PL 480 agreement with India that was drawing to a close.[35]

Johnson was feeling his way. Frequently Bundy, Komer, and other advisors, in turn, responded to his limited cues by telling him what they knew about the implications of where he was leading them. Both he and they accepted this procedure as a matter of course. They regarded it as a legitimate way for a president with other priorities to proceed. But it caused much discomfort when it raised issues requiring urgent clarification and the assessment of the utility of economic sanctions in foreign relations. Such questions as "What should be asked of India and Pakistan before assistance of any kind is resumed?" were difficult to address.

At about the same time, Ambassador Nehru had come up with the question, "What must we do?" Bundy and Komer, assessing possible answers to their related question of what to expect from economic sanctions, rejected the idea of applying leverage through the withdrawal of military and economic aid in the Kashmir dispute: "We cannot tie our economic aid to positive progress on Kashmir. We can tie it to reasonable progress under observance of the UN ceasefire resolution and to the acceptance of political process. We can also tie it to other basic US interests."[36]

Another question regarding the U.S. approach to the food pipeline could be handled in such a way as to preserve the possibility of future leverage. The United States would not have to decide in advance exactly what ends that leverage would serve or how to apply it. Johnson reviewed the leverage questions with Secretary Rusk, and also with two outside advisors (or "Wise Men"), Arthur Dean and Clark Clifford, who acquiesced in employing leverage against India (and Pakistan as well). They raised passing questions about the appropriate means and scope, but quickly narrowed their concern to one point: Only on issues of undisputed parallel interest should leverage be applied. Johnson authorized a one-month extension of food shipments on September 23.

When the next renewal fell due, Bundy reported that he had again reviewed this matter with Dean Rusk, Clark Clifford, and Arthur Dean: "They all believe strongly that a one-month extension is the best arrangement. . . . [W]e are . . . beginning to get to the Indians that their agricultural performance is weak. They are on notice to respond to this challenge. Until they do, month-to-month action makes good sense. . . . But none of us sees any point in letting the pipeline break."[37]

In the Rudolphs' valuable theory,[38] global power politics employed by the president clashes with the regional and local interests of smaller powers and with the perspectives of the regional experts in the permanent ranks of the U.S. government who manage the functional ties of the United States with these smaller powers. One cannot deny that in October 1965, American interest in South Asia was related to global power politics. Until the summer of 1965, the United States had been supplying arms to both India and Pakistan as a counter to military pressure from China and the Soviet Union, respectively. Washington had cut off aid to both countries because of their own border war, not because of any change in estimates about Soviet and Chinese interests and intentions. But the immediate concern in Johnson's staff turned the regional-global construct of the Rudolphs upside down. Bundy and Komer feared that India and Pakistan would try to counter American pressure by maneuvering between the United States and its global competitors in South Asia, a fear that was not unjustified. They recognized that, in effect, regional powers could employ Washington's concern with global power politics to protect themselves against American pressures. Johnson was evidently more concerned with the performance of India's economy than with an American role in settling South Asian military conflicts. While this faced him in a different direction from his national security staff, his position did not fit the Rudolphs' distinction between regional and global concerns much better. The Soviet Union had played the role of intermediary in settling the Kashmir War. Had it not, Johnson would have undoubtedly given more priority to that role for the United States. We thus have a ready explanation for why he did not do so; but that does not eliminate the importance of his non-security objectives in dealing with India, given his deep involvement in accomplishing them. He demanded performance from India and was unwilling to let anyone else define the political limits of his demands.

Komer shared the prevailing view in Washington that one must not use economic assistance to interfere directly and overtly in politics, but he recognized that the U.S. government could not apply leverage effectively to achieve the substantial increases in food production that India needed unless it was prepared to challenge the Indian government's interpretation of what was political interference. Komer's sense of this is indicated in a letter he signed in June 1965. Speaking of "the job of rethinking our Pak/Indian policy," he said:

> First is the question of what we're trying to accomplish with our massive aid program. Many regard it basically as a long term investment, and one in which we should not be unduly concerned about the limited short run returns. This has been our basic philosophy, especially in regard to India [where we have done it] consistently despite the fact that India's particular brand of isolationism and Asian neutralism has often worked against our shorter term interests.
>
> Essentially this rationale would argue for attempting to help

meet [India's and Pakistan's] basic needs for growth without attempting to use our aid too much as political leverage. Resist using aid for political purposes, in other words. *Without contesting the long term goal of our effort, I would still ask whether our day-to-day policies won't have much more effect on our ability to realize our longer term investment than some of my colleagues suggest.*[39]

By stating his doubts about the seriousness of attempts of the Indian government to solve its grain problem, Komer set Bundy and himself apart from what might conveniently be called the Bowles or pro-India group in the government.

George Woods and the World Bank: Discovering an Ally

The World Bank initiated its own reappraisal of lending policy toward India. The relationship between that reappraisal and AID's evaluation of foreign assistance later became a matter of controversy in New Delhi, and it is therefore important to understand what the World Bank actually did.[40]

Like AID the World Bank depended upon building relations of trust and confidence—what George Rosen called "technical persuasion"[41]—with officials of client governments. In meetings held during June or July of 1965 in New Delhi, bank officials told the Indian government that the AID-Indian consortium, which the Bank chaired and convened, would not be able to increase its loans to India unless the Indian government adopted a set of economic reforms, including measures to liberalize trade. Since the World Bank's principal shareholder was the United States government, it was often accused of following U.S. recommendations, a charge that attacked the World Bank's multilateral status. Indian officials repeatedly made this charge public. In the privacy of the New Delhi meetings with the World Bank, however, India's negotiators were more realistic. They faced an immediate demand from international bankers, who claimed to be acting on behalf of governments which were consortium members, to consider ways of improving India's economic performance. This demand, it should be noted, came just at the time when Indian officials were nervously awaiting the results of Washington's review of its bilateral aid programs with New Delhi. With Washington's hand still undisclosed, the Indian negotiators challenged the bankers: Were they speaking for themselves, or on behalf of the consortium? The question referred to the Americans, in particular. Would they take a less firm stand than the Bank, as they sometimes had in the past? The reply was that the Americans were in line with the Bank's position.

The meeting in New Delhi in late June 1965 occurred at a time of rising nationalist sentiments in India. Shastri's government faced border conflict with Pakistan in the Rann of Kutch, a barren sector on the western Indo-Pakistani border. In public, some Indian political figures attacked the Bank for serving as an agent of Washington and "Wall Street," a particularly serious charge because it appealed to inherent fears about capitalism and challenged the multilateral structure of the Bank. The conventions of public judgment were that the Bank must be wholly independent of the United States. Privately, however, the Indian delegation indicated that it would not take seriously the Bank's new, tough line about economic performance unless that line had the support of the U.S. government. The delegation took this stand not because it believed the Bank's position *ought* to run parallel to or be backed by U.S. policy, but because it would be more practical. In the past, India had been able to use AID's more lenient policies to force the World Bank to moderate its own.

Bank officials were able to respond as they did because they were aware of the direction being taken at that time in the "quiet review" of American aid policy for India. That review, in turn, evidently served to orient David Bell, the AID administrator, to a new way of dealing with India. The Johnson administration had already decided to take a firmer position about India's economy. When the World Bank finally ended its meetings with Indian officials, that moment marked a milestone. The World Bank had broken out of a pattern of accommodation with the Indian government that had left it with little leverage and that had also weakened American leverage.

The relationship between Johnson's decision and George Woods's about how to deal with India became a matter of extreme sensitivity in New Delhi, because the Bank stood for multilateral independence. The evidence indicates that the influence was mutual, but that the World Bank was further along with the formation and implementation of policy. If one direction prevailed, it was the Bank that precipitated the White House's resolve to take action and change direction. In fact, at this point the president had not made clear to his staff where he was going, and he probably did not yet know. As noted, Johnson was not only reticent about his goals. He did not make them clear to Bundy and Komer, to Bell of AID, or even, as we saw at the beginning of this chapter, to Freeman, who was to become a major and extraordinary participant later on when Johnson did act.

Johnson's failure to decide precisely and explain his goals clearly to his staff is partially explained by the numerous priorities he had to address. South Asia occupied only a small amount of his attention and figured in a very limited way in his programmatic interests. But events there forced a change in both the growing antagonism between India and Pakistan that summer and the growing food crisis in India. The delayed passage of the foreign aid bill in Congress that summer and the record of congressional discomfort associated with it doubtless also registered with Johnson. These events threatened Johnson with further trouble at home in any case. The mini-war between Pakistan and India further threatened to produce acute embarrassment for him with Congress because the United States had been supplying both countries with economic and military aid. Johnson may have kept his own counsel in part because he feared leaks from the White House that would complicate his efforts to manage congressional action.

Woods, once he had resolved to take a tougher position with New Delhi, faced much less of an implementation problem than Johnson's because his staff was smaller and more controllable than Johnson's. Implementing a tough stance with India could be expected to bring the World Bank under attack from almost every quarter in India, and it did; but the Bank, even though its staff was multinational, could count on a degree of cohesion lacking in the much larger arena of the U.S. government. That itself would have been sufficient reason for Johnson to want to delay signaling a parallel decision, and since it made sense to delay, he also had reason to avoid much discussion even among his immediate staff. Johnson also had less prospect than Woods of changing such a policy without drawing notice and causing dissension. The pro-India factions within the State Department, AID, and indeed, the White House—career and appointive officials with a record of advocacy in favor of economic, commodity, and (since the Chinese attack in 1962) military assistance—had to be reckoned with. Johnson did not choose what would doubtless have been a laborious and costly process of persuading the Indophiles. Instead, he chose reticence.

But there was more to Johnson's reticence than these circumstances reveal. This personal characteristic merges with a more general one. Johnson was not the first president to withhold information from his staff in order to protect his own options.[42] Johnson habitually left to his associates the task of figuring out what he wanted. The truth was not something to give away to anyone; they (and "they" included his closest staff associates) must find it out for themselves.[43]

The Rome Agreement as a Performance Contract

Freeman and Subramaniam met as planned in Rome on November 25, 1965, and signed a secret agreement dealing with what India would do in the immediate future and in the longer term to increase production of food. The Rome Agreement restated India's oft-stated intention to achieve self-sufficiency in food production, but its importance scarcely lay in that fact. It was significant because it transposed this general intention into distinct performance commitments that remained the basis for a working understanding between India and the United States over the critical year that followed and beyond. At last, Washington had a distinct understanding with a responsible Indian official about what India would have to do to receive the U.S. aid it wanted.

Immediately upon his return to Washington, Freeman wrote to Johnson expressing his view of the Rome Agreement as a *performance contract:* "For the first time the Indian Government, through its Agricultural Minister Subramaniam, has made concrete specific commitments to the United States which will if carried out vigorously significantly improve India's agricultural performance. The critical question remains: How can the United States make certain that pledges are followed by performance."[44]

Freeman expected that the next steps in publicly committing the Indian government to these specific terms would be taken now that Subramaniam was back in New Delhi. First, "the Indian Government in the near future will make a public pronouncement on agriculture incorporating the agreed upon actions and targets with a commitment to accomplish them." Second, Subramaniam would spell out to the council of state "a plan of action to meet the current crisis and incorporate the commitments made at Rome in such a presentation." Freeman spelled out, in turn, what the U.S. government could do to reinforce Subramaniam's efforts to move the Indian government in the direction of agricultural reform:

(a) Length of Public Law 480 agreements can be conditioned to the performance of the Indian Government.
(b) The agricultural action commitments can be incorporated into the AID arrangements with disbursements conditioned on the Indian Government meeting its agricultural commitments. Precise detailed criteria to measure performance and insure action can be negotiated. Failure on the part of the Indian Government to perform will be surfaced under such a procedure and the appropriate action decision can be made accordingly.[45]

Freeman even proposed a "sequence of actions," or a scenario:

(a) Communicate to Prime Minister Shastri that spelling out as the plan of the Indian Government the commitments made in Rome would be favorably received by the United States Government.
(b) United States announce another short term PL 480 agreement.
(c) Following Indian Government public commitment perhaps through Subramaniam's proposed December 8 speech to the Council of State, U.S. Government would then compliment the Indian Government on strong new efforts and announce the opening of negotiations for a further extension of PL 480 for a longer period (but still limited).
(d) When the U.S. Government resumes negotiations for economic assistance it will be made perfectly clear privately that assistance will be geared to the Indian performance in meeting their agricultural commitments and targets.[46]

Freeman notified Bowles of the understanding he had with Subramaniam about what steps the Indian government would take to strengthen agriculture.[47] Bowles, in turn, reported back on December 6 the Indian Cabinet's approval of the program for strengthening agriculture.[48]

USDA was now at the center of action. Johnson, to acknowledge this fact, issued National Security Action Memorandum No. 339 (NSAM 339). Referring to the "critical Indian food situation," it instructed Freeman to establish a special interdepartmental committee to coordinate American efforts directed at the Indian famine. USDA had now achieved its goal as a major player in foreign commodity aid programs. NSAM 339 took the action away from AID and State and away from Bowles and put it in the hands of the Secretary of Agriculture. He intended to employ his new authority to induce the Indian government to do what it had been saying it would do to achieve self-sufficiency in agriculture by 1971.

Subramaniam's December Visit to Washington

Subramaniam arrived in Washington in mid-December, where he met with Rusk and with the president himself. He also had extended talks with Freeman, with AID, State, and Defense officials, and with representatives of the World Bank. He dined with twenty-five members of the House and Senate. He met with representatives of American fertilizer companies. Before Subramaniam left, Freeman summarized the visit for Johnson.[49] The senators and congressmen, he noted, questioned Subramaniam closely on self-help efforts (a term that referred both to short-term efforts to cope with the famine and long-term efforts to increase food production). "They also pressed for information on what countries other than the United States are prepared to do to provide food, fertilizer and other assistance to India in the crisis months ahead." Johnson had already made this concern his own.

Implementation Procedures

Subramaniam's visit served several purposes. It built a public record and a more complete internal governmental record of feasible commitments to be used by both governments, a record that would facilitate monitoring India's performance. If the U.S. government was going to influence the Indian government to follow a course of parallel interest—to do what both governments wanted India to do, but *to do more than India would have done in the absence of U.S. influence*—then more had to happen than reaching a meeting of minds with Subramaniam, even though he was a Cabinet officer who had the backing of the Cabinet, even though he agreed with Washington's viewpoint, even though the agreement was in writing.

Where parallel interests are recognized, and agreement occurs on common objectives, persuasion has already achieved its main purpose. The problem then shifts to implementation: What can be done to achieve these objectives, given the resourcefulness of each government's officials? This was where Freeman and Subramaniam now stood. The question had become how the U.S. government should deal with the Indian government so that not only Subramaniam, but other Indian officials who did not share his sense of the priority needed for agriculture policy or his stake in a successful agriculture program, would go along with agricultural priorities. The design of the Rome Agreement itself and of the meetings with Subramaniam in Washington seems to have been directed at answering this question.

Subramaniam had more at stake than did Freeman or Johnson. It would not be surprising if he saw this quite clearly, nor surprising if he was disappointed with some aspects of the Washington visit. According to Freeman's report to Johnson, Subramaniam "asked what he might say on his return to India[,] expressing concern about possible political attacks from the Communist and fanatic Hindu party if there were no definite and measurable assurances of further

United States availabilities [i.e., general economic assistance]. I responded that he knew his own politics best and I couldn't tell him what to say."[50]

Freeman's goal was to have detailed operational arrangements with the Indians that could be monitored and enforced: Subramaniam detailed the *long-term* policy and program commitments which the Indian Cabinet had agreed to later. The program follow-through was "not as precise or detailed as the plans to meet the short-run logistic problem," according to Freeman. But Freeman and Subramaniam established methods by which to evaluate India's progress. Working with AID and the Indian government in Washington and in New Delhi, the program would be jointly reviewed each quarter. Freeman hoped this would make it possible for the administration to know whether the Indians were "just talking or making tangible progress." Freeman stated that "such a procedure will make it possible for the U.S. to make long-term aid and technical assistance contingent upon specific actions and measured progress by the Indian Government," and Subramaniam acknowledged this proposal.[51]

Mrs. Gandhi and the Question of Partnership

Indira Gandhi, India's new prime minister, came to Washington in late March 1966 on a state visit. She had been in office for scarcely two months. Her state visit provided an opportunity in Washington to assess her potential as India's leader and explore in Johnson's terms whether a working relationship could be established with her. The main premise of the American response to the Indian famine was that the Indian government could be induced to commit itself and be held to its commitments. India's prime minister occupied a critical role in economic development and foreign relations, and Mrs. Gandhi was a new factor in this strategy. A working relationship with her was essential to validate this premise.

The Johnson administration's objectives in preparing for Mrs. Gandhi's visit revolved around her role as the critical player in a working political relationship. The background and position papers prepared for the visit confirm that the relationship "at the top," between the two heads of state, needed to be strengthened and verified—a striking change from the preparations that had been made for a canceled Shastri visit nearly a year earlier.[52]

Expectations in the Department of State about what India should and could do had been raised significantly since the previous summer. A year earlier India's "best efforts" in food production had been accepted at the State Department's headquarters and at the embassy in New Delhi as adequate performance. Two years earlier Bowles had reported that Subramaniam was carrying out what Freeman had proposed in their first encounter. In March 1966 the situation looked much different. Subramaniam's "program is still largely on paper,"[53] and "[i]f put forcefully into effect . . . promises the first frontal attack on the intractable problems of raising agricultural production."[54] Where it had been common to accept India's choices about internal economic policy, now there is "general agreement among us and other major Western donors, including particularly the World Bank," that India must "loosen up the web of bureaucratic controls over economic activity, and rely more on the private sector and the market."[55]

The new perspective in the Department of State was now in line with the USDA view. Johnson wanted to employ Mrs. Gandhi's visit in the leverage effort to achieve increased food production in India. In early January, Freeman, as chairman of an interdepartmental committee to coordinate economic and commodity aid to India, sent a team of specialists to India to obtain "more solid information on the crop short fall, . . . port facilities, planned improvements and internal distribution plans."[56] The committee then turned to consider whether to send a team headed by Freeman that would carry political weight, one that included congressmen and possibly representatives from other countries that supplied India with wheat. The questions raised about this proposal revolved mainly around applying and protecting U.S. leverage. The committee considered directing attention "to overall agricultural needs in the less developed countries in general by visiting a country other than India" as well. Its tough regard for protecting Johnson's U.S. options is demonstrated by this question: "Would a prominent team so dramatize the United States' interest and contribution that if next summer it is widely reported that Indians are starving (which is likely no matter what we do) the United States would be insulated from the charge both at home and abroad that we failed to act promptly despite the fact we had heavy reserves of wheat on hand?"[57]

Johnson by this time had communicated something about his own aims with respect to India. In mid-1965 he was enigmatic; by the end of the year, Freeman and the committee seemed to be working with a fairly clear idea about what Johnson wanted. By March 1966, the Department of State's staff work in preparation for Mrs. Gandhi's visit showed even greater clarity in the president's goals. Now reflecting Johnson's viewpoint, State's strategy paper spoke of striking a bargain "at the top" about a basic economic reform program. Nothing like this had appeared in the visit book prepared for the previous summer's scheduled visit of Shastri.

The purpose of the visit, as defined in the Department of State, was to insure that Mrs. Gandhi understood that "the future of our relationship depends on reciprocity. . . . India has an obligation to do everything in its power in its own behalf . . . to strengthen its economy . . . and give higher priority to efforts to achieve *self-sufficiency in food production*."[58]

Acknowledging the value of India's connection with Moscow, the strategy paper was critical of India's public stance about China. The United States had supplied India with needed war material in 1962 when China attacked India through the Himalayas. Now, the United States was involved in containing China by supporting the regime in South Vietnam, and it wanted equivalent support from India: "*We need some public sign that in any major conflict of interests between China and the U.S., India stands with the U.S.* India must refrain *from publicly criticizing U.S. policies.* . . . When disagreements occur, they are dealt with privately."[59]

Both papers paid much attention to a reciprocal recognition of constituency constraints. "The important thing," as the talking paper put it, "is that we each understand each other's internal situations, particularly as they limit or otherwise relate to the conduct of our bilateral relationship. As working democracies, *we each have a constituency in the other's country*, which we each must heed in the future."[60]

Consistent with this position, another background paper noted that the agricultural reform program had encountered stiff resistance from the Indian states and warned that Subramaniam "will run a considerable personal political risk."[61]

In Washington, Mrs. Gandhi's state visit went well. Johnson was impressed with her, or said he was. He lavished praise on her. Evidently he thought he had succeeded in establishing a working reciprocal relationship with a skilled and tough political leader. On March 30, following up, he sent a gracious message to Congress endorsing India's "sound plans for strengthening its agricultural economy and its economic system."[62] The message emphasized the importance of self-help and the need for other governments to share in the effort. Foreign economic aid was in trouble in Congress. Johnson, using the Gandhi visit to advantage, won a unanimous vote on a joint resolution supporting emergency food aid to India.

The Gandhi visit also served as the stage for Johnson's announcement that he would send 350 million more tons of PL 480 grain and commit $88 million more in economic aid grants and loans. As had long been planned,[63] the short tether now ended, only to be reimposed five months later, in August. During the interval, relations soured on both sides. What accounted for this souring?

On the Indian side it was the failure of the Indian consortium to provide India with the foreign exchange credits it expected when New Delhi devalued the rupee in June 1966. The rupee devaluation all but failed. Rapid domestic inflation wiped out the foreign exchange advantage initially gained by devaluing. The government blamed the consortium and especially the United States because they did not provide prompt debt accommodation.

The consortium was not entirely to blame. Its behavior reflected in part the fact that the Johnson administration had already quite deliberately changed, and would change further, the terms of its relations with India—what one staff paper, written in preparation for Mrs. Gandhi's visit to Washington, called "the economic bargain with Mrs. Gandhi."[64] The U.S. position would continue to evolve and to be a source of strain between the two governments.

Johnson's Disappointment

On the American side, the main problem with India for Johnson was Prime Minister Gandhi's public behavior after she visited Washington, which Johnson evidently considered improper for working partners. In his eyes, her denunciation of American imperialism in Asia during a visit to Moscow that June was probably her greatest misstep. It may be a measure of how much Johnson was isolated among the officials of his own administration that no one seems to have stated the view, which was wholly compatible with the American planning position for the Gandhi visit, that Mrs. Gandhi's behavior undermined confidence in the main premise of the American response to the Indian famine. The premise was that the Indian government could be induced to commit itself and be held to its commitments. Her shrewdness served different purposes, or so it evidently appeared to Johnson. She not only sought to distance herself and her government from the United States, which was a requirement for any nationalist leader in India, but to discredit Johnson's Indian policies to a degree which would insure that her government would not have to fulfill its commitments to the Johnson administration, or so it seemed. In high politics, it is a short distance from trustworthy guile to untrustworthy malevolence. Johnson, the preeminent politician, evidently found Mrs. Gandhi attractively guileful, only to reconsider and judge her malevolent—too clever to trust.

In New Delhi, just before coming to Washington, Mrs. Gandhi had signed an agreement with the Soviets to have them build a large steel plant at Bokaro. In Washington, the project appeared to be a showpiece, one that would give Indians an exaggerated impression of the extent of Soviet aid in comparison with American aid. This event did not seem to dampen Johnson's enthusiasm during her visit, but it may have been reassessed when she went to Moscow and criticized Johnson's Vietnam policy. One of Johnson's critics, Mitchell B. Wallerstein, has observed: ". . . Lyndon Johnson *never* understood the Indians (although he was remarkably conversant with the nature and extent of their food problem), and he would accept no advice from those in the government who did. His misapprehension prevented him from realizing that much of India's public reaction to the short-tether policy (e.g., Mrs. Gandhi's statement in Moscow) was political posturing meant more for domestic consumption in India than as a meaningful foreign policy statement. . . . But, by this time, Johnson was increasingly obsessed by his own personal demon, the war in Southeast Asia, the war which was consuming his presidency."[65]

What is even more to the point, the guidance that Johnson received from the foreign policy and foreign aid segments of the government (i.e., the Department of State and even the NSC staff, and at times AID, Defense, Treasury, and the intelligence community) proved unconvincing on the question of domestic political constraints, or regime capabilities, in India. If his critics are correct about his failure to understand Indian politics, then it should also be recognized that the problem can be put in reverse. Over time, the foreign policy and foreign aid segments of the government lost the confidence of the White House regarding their handling of foreign aid; and a critical element of that loss was their assessment of what the United States could reasonably expect the Indian government to do in response to U.S. demands. "Best efforts," the seemingly casual phrase that justified India's performance (and the performance of other aid recipients), referred to important conclusions about Indian governmental behavior that had now lost their credibility for Johnson and for his restive colleagues on the Hill.

Johnson proved to be wrong about Mrs. Gandhi, by his own apparent rating. But he did not prove to be wrong about another estimation vital to famine policy: the claims from Indian sources, usually endorsed by American officials until American policy changed, that unless the United States made at least annual commitments of grain tonnage well in advance, famine relief would prove to be unmanageable. Early in the famine crisis, Johnson instructed his staff to inform him immediately of a single death from the famine that was attributable to American delays.[66] They were never able to. Their failure, of course, only proves that it was either difficult to acquire reliable bad news, or that it was difficult to determine the sincerity behind India's pleas for long-term aid in the first place. Johnson successfully challenged these pleas for aid.

Shortening the Tether Again

In late August 1966, Johnson scrawled across the cover letter accompanying a State-AID-USDA recommendation on PL 480 allotments for India and Pakistan, "We must hold onto all the wheat we can. Send nothing unless we break an iron bound agreement by not sending."[67] This was the beginning of the second phase of the "short leash policy," which consisted of another period of short-term commitments and monthly bargains with India. This policy lasted, with some variation in intensity, until the day before the American presidential election in November 1968.

Freeman continued to monitor India's efforts to meet the Rome Agreement performance goals throughout 1966, and to insist that these commitments be met. But by November, he shifted his position and began advising the shipment of more grain.

He was not alone in this view. Rostow, who had reluctantly gone along with Johnson's short-tether policy, by then had also shifted, as can be detected by his report to Johnson on a meeting with Bell, of the World Bank, and with one of Bell's associates, Sir John Crawford. Rostow reported to Johnson that "Crawford on balance felt that our short-leash policy last year helped Subramaniam in pressing for his programs within the Indian Cabinet. Now he feels that Subramaniam has won most of his battles and would be better served by having an assured supply to work with."[68] Crawford also advocated multilateral arrangements to build India's buffer stocks.

The National Election of 1967

Johnson lost the initiative with India in late 1966. As the election of 1967 approached, it was prudent to let up on the demands for performance. American internal staff papers said this in December 1966, and probably earlier. The outcome of the elections themselves served to stay the hand of American pressure. They were a setback for India's Congress Party and they put Subramaniam out of elective office, an outcome that gave Bowles's complaints against Johnson's

India policy increased weight. They of course forced Subramaniam out of his appointive post as Minister of Food and Agriculture. Johnson, as noted, nonetheless continued to limit grain shipments until late 1968.

It might appear that the election of 1967, because of its outcome, marked the limit of effective American pressure. It has been charged that Johnson's pressure on Mrs. Gandhi's government produced a political setback for those Indian officials who were associated with the agricultural reform program. It would be difficult to disprove a connection between American involvement with India at that time and specific outcomes in the 1967 national elections in India; it would be equally difficult to prove a significant association. The setback in Subramaniam's political career from defeat in the 1967 election proved temporary and his "pro-American" stance as Minister of Food and Agriculture, if indeed it figured in his defeat in 1967, did not remain a significant political handicap to him. Major interpretations of India's political history in this period do not define Johnson's policies as a significant issue relative to a great many other forces at work in India's political and economic system.[69] The 1971 general elections in India disclosed that the Indian political system was continuing to change significantly,[70] and during the seventies Mrs. Gandhi herself took the initiative to deregulate other administered markets besides agriculture as a remedy to economic stagnation, the very remedy that she had resisted when pressured by the World Bank and the U.S. government in the mid-sixties.

Beyond the Famine: Parallel Interests and Regime Limits

The Indian food shortage case is an extreme example of presidential initiative overriding established cross-national relationships among experts involving "deliberative coordination," as the Rudolphs have termed it,[71] and other routine procedures. It should be clear by now, however, that Johnson's behavior in handling the Indian grain shortage did not lack serious purpose, and that he was lucky. As it happened, the threat of famine arrived in India just as Freeman and USDA could offer him a credible alternative to the established policy of disposal of surplus American grain production through soft loans, mainly to India. At the very time that the grain crop failure and the prospect of famine in India became known in Washington, American farm policy, under Freeman's leadership, was changing in a direction that facilitated Johnson's response—that indeed made a real change in U.S. policy politically and administratively feasible.

At the same time, within the concessional aid community in Washington, a rationale for changing the terms of reference for such aid had been developed and was known to Johnson. It emphasized the importance of economic incentives for increasing agricultural production. The elements of a major policy innovation were in place. To understand the import of the resulting innovation will require more attention to the situation that existed before the status quo was altered.

Functional, Technical, or Administrative Integration and Asymmetrical Bilateral Relations

The routines of regular business between the Indian government, on the one hand, and foreign governments and the international agencies, on the other, had evolved into resilient and stable links that facilitated routine communication and deliberation. Unfortunately they were also capable of facilitating misunderstanding and miscalculation when stakes and objectives changed. The standard operating procedures, or SOPs, that served as intergovernmental links had narrowed their business to technical matters. Harmonious working relationships were often achieved and maintained by ignoring or avoiding issues of policy and interest conflict.[72] Such linkages can be extraordinarily valuable because they operate at a working level on a routine and continuing basis, partially integrating elements of the U.S. government with elements of the governments of allies and client states. Integrative relationships became normal means of communication and influence in both directions. They work in part by isolating technical administrative functions from political and policy functions, or by defining mixed problems as technical whenever convenient. Domestic government and private agencies work in a similar manner.[73] This complex relationship between policy and politics, on the one hand, and administrative and technical matters, on the other, may be the oldest acknowledged problem of public service.[74]

Policy can be submerged in administration, and submerging it can help stabilize governmental programs by stabilizing the politics (the players and their stakes) that underlies policy. In domestic programs, policy maintenance depends upon stable alliances within the governmental process among governmental and nongovernmental players. The same statement applies to foreign policy, but policy maintenance there also depends upon stable arrangements with other governments. These are a form of functional or administrative integration.

Asymmetry and Access

The process of issue management can have quite different implications for the United States in foreign affairs than in domestic affairs. Whether the United States is dealing with other governments
through multilateral channels or through bilateral channels, there
is often an asymmetry in the stakes and attention of the governments involved. American officials who normally dealt with India
in the decade before the famine rarely had the same access to the
president that their colleagues in the Indian government had to the
prime minister. These differences are readily demonstrated and explained. Three exceptional people, B. K. Nehru, John Kenneth Galbraith, and Chester Bowles, show the difference.

Nehru had been India's ambassador to the United States since
1961. Much earlier, beginning in 1947 and for seven years, he had
been a special envoy to Washington. He was a cousin of India's
founder and first prime minister, Jawaharlal Nehru.[75] Galbraith was
ambassador to India from 1961–1963; Bowles, from 1963 until 1969
(and previously, from 1951–1953). Galbraith and Bowles both were
political friends of President Kennedy's, to be sure, and their assignment to New Delhi during the sixties was the result of Kennedy's
intention to give India special attention. But while India was an important sideshow, it was not the main event.

India was simply not as important in Washington as the United
States was in New Delhi throughout the sixties, and indeed, is not
today. The initial response from Washington to the Indian grain crop
failure only underlines this point. The pro-India factions within the
U.S. government, when confronted with a request for more than ten
million tons of grain in 1965, were strongly inclined to treat the
request as a technical challenge and thereby to contain the way this
extraordinary request was handled within the government. To treat
it as extraordinary would have been to acknowledge that it was
political and demand more attention for it, which would complicate the administrative process in the executive branch and cause
the administration problems in the Congress. The initial response
avoided or at least minimized all of these possibilities.

Diverging Expectations

Another asymmetry was the expectation of each government about
the other. These expectations had been stabilized and were relatively congruent in the early sixties, but had now changed character.
Given the close working relationship that had evolved among India,

the United States, and the World Bank, the size of the U.S. and World Bank's offices in New Delhi grew, as did the offices of India's government in Washington. This growth in staffs seems to have generated exaggerated expectations about common interests and cooperation, because the cooperation that occurred between them was largely on technical matters. As is often the case, technical cooperation in bilateral relations was working to hide more fundamental issues.

These factors had an immediate bearing on Indo-American relations as they developed under the stresses of the grain shortage and pressure from Johnson. They also affected multilateral relations, particularly the critical difficulties between India and the Indian consortium over rupee devaluation and consortium help. From previous experience, the Indians were entitled to expect the consortium to talk tough, but eventually to provide the credits. This assumption now proved to be in error. The consortium changed its accustomed behavior, catching India's officials by surprise.

Development Politics and Relative Desperation

Finally, another asymmetry was the degree of desperation or risk proneness that governed India's dealings with its outside sources and set it apart from the political environment in which American officials worked to offset the U.S. advantage. *Risk prone* and *risk averse* are terms of political art usually employed to differentiate individual players within the same economy or polity. I apply it, respectively, to Indian officials and American officials collectively. Their different behaviors reflect the uncertainties present in their different national political environments. No doubt some Indian civil servants and elective officials were more risk averse than comparable Americans. But others seem to have been more risk prone. India's political leaders dealt in large value allocations and uncertainties regarding their own political fate. That is what was so striking about Subramaniam. Comparisons across polities regarding this uncharted factor are difficult, to say the least, but scarcely avoidable if we are to understand the roots of the Indo-American relationship during this period. Indeed, Bowles and other critics of Johnson have made a strong case that his short leash exposed America's friends in Indian public life, and Subramaniam in particular, to such severe political risks that it amounted to punishing them for being our friends. Yet, on the face of it, Subramaniam understood from the Rome meeting on that he stood between his own government and a foreign taskmaster.

Collectively, India's rulers dealt with questions of life and death of a tragic magnitude. They planned India's development throughout the fifties and sixties and beyond with the knowledge that roughly 40 percent of their population was, and would remain, in absolute poverty.[76] Since they lacked the capacity to change this situation very much, it was unavoidable that their decisions dealt with this massive poverty only on the margin, and therefore, that they made life-and-death decisions about India's populace on a scale scarcely imaginable in the United States. By choosing egalitarianism in the rural sector, they chose against food production efficiencies and therefore, against lives. It seems that they also chose to advance industrialization to achieve greater autarky for the sake of national independence and national security, at the cost of lives at the poverty level. Doubtless the issue of life and death usually remained in the background, to be handled tacitly, but it was not invisible within the Indian government and most certainly not when India pressed the U.S. for increased aid after the failure of the grain crop in 1965 and 1966.

In this case, as in others, desperate political actors may have been unreliable because their rational interests were forcibly narrowed and they acted on a different time scale from the time horizons of their allies and mentors. A common assumption governing Indo-American relations was that India's democracy and development objectives (though not always India's plans) ran parallel to American interests. The grain shortage and Johnson's probing raised a question about whether India and the United States could actually move along in the same direction harmoniously, a question that went well beyond the premise of shared democratic values. India's political leaders were too desperate to be able to deliver in order to meet their part of a bargain. Given what an American president needed from foreign political "partners" to assure that he did not have to expend a disproportionate amount of his own political capital to pursue their parallel interests, this desperation made the foreign partners unreliable. This observation applied to India, with the noteworthy exception of Subramaniam. The desperation of Indian officials, according to this interpretation, made them too prone to play for short-term political gain, too preoccupied with holding their domestic political coalition together, too reliant on nationalistic appeals at the expense of the foreign partner, too committed to the status quo of internal political power and governmental performance to respond themselves to the crisis of food and dependence, perhaps too locked into the status quo even to recognize that they had become utterly dependent upon the United States for regime survival. If Johnson developed a personal hostility to Mrs. Gandhi, as seems probable, it was very likely as a reaction to this sort of desperate behavior on her part. No one can disprove this charge, made by Johnson's critics. The argument in this chapter does not seek to. It is that other, more substantial grounds for his short tether policy can be demonstrated.

Arnold Wolfers and Laurence Martin noted a fundamental difference in perspective between the traditions of European politics and the American tradition of foreign relations about the exercise of power by national states in the international system. The European tradition was governed more by necessity—by the absence of policy options—than the American. It recognized less opportunity for choice.[77] For Wolfers and Martin, necessity arose from the close intersection and overlapping of national interests in a Europe crowded with modern states. It defined a distinct international political culture, which they termed the European tradition in statecraft. But necessity—domestic necessity, the necessity of regimes on the edge of their own survival—could also constrain the motives and behavior of developing states, rendering them unreliable allies and clients, even when they are democracies. Something similar could also be said of democracies in politically and economically developed states, particularly where the government of the day rules with narrow margins. Critics of the United States concerning the Vietnam War made similar charges, that it was desperate and therefore unreliable.

Johnson confronted a severe constraint of necessity in dealing with India: a government that had to make decisions that condemned millions of people to poverty in order to hold the state together. John Mellor writes of the consequence of these decisions:

> The failure to raise the incomes of the poor resulted in their continued alienation from the economic system. While the chosen strategy probably was effective in binding disparate geographic regions of the nation together it did not harmonize the interests of the different economic classes. Geographic barriers to food movement would become an important issue in late 1966. . . . This damaged India's image in Western countries which are not enamored of growing industrial power in Third World nations and tend to judge economic progress in the Third World largely in terms of poverty alleviation. The question for the future [he wrote in 1979] is whether India can formulate a development strategy that improves the lot of the poor and also adequately serves other national and international political needs.[78]

Comprehensive Political Assessment: Limits Not Assessed

Supplying assistance, whether commodity, economic, technical, or military, is never a neutral act. It helps the recipient regime. Rulers and their governments must manage with what they have; supply assistance adds to what they have to manage with. Rarely does an aid-recipient government lack the minimum of governing viability, which is a capacity to shift at least some of its resources to offset the direct effect of outside aid that comes with strings attached. India was no exception. "To the extent that the aid recipient can transfer resources from one sector of the economy to another," Myron Weiner has asked, "does it matter which projects, which sector of the economy, or even which region received *foreign* assistance? The total performance of the Indian economy was so linked to the strategy pursued by the government, which in turn was facilitated by foreign assistance, that it is not very useful to explore the political effects of specific foreign-assisted projects."[79]

At the very least, if the provider government is interested in the effects of its grants within the recipient country, rather than confining its interest to generating and implementing the grants themselves, its foreign aid officials need to know enough about how the recipient's political economy or polity works to assure themselves that the intended effect of the help is not nullified by the recipient's employment of autonomy-protecting countermeasures. The functional or technical perspective that Johnson thrust aside when he intervened in aiding India made it appear that the issue was feeding starving people. But India, earlier, had made choices which brought on the threat of starvation,[80] and it used food from outside to maintain those choices. Just as arms purchased from outside can maintain a status quo, so can food from outside. The bilateral aid relationship reflected normal organizational behavior within the constraints of that relationship. India sought to preserve its autonomy and to reduce risk and uncertainty.

Bargaining, Leverage, and Diplomacy

The symbiotic relationship at the working and technical level of foreign aid generated a powerful drag effect. Policy innovation could scarcely be expected to arise out of that situation in the way, say, that it does in the private sector where customers or users often are a source of innovation for suppliers.[81] It is no surprise that innovation came from outside the working relationship, or even from the top, spreading down in the executive branch of the U.S. government.

The president also had a leadership role to play with respect to foreign aid in dealing with the Congress. Johnson habitually expressed his own sense of his limited choices or power by speaking of his problems with handling Congress. As indicated, that is what he did when he refused to continue AID and consortium funding. But his references to Congress were sometimes misleading. Sometimes, when Johnson said he had to adjust his policies to coincide with what Congress would support, he meant no more than that. In the Indian famine episodes it appears that he also intended another meaning. He meant to remind his listeners that it was he, not they, who had to come to terms with the Congress over his programs. It was his way of saying what Harry Truman meant when he put the sign on his desk that said, "The buck stops here." It was evidently this assessment about his political exposure that alerted him to the rising stakes for him in India.

Johnson's references to Congress also served as a bargaining device. He reminded his listeners that he was subject to constraints that must limit their expectations about what he could do. In particular, Johnson's references to the congressional vulnerability of foreign aid positioned him to do business with foreign government officials who commonly protected themselves against American demands for performance on similar grounds. For the authentic political player, and Johnson was one, the claim of political constraint is nothing if not understandable. But when it is employed disingenuously it challenges the principles of reciprocity upon which a sound political relationship depends and requires a response such as the following hypothetical comment:

> You tell us that you are doing all you can to meet our demands for your economic development because to do more is politically impossible. If we are to accept your estimation about what is possible for you to do, then you must accept our estimations of our own limits. If you want to do business with us, we both must recognize that each incurs political as well as economic costs. If you put your political costs and limits beyond discussion, but will not allow us to do the same with ours, then we cannot do business.

This comment of course does not address the options of players who have no choice but to do business with one another.

Nothing was more important for the reviews of foreign aid programs that took place in AID, in the Department of State, in the USDA, or in the World Bank and other multilateral agencies in the spring of 1965 than the way this question of political feasibility, or the political limits of performance, was handled. Governments claim they are doing the best they can and rarely if ever can anyone prove that they are wrong. The question was, how much should one trust the other government when it said this? Where there was a basis for trust, political constraints could be accepted, as one senator accepted the judgment of a trusted colleague that he must vote his constituency's interests on the bill in question. Where no experience served to establish the needed trust, the claim rang hollow for a political player of Johnson's experience. As much as anything, this consideration may explain Johnson's seizure of the Indian food shortage issue.

After Mrs. Gandhi's visit, Johnson continued to demand what amounted to a coordinated policy on famine aid to India. The task of overseeing it fell largely to Walt Rostow, who had succeeded McGeorge Bundy as Johnson's National Security advisor. Rostow performed his job enthusiastically until late in 1966 when he joined the loyal opposition among Johnson's White House assistants and tried to persuade Johnson to release India from the short tether. In August (or earlier), with domestic wheat prices "unusually high,"[82] Johnson asked Rostow specifically whether PL 480 shipments to India should be stopped in order to bring wheat prices down in support of his administration's anti-inflation policies. Under Johnson's prodding, domestic price tracking proceeded on a weekly basis, and with it, the tracking of world production and prices. Johnson also persisted with his demand that other governments participate and was particularly incensed when India bought 200,000 tons of wheat from Australia on commercial terms.

Parallel Interest and Political Influence

Finally, we return to the first question that must be addressed in a bilateral relationship, the question of parallel interests.

With respect to India, a parallel interest seemed obvious. The United States wanted the Indian economy to develop and prosper. Given India's poverty, there was little to lose and much to gain for U.S. interests from such a change. At the same time, the routines of U.S. relations with India masked some serious persistent differences of interest between the two governments. The principal questions confronted in administering foreign aid programs, which quite naturally were addressed on the basis of the prevailing wisdom about development strategies, concerned efficiency. They dealt with how to allocate foreign aid resources to optimal effect within recognized political constraints. More fundamental questions, however, lurked behind the allocation question.

Increased food production had become an accepted norm of American economic development doctrine by the late fifties, a norm on which Bowles and Freeman, for instance, could agree. Developing countries could make more productive use of their investments in agriculture than in heavy industry, as many of them were doing. It was not disagreement about this policy statement that separated factions within the U.S. government, but disagreement about how much should be done to implement the policy.

The Indian government had more to worry about than the optimal adjustment of resources according to some macroeconomic model of its national economy. It was also concerned with governing India, a job which tended to force the government to lean toward satisfying the urban population at the expense of the rural population because the latter could less effectively protest. (The Chinese government evidently forgot, or never learned, this rule, until student protests in Tiananmen Square instructed it in 1989.) It also had to worry about the rising expectations among those people in absolute poverty; they comprised roughly 40 percent of the population throughout the sixties. The economic analysts could consider the optimal distribution of investment resources between industry and agriculture, but for the Indian government, investment in industry was indeed an investment, while investment in agriculture could increase the demand for food among the rural poor enough to offset any gains actually made in food production. For the governors of India, investment in agriculture carried a risk of rising consumer demands that would set back their hopes for economic development. India's economy stagnated in the mid-sixties; and it is noteworthy that increased consumer demand has not been held responsible. The demand for food increased during the first half of the sixties, prior to the grain shortage, and this demand has been attributed to increased industrial employment during this period.[83]

Even the Rome Agreement, to say nothing of the short tether, posed starkly the question of a parallel interest. Assuming that the United States had an interest in ending the Indian famine, did India have an interest that paralleled Washington's in being coerced into major changes in its food production policies? Was it a good idea to push India into giving such priority to food production by this method, i.e., by increasing its reliance on market incentives? This would (and did) mean significant changes in India's allocation of resources among its national accounts. Johnson would have been justified in adopting a coping strategy, rather than a fixing strategy, given the lower priority India's problems held in the U.S. government. But considering the magnitude of the food crisis, and of India's demand for American grain, stronger action was supposedly justified in order to preserve American policy options. When Freeman asked whether the United States would be blamed for famine in India if it strictly enforced the requirements for those deliveries, he was describing the perverse situation in which the U.S. found itself. Since the U.S. had come to India's rescue, it could be blamed if the rescue failed. Viewed in this light, Johnson's behavior was option protection.

Answering the question Freeman posed about risking blame by helping required an assessment of India's economic predicament in the mid-sixties. A decade after the food crisis of 1966–1967 and five years after food aid ended, a group of India specialists considered whether or not the U.S. should resume aid to India. (India stopped purchasing U.S. commodities at concessional prices at the end of 1971.)[84] Lloyd Rudolph, an expert on U.S. foreign policy toward India, viewed Johnson's actions as wholly unnecessary, much like Bowles's assessment from New Delhi in 1965.[85] Myron Weiner, an India area specialist took the contrary view. The external coercion of Johnson's leash was valuable. India, he claimed, was a complex, polyarchic government and political system that would not change its direction and move consistently toward increased food production as long as food was available from outside sources. Mellor, an economist, concentrated on the background conditions of India's economic development strategy and, like Weiner, depicted the Indian government as (a) sufficiently pluralistic and complex to be unable to move purposefully in a new direction except slowly and incompletely and (b) sufficiently effective in protecting its own options against outside pressures—including specifically from commercial as well as concessionary suppliers—to be able to resist most pressures for change.

How Much or Which? Vertical and Lateral Options

We come finally to Johnson's choices: how they came to him and what he did about them. It is particularly noteworthy that his important options in the Indian case are more readily depicted as vertical than as lateral, as answers to the question "How much?" rather than "Which?" How strongly should the president have become involved in the face of an executive branch inclined to handle the Indian crisis through routine procedures? How much personal effort and political capital should he have put into (or what priority should he have given to) building consensus within the U.S. government, and therefore into sharing blame and praise over India with others? How hard should the Indians have been pressed? How much should Johnson have relied on those Indian officials identified as sympathetic with major agricultural reform? How united a front should have been forged, and how conspicuously, with the World Bank? How relentless or accommodative should the U.S. government have been toward India's problems of government? What risks should the U.S. have taken with regard to grain price increases in the U.S.? Or with regard to the fall of grain prices and increased trouble with the farmers? Or with the darker prospects: political backlash in India and—the darkest of all—Indian starvation? How long should grain shipments have been kept on a short leash?

These are "how much" questions. They can be stated as "which" questions, of course, but that is to disguise the vital vertical dimension of foreign policy decision making by the president so evident in this case. What implications does this vertical dimension of choice have for the management of foreign relations, particularly with reference to the president's role?

We will in the next chapter inquire further about the shaping and sustaining of foreign policy as a dynamic, but stable and continuous, situation of foreign relations (the "sunk" costs, as it were). We will also inquire about the modification of these policies.

How Much Could India Take?

Johnson's short tether on grain shipments to India and his public statements about foreign aid and India raised the question that Chester Bowles, the American ambassador in New Delhi, was quick to put: Are we harming our particular friends in India? The question correctly identified an important risk, but the possible effects of Johnson's tactics went further. They challenged the conventional norms about how much India might be expected to do. The goal was agricultural reform. The issue became, in order to achieve that goal, how hard and how far could India be pushed in this crisis without risking political disintegration? It was recognized that administrative capabilities set limits on India's capacity to respond, but that behind administrative capacities lay more fundamental constraints that were political. The magnitude of the food crisis justified a concern about the political limits of India's regime.

Any government of the day, in dealing with another, trades on its own competitive advantages as compared with the political opposition. In the commercial world of contract, there is a phrase that captures the issue: "If the person in question cannot do it, let's get someone else." Governments that are not simply satellite regimes rely on international norms and domestic nationalism to protect themselves against their casual displacement by foreign meddlers. But those norms, in turn, rely on the presumption that "getting someone else," i.e., overturning the government of the day, or even the regime, is a dangerous and unreliable way for governments to do business with one another. Yet, to escalate the game of influence as much as Johnson did with India, was to risk disrupting the configuration of domestic forces which had shaped the other government's behavior into familiar patterns. This had the effect of producing more adverse behavior, not less, and putting at risk the substantial assets which were part of the bilateral relationship: stability, mutual confidence, reciprocity, protection of national identity, and—a particularly salient asset—discreet, sustained influence over the other government. Yet, a government must be willing to run such risks in order to bring about substantial changes in another country through bilateral relations. If it is not willing, change will be deterred and the habitual ways in which it deals with its ally, client, or adversary will prevail, and its diplomats and program administrators will remain prisoners of normal relationships.

Caution about risk is rooted in these relationships. In a complex environment, where players must deal with complex policies, they limit change in part to cope with the limits on what they know and can figure out. Recognized methods of search and satisficing that predispose decision makers to minimize policy change are designed to cope with these cognitive limitations.[86] They also predispose organizational behavior toward policy maintenance. Foreign aid programs and other programmatic elements of foreign policy do not escape these patterns of organizational behavior, and in fact come under additional pressure to maintain policy unchanged. In the early years of postwar American foreign policy programs, as Hans Morgenthau noted, the administration often made exaggerated claims about what could be accomplished with foreign assistance programs in order to win the support of Congress,[87] claims that later became an embarrassment to the administration. By the sixties, as noted, justification of these programs had shifted to indeterminate, long-range goals which were less serviceable to program critics. The Indian program was typical in this respect.

As long as the bilateral relationship remained unmodified, or underwent only minute change, the requirement for comprehensive political assessment was minimal. Conversely, by introducing major changes in the bilateral linkage in order, in turn, to induce major changes within India, the short tether generated a demand for comprehensive political assessment of India's regime capacities.

Johnson's staff included Asian experts of some stature: Walt W. Rostow, Robert Komer, Howard Wriggens, and Harold Saunders (not all of them at one time). The demands of White House staff work spread the talents of these experts thin, particularly when compared with what was available among the embassy staff in New Delhi, at the Indian desks in the Department of State and in AID, and to a lesser extent in the Defense Department (OSD/ISA).

When Johnson took the initiative on India, his national security staff followed him loyally even though its members continued to have misgivings. Eventually they arrived at the fundamental questions about the political limits of the short tether. If Johnson is to be criticized, as Bowles and other critics claimed, for squeezing until his pressures were counterproductive, harming the friends of the U.S. government in India and conferring advantages on America's enemies, then why did not the record show convincing evidence that this was what was happening, or—more to the point—was about to happen? Political reporting from and about India did not come near this level of performance; it scarcely touched upon the question of the limits of the regime. Yet that was the question that Johnson's policies posed from the beginning of his intervention, in the spring of 1965, until November 1968; and that is the question that Bowles and the South Asia specialists in Foggy Bottom, McLean, and at the embassy in New Delhi had to answer directly. It is not unfair to note that, whether Johnson had intervened or not, the magnitude of the grain shortage should have raised regime-limits questions anyway. With respect to India one can agree with Neustadt's observations about Britain: Political reporting was good at telling about routine things that were of little use, while the vital issues of policy remained unilluminated by political reporting.[88]

Eventually, in the fall of 1966, the White House staff made some effort to look at regime limits.

The Jacobson Mission and Heck's Assignment

The Johnson administration sent several special groups to India to survey progress there toward increased food production and more efficient and equitable geographic (and to a lesser extent, socio-economic, or vertical) distribution. Two groups went in late 1966. One was composed of agricultural specialists from USDA. The other consisted of members of Congress. Neither excursion lacked either serious substantive purpose or political theater. As should be expected, these visitors complicated the embassy's task of representing the U.S. government in New Delhi. Unavoidably, they provided competitive channels of communication with Washington and reflected adversely on Bowles's standing with the Johnson administration as it was accurately assessed by the government of India.

The first of these groups descended on the embassy in mid-November 1966. It was led by Dorothy Jacobson, Assistant Secretary of Agriculture, and it included three other members, two agricultural economists from the Department of Agriculture and the country director for India from the Department of State, Douglas Heck. Heck was there by arrangement of Howard Wriggens, a member of Rostow's staff. His inclusion was not extraordinary. It was intended and it probably served to soften the antagonism with Bowles, which was considerable. Bowles readily understood why congressional groups came to look. He had been a congressman himself. The experts were a different matter. He had experts on his staff, some of the best—John Lewis, for instance, and an academic economist of considerable stature and breadth, C. E. Lindblom. Heck's inclusion is nonetheless noteworthy. His assignment was, in effect, to consider the political limits to which India could be pushed in the effort to force agricultural policy change.[89]

Freeman, it will be recalled, had accounted for why the Indian government favored the development of heavy industry and resisted the employment of commercial market incentives to achieve increased food production with the "Fabian prejudice" theory. Without rejecting the theory, Wriggens's instructions to Heck reflected another theory that was more congenial with the experience of American politics and more congruent with contemporary theories about political development. It dealt with the structure of power in rural India. The Congress Party's control over rural constituencies, it held, depended on the present inefficient system of small landholdings and traditional methods of cultivation. It came down to what the Congress Party's domestic power base was, and hence, the regime's. If the Fabian mind-set was secondary, and the primary constraint on the development of Indian agriculture was the power structure of the Congress Party, then the requirements for inducing a major change in national policy were much greater and required much heavier pressure from outside to accomplish it. Pressure of such magnitude could be expected to produce substantial political effects in India, many of them adverse and most of them hard to predict. Would these effects be disastrous? Given the uncertainties involved in anticipating them, was Johnson, with his short tether, courting disaster in India? More generally, how far could the Indian government be pushed to implement the Rome Agreement provisions before it was itself at risk? Before mid-1965, the Indian government had managed to keep the consortium, the World Bank, and the United States limited in their expectations to the same marginal concerns that the Indian government contended with. By doing that, it had held them to underwriting India's national policies. Having broken out of that pattern, they now faced the question of how far India could be forced to change. The question led to estimating the limits of influence by estimating the limits of India's capacity to change under pressure from outside, what amounted to the limits of stress endurance by India's regime.

Bowles resisted the very idea of testing the political limits of India's regime. Wriggens instructed Heck to address the stressful effects of the short tether on India's political system. He cast his questions in terms of systemic effects rather than the fate of individual politicians, and therefore put the question, what were the *system's* limits? Thus, he instructed Heck that the White House needed ". . . a better understanding than we have of the way the Congress Party rural machines are held together by patronage made available through present—and agriculturally inefficient—institutions. Unless we have a better fix on how such (and other) political factors encourage or impede agricultural innovation, we cannot expect to communicate accurately to the President the true nature of India's problems and what we can honestly expect."[90]

Another implication of this "deeper" theory about Indian policy determination ran in a different direction. Since wheat was a major patronage resource for the Congress Party, the Indian government was not going to provide the kind of reliable information about it that would confer the power to control food distribution on its Centre—or on the Americans. The Congress Party was powerful at the state level and relatively weak at the Centre. Even if the states knew how much wheat they had (which would be unlikely), they were unlikely to tell the Centre. The Centre itself, therefore, would not have reliable information about wheat in the states.

Rostow had mentioned this line of thinking two months earlier to Johnson. At the beginning of the drought in 1965, the president had been warned that his short tether would interrupt the outflow from the grain logistics pipeline and Indians would starve. The pipeline was interrupted briefly more than once. Under severe pressures, state governments and the forces of the marketplace managed to find grain no one at the Centre knew existed. Predicted famine never actually occurred. Grain appeared as if from nowhere when a region really became desperate. Thus, fears never wholly materialized.

Johnson knew this. He instructed his staff to tell him when any Indians had starved as a result of his holding back on grain shipments; they never did—never could—respond affirmatively to this callous and insightful challenge.[91] Now, well along a learning curve, Rostow warned of "a gap in December arrivals if we don't go ahead with the new agreement in the next week," but added: "No one argues that Indians would starve. Not even the Indian government knows how much food may be tucked away in that vast nation."[92] (Johnson's response was to hold off for another week in the hope, or so he claimed, that domestic grain prices in the United States would drop.)

This perception of wheat and information as integral elements of a vast and resilient national political system might have taken shape and been articulated much earlier by government officials in AID or the Departments of State and Agriculture, had these agencies defined their role differently. It is quite likely that many career foreign assistance officials understood at an intuitive level, or even more rigorously, the resilience and the shielding or defensive capacity of India's political system, but their ability to share their wisdom on this subject had become severely limited. For more than a decade they had been dealing with Indian officials in terms of Indian government performance, measured by Indian government figures. Their work required that they question and challenge—within limits. Within the United States government, they were usually cast in the role of advocates, justifying the programs they administered and the performance of the governments these programs aided. Program implementors are rarely effective evaluators of what they implement for this very reason.

It is one thing to imagine regime limits and quite another to take the concept seriously as an empirical or analytical question. The Jacobson survey group became an occasion to raise or try to raise such questions.[93] Heck provided the intended political inputs into the Jacobson group's conclusion, but did not rise to Wriggens's challenge about estimating the political limits of India's regime.

From the beginning of Johnson's interest in India, in the spring of 1965, until his interest diminished in 1967, neither the career foreign aid, agriculture, or diplomatic staffs in the government nor his own NSC staff caught up with him in addressing the large questions about bargaining with India which his behavior itself required. If nothing else explains Johnson's handling of the Indian food shortage of 1965–1967, this fact explains much of it. Except for the early period when Woods and Freeman generated options for him, Johnson acted alone in bargaining with India's government. To be sure, he showed no clear vision of what he wanted or where he was going, and probably had none. What he showed most clearly was that he would not accept the business-as-usual options that confronted him.

Innovation

There seems to be some value in foreign relations that have been reduced to routines, that are institutionalized. Routines are stable and predictable, and therefore colorless and inconspicuous or at least seemingly unavoidable; and because they are all of these things, they permit politicians to put distance between themselves and unattractive policies and governmental activities. Presumably, the management of foreign policy can be defined in two modes. The first is the construction and maintenance of institutionalized relations. The second is the management of innovation—the effecting of changes in the way foreign relations are perceived, analyzed, and handled. These changed perceptions include the way in which the terms of cooperation and competition with other international players are perceived. The Indian case starkly illuminates both the stability of institutions and the possibilities of innovation that are sometimes available. It also illustrates how defining an issue as critical translates into challenging the policy routines of perception, analysis, and handling at the expense of stability. In a normal management world, where small things break and the job of managers is to fix them, where problems arise and managers solve them by searching for a better way within resource and cognitive constraints,[94] foreign policy usually centers upon the fixing process, which in fact includes the design and maintenance of normal procedures, or the status quo. Critical issues which open the prospect or impose the necessity of innovation, of going beyond normal procedures and normal outcomes, lead beyond normal behavior.

The normal processes of government and the normalities of bilateral and multilateral foreign relations can have, by accident or design, adaptive capabilities. When these capabilities exist, they reduce the need for intervention, at least for conspicuous intervention directed to achieve innovation of the sort entailed in the Indian grain shortage. Adaptive capabilities are attractive alternatives to innovation because they offer the prospect of discreet change, that is to say, change that is constructive and selective and does not generate costly side effects. The directive, top-down innovation entailed in the case of the short tether, with the president as conspicuous chief innovator, was politically costly in both New Delhi and Washington. In both capitals, he was the "heavy." He appeared to be willing to let Indians starve in order to punish an Indian prime minister for her independent foreign policy. No doubt Johnson was irritated by Mrs. Gandhi's opposition to his Vietnam policy, and by the way she expressed it, which lent substance to this exaggeration of his motives.

The next chapter describes an effort to nurture change in American policy in Western Europe through an innovation that gained limited presidential endorsement, that was left to the mercies of middle-level government sponsorship in the interest of avoiding the costs (and risks) associated with conspicuous, directive presidential action.

4. Johnson and Europe: The MLF and Alliance Politics

WE NOW TURN TO Europe and back to the beginning of the Johnson era. This chapter recounts an effort by American officials to create a special force of nuclear missiles under arrangements that would achieve several objectives. The primary goal was to reassure NATO allies that nuclear forces would be available to defend them if necessary. To this end, the force would be under an integrated military command that would, in turn, be guided by a unified political authority. Manning and command arrangements—what came to be called mixed-manning—would be employed to make it difficult or impossible for any member to withdraw its national contribution from the common military force. Further, the effort was intended to transform NATO and to change the range of American choice by inducing greater political integration in Western Europe through greater military integration. It was an audacious attempt to change NATO that did not succeed. From the standpoint of two presidents, Johnson and Kennedy, it was a policy innovation that did not happen. Chapter 5 will draw upon the details of the MLF case to extend further the more general discussion found in Chapter 3 about foreign policy management viewed as an organizational process.

Johnson's Takeover of the MLF Commitment

During the first weeks after John F. Kennedy's death, President Johnson devoted much of his time to establishing his presence at the head of the U.S. government with the Congress and with executive branch officials. He also gave a limited amount of his time to foreign officials. The issue of his exposure to foreign officials arose immediately in connection with Kennedy's funeral, which drew many foreign dignitaries. On advice, Johnson met privately and briefly with fourteen of them, including the West German, British, and Japanese prime ministers, Anastas Mikoyan, the Deputy Chairman of the Soviet Council of Ministers, and the French president, de Gaulle. The meeting with de Gaulle was longer than the rest, and it produced an aggravating misunderstanding. Johnson invited de Gaulle to return on a state visit for longer discussions, thought he had accepted, and promptly announced it. De Gaulle denied it and demurred.

In addition to greeting funeral visitors, Johnson addressed the Latin American ambassadors about the Alliance for Progress, spent a day at the U.N. (December 17), two days with German Chancellor Erhard (December 28–29), held a reception for foreign correspondents (December 12), received the diplomatic corps (December 13), met with the Italian premier, Antonio Segni (January 14 and 15), the Canadian premier, Lester Pearson (January 21 and 22), lunched with the Dutch queen, Frederika (January 27), and saw the British, Japanese, and Finnish ambassadors briefly.[1]

During a brief takeover period Johnson spent time conspicuously working at international tasks, but after a few weeks he struck a bargain with the Special Assistant for National Security Affairs, McGeorge Bundy, to set appointments with foreign visitors so that they consumed no more than one hour per week of his time.[2] In the following twelve-week period (from early February to mid-May 1964), by close reckoning from Johnson's appointment calendar, he spent only six hours and twenty-seven minutes in that way.[3] He disliked spending time with official foreign visitors, with certain exceptions; German Chancellor Erhard was one of those exceptions. Instead, he increased the time he spent with unofficial advisors on foreign policy, such as Barbara Ward and W. Averell Harriman. But mostly he attended to his domestic agenda.

Kennedy had assembled an impressive domestic legislative program. Johnson resolved to push it through Congress and did so with stunning speed. He embraced Kennedy's program while demonstrating his superiority as a legislative leader. As a corollary of this choice, Johnson asked his foreign policy aides, in addition to protecting his time, to avoid international crises that might deflect attention from his plans for Congress.

The awkward encounter with de Gaulle and the political chaos in Saigon after Diem's and Kennedy's deaths were two of the threads of foreign policy that Johnson could scarcely fail to grasp immediately. Another early encounter was the MLF, or multilateral force, a proposal for a supranational nuclear force in Europe that, by the time of Kennedy's death, was supported mainly by a small and highly effective faction associated with the Policy Planning Staff of the Department of State. Johnson himself acted in support of the MLF shortly after assuming the presidency, and spoke publicly in support of it several times. A year later, in December 1964, he backed away from supporting it and eventually abandoned it. While presidential involvement with the MLF proposal was essential to its survival and success, Europe's active support of the proposal was also critical. The MLF project required limited presidential sponsorship, and in the end, Johnson used this logic to allow its demise.

When President Kennedy died, preparations were well underway for the annual NATO meetings that would take place within a month in Paris. Johnson immediately met with Rusk, McNamara, and others to consider guidelines for those meetings. In this context he was also asked to consider, as Bundy stated it in telegraphic style, whether it was prudent to do one of the following: "(a) to let staff advocates of MLF brief selected Congressional leaders on current state of Paris negotiations with seven other interested nations; (b) to let the same people brief General Eisenhower in the hope of holding his support for this force."[4]

The MLF was to be a European nuclear force—European in its manning and command but not in the ownership or authority to fire nuclear weapons, at least not at first. Its nuclear weapons would be supplied by the United States and possibly also by the British with some expectation that in the future the European command authority could own them. The proposal was mainly American, and for the previous six months it had been kept alive largely through the enthusiasm of a small group in the Department of State, with the assistance of a small group of supporters in the U.S. Navy. These were the MLF advocates, or promoters.[5]

Questions about what happened at this meeting in early December 1963 would arise a year later when Johnson faced the potentially embarrassing prospect of withdrawing his own public commitment to the MLF. The most probing question was whether he was aware of Kennedy's reservations about it. The available evidence is inconclusive.

We have Bundy's memorandum to Johnson in preparation for the meeting. Significantly, it addressed the peculiar status of the MLF. It alluded to much of the background about the MLF, but did not present the pros and cons of the proposal itself. It referred to "a tension which existed for many months between MLF advocates in [the] State Department and President Kennedy," and mentioned differences over how much to press the Europeans for their support.[6]

Bundy referred to the "MLF advocates" and linked former Secretary of State Dean Acheson to them. Acheson had easy access to Johnson as well as to the senior officers of both State and Defense.

Bundy also reported that Dean Rusk, Johnson's Secretary of State, was not an advocate of the MLF, and he noted that the Secretary of Defense, Robert McNamara, was "cool" to it. He also mentioned the lack of support in Europe for the MLF. Most important, Bundy reported that Kennedy had not wanted a "debatable treaty in 1964," doubtless referring to the presidential election scheduled for the next November.

If there were warnings in this memorandum, Johnson failed to heed them. Quite by accident, he had publicly favored the MLF in a speech in Brussels earlier that year. As vice president, he had been speaking for the Kennedy administration, but in doing so, he had also committed himself. However, circumstances had changed since his visit to Brussels. With his accession to the presidency, he could have stepped back from commitments made under such circumstances. Instead, he felt predisposed to pick up Kennedy's "fallen torch." This predisposition applied with particular force to European policy, an area in which he seems to have judged that the Kennedy holdovers possessed special competence. Johnson approved the briefings for congressional leaders and evidently regarded this decision as his own endorsement of the MLF; in the months that followed he made additional public statements in support of it.[7] By these actions, Johnson co-opted a prominent Kennedy proposal which was an innovative idea—an innovation that would fail. To understand the full meaning of this action requires a further inquiry into the origins of the MLF proposal and into the way the Kennedy administration originally employed it.

Kennedy's Involvement with the MLF

One can track the MLF concept back at least to the deliberations of a study group in London sponsored by the International Institute of Strategic Studies in the late fifties. Among the participants was Walt W. Rostow, who would become a supporter of the MLF in the Kennedy administration as head of the State Department's Policy Planning Staff and would remain a supporter under the Johnson administration. He eventually succeeded McGeorge Bundy in 1966 as Johnson's Special Assistant for National Security Affairs (although with a slightly altered title).

The MLF became an American proposal when an experienced American official and law professor, Robert Bowie, prepared a study in 1960 to address the growing problem of NATO Europe's lack of confidence in the U.S. nuclear deterrent. He prepared the study at the behest of Gerard Smith, Assistant Secretary of State for Policy Planning under the Eisenhower administration. Bowie proposed the creation of a NATO strategic nuclear force composed of the then newly developed Polaris submarines and missiles. The critical principle in the Bowie proposal was a nuclear force in the possession of Europeans. Three years earlier the ranking military official in NATO, General Lauris Norstad, also Commander-in-Chief of the U.S. European Command (EUCOM), had proposed the establishment of a European-based medium-range nuclear missile force (MRBMs) under his NATO command as the Supreme Allied Commander, Europe (SACEUR), that would supplement American nuclear forces. Norstad sought to increase the confidence of Europeans in American promises to employ U.S. nuclear weapons in the defense of Europe. Following established NATO practices, Norstad proposed that national forces be contributed, more or less intact, to SACEUR. Bowie proposed the creation of a force separate from any national military command composed of personnel from all contributing countries; it would be an integrated *force* much as NATO's command headquarters was an integrated *staff*.

Kennedy adopted the MLF proposal, presenting it in Ottawa in a speech before the Canadian parliament in May 1961. He announced that he was committing five Polaris boats to Europe for a multilateral force, but set difficult preconditions that would have to be met. First, NATO would obviously have to decide if it did indeed want a multilateral force. Second, NATO members would have to agree to a set of guidelines about making decisions for firing the Polaris missiles. Most difficult of all, NATO members would have to agree to the buildup of NATO's conventional forces.

Kennedy's own position on the MLF, particularly the strength of his commitment to it, was, in Bundy's careful statement to Johnson, "never entirely clear," but several of its dimensions can be described. Kennedy was drawn to dramatic foreign policy initiatives. The MLF became one such initiative. Later, even after he backed away from the MLF, Kennedy remained interested in it as a technical proposition. He followed with interest the experiment of the mixed-manned ship named the *Admiral Ricketts*. His behavior was consistent with the combined requirements for imperative direction in that he forced the U.S. government to provide leadership and deliberately coordinated efforts to persuade European allies to accept and respond to the challenge of this leadership. By sponsoring negotiations with them persistently at the technical or working level, he in effect tried to evoke a response from the allies. As we shall see, he understood that such negotiations, at least as they might be conducted by the skillful and aggressive MLF promoters, might commit his administration's prestige to the point of injuring him politically.

At this point Kennedy, Rusk, and others in the Kennedy administration, not unlike officials in the Eisenhower administration, evidently saw the MLF as an example of what Europeans might want and not as a goal or requirement of U.S. foreign policy. Europe's failure to respond had already indicated that further initiatives were required from Washington. However, the strict provisos included in Kennedy's Ottawa initiative signaled that the important initiatives still lay with Europe. With these provisos, the MLF lay dormant until after the Nassau Conference, at the end of 1962.

Kennedy met in February 1963 with Livingston Merchant, Gerard Smith, and Admiral John M. Lee, the MLF negotiating team. Merchant was the Special Ambassador for Multilateral Nuclear Affairs. At the time of the meeting, the MLF enjoyed the status of a proposal recommended to Europe by the president. Yet Kennedy expressed his misgivings about their impending tour of European capitals: "You should so conduct this mission," he told them in writing, "as to avoid serious damage to U.S. prestige if our allies do not wish to proceed with an MLF."[8] Thus, despite his endorsement of the MLF, Kennedy was evidently skeptical of the proposal; if not about its substance, then at least about the potential political costs of achieving it.

Bundy himself had been hospitable to the MLF proposal—more so than Rusk, less so than McNamara. Its goals were compatible with his own outlook on Europe, and he knew and respected most of its key supporters. One of them was Henry Owen, a member of the Policy Planning Staff under Walt Rostow. Bundy often co-opted Owen as an informal member of his White House national security staff, an arrangement that was exceptional, but not unique. It was intended to avoid staff layering, and reflected Johnson's conviction that it was useful to penetrate the line departments as well as keep White House staffs small for political reasons. Bundy made it a practice to depend upon officials in the Department of State and sometimes in other agencies as extensions of his own staff.

In mid-June, as Bundy prepared for Kennedy's European trip that July, he presented Kennedy with a negative estimate of the MLF situation. He judged the British government unable to act because of scandals and held that "almost no one with any political standing is personally favorable to the MLF." A decision to support the MLF "would be regarded as an extraordinary case of subservience to U.S. pressure. We should not believe those who tell us that the Foreign Office is favorable." He found, in fact, little enthusiasm in any allied country, including the Federal Republic of Germany. In France he saw a prospect for serious hostility, while in Italy, he saw divisiveness in an already divided government. Not the least of the problems with the MLF in both countries was the fact that the U.S. government could not, under the terms of its own statutes, give up custody of its own nuclear weapons. At the minimum, this meant that it must maintain the right to veto their uses. "Only among the passionate pro-Europeans like [Jean] Monnet," Bundy observed, "is there real sentiment *for* the MLF, and this sentiment itself is conditional upon a clear offering to abandon the veto [at] an early state if a genuinely European force becomes practicable." He estimated: "If we press the MLF through in the next 12 months, we shall have only grudging support among the very people in whose interest the force has been designed."[9] In the United States, Bundy anticipated a serious "drain on the Presidential account" from "amending the McMahon Act for the purpose of arming people who are themselves uncertain and divided on the need." With respect to the Soviet Union, he saw as "a new factor of real importance" the prospect that the MLF would be "increasingly held up as a militaristic maneuver which prevents serious progress toward peace in Europe."[10] He concluded: "I think we need a sharp break in planning for the political discussions of the MLF in Europe. In Bonn, Rome, and London this will be a major topic, and I think it is important to switch from pressure to inquiry. I also think that quite possibly the shift should be signaled before we leave Washington."[11]

Kennedy responded to this recommendation with the affirming question, "What took you so long?"[12] Later, Bundy would describe Kennedy to Johnson as "tentative and careful about the MLF" and reported that there were "different reasons [for this] at different times." Bundy said: "In the last half of 1963 the reasons were, I think, dominated by his feeling that if he could only get the MLF by major and intense U.S. pressure, it was not worth it."[13]

The MLF promoters had descended on Bonn and London in anticipation of Kennedy's European trip. Adenauer's support was critical. Ball urged Kennedy to permit full congressional consultations on the MLF, which would have meant risking a serious confrontation with the Joint Committee on Atomic Energy (JCAE). The JCAE oversaw the enforcement of the McMahon Act. It was highly attentive to that law's provisions for maintaining U.S. control over American nuclear weapons. Soundings at the JCAE were discouraging. Committee members had recognized in the earliest stages of the MLF promotion that satisfying Western European interests in possessing nuclear weapons would require altering custody arrangements. The JCAE was on record as opposing such an alteration. Given the committee's perspective, full congressional consultation would have involved a very serious commitment of the administration to the cause, just when Kennedy's influence in Congress was limited. Bundy's assessment that little enthusiasm for the MLF could be found in Western Europe, even in Bonn, suggests that he discounted favorable indicators, such as the cables from Bonn, London, and perhaps from Rome, as well as direct messages from those governments themselves. These messages were often planted by the MLF promoters.

Kennedy's conduct on his European trip was consistent with what he told Bundy.[14] With Britain paralyzed, Italy divided, and de Gaulle following his unique agenda of national independence for France, the critical stop was Bonn. There the MLF suffered a discreet and intentional setback. Earlier, Adenauer had written Kennedy endorsing the principle of the United States's maintaining positive control over the nuclear weapons supplied to the MLF, but reserving the right to reopen the question of control once initial agreement had been reached. This position was underlined through a quite separate channel by Adenauer's defense minister.[15] Evidently intended as a positive response to Merchant and his associates, these messages signaled a different meaning which may have been detected in Bundy's office. Merchant and his associates, in pushing the MLF proposal as hard as they did, forced Germany to address an issue which it thought would not arise until much later. The issue was whether or not Germany, by participating in the MLF, would have more access to nuclear weapons than they already possessed under NATO.

Kennedy's discussion with Adenauer was the occasion for the setback.[16] The MLF promoters had been preparing for Kennedy's trip to bring about decisive action in support of the force. They failed. Kennedy and Adenauer issued a communique that promised "best efforts" to pursue the MLF, but agreed to an indefinite delay. A similar communique followed Kennedy's consultations with Macmillan in London.

After Kennedy's trip to Europe, Merchant and the other MLF promoters worked to keep the proposal alive. They seized upon what may have actually been a palliative in the Adenauer-Kennedy agreement, i.e., the agreement to continue with quiet discussions.[17] "Quiet discussions" became the basis for proceeding with working level negotiations in Paris, under the sympathetic eye of Kennedy's NATO ambassador, Thomas K. Finletter. It was because of the results from these negotiations that Merchant and his associates sought Johnson's permission to brief congressional leaders at the end of 1963. Meanwhile, the MLF advocates proceeded to demonstrate the feasibility of mixed-manning by employing a U.S. destroyer renamed the *Admiral Ricketts*. The project had caught Kennedy's interest, despite the fact that he had not wanted to face a debatable treaty until after the 1964 elections.

Johnson's favorable public references to the MLF after his decision in December 1963 to permit congressional briefings, which was his first action in support of the MLF after becoming president, gave presidential grounding for the Merchant group's continued diplomatic actions. They pursued them with impressive effect. "Sometime between February and April 1964," the distinguished British defense analyst Alastair Buchan later wrote, in what proved to be a premature observation, "the MLF ceased to be an American proposal and became a central objective of American policy."[18] The skillful moves of the MLF promoters brought about this important change of status.

The Momentum Builds

The congressional briefings that Johnson agreed to in December 1963 failed to generate any significant support on Capitol Hill. Nor did Johnson's public support of the MLF during his first six months as president translate into much progress in the working group of eight nations in Paris. The British bore some responsibility for the lack of progress there. They had agreed to participate only on the condition that they would not have to participate in the force itself! But there were other explanations for the slow pace in Paris. De Gaulle's opposition and Adenauer's retirement produced cleavages in Bonn. Erhard and Kai Uwe von Hassel became unenthusiastic about the proposed multilateral force, possibly reflecting German pressures. More broadly, negotiations in Geneva, which had turned from the test ban to nonproliferation issues, produced ambivalence in most NATO capitals. In Belgium, for instance, Paul Henri Spaak, a leading Europeanist, declared that Belgium would not participate in the force, but like Britain, would retain its place in the negotiations.[19] Finally, when the Labour Party won power in Britain that October, British policy toward the MLF, which had previously been politely obstructionist, became overtly obstructionist. Despite these developments, the negotiations in Paris continued actively until the Grewe fiasco, which will be described below, and beyond, until the end of 1964.

One might be puzzled why, with so little support, the MLF proposal survived so long. Yet the answer is quite clear. Survival was due to the ingenuity and drive of the MLF promoters. In particular, although progress was slow, they were able to seize an opportunity that presented itself in April 1964 to commit the president to a timetable for negotiating an MLF treaty. The occasion was an appointment with the president arranged by Thomas K. Finletter, ambassador to NATO and a strong MLF advocate. It was to be a ceremonial occasion, to say good-bye before returning to his post in Paris. Finletter took with him Smith, who had just succeeded Merchant as head of the Paris negotiating team, and George Ball, the Under Secretary of State, who was handling the matter for the Department of State. They talked with the president about the MLF.[20] Bundy and McNamara were out of town. Quite possibly Finletter scheduled the meeting with this fact in mind. The outcome was that Johnson agreed to an end-of-year deadline for the negotiations. Without Bundy present to warn of MLF deadlines, it is quite possible that Johnson was not fully aware of the agreement's implications, although he was to reaffirm the deadline in June.

Cables went immediately to European capitals. They declared the intention of the U.S. government to seek agreement by the end of 1964. In Bonn, there was renewed interest. Ludwig Erhard had succeeded Adenauer as the German chancellor the previous October. Erhard had favored the MLF at the time Kennedy met with Adenauer in June 1963, when the German government was in fact growing more acquiescent about it.[21] The American promoters had worked at distracting the Germans from the sensitive voting issue, but it was plain in Bonn, and particularly to Adenauer, that the Federal Republic would have to enter upon the MLF project with no distinct promise of sharing in the custody of nuclear weapons or having the authority to fire them. The U.S. government, given the opposition of the JCAE, was in no position to agree at this time to turn nuclear weapons over to the Germans on any terms.

As noted, Kennedy had used his meetings with Adenauer to postpone German action on the MLF. Adenauer was evidently sensitive to the custody and control, or voting, issue, perhaps more than was Erhard. In any case, when Erhard succeeded the venerable Adenauer as chancellor four months later—in the first leadership succession since the founding of the Federal Republic—German defense issues became tangled with intraparty rivalries.

This was the situation when Erhard paid a state visit to Washington and Johnson's Texas ranch in June. It was a time when Erhard was not in a position to act decisively on the MLF, but neither was he disposed against it. Consequently, his visit to Texas became the occasion for a public commitment from both heads of state. In their communique, Johnson and Erhard "agreed that the proposed multilateral force would make a significant contribution to this military and political strength and that efforts should be continued to ready an agreement for signature by the end of the year."[22]

The end of the year was six months away, conveniently after the American presidential election in November and conveniently before the next German parliamentary elections that would occur in September 1965. The communique, much like Kennedy's understanding with Adenauer, took the pressure off the American promoters of the MLF, but established an action-forcing deadline against which proponents in both governments could work.

Regenerating Presidential Options: First Preparations

McGeorge Bundy's stand on this issue is instructive. He told Kennedy in June 1963 that he had been hospitable to the MLF, but in an effort to protect the president from attempts by MLF advocates to force action in 1963, warned Kennedy against giving the proposal full support. Yet its promoters continued to regard him as an ally. Further, Bundy evidently did not protest the outcome of the Finletter meeting or the Johnson-Erhard communique. Not until late November 1964, in the course of preparing for a meeting between Johnson and the new British prime minister, Harold Wilson, did he again show clear opposition to the MLF. Yet he had begun to prepare for an independent appraisal of the MLF as early as April 1964, an action suggesting that he harbored misgivings on the direction of the MLF promotion.

Enlisting Richard Neustadt

Bundy brought Richard E. Neustadt in from Columbia University to assess how to deal with the British on the MLF. Neustadt was prepared for his assignment. Kennedy had commissioned him to conduct a postmortem of the Skybolt affair, which was a major misunderstanding with the British government settled at the Nassau Conference at the end of 1962. Neustadt had talked with participants and observers in London and Washington and reported the result in a carefully drawn report to Kennedy himself. Now, with Bundy's commission, Neustadt again visited London. His findings were completed by July 6, too late to be of any use to Johnson in preparation for Erhard's visit. They were, however, useful in preparing for the Wilson visit in December.

Britain, always a key player in U.S. nuclear weapons command policies, had become a spoiler of Washington's MLF goals. Well aware that the MLF promoters did not represent a broad consensus in Washington, the British had themselves promoted a European nuclear force. It was based on two premises that contradicted features of the MLF. One was that it would be a common force combining national contributions, rather than an integrated multilateral force. The other was that strict U.S. control would be maintained rather than holding out the hope of eventual transfer of U.S. control to the multilateral command. For peculiar domestic political reasons— they trusted Europeans less than Americans—the British wanted a guarantee that the U.S. veto would never be given up. (The Germans, of course, took the opposite position.) Whether intentional or not, the British government's determination to maintain an American veto over the use of nuclear weapons not only placated British fears about continental insanities, especially German, but also shrewdly placed Britain in a position for dealing with the United States in that it appealed to the hard-line protectors of nuclear weapons custody in the JCAE.

Neustadt's task in London can be defined by reference to a confidential report by Alastair Buchan that found its way into Bundy's hands as Neustadt worked. Buchan was a prominent British intellectual, well-connected in Whitehall, and the founding head of the International Institute for Strategic Studies. He was an international authority on defense matters whose opinions carried much weight in Washington as well as in Europe. He had long been aware of the multilateral force idea and had in fact claimed credit for it.

Summarizing current European opinion, Buchan saw foreign offices favoring it as an antidote to Gaullism, which supported a European nuclear force at the expense of NATO military integration: "Ministries of Defense, however, are, with the exception of the German Defense Ministry, extremely dubious about the surface fleet concept," which was what the MLF had settled upon by then. "They are alarmed at the money which a significant share in it will cost, and at the drain on skilled manpower it will involve." The Germans, he inferred, did not understand this. While sympathizing with "the Erhard Administration in their enthusiasm for the MLF solution," and "the hesitations of the British government," and believing that the MLF, or something like it, could serve "a useful if limited purpose," he wrote, "I am equally certain that an attempt to force the issue at this stage, on a narrow plan, using techniques of cabal rather than diplomacy, will create a series of reverberating domestic crises which will weaken the sense of confidence which the MLF is designed to promote, without creating any permanent solution to the real political and military problems which we face."[23] Buchan's reference to "techniques of cabal" was strong stuff. It stated his judgment and doubtless a common view in Whitehall of the methods employed by the MLF promoters.

Like Buchan's, Neustadt's report described political assessments at variance with those commonly reported by the MLF promoters. His principal findings, however, had to do with timing. On the premise that Labour would win the election the following October (which it did), and noting that it had not been in office for twelve years, he identified a sizeable gap between defense policies it was comfortable with and those policies it would have to adopt once the party came to power: "Power breeds realism, no doubt. But there *is* a gestation period." He concluded that if Labour won the election it would be under no pressure to reach an early deal with Washington. The Labour Party would first test America's continued support of the MLF by waiting to see if the developing situations in Vietnam, in East-West relations, or a change in the status of the "cabal" would shift U.S. priorities away from the year-end deadline for the MLF.[24]

Neustadt recommended, first, pre-election restraint. According to him, Wilson knew that President Johnson had said he wanted the MLF. Neustadt recommended that American officials, particularly the cabal, refrain from needling Wilson on this subject during the election. Second, after the American election, Neustadt wanted Wilson to be invited to Washington as soon as Johnson was ready, perhaps at the end of January. Neustadt expected the Labour government to take at least that long to sort out its defense policies. The purpose of the invitation should be made clear: "action on the MLF, if possible, in company with Wilson." It should convey "explicit determination," but "no pressure, no gun-to-the-head on timing." Its purpose would be to move the new Labour government much closer to the realities they would encounter in Washington.[25] It should be noted that Neustadt's position, while not anti-MLF in substance, was distinctly in opposition to that of the MLF promoters. Their main point of advocacy, based on the Johnson-Erhard deadline, was "now or never."

Neustadt and Ball, instead of Bundy, went to London immediately before Wilson's visit in the first week of December, much earlier than Neustadt had anticipated. But before that, Bonn acted in haste to force the pace of negotiations over the MLF. The Grewe fiasco, as we will call this episode, is important to us here because of what it indicates about the behavior of the MLF group.

The Grewe Fiasco

The Johnson-Erhard communique had referred to "efforts [which] should be continued to ready an agreement for signature by the end of the year." The only efforts in progress were the negotiations among the eight governments represented in the working group in Paris, where Smith headed the U.S. team. But the pace in Paris remained slow, owing largely to what was interpreted as British delaying tactics. Meanwhile, the communique came to mean something else to the negotiating teams from Washington and Bonn. As Thomas Hughes, the director of the Bureau of Intelligence and Research in the Department of State, explained it, "Unbeknownst to the sluggish six," and, indeed, to many in the U.S. government, including the White House, "the American and German representatives on the working group in Paris undertook private meetings to accelerate the drafting. On this bilateral basis, *ad referendum* texts of various necessary documents have been prepared which, while still leaving a few major political issues unresolved, nevertheless represent much more of a final MLF proposal (if approved by Bonn and Washington) than anything yet turned out by the full eight nation group."[26]

This progress toward a bilateral agreement had been accomplished between Smith and his team and an equivalent delegation from Bonn. The next move now came through Bonn. Finletter's opposite number, Wilhelm Grewe, the German ambassador to NATO, carried a letter from Erhard to Johnson. It expressed concern about the lack of progress in the committee of eight, restated his commitment to the original time schedule, and recommended that Washington and Bonn sign the treaty alone. The letter, supplemented by Grewe's commentary, mentioned additional reasons for Bonn's interest in an early signing of the MLF proposal: There were complications with United Nations action on a non-proliferation treaty (which would be hard for West Germany to accept without the MLF) and a need to reach an agreement well before the German parliamentary elections scheduled for September 1965. Erhard was clearly fearful of the growing influence of German Gaullists in his own Christian Democratic party and anticipated that closer cooperation with France would be a major issue in those elections.[27] The MLF could serve to demonstrate the advantages of Erhard's Atlanticism.

De Gaulle had visited Bonn that July. His visit marked a change in French policy from tolerance of the MLF to outright opposition. His shift sharpened the choice for Bonn between Paris and Europe, on the one hand, and Washington and the Atlantic, on the other. He won Adenauer's support (in retirement), a coup that strengthened the German Gaullists in the Bundestag. The MLF would help the Erhard government respond to German grumbling about the status of the Federal Republic in NATO. But it would also reduce the government's ability to maneuver around the Gaullists, who were not only attacking the MLF, but NATO itself. In this situation a German-American MLF may have appeared to the Erhard government as a way to beat the Gaullists at their own game, providing it could be carried through expeditiously. If the Americans would agree to starting the MLF bilaterally with Bonn, the German Gaullists would be undercut. Such an agreement would assure Bonn a seat in de Gaulle's Atlantic directorate that de Gaulle would otherwise deny the Germans. (He had proposed a French-British-American directorate.) But to succeed, this maneuver required prompt American agreement. Any delay or equivocation in Washington could serve Gaullist interests; indeed, this is precisely what happened.

Grewe arrived to see Johnson on a few days' notice with the barest indication of his purpose.[28] Washington—and this is the most critical fact—was wholly unprepared for this German initiative, suggesting intentionally poor communications from Finletter's office in Paris, for circumstantial evidence strongly indicates that he and Smith knew in advance about the Grewe mission. The German government's failure to prepare the way in Washington for Grewe's visit also suggests that the Erhard government thought that Johnson was already on board, a misperception that, again, would have originated with Finletter and Smith.

There was no time for the U.S. government to explore the matter with the Germans or, just as importantly, with the other six nations participating in negotiations in Paris. By the time the letter had been read in the White House, the substance of it was public. Grewe's background remarks to a friendly German newspaper reporter in Paris on October 2 (immediately before his trip to Washington) generated hard questions for Erhard, who disclosed the substance of the letter.[29] But the problem of timing would have existed even without Erhard's leak. Grewe's visit with Johnson was no way to accomplish the goals sought by Erhard. Under the circumstances, Erhard had to be refused. Johnson's reply, stating a commitment to broad participation, went off the next day. The following day Rusk rejected the bilateral agreement at a press conference.[30]

It was a clumsy performance by Grewe and Erhard that proved

embarrassing all around. At the very least, the Germans needed to get the Johnson administration aboard before going public, but getting the administration's support would have taken more time than Grewe's visit permitted under any circumstances. While informed observers at the time interpreted these events as the products of carelessness, which was certainly involved,[31] a more fundamental error had occurred. The Germans erred in assessing the current position of the president on the MLF. Evidently the Erhard government had relied, through Grewe, on statements by Finletter and Smith, and failed to recognize that a split still existed in the U.S. government over the MLF. If this line of interpretation is correct, an even more interesting observation is justified. Smith and Finletter were using the Germans in an attempt to commit Washington as well as Bonn to the MLF.[32]

It would be difficult to imagine a venture more dangerous to the Erhard government than proposing a German-American MLF, one that staked so much on the bilateral connection with the United States while presenting serious difficulties for NATO.[33] Unless Erhard could be certain that the proposal would be accepted and implemented, it was folly to make it. It sharpened the requirement that he choose between Washington and Paris too much to do him good. In fact, as Catherine Kelleher notes, Erhard's fumble triggered the Gaullists to "make their first major challenge to foreign policy within the Bundestag itself."[34]

The bilateral option appears to have been a gross failure of political assessment in Bonn and in the bilateral talks in Paris, where it originated. Its American advocates promptly employed it in an attempt to coerce other NATO governments, especially the Italians and the British Labour government, to stop stalling.[35] This ploy backfired in Europe because it backfired in Washington.[36] The Grewe fiasco, together with a growing skepticism about the MLF in Europe,[37] precipitated Bundy's final effort to protect the president's options.

Bundy was more sympathetic to the MLF than were some of his staff.[38] The Grewe fiasco aroused one of them, David Klein, to recommend a complete review of MLF policy and strong measures to control the MLF promoters. Klein informed Bundy that the Paris discussions with the eight powers were moving toward the elimination of NATO nuclear forces, yet not broadening the discussion to include British forces. Klein also charged that the MLF promoters had for at least six months been willing to sacrifice NATO to the MLF.[39] Bundy's sympathies with the MLF would not have extended that far.

The Wilson Visit Anticipated

Much earlier, anticipating Wilson's post-election trip to Washington, Neustadt had proposed that Bundy visit London first to prepare the way for the MLF. In his view, it would not be proper to send a cabinet member ("too prominent") or a "cabal" member (this would be "fatal").[40] Ball, who barely missed disqualification on both of Neustadt's criteria, actually made the advance trip to London accompanied by Neustadt himself. By then, they could anticipate that the British foreign minister, Gordon Walker, would come to Washington in mid-November, after the American election, and that Wilson would follow in early December. In London, as Ball later reported it, they told Wilson that "agreement in principle on British participation in surface ships is a *sine qua non* for a success in negotiations with the Germans."[41]

Ball had intended to have Henry Owen, an ardent cabalist, handle the preparations for Gordon Walker's visit. When Bundy learned this, he acted to broaden and balance the staffing effort for both the Gordon Walker and Wilson visits by establishing an interdepartmental committee composed formally of himself, Ball, Rusk, and McNamara, with Neustadt as full-time support. Rusk may never have attended. Bundy instructed Neustadt, according to John Steinbruner, to "manage the MLF proponents so that they [will] not run away with the action."[42]

The Ball/Bundy committee not only reflected Bundy's cautious manner of asserting his role as the president's National Security advisor,[43] but also his determination to leash the MLF promoters. It was perceived in State as Ball's committee, since he bore primary responsibility for drafting the final report.[44]

Ball and Bundy agreed that many of the vexing details which were delaying the MLF negotiations with the British were of little consequence. They at first disagreed on the amount of time needed to resolve the issue. Ball, like other MLF promoters, wanted quick action on the matter to prevent erosion of the MLF proposal. Bundy went along, but only after indicating that he wanted to see a full review and assessment of the administration's commitments to the MLF.[45]

The main function of mixed-manning was to so integrate the national components into a common force as to make it impossible to withdraw the one from the other. The British had been insisting on what they termed an Atlantic Nuclear Force (ANF), to which they would contribute their Polaris submarine force without giving up its national identity or their right to withdraw it from the ANF. The failure of the German and American MLF promoters to pin down an American commitment before the British post-election visit to Washington now posed for the U.S. the problem of coping with the British while maintaining the support of the Germans. Ball wanted to hold the British to the terms of MLF participation, i.e., the funding and manpower contributions to a mixed-manned, surface ship force. He noted that MLF participation would be cheaper for the British than their proposed Polaris contribution to an Atlantic Nuclear Force. Bundy, again, argued that the new Labour government "merely wanted to be able to say to its people that it had part of the British Navy attached to the NATO Command."[46]

While the committee worked to establish an American position which reconciled German and British constraints, Bundy drafted and obtained Johnson's signature on NSAM 318, a presidential directive that, in effect, formalized the Ball/Bundy committee's main task. The task was not only to prepare for the Wilson visit on December 7th and 8th, but also to control press briefings and diplomatic contacts concerning the MLF more generally.[47] This did not mean a press blackout; quite the contrary. Some background press interviews occurred which made Johnson's ability to withdraw his support for the MLF easier when it did occur. Thus, the *Bulletin of the Atomic Scientists* published in its November issue a report on the MLF that cited "a member of the White House staff." It eased the way for Johnson to reverse his position by noting that Johnson's primary public commitment to the MLF was the speech he had given in 1963 as vice president.[48]

Ball, Bundy, and Neustadt

Ball managed to dominate the Ball/Bundy committee, if not by force of personality, which was strong enough, then by energetic participation. He volunteered to write the major working papers and arranged to visit Bonn and Whitehall with Neustadt. The main document from the committee reflected Ball's most important position, that the MLF or some kind of Atlantic force must proceed without delay, with or without the British. Meanwhile, Bundy had acted upon a suggestion from his staff assistant, David Klein,[49] to open up another possibility. Writing to Rusk, McNamara, and Ball—and taking the greatest care to see that his message reached only them[50]—Bundy stated:

> Against my own expectations of two weeks ago, I am reaching the conclusion that the U.S. should now arrange to let the MLF

sink out of sight. Whether this should be done quickly or slowly is an important tactical question, but the overriding point which I wish to suggest in this tightly limited group is that we should now ask the President for authority to work toward a future in which the MLF does not come into existence.

I reach this conclusion because it seems increasingly clear that the costs of success would be prohibitive. They would include at least the following:

1. A deeply reluctant and essentially unpersuaded Great Britain.
2. A Germany whose governing party was divided on this issue and whose participation was ambiguous in meaning.
3. Additional strains on an Italian government which is weaker and not stronger as a result of its last election.
4. At least a temporary setback in efforts to limit the spread of nuclear weapons by international agreement (those who believe strongly in such agreements, in all countries, are skeptical of the MLF).
5. A protracted and difficult Congressional struggle in which we would be largely deprived of the one decisive argument—that this arrangement is what our major European partners really want.
6. A constitutional debate in NATO which, even if successful, would provide justification for further Gaullist outrages against the organization.
7. A genuine and enduring blow to Franco-German relations which the Germans will blame on us.

This is not an attractive prospect, and the MLF is not worth it.

From my own conversations with the President, I am sure that he does not feel the kind of personal Presidential engagement in the MLF itself which would make it difficult for him to strike out on a new course if we can find one which seems better. I believe we can.[51]

Bundy proposed a meeting among the four that weekend (not an uncommon practice)—one week before Wilson's scheduled arrival. Meanwhile, Bundy did not stand still. Johnson was under increasing pressure to declare his involvement with and support of the MLF. That Friday, advising Johnson about his Saturday press conference, Bundy warned him against taking Dean Acheson's advice on what to say about the MLF. "In my experience he has more than once sought to commit Presidents to his own policy without fair warning of all the problems involved. In particular, Rusk and I agree that there is a serious problem of the timing and content of any MLF agreement, and that you should not tie yourself to any particular mast until you have a chance to weigh all the evidence."[52]

Johnson delivered a foreign policy address at Georgetown University the next midweek. He artfully endorsed European unity, Atlantic unity, and German aspirations, and included a paragraph that could be interpreted as endorsing the Grewe proposal for a German-American MLF, or at least reassurance that de Gaulle would not be permitted to paralyze the Atlantic alliance.[53] Bundy promptly reported "a warm and grateful phone call from the German Ambassador and one or two favorable comments from European correspondents."[54] At the same time, he forwarded an intelligence report dealing with the MLF which he considered "a little bit more bearish than is justified."[55]

Dealing with the press the following midweek under pressure to state Johnson's support of the MLF as a foregone conclusion, Bundy gave an answer that provided a *Newsweek* reporter the basis for saying that he took a cool line on the MLF. (Ball, reading the report in Paris, cabled Bundy asking whether the report was true and adding that it indicated the administration was divided—a fair comment after NSAM 318.)[56]

Klein, as we know, had been warning Bundy of MLF developments, including the exaggeration of European support for it that had crept into the cable traffic from NATO capitals. He had called Bundy's attention to cables and intelligence reports pointing in the other direction and showed him INR papers that presented a more balanced position. Germany was the critical country. On November 30 Klein asked Martin Hillenbrand, the ranking professional diplomat at the American embassy in Bonn, for a candid and personal evaluation of German support for the MLF. Hillenbrand's response arrived at a critical moment in Johnson's discussions about how to deal with Wilson.

The Eve of Wilson's Visit

By Saturday, December 6, with Ball and Neustadt back from London, and Wilson about to arrive, the MLF posed severe dilemmas for Johnson. Wilson had read American bureaucratic politics well. The U.S. needed his agreement if prompt action was to be taken on the MLF without making it a German-American force—something which Washington had recently and clearly opposed. Wilson's narrow parliamentary majority of four left him weak, while Johnson's landslide election on November 3 had provided him with a much stronger political base. But Wilson had much more at stake than Johnson, and the value of agreement between Downing Street and the White House about a European nuclear force was therefore much higher for Wilson than for Johnson.

The British could not dominate, but they could spoil. They had delayed the working group negotiations in Paris until agreement there by the end of the year became impossible. By December, they had fashioned a position that might be able to embarrass the Johnson administration because of its potential for causing trouble within the U.S. government while strengthening Wilson's own position domestically. British officials were alert to the polarizing force of what they called the "cabal." It had caused them trouble, but it also presented Wilson with opportunities, because the U.S. government was divided.

Wilson's position, put together with surprising speed after organizing his government in October, provided for broadening the MLF to include Britain's aging V-bombers and new Polaris submarines, Germany's Pershing missiles, and U.S. Polaris and Minuteman forces. A clever combination of national manning and mixed-manning (the latter involving the American Minutemen) would assure the opposition of the U.S. Air Force. The proposed involvement of American Polaris submarines threatened to torpedo the truce the U.S. Navy had struck with the MLF promoters over a surface sea force. The proposal of a mixed-manned Minuteman force opened up the prospect of sharing control of nuclear weapons with the Germans. To American experts this was the central issue, or as Steinbruner put it, "the real thing."[57] It assured the opposition of the JCAE. Despite the enthusiasm generated by the American promoters of the MLF, it took little acuity to observe from London that none of the NATO forces, especially those of the United States, preferred such a weapon system. Wilson, whose actions were severely constrained by his government's attempts to preserve popular illusions about British nuclear strength and independence, still managed to challenge the rationale behind the MLF. He did this immediately and more thoroughly than had Macmillan's government in the two years after Nassau.

The Showdown with Johnson

Ball, with Neustadt's help, drafted the main proposal to Johnson. It defined the basis for a deal with Wilson.[58] With the MLF promoters restrained by NSAM 318, the pace of settling with the British set by

Wilson's scheduled visit, and Bundy discussing the MLF with Rusk and McNamara in a quite different procedure, it was not difficult for Ball and Neustadt to come to agreement. The document began forcefully, declaring the general principle that in "dealing with the British we must impress upon them that the final scheme must be so arranged that their participation is on a parity with the Germans and other Europeans rather than with the United States." Military policy must not concede a "special relationship" with London. It rejected the mixed-manned Minuteman and Wilson's preference for a small mixed-manned force outside SACEUR jurisdiction without British participation. Britain must participate in the multilateral seaborne force enough "to satisfy the Germans," whether or not it participates also by contributing national forces. Having established these points, it suggested possible concessions to Wilson: state a U.S. intention to maintain a U.S. veto; "graciously accept" the contribution of a nationally commanded British V-bomber force and consider other nationally commanded forces, including the possibility of a U.S. Minuteman force; "assure Wilson that participation in the surface fleet is on a no-extra-cost basis to him." It acknowledged the principle, attractive to the British, that the contribution of nationally commanded forces would let the U.S. reduce the number of surface ships to "fewer than 25." It conceded that the issue of SACEUR's command over the new Atlantic force could be left open for the present, to be resolved later.

Johnson, as he preferred, faced a consensus document, one that Ball, Bundy, McNamara, and Rusk had agreed to at their weekend meeting. It was composed of a memorandum by Ball and a cover letter by Bundy. Ball's memorandum advocated seeking Wilson's support for a modified MLF which would satisfy the Germans. Bundy's cover letter supported Ball, but offered the option of withdrawing from previous commitments as a fallback and recommended that, in the event that Wilson failed to agree to join a surface ship multilateral force, Johnson adopt the back-away option that Kennedy had once pursued. He outlined procedures designed to place responsibility for the demise of the MLF on the European allies rather than the United States.

In the discussion with Johnson, all present supported Ball's position, but McNamara indicated that he was more inclined toward the back-away option. Since Johnson already knew of Bundy's and Rusk's doubts about it, and Bundy's concern that Acheson (who was also present) was pushing Johnson too hard, the disarray among his advisors must have been quite clear to Johnson. By this time, also, he may well have seen other evidence, in the form of cables from

Europe and reports from Capitol Hill, that confirmed Bundy's and Rusk's concerns. Accounts of his reaction at this time indicate that it was remarkably congruent with Bundy's warnings.[59]

While Johnson would probe deeply into the technical accuracy of the analysis of grain shipments to India within a year, as noted in Chapter 3, he did not challenge the MLF on technical grounds. He concentrated his analysis on political feasibility. Noting the opposition in Europe, and sympathizing with Wilson's opposition because of his political situation, he turned to the problem with Congress. Ball admitted trouble there and argued that a major effort would win congressional approval. McNamara agreed, offered to help, and predicted success.[60] Bundy, in his cover memorandum, had compared Johnson's position vis-à-vis Congress ("strong") with Wilson's vis-à-vis Parliament ("weak"). Congress was Johnson's territory; advice about it from Kennedy holdovers carried little weight with him. He seized, instead, upon the following question: What had actually been Kennedy's position? Bundy responded that Johnson had not been fully exposed to the position against the MLF. He offered to prepare a paper that dealt with both subjects.

By the time the meeting resumed the next day, Johnson had checked congressional reactions for himself. Sen. Fulbright was fresh from a NATO parliamentarians' meeting, where corridor talk about the MLF was invariably negative. A cable had come in from Bonn, probably in response to Klein's back channel inquiry to Martin J. Hillenbrand, the Deputy Chief of Mission, on November 30.[61] It assessed German support for the MLF much differently and less favorably than had the documents submitted to Johnson, as Bundy had anticipated. Evidently Klein's inquiry had signaled the Bonn embassy to be more candid than the cable traffic had recently been. Bundy submitted a new paper that began: "You asked yesterday why President Kennedy was tentative and careful about the MLF. It was rightly pointed out that there were different reasons at different times, but in the last half of 1963 the reasons were, I think, dominated by his feeling that if he could only get the MLF by major and intense U.S. pressure, it was not worth it. His exact reasoning I do not know, but I do know that he reacted very strongly and affirmatively to a memorandum which I sent him on June 15, 1963."[62] Bundy attached this memo to the above paper for Johnson's consideration.

He warned Johnson about the dangers of going ahead with the MLF, saying that the newest version of it, "even though wider and better" than the old one, "will have many opponents, and their voices will be heard, whatever specific leaders of governments say." The earlier memorandum to Kennedy dealt mainly with foreign opposition, but

Bundy now addressed the problem of domestic opposition. He listed the "most important" opponents as French Gaullists, most professional military men in the United States, "American commentators like [Walter] Lippmann and George Kennan," the JCAE and the Senate Armed Services Committee, and the Senate more generally.[63] Lippmann, he wrote, "believes that there is no serious support for this force anywhere except among a few faddists in the State Department." His paragraph on military opinion discounted McNamara's offer to help persuade the Congress: "Most professional military men are cool at best, and many are openly opposed. [General Lyman L.] Lemnitzer [SACEUR and CinC, EUCOM] is warning against this enterprise as divisive within the Alliance. Norstad [Lemnitzer's predecessor, now retired] is publicly against it. The JCS will be loyal but probably not enthusiastic. General Eisenhower may not be any better than neutral and could be opposed."[64]

In essence, Bundy discounted the claims of his colleagues that Congress could be won. Johnson found the fact that Kennedy had cooled to the MLF particularly significant, and in the second meeting he announced his rejection of the negotiation objectives set out in Ball's memorandum. He "would not deliver Wilson."[65]

The discussion now centered upon the cost of reversing previous commitments. Earlier, Klein presented the problem to Bundy: While the president seemed wholly committed, his public commitments were, as Klein phrased it, "promises [of] *efforts* for *agreement*, rather than *agreement* itself, and by December 31, there may *not* be agreement."[66] Whether this line of retreat drew any attention that Sunday is unclear; the recollection of participants runs instead in another direction. Ball, with Bundy and McNamara joining in, warned of the costs of withdrawing support.[67]

Steinbruner has summarized what he learned from his interviews in light of Philip Geyelin's account. Johnson, he relates:

> insisted that he did not feel personally committed, and he re-
> fused to be bound by the record. Elaborating on his lecture to
> them the previous day, the President spelled out his own in-
> terpretations of his political position. His election, he argued,
> had been a defeat of Goldwater extremism and not a solid liberal
> mandate. The swollen Democratic majorities in Congress would
> pose discipline problems, and public expectations were likely to
> outrun what he could realistically do. His enemies would be anx-
> ious to catch him in a major defeat, as had happened to Wilson in
> 1919 [and] to Roosevelt in 1937. His immediate problem was
> avoiding such traps, and he made it clear that he wanted much

more respect for his problems from his advisers than he felt he was getting.[68]

Geyelin, who had the benefit of fresher memories, reported an extraordinary scene:

> Johnson assailed the men around him, questioning their competence as well as their counsel. . . . [H]e ticked off each man in turn. Ball was upbraided for the "disgraceful" caliber of ambassadorial candidates served up by the State Department. Dean Acheson, sitting in as a private consultant, was needled "as the man who got us into war in Korea" and had to "get Eisenhower to get us out of it." McNamara was derided for his easy assurances that the MLF could be sold to Congress; commended, sarcastically, for his command of Senate politics, and reminded that if MLF was to be sold to Congress, the job would have to be done by the President himself. Acheson, according to reports, finally broke the mounting tension by declaring: "Mr. President, you don't pay these men enough to talk to them that way—even with the federal pay raise."[69]

Johnson decided that he should listen to Wilson, tell him that his proposed arrangements would not solve the German problem, and send him on to Bonn where he would have to try to satisfy the Germans without American leadership or mediation. Wilson would not be required to make an explicit commitment to the surface fleet— nor would he receive, in turn, any concessions from Johnson. In particular, he would not be permitted to claim that he had killed the MLF.

Johnson, Wilson, and the Aftermath

When they met, Wilson conceded support for surface ships, but Johnson stuck to his script. The Anglo-American inter-Cabinet discussions that followed the Johnson-Wilson meeting, accordingly, explored but did not settle differences.[70] After the British left, a message went to Bonn, The Hague, and Rome reporting the American reaction to the British proposals. It referred to the discussions with the British government and stated, "We believe that it would be appropriate to have discussions with other interested NATO governments of a concept of an Atlantic nuclear force" composed of three or four British Polaris submarines, elements of the British V-bomber force, and "such strategic nuclear forces as the United States or

France might be prepared to subscribe," in addition to a Polaris surface fleet that might be down-sized "from the initial proposals in
the light of other contributions now in contemplation."[71]

The British, in place of the faction that had promoted it for so long
from within the U.S. government, now carried an American license
to promote an Atlantic Nuclear Force. But the terms were more
strict than a casual reading of the report on the Wilson visit might
indicate. Johnson, at Bundy's suggestion, signed NSAM 322, which
extended the controls that he had established with NSAM 318 over
diplomatic contacts and press briefings in connection with the Wilson visit, controls that had constrained the MLF promoters. It went
further: no pressure for agreement; no agreement without the substantial support of Britain, Germany, and other allies; no action
against the direct interests of France; and sympathetic attention to
French sensitivities.[72] Johnson had adopted the back-off option. For
minimum damage to U.S. prestige, NSAM 322 would have been
kept secret and remained an internal control document. Johnson,
however, leaked its substance, a prudent measure in light of the previous record of MLF promoter initiatives and the promoters' reaction to Johnson's decision. Geyelin, who is a primary source, reported the latter as follows: "At the State Department, it was still
possible for the embattled men advocating the MLF to put up a bold
front. Their formula for NATO's nuclear reorganization, so long es-
poused by American officials and American Presidents, was not
dead, newsmen were advised. Rather, 'what is emerging is a broader
view, an expanding concept, bigger than anything we have talked
about.' A high official insisted that the idea of mixed-manned surface ships remained a significant part of this larger package, indeed
'an indispensable element which we are in no sense abandoning.' "[73]

With the publication of NSAM 322, the MLF office was abolished
and Gerard Smith, its head, resigned from the government. Congressional leaders needed to be briefed about the outcome of the Wilson
visit; Bundy eased Ball out of that role. He also warned Johnson
when Ball sought clearance for a speech in New Orleans in which
he planned to restate the administration's Atlantic nuclear policy.[74]

Bundy originally sought a process that would, ideally, have been
invisible. Johnson had become too involved and was too skeptical of
the MLF promoters to expect invisibility as well as compliance.
Hughes, the intelligence chief at State, wrote of the MLF in late
October 1964, stating that, "both Washington and Bonn are too committed to its realization to be able to abandon the project. Furthermore, its lack of success could have serious repercussions for the
standing of the United States vis-a-vis Germany, its other close

friends in NATO, France, and the USSR. It might even cause Germany to question its Atlantic orientation."[75]

Johnson could scarcely have had much confidence in late December about effecting a discreet back-off without risking a resumption of U.S. initiatives. He chose—we cannot know with how much calculation—to go public by showing James Reston the document that happened (or he had arranged) to be on his desk. Reston's report, published by the *New York Times*, was read in Bonn, where the Erhard government was already embarrassed over the Grewe fiasco. It caused such a row in Germany that Johnson's ambassador there feared it would cause, in turn, an escalating reaction from Johnson.[76]

Steinbruner dates the death of the MLF as December 1964.[77] His point is well taken. No doubt the actions taken that month contributed to its death by bringing the promotion of the MLF by its American advocates under more control and by shifting the initiative back to where supposedly it had been intended to be, in the hands of the Europeans. Kelleher observed: "[T]o some in Bonn [though not all], the MLF proposal as the central focus of American nuclear policy for NATO was moribund. It was now just one possible proposal to be discussed, debated, and compared, without haste or pressure. A German commitment was interesting, welcome, and worthy of consideration, but it was a necessary rather than a sufficient condition."[78]

Bundy stuck close to Johnson on the MLF throughout its life, carefully preparing for the back-off option, but not pushing Johnson toward it. McNamara had been opposed, but supported Johnson and bided his time. Before Johnson became president, McNamara had offered what became the alternative to it, more participation for NATO members in American nuclear target planning. He sometimes challenged the MLF proponents within the government, but he was not an active opponent of it. He, too, stuck close to Johnson. Even at the end of Johnson's active support, during the showdown in December 1964, he volunteered to make a new effort to win support on the Hill for it. Ball had been an open and strong advocate of the MLF from the time of the Nassau Conference (if not earlier) and remained an advocate after 1964.

There is no evidence that Bundy sought to discredit Ball (in fact, quite the contrary), or that Ball's status with Johnson was weakened by his being so obviously on the losing side with respect to the MLF. He remained in place in the Johnson administration, although he was the most conspicuous and persistent dissenter with respect to Johnson's Vietnam policies. His role as the in-house dissenter over Vietnam led critics to claim that he was used (meaning misused) by Johnson in this role. He may have been. But it was not only with respect to Vietnam that Ball advocated policies Johnson did not adopt. The MLF was another instance of this.

There are two features to the MLF episode in this respect. Ball was an advocate of the MLF before and after Johnson adopted the back-off option. When Johnson criticized his subordinates for the way they had handled the MLF, he did not single out Ball as an advocate (the only advocate present who was a government official) for special criticism. Yet Ball, at least by association, could have been linked to leaks and misleading political reporting from the field. Further, even after Johnson decided to reduce his support for the proposal, he did no more than deny Ball convenient opportunities to advocate the MLF.

In all of this, Rusk figured very little. Yet perhaps he made the most critical move of all. He had absented himself from Nassau, an Anglo-American summit that had thrown American nuclear policy into chaos, and when the showdown sessions over the MLF came in December 1964, he was inconspicuous. He placed great weight on his personal communications with the president and may have chosen to let Bundy handle Ball. His public response to the Grewe mission in November may have been a critical action against the MLF, sealing its doom well before Bundy and Ball laid out the options to Johnson in early December. His response shattered the most audacious move of the MLF promoters, a clearly ill-considered effort to set the Germans to persuade Johnson directly. Rusk remained committed to the original concept—and ultimately, the back-off position—that the MLF was one of several ways Europeans could solve their problem of nuclear credibility.

The Politics of Leadership: "Having It Both Ways"

Harlan Cleveland, who succeeded Thomas K. Finletter as U.S. Ambassador to NATO and opposed the MLF, explained the episode further in terms of a particular presidential posture. He interpreted Kennedy's support for the MLF, and Johnson's as well, as "having it both ways."

> If the enthusiasts for the MLF could bring it off, it might prove a good answer to a really serious problem—the abrasive complaints from our allies about our reluctance to engage in any real nuclear sharing. If in the end MLF did not float, the President could always walk away from it, saying it had always depended for its success on European initiative—thus exposing the diplo-

matic advocates rather than the Presidency to congressional and journalistic I-told-you-so's.[79]

The phrase "having it both ways" refers to the relationship of the president to the MLF promoters. It denotes, first, their dependence upon one another regarding the MLF; second, the distinct difference in goals between them; third, the known prospect that the group might or might not achieve its goals; and fourth, what the president's stakes were in the two alternative outcomes. He could "win" either way, and he could also lose.

Having it more than one way is a common method of coping with the uncertainty that abounds in foreign relations. The scale, complexity, and disjointedness of U.S. government actions generate some of the uncertainty. Factional behavior, another source of uncertainty, can also be employed by the president to cope with it. That is what happened in the MLF case.

The MLF promoters, although exceptionally effective performers, were ineffective in building a power base. Their weakness became evident in the relative ease with which Johnson undercut them. They had not built a wide base of support in the foreign policy bureaus of the executive branch. In Congress, the nuclear issue had blocked them. In Europe they had built some support in foreign ministries, but ministries of defense generally resisted them. Political and military staffs in NATO were neutral or resistant.[80] In Washington, the Department of Defense, with its outside constituencies linked to the services and to weapons procurement, was unenthusiastic. For Defense, or at least for McNamara, the MLF was an inconvenience, or worse. State, at first sympathetic, likewise became unenthusiastic, except for those few proponents of European integration who saw the MLF as a valuable tactic. The more aggressive the MLF promoters became, the more they isolated themselves from the larger groups sympathetic with European political and economic integration. We do not need to decide whether the cabal dissolved from self-inflicted wounds; we can still observe that it had a hand in setting up the deadline for the end of 1964 and in seeing that it remained in effect, and that working against that deadline proved its downfall. We can also observe that its longevity was more remarkable than its counterproductive aggressiveness.

One reason for the cabal's survival was its vulnerability. While its activities might produce embarrassing effects, it could be stopped. The group lacked a reliable constituency within the U.S. government (time had proved that, unless something changed drastically, the cabal would remain a small, isolated group) and in Europe, where even at the working level, only the Germans proved support-ive enough to be troublesome. The MLF promoters remained a small group that could be brought under control with few repercussions.

There are, however, three things wrong with this perspective. First, only Johnson was in a position to dissolve the cabal, and it is doubtful that he thought much about it. The attention he devoted to it was, until the showdown, too little to have plausibly involved such a calculation. Second, letting the MLF promoters run as they did risked embarrassments too serious to ignore, and Johnson was not inclined to ignore such embarrassments. Third, the object was to build support for the MLF. Johnson, and those who tried to "stand in his place" on MLF policy, wanted to see the cabal—the pro-moters—build support, particularly in Europe.

A more interesting view of the MLF promoters' license recognizes that two presidents were at first promoters themselves. It views the cabal's role as a change agent. It seemed likely that this group would be able to induce a major change in NATO with a minimum of U.S. government effort (an efficiency factor) and without much of a com-mitment or involvement by the president or his administration (a limited involvement factor). The hope was that a faction in the U.S. government would serve as a change agent. It would induce changes in a complex system of alliance politics, actions that would be much more costly, if not self-defeating, when taken by the president.

The MLF case also demonstrates a special problem of internal per-suasion. In the MLF case, two presidents risked entrapment, each with some general awareness of the risk. The problem of presiden-tial entrapment is scarcely confined to foreign relations, but it takes on special features there because of the cross-national dimensions the game of entrapment can assume. What is more important, it has special importance because of the risks that can be generated in the international context by entrapment. The policy issues that the Johnson administration faced with respect to NATO turned criti-cally on dynamic relationships, on the anticipation of trends such as nuclear credibility and fear, on trends in complex political factors such as these questions pose: Where was German nationalism go-ing? What was de Gaulle up to? Would the British abandon their military presence east of Suez? Their strategic nuclear forces? Which among the smaller powers would waver in their NATO par-ticipation if they could not participate in a nuclear force? More particularly, as it turned out, the Germans were drawn into a pre-mature commitment to a two-power MLF—a form of entrapment that, if it had run its course, would have also drawn in the Johnson administration.

Questions like these deal with relationships between Washington and the European capitals and for all NATO members, with their relationship to NATO and to other multilateral organizations. At some risk of taking ourselves too seriously, and in any case, to belabor the obvious, we can describe these relationships as occurring at the conjunction of three systems: (1) one's own pluralistic governmental system in which factions form and change, (2) other more or less pluralistic governmental systems, in which we can account for and describe foreign relations or foreign policy in similar terms, and (3) nongovernmental and intergovernmental organizations, together with the rules of the game that govern relations among the elements of these three systems. The questions that interest managers of foreign relations usually concern relationships among elements of these three systems, but they are rarely system-level questions. Most often they begin with some event or development, and their wider effects are dealt with speculatively.

Those of us who have explained governmental outputs by describing organizational processes are like manufacturing engineers who can account for what a widget looks like, and even how reliably it meets specifications, because we know how it was made. Yet the manufacturer wants to know, with respect to this output, whether a different kind of widget ought to be produced instead, and in any case, what to do with these widgets once produced. To answer these questions the manufacturer must look not only inward and consider the interests and goals of the organization, but also outward at the company's market position and what its customers want. There is more to be known about widgets and policies than how they are made.

There is more to foreign policy than the steps leading to its creation. But unlike the process of manufacturing widgets, the foreign policy process is not always as clearly defined, nor is the relationship between processes and the quality of the product as simple to understand; one cannot assume that a policy created by several experts in and out of government will be more successful than a policy implemented by a few, perhaps less experienced officials. Nor can it be assumed that time is always a factor. In addition, changing and unpredictable circumstances may undermine what was generally considered a "good" foreign policy and give life to one which was poorly conceived.

Moreover, for both widgets and foreign policy, knowing the process indicates nothing about the product's marketability. Foreign policy encompasses more than the concern for processes. It also encompasses a concern for the products and their effects. This means policymakers must anticipate: first, the actions or outputs of their own government; second, the effect of these actions on other governments; and third, the effect of these measures on elements of the pertinent international regime. Foreign policy management is successful or unsuccessful depending on the instruments available and the way they are used to affect each of these three domains.

Which brings us again to the MLF venture and its ending in default. The MLF episode can be seen in highly pragmatic terms: "Try it out; see what happens. If the results are doubtful, abandon it. If the status quo works and if normal processes are tolerable, or satisfactory, they can, indeed, serve as a fallback." To state this point in terms of the MLF case, the option of withdrawing support for the MLF proposal had the anticipated effect of reverting to a default or normal condition,—to "square one," in the vernacular—which was tolerable. The MLF was a venture. Had it gone much further, had the effort to promote it discredited the status quo by design, or unintentionally, the damage that would have been done to NATO and to the U.S. connections with NATO would have been serious, and its failure would have been very costly, indeed. But that is not what happened. Most of the attention on the costs of back-off was directed at the president's reputation; some, more broadly, was directed at the prestige of the U.S. government. What critics of abandoning the MLF underestimated was the capacity of the U.S. government to change its course from a policy supported by a small, isolated group of promoters, and the ability of a resilient alliance system to absorb such costs to the alliance as this venture incurred.

It will be helpful, as a concluding point to this chapter, to note as a comparison the efforts of another head of state who was venturing to change the alliance and the relationship of his government to it. This comparison will permit us to deal briefly with the broader political stakes that the MLF entailed for the Atlantic alliance, for the United States, and for Johnson.

De Gaulle, the MLF, and the Heroic Presidency

The discussion about Charles de Gaulle in this section has two purposes. The first is to explain what France generally and de Gaulle in particular did to influence American actions with regard to the MLF. De Gaulle considered the MLF a threat to his goals for France. The second concerns heroic head-of-state leadership in foreign relations, a phenomenon that is central to Lyndon Johnson's foreign relations. The American form of government, when it comes to foreign relations, combines relatively broad political participation with a relatively strong political executive. The American presidency has enjoyed certain advantages in exercising leadership in foreign relations, at least when it is compared with chiefs of government in parliamentary governments. This advantage was apparent after World War II until late in the Johnson administration. How much that advantage has been revived in more recent years is another story.

Among America's European allies, competitive national politics, fitted into the various forms that parliamentary government took in Western Europe after World War II, and the shattering experience for popular government in Europe during the interwar era, limited the discretion and maneuverability of heads of state in Western Europe. NATO, as already noted, served the interests of political leaders of almost every political complexion in Western Europe in this respect. Their participation in NATO reduced their political exposure with reference to national security and military affairs—reduced the "politicalness" of foreign relations. NATO helped restore the legitimacy of national security policy throughout Western Europe.

Nowhere was the problem of maintaining a stable course in foreign relations more conspicuous than in France through the fifties. France's premiers, presiding over a nation ruled by shifting parliamentary coalitions, were dominated in foreign as well as domestic policies by the expediencies of coalition politics. Under de Gaulle, France in the sixties changed course. Under de Gaulle, French foreign relations came to rest on a national consensus based on nationalist sentiments, on national pride, on *grandeur*.

Charles de Gaulle had returned to power in France in what amounted to a right-wing coup in 1958. To achieve his long-stated goals for France and cope with the immediate problems that had brought him to power, he changed the French constitution into a presidential form based on indirect elections. By doing so, he partitioned the conduct of foreign from domestic politics, which enabled him to salvage France from the quagmire of the Algerian War. Then in 1962, after settling the Algerian question, he changed course, making the French presidency subject to plebiscite, a procedure designed to increase the legitimacy of the office by tying it directly to popular sovereignty. (Subjecting the presidency to plebiscite was nothing new to French politics. Napoleon III used such a strategy in the mid–nineteenth century to gain public approval after every foreign adventure or whenever his hold on power was shaky.) With this move, de Gaulle could be the single national representative in both foreign and domestic functions.[81] For the time being, he could at least use his capacity to dominate domestic politics as an asset in dealing with the closely divided partisan regimes of his neighbors.

De Gaulle's foreign policy served to export France's problems and to stabilize the domestic order of the Fifth Republic at the expense of the expanding European Economic Community, a strong NATO, and American ties to Europe. In mid-December 1964, after Johnson had taken the pressure off the German-American effort to produce an agreement on the MLF, Dean Rusk called on de Gaulle in Paris. According to Charles Bohlen, the American ambassador to France, who accompanied him, de Gaulle told Rusk: "No one in Europe believed in the imminence of a Soviet attack, nor he felt did the U.S. It was not considered likely that the Soviet Union, Brezhnev and Kosygin, would launch an attack on Western Europe, nor that the West would attack the Soviet Union."[82]

De Gaulle could not have made it clearer that politics, not security, dominated his military policies. Betting that the French claim to nuclear military independence would not be put to the test, he could employ the *force de frappe*, France's nuclear strike force, for another purpose, to further France's interests within the alliance.

These developments, from the standpoint of American interest, while irritating, were not all adverse. The instability of France's Fourth Republic had been costly to the United States in measurable ways that were now gone. Washington had subsidized France's war in Vietnam during the late forties and early fifties with more than $3 billion, as dollars were then valued. De Gaulle, in the early and mid-sixties, was aiming toward a stability in France that rested on a popular base and a reduction of dependence on the rightist political and military forces which had put him in power. Even France's *force de frappe*, which to the Kennedy administration appeared to be wasteful and dangerous, was part of a scheme to bring the French army under control.[83]

In altering France, de Gaulle changed patterns of political behavior which had defined the country as the "basket case" of Western Europe. Although evidence of this development was inconclusive at the time, it was not totally obscure. The United States had much to gain from de Gaulle's success.

De Gaulle's approach to solving France's problems involved two closely related elements, one exemplified by his vetoing twice Britain's entrance into the Common Market, the other indicated by his plebiscites, or earlier, the presidential features of the 1958 constitution. Resisting Britain's entrance into the Common Market was narrowly nationalistic and wholly within de Gaulle's means. The plebiscites, as noted, were a major part of de Gaulle's effort to construct a national political system rooted in the direct participation of the electorate in the choice of a powerful president. By doing this, and employing the base of domestic political power it provided, he had more flexibility, more discretion in exercising what power France possessed than previous postwar leaders of France. De Gaulle's situation was even more favorable than that of contemporary leaders in most of the allied nations. He could and did employ diplomatic leverage against his European allies and the United States more aggressively than any of them did.

De Gaulle claimed opposition to the European integration movement and support for national independence, both of which collided with an American sentiment favoring a united Europe. He exploited France's advantages in the alliance and his role as founder of a new regime in France to further France's interests. De Gaulle's policies were, as much as anything, the reason why the MLF's American promoters had advanced its fortunes so persistently. They sought to counter France's retreat into a unilateral, nationalist military policy, a retreat the Gaullists in the Federal Republic also supported.

De Gaulle's diplomacy of *grandeur* was at times something like a game of "chicken" in which the French diplomatic machine, unmistakably driven by de Gaulle himself, bestride the center line, drove with a will until it forced its adversaries—who were usually also its allies—to give way. At the end of de Gaulle's rule in 1969, the long-term drawbacks of the short-term benefits of diplomatic escalation began to show;[84] but there were also some long-term benefits to France and NATO. France was the least concerned among the West European states with public agitation over nuclear policies in the early eighties.

De Gaulle's behavior revived fears on both sides of the Atlantic of a Europe returning to the nationalistic authoritarianism of its pre–World War II history and turning away from the positive developments of the postwar era, which included movement toward a vision of a united Europe. The MLF proposal was one of Washington's ways of encouraging that movement, and therefore a source of conflict with de Gaulle. As perceived by its determined American promoters, it was a tool designed to unite de Gaulle's opposition in Europe and embolden it within France. Outside the MLF group, the proposal appealed more broadly to Europe as an antidote to frustrations over de Gaulle's intransigence and nationalistic opportunism. Many of those who lacked conviction about the MLF—the unbelievers, the nonpromoters—could support the MLF as a counterattack against de Gaulle.

The U.S. approach to NATO reflected an American prejudice in favor of European integration, one that with surprisingly little self-awareness encouraged indirect over direct electoral politics in Europe. At first it served de Gaulle's purposes in this respect, but once he had shifted to a plebiscitary presidency, it no longer did. The MLF, as long as it survived as an American proposal, served the prejudice favoring integration and indirect politics. To the extent that the MLF proposal was linked to the Monnetists—the tenacious proponents of European integration—it depreciated the value of strong political leadership and nationalism in Europe and appreciated the value of indirect, bureaucratic policies among the integrated multinational staffs of NATO and the agencies within the European Economic Community.

De Gaulle, as a charismatic leader—an heroic head of state—transformed France's constitutional regime and created a new, relatively stable political structure for France, one that survived his own loss of authority and power in 1969. During Johnson's presidency de Gaulle was able to marshal the political forces of France behind his nationalistic foreign policy almost at will. Johnson, who was prone to resist the anti–de Gaulle moods of his foreign policy officials, appreciated de Gaulle's situation, if he did not particularly like de Gaulle's opposition to the Atlantic community goals of his own policies. Johnson, like other presidents, had inherited an Atlantic infrastructure built upon a relatively stable network of bilateral and multilateral relations associated with NATO that the MLF sought to reinforce—and alter. The American presidency provided Johnson with many of the advantages of the domestically-based political leverage de Gaulle held at the height of his own political power in the mid-sixties; but Johnson's policies in Europe were those of a conservator. For a conservator, the MLF was an audacious effort to make changes which could be—and was—abandoned. Were Johnson not a conservator in Europe, one could have expected a confrontation between the two presidents. On the continent, only de Gaulle had a sufficient political base and incentive as a national leader to challenge American foreign policy during the Johnson presidency. De Gaulle lost the political base for his governing in the student riots of 1968. It is more than a coincidence that his political support faded at about the time Johnson decided not to run for reelection.

5. Influence, Strategy, and Western Europe

WE HAVE NOW LOOKED at Johnson playing two quite different roles in foreign policy. With respect to India, we have seen him take direct action to seize direct, literal control over the critical instrument of grain shipments and employ that control to force India into a fundamental change in its economic development strategy. One could scarcely imagine a more direct and forceful exercise of presidential power in foreign relations. With respect to Europe, we have seen Johnson responding with measured action to the initiatives of others—to the efforts of American officials to promote the MLF options, to de Gaulle's efforts to obstruct at once the exercise of American hegemony in Western Europe and the integration of Western Europe's military functions. The quite different presidential behavior that we observed reflected the greater prospect, in the Indian case, of employing presidential leverage to induce changes in India's agricultural policies that could be monitored at a working level. In Europe, it was also the case that a distinct alternative to the status quo presented itself in the form of the proposed MLF, an alternative that had the support of a small, influential group of American officials. In the end, however, far from seizing the initiative and imposing this potential innovation, Johnson removed its "life support" system and let it die. The differences, from the standpoint of U.S. policy, between India—and indeed, other Third World countries— and Western Europe are large and obvious: The United States was (and is) linked to Western Europe through a thick, strong network of economic, political, military, and cultural ties, while its ties to India have been thin and relatively weak. It is noteworthy that at this writing, a quarter century later, the difference is equally obvious. The MLF is today interesting because it was an effort to change things where the American foreign policy infrastructure was at its thickest, where the status quo was anchored most strongly, or so it would appear. In this chapter, we will explore further the implications of this conception of the foreign policy infrastructure.

In all respects—in its diplomatic, economic, security, monetary, and other ties—the United States has been more closely integrated with Western Europe than with any other part of the world. During the late sixties, long-anticipated trade negotiations between Washington and the European Economic Community produced bargaining positions which tested and applied influence in the conventional sense of that term. In the military security area, however, the constraints that could be attributed to common interests and the convenience of a common military program prevailed as the basis of American influence. De Gaulle's withdrawal of French military forces from NATO stands as the major exception. Trans-Atlantic security relations reflected a mutual appreciation of the status quo, or at least a reluctance to force major changes in it. Influence worked at the margin, with modest expectations of change. The MLF promoters pursued their goals at the working level. From the standpoint of two presidents, if the bureaucracy could have made headway, this would have been a satisfactory outcome. The kind of headway the MLF promoters sought and seemed to be achieving would have amounted to larger than marginal changes through channels ordinarily serving minor adjustments.

The second basis of American influence is the American role in a common strategy. The MLF was not an attempt to change strategy. In fact, it may be regarded as an effort by State Department officials and a minority interest in the Navy to offset the political effects of changes in strategy carried out as the result of strong initiatives taken in the early sixties by the Secretary of Defense. The MLF was the major prospect for Johnson to change extended deterrence, with the possible exception of the strategic arms control moves that aborted much later in his administration. The strategic arms limitation initiative was, like the MLF, promoted by a small, relatively cohesive group of highly skillful American bureaucrats with their own agenda. Unlike the MLF promoters, the strategic arms limitation promoters did not adopt policies that isolated them from the larger foreign policy community in the executive branch, and the methods they employed to promote a treaty, likewise, did not isolate them. The fortune of their initiative was bad luck. The Soviet invasion of Czechoslovakia in August 1968 put an end to plans for a summit meeting at which a strategic arms agreement might have been negotiated.

The MLF, though flawed, offered a prospect for major innovation in American policy toward Europe during the Johnson administration. There were other attempts to innovate that also failed. The most ambitious was to soften the division of Europe by strengthening ties to Eastern Europe. In his State of the Union message in January 1965, Johnson spoke of restless nations in Eastern Europe and announced: "Your government, assisted by leaders in labor and business, is now exploring ways to increase peaceful trade with these countries and with the Soviet Union."[1] Johnson would expand his vision of improved commercial relations to include cultural and political "bridges to the east." But it was Western Europeans, principally in the German Federal Republic (FRG), who expanded commercial links eastward. The United States lagged behind Western Europe in this respect. "Bridges to the east" never got much further than a slogan during the Johnson administration, an item on its policy agenda that remained largely unimplemented.

More to the point, the Federal Republic was "left out on a limb" as "American interest turned from Europe to Vietnam and from MLF to NPT"[2]—the Nuclear Non-Proliferation Treaty, another legacy from Kennedy which Johnson pursued with little regard for European sensitivities. German diplomacy, under a new coalition government in 1966, became less reliant on the United States and less disposed toward European integration. The British Labour government, in turn, governed as was common in the U.K. with narrow electoral margins that prevented it from taking any initiatives to resolve Britain's own foreign policy dilemmas. De Gaulle, with an ample margin of domestic political support until 1968, took France out of NATO and applied pressures on the United States through the dollar. The Johnson administration, in turn, elected to wait de Gaulle out.

The prospects for substantial policy innovation in NATO, carried through under U.S. leadership, passed with the demise of the MLF. With the exception of the Nuclear Non-Proliferation Treaty, which was finally completed and signed in mid-1968, "the initiative on European security affairs would be left to others, or encouraged indirectly."[3] Existing security arrangements would be adapted but remain unchanged, and would in fact remain largely unchanged for more than a decade, until another German chancellor, Helmut Schmidt, again raised the nuclear issue and asked for the modernization of theater nuclear forces in Europe.

The Johnson administration lost the initiative to others. It defended the status quo of American commitments and deployments in Europe against pressure in the Senate to reduce the number of American troops located there. Defending the status quo would, in turn, require the Defense Department to pursue a more active arms sales effort in Western Europe to reduce the export deficit. The fiscal consequences of trade imbalances in the face of de Gaulle's monetary manipulations, which he employed to attack the dollar, required new arrangements with the Germans for offsetting dollar credits. A weakening dollar led to export controls and the development of new arrangements for maintaining international liquidity in Western Europe. U.S. policy became largely reactive but scarcely static.

The MLF may have been an unrealistic goal for the U.S. government, given Kennedy's and Johnson's unwillingness to give up their veto over the use of U.S. nuclear weapons, and congressional opposition to that happening. An additional barrier was the fact that neither president was willing to make the MLF proposals a high priority. Yet it qualifies as a significant attempt at policy innovation and assists our analysis of the problems associated with such efforts by affording us a view of change attempted while minimizing costs associated with succeeding or failing in a situation where a high value is placed on the status quo—the prevailing conditions of the infrastructure.

Entanglement, Search, and Reassurance

The entanglement of U.S. military commitments and forces in Europe limited U.S. options and reassured NATO's European members about what the U.S. would and would not do. Robert Osgood wrote in this vein of NATO as an entangling alliance, addressing the symbols, the commitments, and the limited structural integration.[4] Smart allies can be certain that when they associate with the United States there is always another point of access in Washington which will allow them to work for an outcome in their own interest; that there is always some surviving advocate who cannot be placated, or yet other potential players who can be persuaded to dissent when the president and his Cabinet are all moving in another direction. At a working, functional level, the U.S. government gives assurance to its allies that it will continue to perform the normal tasks associated with its commitments to them by making it manifestly difficult, in the large, disjointed, and highly visible processes of American foreign policy, to change that performance.[5]

Such considerations, much more than verbal promises, reassure Europeans about what the United States will do in the future. These same considerations, however, give particular significance to the president's function in foreign relations. If de Gaulle could move on the diplomatic game board with the superior mobility provided him by the French political order, a base he had fashioned for himself, Johnson could boast comparable advantages in a much more powerful state. Like de Gaulle, he was also a president, possessing the considerable constitutional prerogatives in foreign relations enjoyed by the American president. And after November 1964, at least for a time, he also had a strong popular mandate. His domestic political base permitted him to match de Gaulle's diplomatic mobility, but his commitment to the Atlantic alliance, and to the infrastructure of American foreign policy in Europe, did not. His choice in Europe was a conservative one, to limit his initiatives and wait out de Gaulle. De Gaulle, with his vision of France's place as a world power, had much more at stake than did Johnson. While de Gaulle sought this power, Johnson wanted only to maintain the Atlantic alliance and get on with his domestic agenda.

We should not take for granted that the option to abandon the MLF proposal, which Johnson took up in December 1964, four years after Kennedy had proposed the MLF in an address before the Canadian parliament, remained feasible over this relatively long period of presidential sponsorship. NATO's nuclear arrangements, already under criticism when the MLF proposals were launched, might have been further discredited if the president himself had worked hard to make the case for the force. As it was, the reputation of Johnson and his administration suffered when he withdrew support from the MLF and left its supporters in the lurch. But the cost to Johnson's political reputation was moderate, and certainly bearable. In the end, the back-off option was taken up, and it worked. Thirteen years later, when President Carter backed off after proposing the acquisition and deployment in Europe of a neutron bomb, his reputation suffered considerably more than did Johnson's over the MLF back-off. The fact that the neutron bomb lacked a group of promoters with the same independence, resilience, skill, and persistence is not the only exception to a parallel between these two cases. Johnson handled the back-off with more finesse than did Carter, for another exception. There was, in fact, as there so often is in the U.S. government, a faction of strong supporters that formed the core of the coalition of supporters for the neutron bomb. But they lacked the special characteristics of the group of MLF supporters, the "true believers," which set the latter apart and enabled the president, in the end, to step back from them at limited cost to himself.

We have the benefit of hindsight. NATO as a multi-governmental organization and an alliance looked little different for the next twenty years as it performed important political functions. It survived de Gaulle's withdrawal of French forces and its failure to re-solve several seemingly alliance-threatening problems. Its members continued to contend with one another over burden-sharing, pro-curement cooperation, strategy, and other matters. During those years the NATO alliance justified for Europeans and Americans the presence of American forces in Europe. It helped Western European governments justify their national military efforts to their own po-litical elites and publics. It softened the domestic confrontation be-tween right and left in Europe by diminishing the identification of nationalism and raising the association of internationalism with military preparedness. It provided an international framework for the rearmament of the FRG and serves even in the early nineties to reassure all of Europe that the German army is under control. It enhanced the credibility of the U.S. commitment to the defense of Western Europe. It distributed the military burden among NATO members (although to no one's satisfaction). In the United States, it enabled successive presidential administrations and the Congress to commit themselves to Europe's defense through routine administra-tive and routine annual legislative measures. It once aroused and in the mid-sixties still encouraged the hope that Western Europe would unite politically, a development that would have important strategic implications. Only in the late eighties did it become a hopeful pros-pect again.

These are important political functions, many of which NATO still performs in 1992. NATO must deal with security issues com-parable to what nation-states face. Yet it lacks the wider structure of national politics that its member states, as modern governments with competitive political systems, have for airing and resolving is-sues. This statement is true even when we take NATO in its broad-est sense, as a regime composed of an international organization linked to transnational and transgovernmental networks of activi-ties and communications—i.e., NATO itself, its member govern-ments with their governmental subunits, other governments, and nongovernmental organizations, such as arms suppliers and public interest groups, are a part of the NATO system.

Reform in this kind of situation is difficult. Who in what govern-ment is to lead off? What is the incentive to change? For all mem-bers, NATO is a convenience. The MLF was supposed to address Ger-man dissatisfaction with a peace treaty that prevented Germany's owning nuclear weapons. Yet the FRG, of all NATO members, was the most dependent on NATO for help in managing its own expec-tations about security and for legitimizing its national security poli-cies. If one takes into account the range of opinion among German political leaders about the MLF, they remained uncertain until the eleventh hour. It was not until de Gaulle had created a problem in the Bundestag for Erhard's government that the latter acted decisively—and unsuccessfully—to meet the deadline that he himself and Johnson had set six months earlier.

Meanwhile, NATO worked. It was an instrument for the practice of satisficing by its members, and although it did nothing well, neither did it perform its job so poorly as to make its restructuring an urgent matter.

As the situation described above illustrates, an important function of politics that is vital to foreign relations is to determine (more often, to influence) which issues will lie dormant or remain undefined, and among the issues that have become conspicuous, which will achieve an active place on the political agenda, and when.[6] Although items sometimes arrive on the public agenda as the unfolding of "fate," political activists, performing roles akin to entrepreneurs in the private sector, often put them there. Governmental processes also determine which agenda items will be pulled off the agenda and moved away from politics by consigning them, if they are still of political interest, to authoritative administrative or judicial handling.[7] If they are no longer politically significant, they will be handled inconspicuously through normal procedures, administrative routines, or standard operating procedures. Political players—politicians—value the routines of governmental administration which help them influence what issues become items on the public agenda and permit them to handle such issues once they must. They also value governmental capabilities which enable them to choose *not* to become closely identified with the handling of particular agenda items. The framework of NATO provided this choice, too.

Management, Policy, and Administration

These broad propositions begin to link the dynamics of political processes with the stabilizing, system-defining functions and the continuity of institutions in the governmental process. Woodrow Wilson, in a famous essay, differentiated politics from administration and noted that administration is and ought to be constrained by politics.[8] A president may have a stake in what happens almost anywhere in the federal bureaucracy, although this does not mean that his stakes are evenly distributed throughout the government. To the contrary, the existence of public agencies to handle issues permits presidents and other political players to avoid full involvement with political issues by referral or assignment, default or neglect. Political management deals not only in the *generation* and *handling* of political issues but also in their *avoidance.*[9] Accountable political executives, if they are shrewd enough to perceive an agency as a burden and a threat, as well as an asset, should be able to employ the agency in a protective and exploitative function. This means they should be able to distance themselves and reduce their visibility when this suits their interests, and be able to identify themselves with the agency whenever this promises to enhance their prominence and prestige. These choices are indicative of a well-organized and well-managed bureaucracy. Such a bureaucracy allows executives to identify with or distance themselves from an issue by first presenting them with the choice of addressing an issue, then by allowing them to determine when and on what terms it should be addressed.

By the time Johnson became president, NATO had long served several functions for U.S. policy toward Western Europe. Most directly, it served a common defense or military *efficiency* function, pooling military resources, organizing a combined military headquarters, and making advanced preparations for defensive warfare. It also served several *political* functions of a nature discussed above. One, associated with the military efficiency function, was to generate authoritative military requirements for the United States, and to a greater extent, for its NATO member allies. Two, NATO was to make visible and operational the American military commitment to Europe. A third function was to make U.S. behavior more reliable, or rather more visibly reliable, by reducing it to a relatively stable routine. The fact that what the United States did as the senior partner in NATO had, by the mid-sixties, come to be accepted as the result of the normal executive and legislative routines of the U.S. government made the process more credible to Americans, NATO Europeans, and most likely, to Soviet observers. All parties believed that the commitment would continue. This is not to deny that most public attention has been devoted to the other possibility of the United States's reducing its involvement, any more than it would be appropriate to deny that most media attention to NATO has been directed at its ailments and possible collapse.

Finally, NATO served a fourth political function, one that diminished the value of its military efficiency function. It provided an institutional framework within which West Germany could be the major European source of military strength for the alliance without becoming an independent military power. Once Germany rearmed in the fifties, there was no way for NATO to abandon this function without redefining the German problem. To perform it, NATO needed to maintain a persuasive rationale for the German forces assigned to NATO. The same requirement applied to NATO's facilitating the American commitment to Europe, the second function.

The American commitment to NATO, in turn, was built initially on support within the U.S. government that depended upon a variant of partisan politics termed bipartisanship. Bipartisanship was a set of rules for consultation across party lines and between the executive and the Congress about foreign policy. It weakened during the fifties and faded further over the Vietnam War. The Truman administration and both the Republican and Democratic leadership of the Congress developed special cooperative procedures in foreign relations to reduce the partisan cleavage over foreign policy. Truman also partially "bipartisanized" the executive agencies involved in foreign relations by appointing to key foreign policy posts Republicans as well as Democrats who had extrapartisan stature. He appointed Republicans such as Paul Hoffman, John Foster Dulles, and Robert Lovett, Democrats such as Averell Harriman, as well as nonpartisan military men such as George C. Marshall, Walter Bedell Smith, and Dwight D. Eisenhower to major foreign policy posts. The Departments of State and Defense and the foreign economic, military, and technical assistance agencies minimized their partisan roles and partisan vulnerability with varying success. After twenty years of Democratic control of the White House, the relatively limited changes wrought in personnel, structure, and the substance of policy by Eisenhower when he became president indicate the success not simply of congressional bipartisanship (or extrapartisanship),[10] but also of administrative extrapartisanship.

During the early and mid-fifties, a further development in the routinization of foreign relations occurred as the procedures for supporting U.S. foreign programs and relations became normal processes in Washington. The bipartisan order had permitted the creation of the Economic Cooperation Administration (ECA) and the European Recovery Program, NATO and the Mutual Defense Assistance Program. It had permitted the Truman administration to convert the temporary occupying armed forces in Germany into the permanent American contribution to NATO forces and had reequipped and expanded these forces, winning annual congressional acquiescence through the military authorizations and appropriations. Time, repetition, and habit strengthened these routines. For NATO members, NATO became nothing if not politically legitimate during the fifties. In that capacity it became an alternative to bipartisan restraint.

NATO as a Demonstration of U.S. Policy

Some of the most important things that happen in American foreign policy—NATO-related happenings are certainly among the most important elements of American foreign policy—are repeated yearly, or more often, or have other routine dimensions to them. They are legislative or executive-branch routines or, with reference to external relations, patterns in our bilateral and multilateral relations. The most noticeable thing about them is their general predictability, their normalcy. Take the behavior of the American generals who have served as the Supreme Allied Commander, Europe (SACEUR). It has been predictable that their service would be rated as distinguished if largely because Western Europeans wanted it to be. This has been due to the Supreme Commanders' demonstrated commitment to act as spokesmen for common NATO interests, to the discomfiture of the Pentagon and the White House. T. R. Milton, a retired Air Force general with extensive NATO and Pentagon service, described this routinization of the U.S. government's NATO policy in terms of the normalities that are internal to that government: "European defense has been the primary US military preoccupation since the USSR made its objectives clear after World War II. Vietnam saw the US Army in Europe go sharply downhill in quality, but the numbers, reassuringly, stayed about the same. As for the Air Force, there has been a similar stability in the number of wings. *NATO obligations have thus become the justification for a considerable share of the Army and Air Force force structure. The Navy has managed to keep its NATO contribution less rigid.*"[11] Milton's observation helps clarify a fact which is usually overlooked about NATO: the Alliance is in a perpetual crisis, yet it survives.

Why NATO survives in the face of repeated crises, however, remains a matter of only passing notice. This phenomenon—noticing but failing to explain NATO's survival—is observable in the best informed of statements about NATO, such as that of Karl Kaiser, director of the Research Institute of the German Society for Foreign Affairs, who has written: "When it comes to popular and elite support for NATO, all available survey data show a remarkable continuity of adherence over 35 years after the creation of the alliance. It is not NATO's problem, but conflict and divergence at the level of elites. Those who view the future of NATO pessimistically usually argue that sooner or later the conflicts and disagreements among administrative and political elites are likely to affect public opinion and erode support for NATO."[12] Such a line of reasoning may at first appear convincing. But a closer look at the history and present structure of the organization reveals that NATO has always lived with internal disagreement and nevertheless survived. It was a "troubled" alliance from the very beginning.[13]

The missing element in Kaiser's observation and in so many other observations about NATO is that NATO serves an important function for its members, a function which presumably ensures the support of the elites in each country despite their constant complaints about it. This function can, for convenience, be described as a baseline or default function. The disagreements among administrative and political elites as identified by Kaiser can be seen as the very situations for which NATO was created. NATO's baseline function is to resolve the sort of issues which are normally resolved by national governments. Some of these issues are relatively partisan and contentious, but others are the normal result of bureaucratic and legislative politics. This comparison will be explained further in order to provide further description of the functions performed by NATO as an important component of the infrastructure of U.S. foreign policy in the Johnson era.

Defense policy can be a chancy business for national politicians, so they often seek ways to minimize the politics of it. But they must minimize politics in an active political arena which is based directly on electoral politics. In NATO, however, the relationship to electoral politics is indirect and the process of reconciliation, therefore, quite different. Rarely is there sufficient consensus throughout NATO about the nature of the threat and the need to cope with it. Never is there agreement about allocating the burden of support for NATO, although statements claiming agreement are periodically tacked together. NATO, as an international agency, cannot provide a forum comparable to that of the national political marketplace in highly developed political systems such as Britain, Germany, Italy, or the United States for airing disputes and reconciling interests. Therefore, when such disputes arise in NATO, they often result in crisis. When there is no crisis, the silence usually reflects the low levels of saliency in military matters, and therefore, of these questions. Rarely does it reflect an agreement among the allies or serious disagreement either.

NATO, by providing collective security according to a founding premise, provided a more efficient way for members to meet their individual national security requirements. It also has provided a more effective way for them to justify their military programs. Legitimizing by collective action the efforts of each NATO member toward the common defense reduces the political burden each bears in justifying its military programs to its public. Justifying military programs to national constituencies has not, however, assured that all issues pertaining to NATO's military function will be answered; quite the contrary. NATO's military objectives are multiple, and they must be realized within multiple constraints because of NATO's multinational sponsorship. Justification occurs without answering some quite important questions.[14] In member states these issues can, if necessary, be moved out of the administrative apparatus into the political marketplace where they are resolved, at least to the degree that anything can be resolved in a national political system. When that happens, the result may be a political crisis for the governing party, but rarely a crisis that threatens the political order. At worst, the government of the day, not the political order, will change. That, at any rate, has been true for NATO members, with the important exception of France, which endured a crisis that changed its political order under de Gaulle in the late fifties. No such course has been open to the Atlantic alliance.

The capacity to reconcile conflicting security factors in modern states is almost taken for granted. When Harold Wilson, the new British prime minister, visited Washington in December 1964, his objectives for the visit were part of an elaborate performance for reconciling Britain's declining capacity to project its military power east of Suez with Britain's lingering aspirations to remain a world power, a political drama that played before a competitive, closely divided two-party audience in Britain. Neustadt, assessing this situation for Bundy, noted that Wilson was in a precarious position. His new government could fall if he misstepped badly in his effort to reshape Britain's defense policy. This being the case, he could scarcely act with the force and resolve that de Gaulle, having consolidated his constitutional and political position in France, could muster. Wilson's Washington hosts that December recognized this fact, as doubtless did he and his delegation. Yet on neither the American nor the British side of the table was the problem defined as a crisis of the political order in Britain. In fact, Wilson's behavior had a certain predictability to it. In opposition, he had denounced Britain's nuclear power pretensions, but in power he adopted them.[15]

Continuity, Resilience, and Survival in Foreign Policy

In the face of concerns about keeping a foreign policy system working as well as possible, the fact that it works at all, and works with at least partial success by performing a variety of functions for its participants, may be overlooked. The elementary functions NATO performs have often been overlooked. NATO, along with other institutionalized commitments of the United States, contributes to the maintenance of American foreign relations from year to year by representing the status quo of American entanglements. This means it is sustained by normal organizational processes—budgets, posture statements, manpower requirements, annual increments to foreign aid programs, ongoing diplomatic representational policies. Where foreign military, economic, and technical assistance programs are involved, or where U.S. armed forces or other programmatic capabilities play a role, budgets, with their powerful inclination to maintain a baseline and incrementalize decisions, sustain levels of effort and smooth out changes in them.[16] Lacking the adaptive features of a competitive national political system, and assigned to perform functions that are much like the national security functions that states perform, NATO appears to be at risk whenever it must handle a significant issue. Yet the fact that it has survived through more than forty years of crisis indicates otherwise.

Viewed in this light, the seemingly precarious life of NATO can be more readily understood. It has so often been in crisis or appeared to be because it cannot resolve important questions regarding its role while operating in a normal mode. When NATO is confronted with what appears to be a crisis of the regime, this merely indicates that it is properly, if imperfectly, performing its fifth or main function. NATO is there to address the interests of its members in their mutual entanglement. In this respect, NATO can be likened to a pair of damaged tonsils whose damage indicates, not that their extraction is required, but that they are doing their job and should be left in place so that they can continue to take damage and be useful.[17]

Integration and Presidential Leadership

NATO's capacity to operate as though it were always or often enduring a crisis of its own serves the foreign policy requirements of its member governments. It reminds them of its importance to them; it permits them to demonstrate their interest in it. One might suppose that the NATO regime—to refer to the larger network of national governmental policies and programs as well as of the organization itself—fits the established model of interdependence.[18] It most certainly addresses a common problem with interdependent means. The common defense of Western Europe and North America, as historically that situation has been assessed, has required an independent effort to meet it. NATO is clearly a functionally based international organization engaged primarily in technical cooperation. The sort of routine technical cooperation that has been its main business most of the time has, as has often been observed, an entangling effect that achieves the two major (informal) purposes of NATO, to assure the involvement of the United States in the security of Western Europe and to provide an international locus for German armed forces. Yet the working-level cross-governmental relationships that figure in the MLF case were often overshadowed by internal relationships within NATO governments themselves. As the Grewe fiasco demonstrated, the working-level negotiations over the MLF proved fruitless without stronger support from political leaders. It involved too much technical complexity to be negotiated between heads of state without resolving details first at the working level; yet the negotiations bogged down in technical details in the absence of clearer guidance from the higher political level. Robert Keohane and Joseph Nye define transgovernmental relations as "sets of direct interactions among sub-units of different governments that are not controlled or closely guided by the policies of the cabinets or chief executives of those governments."[19] The MLF negotiations were not on the American side closely guided or controlled. From an American perspective, the most important thing that happened at the technical level occurred after the negotiations failed. The technical link was then used to forge a bilateral partnership with the Germans. Its purpose was to win support at the highest level first in Bonn, where it worked, and then in Washington, where it failed. Ambassador Gerard Smith's negotiations in Paris during the latter months of 1964 could have succeeded only with carefully designed reinforcing actions from Washington. When the test came, however, no reinforcement was provided. The way had not been prepared for positive Washington action.

Adaptable organizations often adapt at least to some extent homeostatically. Their leaders do not control and may not even be aware of all the challenges they respond to. Consistent with its behavior in other fields, the U.S. government is relatively adaptable. Formal subunits and informal factions of the government involved in foreign relations are relatively accessible to other actors in the foreign environment and to other agencies in Washington. But their effectiveness in responding to these lateral stimulators may depend on their vertical support, on what sort of guidance and reinforcement they get from the president and his spokesmen. In the case of the MLF, there was a lack of presidential supervision and support, a situation originally preferred by MLF promoters. Later, when their attempts to build a coalition in the government failed, the promoters turned to devising ways to force presidential action. Certain kinds of action-forcing schemes are accepted devices in government; the Johnson-Erhard communique in July 1964 was an acceptable form of action-forcing technique. The Grewe visit was not.

We come back, then, to the MLF as an effort at innovation sustained by a small coalition of like-minded officials with more enthusiasm than the president, who pushed their hardest while the president's staff prepared the way for his withdrawal of support. As we saw, the arrangement suited the need to keep the MLF proposal alive while limiting the president's involvement with it. By the early sixties, when the coalition of MLF promoters formed, European governments had acquired some experience coping with the disjointed American foreign policy apparatus. As one might expect, they were not equally skilled at coping with it. Germany, in particular, lacked the experience that comes with an independent foreign policy. But the MLF presented the NATO European governments with an exceptional situation in two respects. The first was the status of the MLF faction. To what extent did they represent the U.S. government? Under the circumstances the answer required an assessment of the foreign policy apparatus in Washington. This was an important puzzle which the British were able to solve but the Germans evidently were not.

The MLF effort also was exceptional because it involved the command and control of nuclear weapons. The heroic role the president is expected to play in nuclear matters constrains how much he can disassociate himself from efforts to alter nuclear command procedures. The MLF effort worked in territory that is uniquely dominated by the heroic presidency but was also uniquely controlled by the congressional Joint Committee on Atomic Energy (JCAE). It will be recalled that the JCAE had been consulted about the MLF in 1963. Committee spokesmen took the position at that time that the United States could not give up its custody—that is, its release controls—over American nuclear weapons assigned to the MLF without amending the McMahon Act, which the committee would not do. Here, then, was a game with internal and external elements closely related to one another. It consisted of seeing how far the American promoters of the MLF could get with committing European governments and involving them in the actual operation of an MLF on subtle promises about future changes in custody without having to confront the JCAE over the statutory restrictions on the custody of nuclear weapons contained in the McMahon Act, this in the expectation that the further they could get with the Europeans, the more likely the confrontation would succeed when it became necessary.

The Johnson administration was not about to tell allies that it was willing to circumvent the position of a powerful congressional committee in order to satisfy them, particularly since there was no settled resolve within the Johnson administration that it would actually do so. But there was an additional problem concerning the handling of nuclear weapons that was even more difficult to discuss. Europeans had come to view America's possession of nuclear weapons in Western Europe as assurance that the United States could be counted on to use nuclear force when necessary. This problem needs further explanation.

Michael Howard once explained what NATO Europe expects from U.S. nuclear power as follows: "The American military presence was wanted in Western Europe, not just in the negative role of a *deterrent* to Soviet aggression, but in the positive role of a *reassurance* to the West Europeans; the kind of reassurance a child needs from its parents or an invalid from his doctors against dangers which, however remote, cannot be entirely discounted."[20]

The reassurance required by Europeans is that the United States assume risks and burdens which Europe would prefer to avoid. To explain the frustration evident on both sides of the Atlantic requires metaphors such as those used by Howard. Some Western European officials have observed a "destructive pattern" in the behavior of U.S. officials who, it is claimed, reassure NATO Europe while in office and then question the validity of the U.S. nuclear guarantee after leaving office.[21]

Imperative Direction and Nuclear War

The president oversees an executive branch composed of numerous groups seeking his endorsement of actions and plans, but on their terms. In addition, there are yet other groups which avoid the executive's attention and control when it is to their advantage. Where the president trusts other players, his reactions and initiatives are supportive; where trust is weak, his actions may be disruptive to them; his avoidance of action may seem thoughtless.[22] Always, trust depends heavily on propinquity and time, as well as on personality and the congruence of a president's and other players' goals. Always, the president wants an earlier warning than what is finally received; usually associates of the executive want a commitment to their enterprises earlier and often they want it clearer and stronger than what the president is willing to give.

Johnson's tongue lashing of his associates on the eve of Prime Minister Wilson's visit in early December 1964 indicated a limited trust in them. They had brought the issue of the MLF to him, or at any rate revealed its complexities to him, much too late. They had permitted him to commit himself too much to the MLF. His listeners, in turn, brought their own viewpoints to those meetings. The self-critical Bundy and Neustadt all but agreed with him. They stood in his place. George Ball and Dean Acheson stood on their own. They were advocates of the MLF and this was the time to gain Johnson's final endorsement. They even wanted him to join with Bonn and launch the MLF force as a German-American enterprise, if necessary. They would have been willing to advise him to do it without warning him of the consequences—at least Acheson would have.[23] As a determined innovator, one might say, Acheson was willing to supply the "hiding hand"—a hand that would conceal the difficulties ahead—which was needed to permit this major undertaking to start.[24] McNamara and Rusk stood aside, willing to help the president, but not to warn or reassure him—at least not in front of the others.[25]

If presidential politics is fascinating to spectators, the game of presidential direction and control over military affairs is especially fascinating. It is also grim because of the stakes and potential dangers. There are two reasons for this, both of which concerned Johnson. The first is the president's unavoidable and undelegable responsibility for nuclear weapons decisions. The second is the challenge of managing the huge and complex military establishment. Both pose the same questions: What is the president's interest, as chief of state, in these activities? How should they be organized and supervised to reflect his interest—and to present him with timely options concerning it?

To work, the MLF proposals would have required a reconciliation of European and American perspectives on the command and control of nuclear weapons. When they failed to do this, the initiative returned to the Defense Department. To understand what followed from adopting the back-off option, we must review the situation in the Defense Department, where McNamara had acted under President Kennedy to increase effective presidential direction and control over the military establishment. This included the areas of strategic use, and command and control, of nuclear weapons. By the time Johnson became president, McNamara had implemented his new policies with a thoroughness unmatched before then or since. He took these steps, at least initially, with so little regard for the perspectives of Europeans[26] that his efforts alarmed them.

Flexible Response and Nuclear Locks

When Johnson became president, "flexible response" was a declared policy of the United States. It meant that plans for the employment of the nuclear-armed strategic forces, and the composition and posture of the forces themselves, would be adjusted where necessary so that the president would be permitted a variety of choices in a nuclear strategic crisis. These choices included different conventional (that is, non-nuclear) responses and different nuclear responses. The latter varied in lists of targets, in types of weapons and delivery systems, and in salvo patterns.

In 1961, when Robert McNamara, the Secretary of Defense, drew "scientific strategists" into his service and adopted their viewpoint about nuclear strategy, the logic of flexible response ran a close parallel with theories articulated by Richard Neustadt about presidential power.[27] Flexible nuclear options were intended to protect the president from the strong inclinations of the Strategic Air Command which, in order to make its own formidable mission more manageable, sought to limit him to an appallingly narrow set of choices. Neustadt defined the predicament of presidential leadership: Presidents must always tend their interests and protect their choices; no one can be relied upon to do it for them.[28] William Kaufmann and the other originators of flexible response had found this to be the case with respect to preparations for employment of nuclear forces, something which had persistently encroached on the president's range of choice. Flexible response was the remedy, just as was McNamara's Program, Planning and Budgeting System (PPBS) the way to define and protect the president's choices for the Defense Department. Both strategies, one for national defense and the other for the Pentagon, provided Kennedy and Johnson with more choices, which were also more salient to both men because they dealt with management issues defined from the top down.

The credibility of the American nuclear guarantee had declined in Western Europe during the late fifties with the buildup of Soviet conventional and nuclear forces, the growing respect for Soviet technical prowess that *Sputnik* had aroused, and the anticipated obsolescence of the currently deployed nuclear bomber forces in Europe. Robert Bowie, during the original development of the MLF proposal, sought greater credibility with a sea-based force under a special multilateral command. SACEUR had, with certain limited exceptions, no command authority in peacetime over the forces assigned to NATO by its members. It would acquire that authority only in wartime. The MLF was to be an integrated force put under multilateral command in peacetime.

The MLF was designed to appeal to Europeans in two ways. One was by blunting an anticipated German demand for nuclear status. The other was by bolstering the credibility of American promises to underwrite extended deterrence by offering hope that the solution was just around the corner. Meanwhile, Europeans could have, if not formal control, then at least possession of nuclear weapons. The symbolic value of possession by a multilateral military command organization would presumably be substantial. But this aspect of the MLF was exaggerated. The symbolic value of possession without control was likely to erode because the Americans were actually bringing nuclear weapons under stricter physical controls.

MLF planning gave extraordinary attention to the building of a multi-governmental military command structure that integrated military personnel from the seven participating nations down the ranks to include junior officers and enlisted men. The MLF promoters imputed considerable significance to these proposed arrangements because they would make it impossible for any member to withdraw its forces, and therefore itself, from responsibility for firing the weapons. But they also created a new relationship between possession and control: the prospect that possession would permit preemptive control. This would be more the case if the controlling military force were integrated instead of, as in the NATO military command structure, a collection of nationally commanded forces. Underlying the MLF proposals was the expectation that possession would be reassuring because it would, in the last analysis, assure use. But possession would not assure use so long as the American rules of custody and control obtained, and these the Johnson administration was not free to bargain away.

Flexible response strategy thus illuminates the central, optimistic assumption of the heroic presidency and the significance of the limited presidential commitment employed in promoting the MLF. With respect to the first, it is assumed that catastrophe can best be avoided by top-down command. It permits presidential steering and maneuver, which in turn, is a way to avoid or terminate war rather than be carried into it accidentally or continue it unnecessarily.[29] The doctrine rests on further assumptions that the president will know and comprehend what is happening and that he will take decisive actions when strategy dictates it. Above all, the strategic theory assumes that his behavior as commander-in-chief and chief of state will be rational, i.e., he would choose deliberately among the options that he faced.[30] To put it as simply as possible, when a catastrophe looms, the president must stand above the organizational and political milieu of the American governmental process, devote attention to coping with it, and be able to act with the valid assurance that the decision to act will not be changed to accommodate bureaucratic or political interests. He must escape the negative constraints of organizational process and bureaucratic politics. These are, indeed, heroic assumptions. The heroic presidency survived as a norm of necessity during the sixties, as it does now in the early nineties, in part because no one has found a way to abandon it. It remained an integral component of the MLF proposal, assuring that its promoters could never get very far from the president.

Summary: The Promise, Risks, and Costs of the MLF

We will, of course, never know whether the MLF, had Johnson gone ahead with it as an arrangement first with Bonn only, could have succeeded in the way that its strongest American supporters hoped it would. Could the MLF have been the impetus for George Ball's vision of a politically integrated Western Europe or Thomas K. Finletter's vision of an Atlantic Community? Or would it have fulfilled David Klein's fears of destroying NATO and discrediting the president? As far as the effort went, its costs were limited. It was an innovation from the inside, much like a technical innovation, conceived by government officials who sought to implement it under presidential license. One needs to distinguish between the grand hopes of its advocates and the limited measures they were able to promote. They were limited by the instruments with which they had to work, which they used to their utmost, with great skill.

The MLF episode illustrates a critical dimension of policy management. In this case, the status quo consisted of a relatively heavy and relatively irreversible investment. One can interpret the MLF episode as Richard Neustadt has analyzed political leadership, in terms of its economy. It involved spending and protecting presidential influence. In the MLF case, there are shades of influence which are visible but sometimes missed. One is the degree of desperation or risk-proneness of the political leader. If Johnson could be described as cautious in this situation, de Gaulle, in his willingness to play a tougher game, was a risk-taker. As was true in this situation, the stakes were higher for one head of state than another; that difference can be, and was, vital.

Another factor is the extent to which the states involved are bound together by common interests and practices, i.e., the degree of political, economic, and military integration. With reference to the NATO context, this would mean comparing the stakes that members had, and still have, in NATO as a vital element of their respective national security policies.

Finally, there is the function of NATO—NATO as infrastructure—in supplying U.S. nuclear reassurance to European members. For the U.S., the alliance assures that it will be able to do so without perverse consequences, such as rendering nuclear deterrence more complicated, unreliable, difficult, and dangerous. Viewed in this light—its very best light—the American promotion of the MLF was a policy innovation experiment, a try at policy change that threatened the president's reputation modestly, not greatly, while avoiding serious threats to the vital function of strategic reassurance to Europeans.

In terms of presidential involvement, the MLF case is distinctly different from the Indian grain shortage case. Johnson's initially limited involvement in the MLF issue benefitted from the disjointed character of the American governmental process, permitting a small group with a limited mandate to keep the MLF proposal alive while European interest was tested. In comparison to the regional and country regimes involved in negotiations over aid to India, the regimes involved in negotiations on the MLF were vastly more complicated, and therefore, posed more constraints on presidential action.

In three important respects, however, the cases were similar. Both involved the intersection of forces of infrastructure and presidential leadership. In both cases, policy formation and execution relied heavily on the infrastructure. Goals, means, and tactics could be readily stated in relationship to a rich, definable status quo. In the India scenario presidential leadership was direct, literal, and forceful; in the opinion of several U.S. government officials it was also misguided and clumsy. In the MLF case, presidential leadership was integral to the function of nuclear reassurance in NATO and to NATO's partnership with American nuclear forces. Even though the president stayed by default in the background, he always figured in the negotiations because of his undelegable role in matters of nuclear weapons control and employment.

Second, presidential decisions were mainly vertical decisions in that they primarily addressed issues related to the level of presidential or Cabinet involvement and the time frame for achieving certain goals. The actions of the president were not, in other words, based on choosing from an array of choices.

Third, in both cases the president's relations with his advisors showed notable gaps in communication. In Johnson's dealings with India, there were gaps downward and upward, but most notably, a serious gap at the beginning in upward communication. No one among Johnson's regular advisors indicated that India's food shortage was very serious, nor did they reveal the opportunity it presented to Johnson or suggest what he could do. He, in turn, and perhaps because of the way things started, acted without explanation. In this case he kept his staff guessing about his actions.

In dealing with the MLF, on the other hand, the communication problem was upward, not downward. Johnson let stand what he assumed was a well thought out policy and missed the warning signals sent at the start. By accepting the MLF proposal and the existing arrangements for pursuing it, Johnson, in his communication downward, was clear and complete enough. Once he accepted it, however, two upward communication problems appeared as disincentives to inform him about what he needed to know. First, to challenge his decision would embarrass him; one senses this in the extraordinary care with which Bundy approached him with the contrary arguments. Second, to challenge the course chosen by Johnson would be to split the advisors themselves. In the final resolution, the split was minimal.

So much for these comparisons of the MLF and India grain cases. We now turn to Johnson's Vietnam policy. Chapter 6 is scarcely a case study about this vast subject. It is, rather, an essay about some case studies that have been written about the Vietnam War.

6. Vietnam: Normality and Innovation

WE NOW TURN TO Lyndon Johnson's handling of Vietnam. We accept failure as a premise, adopting David Barrett's view that Johnson's decision "to commit hundreds of thousands of American combat troops to fight in South Vietnam was a mistake of gigantic proportions," which Barrett claims to be "an almost undisputed consensus in the present era,"[1] and Leslie Gelb's and Richard Betts's statement that "America's war in Vietnam was obviously a failure," which they also claim is widely believed, although they note that what kind of failure, whether a "strategic, political, diplomatic," or moral failure, "or all of these, will remain in dispute."[2]

Viewed in terms of what the Johnson administration set out to do with respect to Vietnam, it fell conspicuously short of its objectives, even allowing that some confusion could be expected in its goals. If Johnson's course in Vietnam was intended to contain communist power, it failed at least in the sense that it failed to contain the communist regime that ruled North Vietnam. If his course was intended to demonstrate resolve in aiding an ally, ultimately this also failed. There can be little doubt that U.S. leaders saw the maintenance of U.S. credibility with its allies as a primary purpose in assisting Vietnam. President Johnson repeatedly argued that the failure of the United States to support the Republic of Vietnam (RVN) would be seen by U.S. allies as a demonstration of a lack of resolve to defend the interests of the non-communist world. Johnson's April 1965 address at Johns Hopkins University provides a typical argument. According to Johnson, "To leave Viet-Nam to its fate would shake the confidence" of people around the globe "in the value of an American commitment and in the value of America's word."[3] Dean Rusk perhaps best stated the administration's view of the role of the United States in the world. Rusk wrote in July 1965, "The integrity of the U.S. commitment is the pillar of peace throughout the world. If that commitment becomes unreliable, the communist world would draw conclusions that would lead to our ruin and almost certainly to catastrophic war."[4]

If the primary goal of U.S. policy in Vietnam was to use the assistance provided as a means of reassuring U.S. allies and permanently deterring communist aggression, it failed. The conquest of South Vietnam by North Vietnam had not yet occurred when Johnson left office, and it was delayed until 1975, which is not insignificant. But however significant the delay, that fact scarcely insulates the Johnson administration from that outcome—or from counting it as part of a failed policy of the administration by judging the outcome against the goal of stopping the communist challenge to the Saigon government.

Vietnam came to dominate Johnson's foreign policy. It led, as domestic opposition mounted, to the stalemating of his political leadership and the premature ending of his presidency. Considering Johnson's success with domestic programs and with managing domestic politics, both of which were demonstrated in a lopsided popular vote that reelected him to the presidency in 1964, Johnson would very likely have been reelected again in 1968 and served in the White House until 1972 but for his handling of Vietnam. Instead, as Democratic voter opposition to him and his Vietnam policies showed up in presidential primary results in early 1968, he announced that he would not run for reelection.

In 1963, Johnson's aim had been to see that South Vietnam would not fall to an insurgency supported by North Vietnam. In 1965 he extended U.S. policy goals in Vietnam to the coercing of North Vietnam into stopping its support of the insurgency in the south where the government was barely surviving. In 1968, with the survival of South Vietnam still in question, by announcing that he would not run for reelection, Johnson acknowledged that North Vietnam had defeated him and therefore his Vietnam policy.

"No more Vietnams!" has survived for two decades as a popular slogan in American politics. Depending on how it is used, it is a warning against fighting unwinnable wars, against being drawn into wars that are too costly, or against fighting under political constraints which allegedly prevent military force from being effectively applied. Much attention has been devoted to a fourth, more modest expectation, to studying the deliberative procedures Johnson employed for Vietnam, in the hope of improving policy by improving policymaking procedures. The first section of this chapter addresses these deliberative procedures, applying standards of static rationality. The following section employs a more dynamic model of rationality that is associated with innovation, the concept that different resources can be combined in different ways to achieve improvements in processes and products, to state it in its rudimentary form. The better product that interests us is Vietnam policy, and policy innovation is therefore the objective. This approach follows from the assumption made here that, if the initial decisions about military involvement in Vietnam were incorrect, it would have been necessary in order to correct them to accomplish major constructive changes, or innovations, in the large-scale operations which their implementation launched or in the policies themselves that guided these implementing operations—in effect, innovations in goals and instruments.

These next two sections evaluate the deliberative processes that Johnson employed with respect to Vietnam and describe how he chose policies that failed. They deal with the first two meanings of "No more Vietnams!" The third meaning of this slogan suggests that success was possible and contends that a different strategy would have won in the sense that it would have forced North Vietnam to leave South Vietnam alone.

Could Johnson's Vietnam policy have succeeded if a different strategy had been employed, if military force had been applied in some other way? Addressing this question is beyond the scope of this chapter. Those critics of Johnson's handling of the Vietnam War who regard it to have been winnable have charged that Johnson made it unwinnable by the employment of gradual escalation, by his failure to permit the targeting of Hanoi's capacity to wage war, and by his imposing of other constraints designed to avoid provoking China to enter the war.

The final section of this chapter will consider the president's leadership role, addressing it as it is exercised within the deliberative apparatus of the executive branch.

Johnson's Advisory Process and Two Decisions to Escalate: December 1, 1964 and July 28, 1965

We now have excellent studies that evaluate how Johnson went about deciding what to do in Vietnam. These include several important studies published in the eighties which take advantage of newly available primary documents and which strongly converge on two judgments. The first judgment identifies as a critical period of decision making a time that began immediately after the presidential election of 1964 and ended in mid-1965. Several studies carefully examine and evaluate Johnson's deliberations and decisions about Vietnam during this period, evaluating them based on the assumption that they ought to have met certain standards of rational deliberation. They are in general agreement on what those standards are and therefore what constitutes deliberative failure. Most of them find procedural errors in Johnson's advisory process. Larry Berman, the most explicitly normative and the most critical of these evaluators, finds that Johnson manipulated the advisory process to exclude dissenting views, that he excluded options which he should have taken seriously, that he made up his mind prematurely, and that he employed advisory procedures largely for show. Each of these judgments is shared by at least one other of the group.[5] Berman's first book on Vietnam, *Planning a Tragedy* (1982), looks at the mid-1965 decision to increase substantially the American involvement in Vietnam. Berman's command of the primary sources is unsurpassed, and he was able to draw extensive comment from participants, no doubt due to the recognized quality of his work as well as the passage of time.[6] His second book, *Lyndon Johnson's War* (1989), takes the account on through 1968 in less detail, but with undiminished quality.[7]

Berman evidently set out to demonstrate that Johnson manipulated his advisors and that the advisory process that aided his early Vietnam decisions was more charade than substance. The critical episode to make this point involved his sending Robert McNamara to Vietnam in early July 1965 to conduct an assessment that would figure heavily in making the decision Johnson faced at that time about increasing the American military effort in Vietnam. Berman demonstrates what critics had previously charged, that Johnson was favorable to the increase before sending McNamara but hid his preference and made it look like he decided after McNamara returned. The implication was that Johnson dissembled and that he decided without benefit of adequate deliberation. Given where Berman started, his own conclusion was surprisingly cautious: "Johnson used the advisory process to legitimize the decision to political elites and the general public."[8] This statement might have been made about Eisenhower by his admirer Fred Greenstein.[9]

What is more to the point, the decision making behavior that Berman describes falls well within the range of normal practice. Measured against standards of judicial or scientific deliberation (e.g., judges and scientists should not make up their minds until all evidence is in, and they should take time to get all the evidence), Berman proved that Johnson's executive search in mid-1965 was faulty.[10] The charge of dissembling falls within the bounds of fair comment, but there is no way to prove that Johnson would not have turned back if McNamara's report had been different. It is also proper, as is commonly observed, for presidents to withhold their views in order not to prejudice the advice they seek. Berman did not prove (or claim to) that this behavior was faulty when measured against more relevant standards—among them, the habits and behavior of more recent presidents, including two who achieved significant foreign policy breakthroughs, Nixon and Reagan. It is significant that Berman, in *Lyndon Johnson's War*, maintained the high standards of his first book but abandoned the attempt to prove distinct procedural error on Johnson's part.

It is one thing to say that Johnson made wrong decisions regarding Vietnam and quite another that he followed the wrong procedures (and exercised his foreign policy apparatus improperly).[11] The following of proper advisory procedures does not guarantee correct decisions and correct decisions can come from poor deliberative procedures. Furthermore, given the difficulty of judging at the time on the basis of analytic standards (rather than with benefit of hindsight on the basis of consequences) whether or not one is making a correct decision, critics of presidential leadership have devoted considerable attention to procedural norms. Johnson's deliberative procedures have been the object of much of that attention.

This section analyzes Johnson's Vietnam decision making in terms of familiar static rational choice concepts: to what extent in deliberating about Vietnam he considered an adequate range of options and goals and weighed with sufficient care the costs and benefits of these options. To do this we examine the advisory procedures which Johnson employed in the run-up to decisions which he made on December 1, 1964, and July 28, 1965.

As astute journalists later came to realize,[12] Johnson had kept American action in Vietnam as inconspicuous as possible during the presidential campaign and was scarcely interested in new initiatives. Immediately after the election his principal security advisors began preparations to have him face up to the deteriorating situation in Vietnam. They arranged for an NSC Working Group on South Vietnam/Southeast Asia to review the situation. The working group was composed of personnel from the Joint Staff, the Office of the Secretary of Defense, and the Asian regional bureau in the Department of State—much like a planning board working group might have been constituted under the more formal procedures of Eisenhower's NSC regime.

In reporting, as Brian VanDeMark notes, the working group followed a "Goldilocks Principle": Option A was too little and Option B, too much. Johnson, after some resistance, on December 1, 1964, approved Option C, the "just right" option. He authorized a retaliatory bombing campaign against North Vietnam called BARREL ROLL which was designed to be limited enough to assure that it would not induce the Chinese to attack as they had in Korea fourteen years earlier, yet damaging enough to relieve pressure against the regime in Saigon. An air campaign was seen to have the advantage of limiting U.S. involvement and specifically, to exclude committing the United States to a ground war on the mainland of Asia.

BARREL ROLL produced no visible results in Hanoi's support for the insurgency in the south or its interest in negotiations. Within a month, plans were afoot in Washington for expanding BARREL ROLL into a sustained program of bombing against North Vietnam that took the code name ROLLING THUNDER.[13]

The November 1964 deliberations that led to Johnson's BARREL ROLL commitment were probably the best opportunity for seriously considering the possibility of withdrawing from Vietnam. Option A, the "too little" option in the working group's paper, had proposed continuing with the status quo. Johnson's advisors—principally General Taylor, the ambassador in Saigon, McGeorge Bundy, and McNamara—were in agreement that the status quo was leading to disaster. Option A, had it been given serious consideration, would have aired the prospect of a negotiated withdrawal in a favorable light, after first establishing a record of support to the Saigon government which would serve to answer critics.[14] It is quite clear that it was not taken seriously.

Why was it not? One can find an answer to this question in the way that Johnson's advisors dealt with him as they faced the deteriorating situation in Vietnam that October and November, and more specifically, the handling of deliberations over the NSC planning paper. Johnson's advisors—in the immediate case, it would appear to be Bundy and McNamara—were seeking Johnson's attention and action. After a period of presidential campaigning, with the president's attention drawn elsewhere, they had to gain his attention to the pressing events in Southeast Asia. To do so, they had to approach him on *his* terms, and his terms excluded conspicuous change in his Vietnam policy, either a conspicuous increase in the American war effort or a negotiated withdrawal, which, if embarked upon, would doubtless become conspicuous.

VanDeMark notes that when the working group presented its report to Johnson, both its chairman, William P. Bundy, and McGeorge Bundy, the president's National Security advisor, directed the president's attention to what amounted to the BARREL ROLL option (Option C), and that Johnson "voiced no objection to the absence of a withdrawal option."[15] George Ball had undertaken to make the case for that option and Johnson evidently knew about it. Ball had not completed his assignment but had already discussed a related paper with McGeorge Bundy, Rusk, and McNamara, one that challenged the assumptions of Johnson's Vietnam policy. Bundy volunteered to Johnson in this meeting, Ball not being present, that Ball's work on the "devil's advocate" exercise on a negotiated withdrawal had made little progress owing to the press of other responsibilities.[16] The incident, which VanDeMark considered curious, demonstrates no more than that Johnson's advisors were intent upon directing his attention to Option C, the limited retaliation operations planned for BARREL ROLL.

Johnson paid no attention to Option A, and the record shows that neither McGeorge Bundy, as his National Security advisor, nor William P. Bundy, the chairman of the working group and Assistant Secretary of State for the Asian region, nor any other advisor encouraged him to do so. Had they done so, it is possible that Johnson would not have taken them seriously, yet what they needed from him was serious attention to the deteriorating situation in Vietnam. Static rationality assumes that the advisors already have the decision maker's attention and that the task is to provide him with an adequate array of options. But in Johnson's world, as has been widely recognized, the largest issue was how to manage the trade-off between his domestic goals and the demands of foreign policy. This view served to frame what he would consider with respect to Vietnam in the weeks following his November 1964 election landslide. Later, in July 1965, it would shape the measures that he chose. In both cases, he chose measures which permitted him to proceed with his domestic programs.

The behavior of Johnson's civilian advisors was in part a reflection of their own negative judgment about the withdrawal option, but also a reflection of their sense of what Johnson would consider. At this time, and later, their behavior seems to have been influenced by the dilemmas of credibility with Johnson: They had to make choices about what to present to him in order to maintain their credibility with him, and therefore their ability to get him to make decisions about issues that mattered to them. It was not, as has often been supposed, that he was their captive, that he listened only to a narrow set of advisors; quite the contrary. Johnson distrusted and manipulated them and listened to others. They had to make their way with him each day, and he never went all the way with them.

In the aftermath of the 1964 presidential election Johnson set a relatively narrow range for the Vietnam options he would consider. The staff work that supported his deliberations about how to cope with the deteriorating situation in Vietnam—the working group's paper in particular—had a potential for considering a wider range of options, but it was an unrealized potential. Withdrawal, had it been undertaken in any form, would doubtless have drawn domestic political attention in December 1964. Johnson did not want that to happen.

Following upon his decision in favor of BARREL ROLL, Johnson instructed Ambassador Taylor: "There must be a stable, effective government [in Saigon] to conduct a successful campaign against the Viet Cong." Further, with respect to air strikes against North Vietnam intended to end the support and direction of the insurgency in the south, he explained to Taylor that he had come to agree with Taylor's own view favoring air strikes against the north: "We should incur the risks which are inherent in such an expansion of hostilities until there is a government in Saigon capable of handling the serious problems involved in such an expansion."[17]

BARREL ROLL failed to slow the deteriorating situation in the south. Soon, McGeorge Bundy and McNamara were again pressing Johnson for action. When, on January 27, Taylor cabled Bundy that another coup was underway in Saigon, Bundy held a "very private" discussion with McNamara about this turn for the worse and reported to Johnson that "both of us are now pretty well convinced that our current policy can lead only to disastrous defeat."[18] Rather than considering the political problem in Saigon separate from the military situation in the field, Bundy argued, the president should see them as closely connected. "The underlying difficulties in Saigon," he wrote, "arise from the spreading conviction there that the future is without hope for anti-Communists. More and more the good men are covering their flanks and avoiding executive responsibility for firm anti-Communist policy. . . . The Vietnamese know just as well as we do that the Viet Cong are gaining in the countryside. Meanwhile, they see the enormous power of the United States withheld."[19]

The main premise of this argument, which dealt with the weakness in Saigon, Johnson firmly believed. Bundy now laid out two alternatives: One was to "use our military power in the Far East," by which he evidently meant the employment of air and sea power, "to force a change in policy" by North Vietnam and its backers. The other was to "deploy all of our resources along a track of negotiation." Bundy and McNamara recommended the first. They wanted Johnson to increase the intensity of the air strikes against the north consistently, as a campaign, and announce the coercive intent and resolve on which the decision would be based. Bundy pressed the case by cable during a visit to Saigon in early February: "The situation in Vietnam is deteriorating, and without a new U.S. action defeat appears inevitable," he told Johnson. "There is one grave weakness in our posture in Vietnam which is within our power to fix—and that is a widespread belief that we do not have the will and force and patience and determination to take the necessary action and stay the course."[20]

Bundy's behavior with respect to Vietnam during January and February 1965 might be compared with what he did a few months earlier with respect to the MLF. As noted in Chapter 4, a Johnson-Erhard communique in July 1964 had created a deadline for deciding about the MLF. Following up from the communique, Bundy arranged for Neustadt's assessment of the MLF and, when the time for decision came, was able to offer a back-off option to Johnson. With respect to Vietnam, he joined with McNamara to press Johnson for a timely decision.[21] Bundy in both cases raised questions that Johnson would eventually have to face. In the MLF case, he could offer Johnson an unpleasant, but quick, solution, the back-off option. Nothing as simple was available with respect to Vietnam. In fact, Bundy's role—and McNamara's—in getting Johnson to face decisions about Vietnam put them in a class with virtually all of his Vietnam advisors. Johnson more than once told civilian advisors that all the generals wanted to do was bomb the north. It would have been more appropriate for him to complain that everywhere he turned, to civilian as well as military advisors, he was urged to bite the bullet—to bomb the north and deploy more troops to the south, call up the reserves, mobilize the economy, raise taxes, declare an emergency, and possibly declare war. It was Bundy's job, and McNamara's, to advise Johnson in this way. Such advice, however, amounted to telling the president to spend more of *his* political capital and commit *himself* more conspicuously in order to solve the problems that, one might say, *he* assigned *them* to handle. His answer to his advisors was a series of decisions that marked out a "middle way." It amounted to less than what they asked for, but enough to show that he took their advice seriously.

As noted, Bundy began to prepare six months in advance for the MLF decision deadline at the end of 1964 but avoided confronting Johnson with the prospect of a change of policy until the very end. The position that he and McNamara took about Vietnam in early 1965 with respect to the possibility of a change of policy was less circumspect. They repeatedly reminded Johnson of the deterioration in South Vietnam and repeatedly warned him that action was urgent. Both considered the air campaign against North Vietnam necessary; Bundy was slightly bolder about targets.[22] Both at first shared with Ambassador Taylor his soldierly skepticism about having American troops assume combat roles in Vietnam. Johnson doubted that air power could defeat the insurgent war in South Vietnam, and his view predisposed him to be more sympathetic than were these three advisors with General Westmoreland's requests for more troops and for more authority to use them.

We can put too fine a point on these individual differences and similarities, for they adjusted from time to time, responding to developments in the field and also evidently to perceptions of one another's views and roles. Other matters were more significant than these shifting differences. At the end of March, Taylor was recalled to Washington for NSC meetings which produced NSAM 328. This was Johnson's decision to permit the deployment in active combat of the Marine battalions already in Vietnam. Further, in the interest of Johnson's policy of minimizing public attention to Vietnam, he kept NSAM 328 secret and denied (usually by evasion) any change in the mission of U.S. forces in the Vietnam theater.[23] Meanwhile, evasive denials about the buildup of U.S. forces in Vietnam, which were proven to be false by Johnson's announcement at the end of July, damaged Johnson's credibility.

Johnson came to credit Bundy's and McNamara's sense of urgency. He remained skeptical about bombing the north but became increasingly involved with the details of operations. The differences between the president and his advisors reflected in part differences in their respective roles. Johnson appeared to worry the most about Chinese and Soviet reactions to bombing the north. Bundy and McNamara may at first have put more reliance on bombing the north as a way around the messy problems of aiding the RVN government and military. Meanwhile, Johnson was moving toward authorizing large ground reinforcements in the south. Taylor, back in Saigon, was advised in mid-April that the "highest authority" in Washington believed that "something new must be added in the South to achieve victory."[24] The following week, at a meeting in Hawaii, Johnson decided that the target for troop deployments to Vietnam by the end of June should be raised to 90,000. But the summer offensive by the Viet Cong, with the support of regular forces from North Vietnam, demonstrated ominously strong enemy forces, and Westmoreland resolved that "Washington had to face the task [at hand] realistically."[25] He called for stronger reinforcements, a total of 150,000, not 90,000, troops. Taylor proposed 98,000.

One of the most serious charges against Johnson's decision making is that he made up his mind regarding Westmoreland's request early, possibly as early as late May, and in any event before Ball's case against escalation had been examined, before the differences between Ambassador Taylor and General Westmoreland had been aired, and before he sent McNamara to Vietnam in July. There is no way to disconfirm this charge, because there is no way to be certain what was in Johnson's mind. But there is also no clear confirmation of it and several key participants believed at the time, and afterward, that he had not made up his mind. Even more important, the advisory process brought to Johnson's attention during June and July a considerable amount of information and advice which was critical and candid about Westmoreland's request. Observers who make these points include not only Jack Valenti, who was a strong Johnson apologist, but also George Ball, who was scarcely that. A serious possibility is that Johnson decided in early May that he would meet (minimally) Westmoreland's request and that the rest of his deliberations were for show.

VanDeMark, in a plausible reconstruction, comes to a different conclusion. He depicts Johnson as wrestling with these issues up to the end of the deliberations that considered them, and then deciding on the escalation that the July 28, 1965, decision amounted to as a trade-off with his domestic programs—as a resource-limiting decision. VanDeMark had already noted that the previous November Johnson had failed to consider the withdrawal option. The differences between Berman and VanDeMark are unimportant when we consider their convergence on the point that Johnson's deliberative procedures involved his considering a narrow range of options, a range too narrow to meet a general standard of static rationality, a range that excluded what, in hindsight (and to a few of his less influential advisors at the time) was an option too important to have been neglected, the option of withdrawing.[26] Describing rational deliberations in these terms puts Johnson's critics in the ranks of the static rationalists, who define rational decision making as the arraying of, deliberating over, and selection from among options.

Richard Neustadt and Ernest May, whose account is informed by interviews with participants as well as access to the documents, agree with the charge that Johnson had made up his mind well before July 28. They think he waited for McNamara's judgment about the "minimum force requirements necessary to prevent the generals from claiming that they were being denied what they needed to do the job."[27]

Johnson's decision had attributes that served to keep his advisors (and General Westmoreland) on board. According to the "summary notes" of the NSC's executive secretary, Bromley Smith, Johnson stated his decision to his advisors as follows: "We have chosen to do what is necessary to meet the present situation, but not to be unnecessarily provocative to either the Russians or the Communist Chinese. We will give the commanders the men they say they need and, out of existing material in the U.S., we will give them the material they say they need. We will get the necessary money in the new budget and will use our transfer authority until January. We will neither brag about what we were doing or thunder at the Chinese Communists and the Russians."[28]

The pattern of Johnson's decisions with respect to Vietnam is illustrated in this statement, to do less than his field commander or his decision-forcing advisors proposed, to take the "middle road." I have noted earlier in this study the inward bias of observers of the bureaucratic political scene, the tendency of investigators who watch the bureaucratic struggle to conclude, with reference to foreign policy, that the internal games of government decision making, descriptions of which they employ to explain foreign policy, often give *less* weight than the players actually did to external conditions. It appears that our accounts of the bureaucratic struggle over Vietnam are quite the reverse. There is more than a little evidence that the decisions which set the course of Johnson's foreign policy in Vietnam reflected more of the bureaucratic game and less of the external world than is commonly stated. Johnson's middle course was a compromise among *his* players in *their* positions, and it had much to do with the Great Society.

Johnson's decisions about Vietnam usually were more cautious than the recommendations of his boldest military and civilian advisors. Characteristically, the options which his advisory process focused on did not actually include the option that in the end he chose.[29] This fact suggests their intended function. They were action-forcing. One unfortunate effect was that they cut short a vital stage in executive deliberations, one that, characteristically, Eisenhower as president less often neglected. It was to state what was likely to become his policy *and then have it staffed out*—i.e., to have his principal advisors, and perhaps first their own assistants, go over it thoroughly.

No doubt this phase of an orderly staffing procedure would have prolonged the deliberative process. Timing was a factor, but the pressure of time could have been managed in November 1964, in July 1965, and later as well if advisory procedures had been employed that anticipated the need for critical decisions, procedures that did not confront Johnson with the action-forcing maneuvers of his advisors, as was the actual case. From the 1964 election until mid-summer 1965, Johnson's national security advisors were playing, with reference to their own sense of the developing situation in Vietnam, catch-up with him. Eisenhower's handling of important national security issues, even the Suez crisis, where he was responding to allies who were deliberately seeking to force his hand in their favor, did not put him into the same relationship with his advisors. But the difference did not lie in Eisenhower's willingness to let all the options hang out. It lay in his willingness to be arbitrary up front in order to direct his advisors to work on options that he really wanted to consider, options that included what he would actually choose.

Eisenhower's deliberative style went unappreciated throughout the sixties, a victim of the new appreciation of Franklin D. Roosevelt's clever method of management by competition and chaos that Arthur Schlesinger and Richard Neustadt had generated.[30] Only in the eighties has this changed. Previously, Eisenhower's attention to the formalities of the organization of the presidency, particularly the formalities of the president's advisory process, seemed politically naive. With a new appreciation for what lay behind Eisenhower's use of these formalities, the shortcomings of Johnson's advisory procedures can be better understood.[31]

The comparison with Eisenhower highlights two factors. The first is the way Johnson's decision procedures permitted him and his advisors to neglect a thorough examination of *what Johnson actually decided to do.* Johnson failed to get his military and his civilian advisors and the intelligence community to say, for the privileged record, what they thought would be the result, for instance, of supplying the forty-four brigades that Westmoreland said he wanted in early 1965, but declining to call up reserves and take other steps that would put the United States on a war footing, and to subject these predictions to critical appraisal. The deliberative procedures of Eisenhower's NSC process, when they had finished with a particular matter, were more likely to have scrutinized *the actual decision that Eisenhower made.*

Second, critical to the possibility that a principal decision maker be able to consider an appropriate range of options and otherwise engage in preferred deliberative procedures is the anticipation of the need to make a decision and to make preparations for its implementation in sufficient time to permit the decision and its implementation to be deliberate. Eisenhower was by no means prescient, nor were his advisors. But he established an anticipatory frame of reference for the advisory processes that supported his decision making.

When these proceeded routinely the result was often ponderous deliberations and policy documents. His procedures were more impressive when he was responding to events and had to act. Then, he often provided specific instructions to guide his Secretary of State (contrary to widespread belief)[32] and others and to frame the foreign policy deliberations of the NSC advisory process. Eisenhower employed pointed questions not only to frame decision options but also, and perhaps more importantly, to anticipate dealing with the probable consequences of the decisions he had under consideration.[33] Eisenhower's National Security Council was scarcely a model of openness even to its participants. Things went on beneath the surface of his own thinking and of his White House staff deliberations that not all participants were privy to. But he did not hesitate to guide his advisors to address the issues he wanted to consider, and the formal procedures he employed enabled him at once to guide without dominating and without becoming prematurely identified with a particular viewpoint or outcome. The greater formality of his NSC procedures made it easier to do each of these things than was possible with the informal structures Johnson inherited from Kennedy.

The standards of static rationality which employ a model of arrayed options[34] fail to come to terms with the real world of decision costs—for instance, with the "limited search" and "satisficing" standards that Richard Cyert and James March demonstrated were a normal practice of decision makers.[35] The comparison with Eisenhower and with other presidents has the merit of applying realistic standards of procedural rationality rather than the ideal standard of static rationality. John Burke and Fred Greenstein compared Eisenhower's decision in 1954 to stay out of Vietnam with Johnson's July 1965 decision to enter the ground war. They claim to show that Eisenhower was more thorough in his examination of issues and options than was Johnson eleven years later. They make an almost convincing case. It is Greenstein himself, in an earlier study of Eisenhower, who supplies the evidence that prevents it from being entirely convincing. In the earlier study, Greenstein noted that Eisenhower had regularly used informal, small meetings in the Oval Office to guide the longer, more formal meetings of the NSC and that the latter served as much to persuade its participants as to provide Eisenhower with advice. Eisenhower, that is to say, not only had his "Tuesday lunch." He also employed formal deliberations to build consensus among his advisors and confer legitimacy on his decisions. This said, Greenstein's observation does not undermine

the claim that Burke and he later made that Eisenhower made skillful use of formal NSC deliberations; it does weaken the distinction
between Johnson's and Eisenhower's deliberative procedures.

Burke and Greenstein insist that their comparison shows the
value of Eisenhower's employment of formal procedures. Their work
is central to the new appreciation of Eisenhower. As noted earlier,
Kennedy dismantled these procedures and Johnson adapted Kennedy's informal system to his personal style while also resuscitating
NSC formalities for nonurgent business.

The comparison with Eisenhower opens the way to noting two
other advantages in Eisenhower's deliberative style to which we
have already alluded: (1) He tended to achieve and maintain a greater
detachment from the deliberative process and from the issues with
which it dealt. (2) He often managed to stay ahead of events, or seem
to, whereas Johnson, when he came to deal with Vietnam, was often
working to catch up with the flow of events.

Eisenhower held himself more detached—sometimes from his
staff, sometimes from particular policies, sometimes from the political forces that supported and challenged him, sometimes only in
appearance, which meant at least political distance. Distance was
not one of Johnson's inclinations, certainly not in his taking over of
the Kennedy foreign policy agenda. His lack of detachment about
Kennedy's policies reflected the circumstances of Johnson's takeover
of the presidency. To establish his legitimacy as president, he was
prone to commit himself to what he thought were Kennedy's policies, an inclination that got him into trouble in the case of the MLF,
as we saw. But Johnson's style tended to lead him in the same direction. He was by no means lacking in the skill to back away from a
liability—the MLF again comes to mind—or to disengage, as he did
after his hasty and ill-considered involvement in the Dominican Republic in April 1965. But the Dominican crisis makes the contrary
point more strongly, his inclination to be there and be noticed when
something is happening. A talent in domestic policies, it proved to
be dangerous in foreign affairs.

No one has yet demonstrated adequately the dimensions of Eisenhower's skill at standing back from people and issues, even while
employing his magnetic personal warmth. But there are enough
events which show the results of his detachment to assure us of its
existence: his tough, persistent skepticism about inter-service politics and about the politics of the military budget that served as the
foundation of the "New Look," his reordering of military policy and
strategy, his persistent interest in arms control, his poised refusal to
permit full-scale investment in the first generation of intercontinen-

tal missiles (the liquid-fuelled Thors and Atlases), his cool response to the post-*Sputnik* clamor for a burst of defense spending and other measures in 1957 and 1958.[36]

As for Johnson, his contrary propensity to attach, to climb aboard, to get close to an issue and to its stakeholders is easy to demonstrate. It is almost as easy to account for as the over-determined result of personality factors and personal leadership style. The latter probably reflected in particular his experience in Congress and the circumstances and results of his takeover of the presidency after Kennedy, with his concern about legitimacy and his reliance on a foreign policy staff which he inherited from Kennedy. Johnson's problems with Vietnam often seemed to be associated with at once an effort to limit involvement and an overly close engagement with it. Vietnam was not the only foreign policy issue on which it was difficult to turn him around. It was only the vastly most important one.

Johnson could scarcely have distanced himself from Vietnam politically. Indeed, it became *his* war, just as, in turn, it became Nixon's war. But within his own counsels, among his advisors and assistants, it *was* his war. No one identified with it more than he did. This is a commonplace observation and the evidence for it is extensive. As much as he preferred to work his domestic agenda, he became obsessively preoccupied with Vietnam, with the details of operations, with the fate of troops, with current intelligence reports. The author recalls interviewing in 1969 the support staff for Johnson's White House Situation Room. They reported that when he got up in the middle of the night to relieve himself he would usually telephone the Situation Room from his bathroom for the latest reports from Vietnam. White House log books are now open and they confirm this fact.[37]

Eisenhower's deliberative style employed, as indicated, directive guidance for his advisors followed by staffing out of issues and implementation problems. Even when he was caught by surprise with the British and French attack on Egypt in 1956 when his Secretary of State was in Latin America, one does not sense in accounts of what followed that he was playing catch-up against uncomfortably close deadlines.[38] Johnson, in contrast, was always playing catch-up with respect to his major decisions about Vietnam. Ball sensed the problem and he spoke out about it and wrote about it more than most observers have noted. He found Johnson's Vietnam deliberations turned inward in the pursuit of a consensus that would protect Johnson from authoritative dissent while events marched on. He was in this respect not simply a "devil's advocate" stating the dovish

position. The significance of his role is missed if he is seen only as
the person who dared to think about withdrawal, as important as it
was to do that. Much of the advice Johnson heard reflected the internal game—what Daniel Ellsberg called the "stalemate machine."
Ball stated instead the *external* options. Where Johnson sought the
lowest common denominator among his advisors in order to preserve his options, Ball's idea of protecting options was to protect
them against the contingencies of the external world. Thus, in his
memorandum of June 18, 1965, which he entitled "Keeping the
Power of Decision in the South Vietnamese Crisis," he warned that
"the more forces we deploy in South Vietnam—particularly in combat roles—the harder we shall find it to extricate ourselves without
unacceptable costs if the war goes badly. With larger forces committed, the failure to turn the tide will generate pressures to escalate. There will be mounting domestic demands that we expand our
air attacks on the North so as to destroy Hanoi and Haiphong. Yet
if our air attacks threaten the total destruction of the North Vietnamese economy, Red China can hardly help but react. And our
best Soviet experts do not believe that the Soviet Union could
stand down in the event that we became involved directly with the
Chinese."[39]

Ball had begun his memorandum with a quotation from Ralph
Waldo Emerson that he had alluded to several times before in presenting his views about Vietnam: "Things are in the saddle, and
riding mankind." To avoid losing control over the events that mattered to the United States, to maintain the president's options, Ball
argued for setting limited objectives and making limited commitments. He advised meeting Westmoreland's request for forty-four
brigades only partially, and on a trial basis. The trial would last three
months. It would be a test of the possibilities of "waging a successful land war in South Vietnam," and of whether the RVN body politic had a terminal case of political rot.[40] He urged intensive study of
"the technique of cutting our losses" and getting out, "a solution
involving concessions on our side as well as the Viet Cong."

Ball has never claimed unique foresight about Vietnam, although
memoranda such as this one look extraordinarily prescient in retrospect. His record of anticipation is limited by the fact that he continued to expect, or to write as though he expected, that the end
would never come without concessions from the other side. The
importance of his advice for us here is the clarity with which he
pursued the objective of defining American policy in terms and pursuing it by means that kept the vital decisions about it in Johnson's

hands. He pursued this objective not by claiming to know whether South Vietnam had a viable regime, or what the probabilities were that bombing the north would bring the Chinese or the Russians in more directly, but by insisting that these uncertainties or unknowns about the external world needed to be factored into U.S. policy if we were not to yield control over our destiny to others and let "things" ride us.

The charge that Johnson's methods of employing advice were distinctly faulted with respect to Vietnam seemed utterly persuasive during the war and the rest of the decade of the seventies. They seem less persuasive now as the record of faulty procedures has grown with succeeding presidents: Nixon's preference for meeting only with very small groups, Carter's preoccupation with technical details to the neglect of the "big picture," Reagan's casual acceptance of delegation, Bush's small circle of national security advisors. Gelb, in his impressive early reassessment based in part on an historical study that he had conducted for McNamara in the Department of Defense—the study that was made public as the so-called *Pentagon Papers* by Daniel Ellsberg in 1971—demonstrated that a wide variety of information and advice came to Johnson in the White House up through the internal channels of the government.[41] David M. Barrett has demonstrated, with particular reference to the mid-1965 decision to commit more troops to Vietnam and expand the American combat role there, that Johnson kept active contact with dissenters, particularly in the Senate. He concluded that "Johnson was not a victim of groupthink and that he received and listened to significant advice warning him against sending troops to Vietnam."[42] William Conrad Gibbons shows us that Johnson continued to have contact with his Senate critics.[43] And Clark Clifford, in detailing his role as an outside advisor to Johnson prior to becoming Secretary of Defense in 1967, depicts Johnson as continuing to be distrustful of the advisors within his official circle and continuing to seek the advice of others.[44]

Continuity and Innovation: A Dynamic Standard of Rational Decision Making

Static rationality has its uses, but few of them apply to presidential behavior. It is necessary to consider other dimensions of the presidential deliberative process with respect to national security matters. One way to do this is to consider rational policymaking as a process of policy change; in the case of Vietnam, the scale of change that came to be needed was not simple course correction or "steering," not minor adjustments, but major policy change, or innovation. In this section we will review the circumstances that, together with Johnson's own decisions, set the course of failing policy and then look at the requirements for policy innovation.

When John Kennedy was assassinated, the American ambassador to Vietnam, Henry Cabot Lodge, was in Washington for an appointment with him. Forty-eight hours after taking the oath of office as president, Johnson kept that appointment. He saw Lodge in the vice president's office of the old Executive Office Building. Also present were McGeorge Bundy, secretaries Rusk and McNamara, Assistant Secretary of State George Ball, and John McCone, director of Central Intelligence.[45] Ngo Dinh Diem, the president of the Republic of Vietnam since 1954, had been killed a month earlier in a coup that Lodge had encouraged, and Lodge was optimistic about the future of South Vietnam. McCone was, according to Johnson himself, "much less encouraging" in briefing the new president. "He said the Vietnamese military leaders who carried out the coup were having difficulties organizing their government." He concluded "that he could see no basis for an optimistic forecast of the future."[46] Otherwise McCone's briefing was reassuring about the international situation, contributing to Johnson's belief that he would be able to subordinate international affairs to his domestic agenda, which he proceeded to do.

The coup was not Johnson's doing, and there is every indication that he disapproved of it. He had met Diem during his tour of Asia in 1961—his first foreign tour. He had likened Diem to George Washington, perhaps with intended extravagance, and had urged that Diem increase the size of the ARVN from 100,000 to in excess of 270,000, largely at the expense of the United States.[47] All of these things only serve to make the larger point that when Johnson became president he faced a situation in Vietnam that, while it did not demand immediate presidential decisions for corrective action, also did not present the new president with an easy opportunity to make a different choice. Much as he had proceeded with the effort to win NATO Europe's support for the MLF, he had accepted the situation in Vietnam. Early in October, before the coup, McNamara had estimated that the United States would be able to phase out its advisory support to South Vietnam by the end of 1965. After the coup, despite this optimism, the question, "When can we pull out?" was displaced by a more urgent one, "What must we do to keep the regime in Saigon from crumbling?" Perhaps the most deleterious effect of the anti-Diem coup was to shift the weight of attention in Washington to this essentially short-run and negative goal, to the neglect of the deeper issues of America's interests and options.

It does not take much effort to explain the direction that Johnson's policy toward Vietnam first took. Given his resolve to continue with Kennedy's policies, which admittedly were not sentimental, and based on the optimistic assessments he received, Johnson held to Kennedy's Vietnam program. The first hours of his presidency, when Johnson met with Lodge, were not the time to reverse a pattern of commitment to Vietnam that went back to the Truman administration. It is almost inconceivable that anyone, as president, would have chosen a significantly different course at that time. As D. Michael Shafer notes, quoting from the *Pentagon Papers*, "the question was what *should* be done, not if anything *could* be done. Defeat was too catastrophic an outcome to bear examination."[48] American involvement in Vietnam was based on concerns about the spread of communism in the Third World and its effect on the security of the United States and its allies. John Lewis Gaddis contends that Vietnam became an important measuring stick for the U.S. commitment to the containment of communism due to repeated statements by American officials insisting that Vietnam was the measure of American willingness to protect its allies and defeat their enemies. In this way, the United States put its credibility on the line in the international community, making withdrawal, or anything less than a full commitment to winning, unthinkable.[49]

The attention Johnson and his advisors devoted to the instability of the Government of Vietnam (GVN) was undoubtedly justified. While the Kennedy administration had despaired about Diem's poor performance in broadening the popular base for his regime, the performance of the series of military and civilian governments that followed him was worse. It was in this period, following Diem's overthrow, that the Viet Cong (the term used for the North Vietnamese–supported forces in the South) became a major military threat to the survival of the GVN. The Viet Cong strengthened their political power in the countryside while the leadership of the RVN engaged in political intrigue in Saigon and ignored the rural population.[50]

Being responsible for the change in leadership in Saigon, the United States became the guarantor of South Vietnam's sovereignty and autonomy. It became Johnson's responsibility after Kennedy's death to reassure the RVN government, and to assure the continued independence of South Vietnam. General Westmoreland may have exaggerated the importance of the American involvement when he observed that it "inevitably contributed to a feeling of obligation among American officials in Washington."[51] A unitary, rational, directive government in Washington intent upon cutting its losses in Vietnam could have estimated the cost of withdrawal and paid it. But for a pluralistic government, a combination of different factions and interests seeking public and elite support, the costs of policy divergence were simply too high. In this sense, Westmoreland's observation is quite correct, and Johnson's reaction,[52] which was both to refer to the coup critically—but discreetly—and to refrain from exploiting this criticism to the degree that it could cause dissension among his inherited foreign policy advisors, is understandable and ultimately tragic. Initially Johnson had little choice but to rely on those officials who had been most involved in increasing U.S. support to the RVN and in encouraging the coup.

When Johnson set his course at the end of July 1965, with the decision to engage American forces in ground warfare in Vietnam, he engaged the United States in a distant war, with parallel military, civil, and diplomatic operations. His problem in foreign policy management then became one of adjustment and adaptation, if only in order to keep all three types of operations together and on track toward U.S. goals. As evidence mounted that none of these operations was successful, that expected goals were not being met, that a much larger military commitment was needed, that more time was required to keep the situation from deteriorating and to meet expected military goals, a more profound question should have become obvious. It should have been clear that incremental adjustments would not turn things around. Major innovations in policy, involving any or all three realms of operation, would be necessary. That was a large-scale undertaking—by far, a much larger undertaking than the MLF project in Europe, and by far much larger than the Indian grain deliveries, if we compare American personnel directly employed and at risk, and American material directly employed. The Indian case, it should be remembered, while it involved the delivery of millions of tons of grain, and was a large-scale effort of its kind, was essentially a commodity transfer operation. It did not involve the elaborate direct operational support that military combat in Vietnam or the direct intrusions into Vietnam of civic actions programs required. Shipping millions more tons of grain to India had sensitive domestic side effects in the United States. The domestic price of grain, and therefore of bread, could go up. (Johnson, in fact, carefully monitored both prices throughout the period covered.) India's domestic problems, mainly the possibility of starvation that could be attributed to Johnson's tight-fisted management of the grain shipments, were scarcely as sensitive an issue for American domestic politics as were American casualties in Vietnam. (Even so, Johnson paid close attention personally to the question of starvation deaths in India.)

In Vietnam, once major operations were underway, it could be expected that new assessments would follow, and with them, adaptations in programs and practices, even to some extent in goals, in response to improved knowledge about the situation in the field, including assessments about the operations themselves, estimates of future costs in relationship to goals, and changes in goals themselves. We have looked at the phenomenon of foreign policy innovation previously in this study in connection with Johnson's handling of the Indian grain shortage and, with respect to European security, by viewing the MLF as an exercise in attempted innovation which Johnson prudently discontinued. Vietnam, because of the scale of the disappointments associated with it, came to demand more than normal adjustments in the implementation process. It came to demand major innovations if it was to succeed.

If the deliberations of April through July 1965, or rather, the decisions they produced, which amounted to committing the United States to a land (and air) war in Vietnam, were mistaken, then the only follow-on policy that made sense was to alter substantially the mid-1965 decision. The commitment having been made, and as the expectations upon which the decision to commit the United States to a land war in order to "win" failed to materialize, the policy problem shifted from adaptive implementation to serious innovation: The challenge became more than the adjustment or tuning of policy. It became necessary to find a substantially different policy—a different set of goals, a different set of means. It is in this sense that I employ the term innovation and in this sense that I define the third problem as one of innovation.

Lyndon Johnson chose in mid-1965 to rely heavily on a military option to achieve the goal of preserving an independent South Vietnam. He softened the narrowness of this choice by promoting civic action and from time to time by pursuing diplomatic campaigns. But the military operations dominated and they proved to have a logic of their own: to reproduce in the field the sorts of warfare that the U.S. armed forces were equipped and trained to carry out. In turn, the kind of warfare that the American armed forces were good at reflected the successful American military experience in World War II and the status of the United States as a superpower. World War II was, for the United States, mainly an experience of successful large-scale mobilization until its forces, at least when added to those of its allies, were overwhelmingly superior in the circumstances. It is not far from the mark to say that World War II was won in Detroit and that World War I was not much different. These observations serve to show the normality of the pressures to expand the American military effort in Vietnam once it began.

Johnson's decisions in mid-1965 about Vietnam amounted to a commitment to his principal field commander, General Westmoreland, and to the JCS and the American armed forces, to permit them to succeed. Success may not have meant "victory" as the term had been used by Sen. Barry Goldwater, Johnson's opponent in the presidential election the previous year. Indeed, it did not. Success would be defined by civilian leaders. But Johnson had made a commitment nonetheless. The leaders of the American military establishment were no less than normal in their expectation that they would be provided with the resources which they needed to succeed *and that, therefore, if they did not succeed with the resources provided, they could get more until they did succeed.*

The import of this arrangement was clear: Vietnam was not a situation in which one should expect American military leaders to be innovative. They had good reasons to expect that they could have more resources if they demanded them. It was safer for them, therefore, to continue to expand what they were doing in Vietnam into a large-scale conventional war of the sort that they had been preparing to fight since World War II than to look for innovative ways to achieve their military missions that might fail. It is in this sense that Vietnam became a problem in innovation.

Innovation: The Civilian Problem

Compared with the "everything was wrong" school, searching for normal expectations is an effort to sort out for decision makers which critical performance factors they can change at little cost from those they cannot. Findings about the normal range of performance can sharpen both the description and the evaluation of presidential foreign policy management by helping to identify the best prospects for counterfactual outcomes as distinct from all imaginable counterfactual developments.

As Robert W. Komer notes, changes in American tactics and strategy during the Vietnam War were incremental, and when they occurred, they were constrained by the interests and practices of the American civilian and military bureaucracies which carried them out. In Vietnam, as Komer points out, on the civilian side of the war, American efforts to build a stronger regime failed largely because of normal bureaucratic impedimenta. American officials failed to take actions in particular which might have helped to consolidate the

GVN politically because they fell outside the normal bureaucratic parameters.

Komer contends that American policymakers realized early in the war that Vietnam was primarily a political conflict, and no doubt he is right. Kennedy adopted a counterinsurgency approach, and Johnson pointedly referred to the building of a viable government throughout South Vietnam as the "other war." In Washington, decisions about escalating military operations during 1964 and 1965 were constrained by a sense of the political weakness of the Saigon regime. Escalation could lead to regime-shattering counterattacks. Victory would be impossible if the GVN was unable to consolidate power and deprive the Viet Cong of its rural base. The ultimate goal was political, making the GVN a self-sustaining government that could cope with its military challenges and compete with its political challengers, yet the American military pursued a policy that divorced the military aspects of the war from the political aspects. Instead of adapting its tactics to the situation at hand the U.S. military, according to Robert Komer, "overmilitarized" the war. This was due to the dominant role of the military in Vietnam, which often precluded political actions by other U.S. agencies that could have strengthened popular support for the GVN. In the same vein, the U.S. military, in its behavior at many levels in the military hierarchy, if not in the perceptions of its highest command, misunderstood the war in the sense that it used tactics more appropriate for a European war than a Third World nation.[53]

There was some expectation that the ambassador to South Vietnam would keep military operations subordinated to their political ends, but he did not. The country team concept makes the ambassador to a nation the primary representative of the president, with all other agencies being responsible to the ambassador. But the country team principle was overwhelmed by the weight of the military effort in Vietnam and by the fact that the military commander in Vietnam maintained a separate, independent communications channel with the Pentagon and the president.

Komer was appointed by President Johnson to coordinate U.S. pacification efforts in Vietnam in response to the president's desire to have a single, knowledgeable official who could advise him on such efforts. On examining his new tasks, Komer asked rhetorically, "Who was responsible for conflict management in the Vietnam War? The bureaucratic fact is that below the Presidential level everybody and nobody was responsible for coping with it in the round. With relatively few exceptions, neither the U.S. government nor the GVN set up any specialized planning or operating agencies to meet atypical needs. . . . [B]oth governments ran the war in largely separate bureaucratic compartments, with each government and each agency within it largely 'doing its own thing.' . . . Lack of any overall management structure contributed to the overmilitarization of the war by facilitating the predominance of the U.S. and GVN military in its conduct."[54]

Komer concluded that "In general, . . . no American ambassador ever imposed consistent, unified control on U.S. agency operations in Vietnam."[55] While Ambassador Maxwell Taylor was given unprecedented powers over military and civilian operations, he chose to ignore them based on his belief that such powers conflicted with the role of the military commander in the field. When Henry Cabot Lodge returned as ambassador in August 1965 he was given similar powers, but chose to let individual agencies do as they saw fit. Divided responsibility existed in Vietnam until the end of the war.[56]

Managing Field Commanders

The main problem of innovation in Vietnam, then, lay with the American armed forces and with the president's directive relationship to them. Johnson's "middle course" was composed of three responses that put the main burden on them. The first was to meet the force requirements of the military leaders in the field, Westmoreland in Saigon and Admiral Sharp in Pearl Harbor, as endorsed by the Joint Chiefs of Staff, but to meet them minimally. The second response was to maintain strict controls over the employment of the air campaign against North Vietnam, including target selection. Targets were chosen on the basis of two general criteria: (1) to induce North Vietnam to stop supporting the insurgent war against South Vietnam, and (2) to avoid provoking mainland China into massive military intervention such as happened in the Korean War. These criteria, which were also applied to other military actions, marked a fine line to walk. They were intended to coerce Hanoi enough while not threatening China too much.

The third response was to minimize the political and economic effects of the war effort within the United States so as to avoid (1) deflecting attention from Johnson's domestic program and (2) generating an impatient "war fever," i.e., a jingoistic public opinion that would force him into fighting it in a way that he and his advisors considered dangerous, as in allowing the military to pursue victory without political constraints—as it happened, the course of action advocated by Sen. Barry Goldwater, the Republican presidential nominee who challenged Johnson in the 1964 presidential race. Korea, again, was the warning example: In 1952, after the Korean War became stalemated, the Democrats lost a presidential election to General Eisenhower, whose popular appeal included the prospect that if elected he would somehow end the war more expeditiously than would the Democratic candidate, Adlai Stevenson.

The middle course placed Johnson in a delicate position, between his generals (and admirals), who were frustrated by not being given a clear mission and the freedom to accomplish it without interference, and a public that could become aroused and impatient for results. Field commanders, who must in any case carry out their missions with fewer resources than they would prefer to have, are prone to recognize that presidents sometimes have difficulty saying "no" to them.

Johnson faced the situation of managing an American general, Westmoreland, who was leading American troops in a distant land against a foreign enemy, a situation fraught with potential political trouble because of the prospect of American military leaders' using the Congress as a forum for venting the usual frustrations of field commanders with insufficient resources to accomplish the assigned mission. Truman had to contend with a far more political general than Westmoreland, Douglas MacArthur, but MacArthur had alienated the Joint Chiefs long before his showdown with Truman, making it easier for Truman to face up to firing him. No split existed between Westmoreland and the Chiefs.

An important aspect of Johnson's middle course was the way it served the special problem of any commander-in-chief in wartime in dealing with his major field commanders. Put in these terms, the middle course lay between what General Westmoreland (supported by Admiral Sharp at CINCPAC and the Joint Chiefs of Staff) asked for in men, material, and bombing targets and the more restrictive considerations advanced by other advisors who worried about domestic political and economic costs and the risk of combat with Chinese and Soviet forces. It was a course that he would continue to follow until March 1968. Johnson's middle course was responsive enough to General Westmoreland's and Admiral Sharp's demands to keep them and the Joint Chiefs of Staff (who usually supported them), as well as other military and civilian officials in his administration, loyally supporting his decisions. But it had two other quite simple and important negative effects: By always responding to the demands of his military leaders, Johnson provided them with incentives to conventionalize the war effort and, in effect, denied them

incentives to find a new way to prosecute the war within the ultimate limits of resources that he would permit and the other constraints that he imposed.

Second, it fell short of the conventional military conception of
strategy embraced by the Joint Chiefs of Staff, which required an
increase in the level of the American military effort in the region
until it succeeded, a strategy quite predictable, given the relative
military power of the two contestants (i.e., the United States and
North Vietnam) and the American doctrines of war, which reflected
the experience of mobilization and victory in World War II. It was a
course that involved relatively large military activities which, as it
turned out, could not succeed and that discouraged the search for
alternatives, including alternative ways to employ military power,
that might have succeeded. The conventionalized military effort of
the three American armed forces failed to produce "victory" or even
the minimum goal of the American war effort in Vietnam, a viable
RVN government able to take over and let the Americans withdraw.
The incentives that Johnson's stream of decisions about Vietnam
created virtually eliminated the possibility that any other course of
action would be given a serious try in Vietnam. Efforts, for example,
to encourage the strengthening of the civil side of the RVN government were simply overwhelmed by the presence of American armed
forces there to fight a conventional war.

Westmoreland, it must be said, was not unrestrained about how
and to what extent he exploited the potential political strength he
had in Washington and the country as field commander. This is not
to say that he failed to exercise what amounted to political leverage
in Washington to get what he wanted. Johnson and his civilian
advisors recognized what is an old problem with warfare, that an
alienated field commander could cause them serious political difficulties on the home front. As much as anything, this explains the
"middle way."

For Johnson, innovation on a scale commensurate with the problem came with his appointment of Clark Clifford to succeed Robert McNamara as Secretary of Defense on March 1, 1968. Earlier,
McNamara's expectations about American goals in Vietnam had
risen as the effect of American deployments became evident, but
then he had turned dovish. He left the Johnson administration quietly to become president of the World Bank. Johnson persuaded
Clark Clifford to take his place as Secretary of Defense. What Clifford brought to the Johnson administration proved to be critical.
When he accepted the Defense post and entered the Johnson administration he came as an outsider with a practiced independence from

Johnson. "The president and I had a frank relationship throughout," he told Herbert Schandler. "He had nothing I wanted. I was older than he. Our relationship was on an entirely different basis than some of his other advisors."[57]

Clifford, by reputation, was a hawk, a hard-line cold warrior who would share Dean Rusk's determination to fight on in Vietnam. Judging by appearances, Johnson had expected Clifford to bring back into line the wavering OSD staff that McNamara left behind under Paul Nitze and Paul Warnke. Instead, Clifford quickly became a dove with respect to Vietnam, much to Johnson's apparent surprise.

It is Clifford's claim that he had always been deeply skeptical about the war and sympathetic with George Ball's views on it. He had stated his own views frankly to Johnson in May 1965, and again on July 25, in a very small "informal but crucial conference" at Camp David, just before Johnson's most critical decision. Available documents show this. Once Johnson made his decision, Clifford went along with it, but continued to harbor the same doubts that he had expressed. When he became Secretary of Defense, and set about reviewing war plans, his skepticism was aroused when he noted the absence of a plan or even a theory for achieving a satisfactory outcome for the war. Whereupon, as he claims, Clifford joined the doves clustered around Warnke and advised Johnson to seek a negotiated settlement.[58]

The conventional view is that Johnson was surprised when, in March 1968, Clifford became the leading advocate within his administration of withdrawing from Vietnam, a position which he advanced largely in the form of a more energetic pursuit of negotiations with Hanoi and a phasing down of American troops in Vietnam. But Johnson is unlikely to have forgotten what Clifford had advised in 1965. Clifford himself has avoided speculating about whether Johnson may have brought him into the Pentagon anticipating that he would reassert the views he had stated earlier. He has carefully explained his own behavior and views from 1965 through 1968 in order to make the point that he was never a hawk on Vietnam and always a skeptic. But he has chosen to remain silent about whether Johnson remembered his earlier advice about Vietnam and therefore, whether Johnson was less surprised when it reemerged in March 1968.

There are no other grounds for claiming that Johnson wanted to quit in Vietnam when he chose Clifford as his Secretary of Defense, but the evidence does suggest a hedging strategy, that Johnson recalled Clifford's dovish views and understood the consequences of bringing him into his Cabinet as Secretary of Defense, that he had intentionally taken the initiative for a major foreign policy innovation with respect to Vietnam.

As disappointments over the progress of the war grew, Johnson repeatedly attempted to negotiate a settlement with North Vietnam. Perhaps it is clearer now than it was then that Hanoi was not interested in any kind of settlement that would have jeopardized North Vietnam's long-term goal of unifying Vietnam under the Hanoi regime's rule, and that these attempts at negotiation were doomed, just as were the tactics of squeezing North Vietnam with limited applications of air power. Some critics have claimed that Johnson was never very serious about negotiating with Hanoi, and they may be right. Whether he pursued negotiations with Hanoi in the expectation that Hanoi would make no concessions which would jeopardize its goal of unifying Vietnam under its own rule has never been entirely clear. Henry Kissinger, to whom the unfinished business of negotiations with Hanoi fell in 1969 after the election of President Nixon, has claimed that he did not understand it either.[59] But it has been fairly clear that until Clifford advised Johnson to abandon his major goals in Vietnam and seek to negotiate his way out, Johnson adhered to the goal of an independent South Vietnam freed from the threat of invasion or serious insurgency.

Johnson announced at the end of March 1968 that he would not run for reelection that fall. He coupled this announcement with an announcement of an unconditional bombing pause against North Vietnam. The bombing pause reflected Rusk's advice, but Johnson offered it with a conciliatory tone that reflected the influence of his new Secretary of Defense, Clark Clifford, and the impact on Johnson of the advice of a group of former officials, or "Wise Men," whom he had consulted previously. Following Clifford's advice, he did so again after the Tet Offensive.[60] They were not unanimous in their views, but generally doubtful about the prospect of progress in Vietnam. Their pessimism evidently had the effect on Johnson that Clifford intended.

Johnson, according to all accounts, was shaken. He reviewed his Vietnam policies and, in a speech on March 31, again chose a middle course consisting not only of Rusk's peace initiative, which "would placate public opinion and allow him to continue the war as before," but also Clifford's outlook by employing "conciliatory language to make it more acceptable to the enemy and coupling it with his dramatic announcement [that he would not run for reelection] to emphasize its sincerity."[61]

The middle course that Johnson took structured the incentives of two important groups. It denied to the first of these groups, the contending elements of the GVN and, more broadly, in RVN society, the incentives that they needed to reconcile their differences and give overwhelming priority to staving off military disaster and, when they could take a longer view, to build a viable, survivable national state. It is an exaggeration, but not a great exaggeration, to say that, until then, the incentives the American war effort created for the South Vietnamese were to let the Americans take care of the threat of military disaster while they pursued other interests. The harshest view of these other interests was that they amounted to wartime profiteering and other personal and family aggrandizements against the public interest.

The second group was the American generals. Johnson's middle course would not permit General Westmoreland all the "men and resources" that he asked for, but enough of what he asked for to dissuade him from the predictable conviction that the safest course was to follow conventional, large-scale American military practices in fighting the Vietnam War.

Johnson's own official advisors, including Bundy, Rostow, McNamara, and Rusk, had—with more than encouragement from Johnson, to be sure—defined their jobs as requiring that they orient their advice and their actions to his viewpoint[62] and that they implement the middle course as he stated it in successive decisions. Outsiders who wanted to be relevant behaved in much the same way. For example, as noted, Clark Clifford, who had spoken out against the course that Johnson would decide upon in mid-1965, got in step and supported Johnson on the war until March 1968, when he became Secretary of Defense. By then the situation had changed, but Johnson once again took the middle course. This time, however, Clifford did not behave like other Johnson advisors. First, he returned to his earlier view that the United States should get out of Vietnam. Second, he told Johnson what he thought and saw to it that others with similar views did likewise. Third, as Schandler put it, "Clifford launched a deliberate public campaign, which was to last until he left office, to interpret the president's decisions [which never wholly abandoned the middle course] in the way he felt they should be interpreted. No public statements by Clifford during this period were accidental. As he stated it: 'This was a conscious effort on my part. It was based upon what I believed the president's attitude should be and what I thought our policy should be. During that period of time during which I touched on it repeatedly, at no time did I get a word of criticism or caution from the president.'"[63]

Clifford had not speculated beyond such cautious hints as are contained in the above statement concerning whether Johnson anticipated what change of policy he was launching when he appointed Clifford Secretary of Defense. One cannot rule out the possibility that Johnson considered Clifford a dove in hawk's feathers at that time.

Business innovations may originate within the firm. They may be adopted from an outside source or be carried into an industry as a firm enters it, bringing new processes or products. When this last happens it is called innovation by invasion. When Johnson partially accepted Clifford's recommendations, and then acquiesced in Clifford's stretching of Johnson's policy statements, this development became the turning point in Johnson's Vietnam policy. It began a reduction in American forces in Vietnam that was never reversed, and it increased Johnson's commitment to negotiating with Hanoi the withdrawal of American forces from Vietnam. A major change—for our purposes, an innovation—had occurred in his Vietnam policy. The "stalemate machine" kept going until a credible outsider induced Johnson to alter it.

Johnson at the same time announced that he would not run for reelection in 1968. We cannot settle here what Clifford's proposed change in Vietnam policy had to do with Johnson's decision against running for a second elected term. Whether there was a connection or not, the decision against running assured that the Johnson administration would not stay the course and contributed to the policy innovation. Just as Clifford had put at risk his relationship with Johnson to bring him along, Johnson had, by ruling out another term, freed himself from the constraints of domestic politics as he conceived it, but he also became a lame duck. It was a massive, negative form of policy innovation, something like a business firm that "innovates" by liquidating its assets, or a businessman who "innovates" by leaving his job.

Power Hubris and Knowledge Hubris

Johnson's handling of Vietnam has often been labeled an exercise in *hubris*. The United States overestimated the reach of its power, or at least its resolve. One cannot escape the charge of *hubris* as a moral judgment about Johnson and Vietnam. *Hubris* as an explanation should be taken further. It is an important characteristic of Johnson's advisory process for Vietnam. The elements of static rationality have drawn too much attention in evaluating Johnson's

Vietnam deliberations. *Hubris*, although closely associated with static rationality, has drawn too little. It concerns how presidents and their chief advisors and assistants, in their handling of national security matters, weigh resource costs against security goals.

The intensive examination of Johnson's Vietnam deliberations, since they do not provide us with overwhelming convergence on explanations that are intrinsic to the processes described, encourage us to seek broader explanations. After sifting through the process descriptions, and particularly the comparisons between Eisenhower's 1954 decision and Johnson's 1965 decision, this author is left with the view that the tone and outcome of Johnson's Vietnam deliberations cannot be explained without employing *hubris* as an explanatory factor. I mean to say that Johnson's advisors, and Johnson himself, in their failure to address from the outset the prospect of failure, particularly under the circumstances of setting severe constraints on the employment of military force, assumed that failure was beyond serious consideration. Eisenhower, on the other hand, by the procedures he employed, and in the manner in which he handled the issues with which he dealt regarding intervention in Vietnam in 1954, *did* take into account the possibility that the United States would be engaging itself in an enterprise that was beyond its capacity or will to carry off. Eisenhower's decision making procedures took account of the possibility that the undertaking in question would fail. Johnson's advisory process, constrained by worry about its internal political costs, nonetheless assumed that the undertaking in question could always be saved from failure by putting more resources into it if necessary. Eisenhower, also concerned about political limits on what he could do in Vietnam, seems to have taken the possibility of failure more seriously.

It does not appear to me that the Eisenhower administration, in the way it handled its Vietnam intervention question, knew any more, or as much, as the Johnson administration did about its adversary, in both cases the regime headed by Ho Chi Minh. Neither administration knew very much about the regime in Hanoi. It is quite possible, from the evidence, that the Eisenhower administration knew much less than the Johnson administration, but took into account this lack of knowledge more seriously. In fact, of necessity this is the case. The Johnson administration adopted policies that depended on its knowing a great deal about how the regime in Hanoi behaved, while the Eisenhower administration chose a policy that did not require it to know much at all about Hanoi. Thus, *hubris* has two aspects. One deals with the limits of American power.

The other with the limits of thought, of knowledge, of wise decision making. We deal with cognitive *hubris* first and power *hubris* second.

Information, Error, and Hubris

Much has been made of the quality of information as well as the advice available to Johnson when he made fateful decisions about Vietnam. In his memoirs, Johnson indicates that the reporting from Vietnam had been seriously biased toward optimism in the fall of 1963, and that this bias was corrected at that time.[64] It was not for lack of awareness about reporting bias that Johnson was misled, if indeed he was.

There was more, of course, to the problem of performance monitoring in Vietnam than being aware of potentially biased reporting. A well conceived, accurate, and rigorous reporting system would have pinpointed weaknesses in performance and facilitated the identification of possible improvements. But such a system would have required a much better diagnosis of how to strengthen the South Vietnamese government at the center and in accessible rural areas. It would have been particularly attentive to performance measuring and performance incentives.

The earliest criticisms of the Johnson administration's efforts in Vietnam originated in the field in the observations of American reporters there of the disparity between normal field office public relations handouts and what they could observe for themselves.[65] These journalists' reports, which were instantly credible and mostly accurate, made persuasive also the quagmire thesis, the claim that Johnson and his advisors made fateful decisions about Vietnam that committed the United States ever more deeply in the mistaken belief that success was just around the corner.

The quagmire thesis provided critics a simple, plausible and inaccurate explanation of error. To begin with, many reports from the field were decidedly negative in tone.[66] The *Pentagon Papers* demonstrates the inaccuracy of the quagmire thesis by documenting the skepticism of staff members in both the Department of Defense and the White House toward claims of progress in Vietnam made by MACV (Military Assistance Command, Vietnam), General Westmoreland's command headquarters, and the military leadership and by documenting the fact that staff members communicated this skepticism to policymakers, including the president.[67] While there is little doubt that body counts were inflated, or that MACV estimates were overly optimistic, skeptics in Washington routinely discounted the information they provided. Inaccuracies were minimized at the decision making level by this tendency to discount information from the field and to project worst-case scenarios. It is clear from the *Pentagon Papers*, and from White House files now available at the Johnson Library in Austin, Texas, which had not been available to the authors of the *Pentagon Papers*, that at all critical decision points Johnson was advised that it would be several years before U.S. forces could be withdrawn from South Vietnam with any chance that the GVN would survive.[68]

Available documents make it quite clear that when optimistic military reports from Vietnam were received at the White House, at least in the early years, they went forward to the president with staff cover memoranda that discounted and offset them. It is less certain that the pessimistic tone of the memoranda Johnson received from his advisors, and his discussions with them, wholly dispelled their hopes. The military in particular hoped that their best efforts under the conditions they encountered would be good enough to save South Vietnam. If that was the case, and it appears to be, it did not settle the strategic issue, how to force Hanoi to terminate the war in a manner satisfactory to the United States. Hanoi's behavior remained for most American officials, even pessimistic ones, in the realm of the hopeful construction of reality: Hanoi, they hoped and believed, could be coerced. Late in the game, in 1968, after the Tet offensive, hope weakened. For instance, when, after Tet, Johnson asked Dean Acheson what he thought about the progress of the war, Acheson replied that he could not advise Johnson because he distrusted what the Joint Chiefs told him about the war. The Chiefs, he said, "don't know what they are talking about."[69]

A common error of military assessments is the "non-net" assessment. It describes the enemy's strength, or one's own military capabilities and deficiencies, without rigorously relating one to the other. Acheson, we can speculate, was troubled by the extent to which the military briefings he received as one of Johnson's "Wise Men" failed to provide a net assessment of the situation in Vietnam based on a careful comparative analysis of the strengths and weaknesses of the parties involved. However, it would be utterly unfair to claim that this was the whole problem, for there are many comparative references in the available documents.[70] The briefings that raised Acheson's skepticism may also have dealt with the wrong gross measures, neglecting the ability of the South Vietnamese government to pacify its populace and gain their support, the "other war."[71]

In all of this, the problem we have as outside observers trying in

retrospect to reconstruct the world of the decision makers is to determine to what extent they understood the "system"—the bureaucratic political context in which they operated, particularly the way
they understood the manner in which information was generated,
disseminated, and prepared for the decision maker to interpret and
decide. Presidential leadership studies have not found much reassurance in these assessments about how much the president knows
about what is going on in the executive branch and is able to control
executive branch actions. These studies are particularly relevant
here. Eisenhower, it turns out, was scarcely the innocent many
claimed he was in managing national security affairs.[72] Johnson, on
the other hand, as suggested by his critics, failed to understand the
system of warfare which his decisions guided and failed to understand their consequences.[73] There is nothing wrong with the sort of
skepticism that the stupidity premise engenders, but it also nurtures
the dangerous expectation that the cause of the error will always be
as obvious as the error itself eventually became, a form of retrospec-
tive *hubris.*

It was in fact the case that Johnson and his advisors were skeptical
about the field reports submitted by MACV and CINCPAC. They
were skeptical about the claimed successes in the pacification program and the validity of Air Force bombing estimates, and they were
reluctant to accept proposals for the expenditure of additional resources based on the promise of ultimate victory. Johnson and his
staff recognized the lack of political support the GVN had inside its
borders and realized that they were losing the support of Congress
and the American people for the continued presence of U.S. troops
in South Vietnam. The problem was not that they were unaware of
these issues, it was in how they reacted to the original assessments
of them and how they responded to subsequent reassessments.

The skepticism of Johnson and his advisors served, or so it appears, to harden their shared resolve to continue with the course
of American involvement unaltered. It therefore lay near the very
heart of the problem. It limited expectations about the prospects
for early success—but by the same token, about the possibility of
adopting alternative strategies. In this manner—by discounting alternatives as well as success—skepticism reinforced the tendency
to agree that if the president was resolved to continue, the best
policy option was to see it through. In effect, the president's resolve
became the determining premise of policy for most *if not all his
advisors.* Even for critics and dissenters such as Sen. Mike Mansfield
and Under Secretary of State George Ball, who doubted the ability
of the GVN to win over its people, dissent faded in the face of John-

son's resolve until the war had become almost wholly Americanized and reversing course meant accepting the defeat of American arms and commitments. But his resolve could not have carried the day were it not the case that his advisors saw the American material power as so large, or potentially large, that it could not be a serious constraint. To understand why, we need to take note of the special perspective that Keynesian expansionism conferred on Johnson and his advisors.

Hubris and Keynesian Expansionism

The commitment of America's political leaders to having the U.S. government take up the burden and the power of what has come to be called the hegemon after World War II—the commitment of the American internationalists—was made largely without reference to American resource limits. American resources relative to other powers was, at the beginning of the postwar era, preponderant, as is well known.[74] The question of resource limits was handled largely as a domestic political question: What level of defense budgets could one get Congress to support over time? How much would Congress permit the president to commit to the Marshall Plan? To foreign aid to other regions? To rearmament during the early fifties? It is true that a conservative wing of both political parties worried about high taxes and high public spending and that this view applied to spending on defense and foreign aid and other external programs of the government. These views were often labeled isolationist, a term of general though not universal opprobrium then, as now. The isolationist viewpoint rarely prevailed, but it was by no means ignored, and it often served as the base on which to build a challenge against the costs of foreign commitments that was more pragmatic at the margin. For instance, as was noted in Chapter 3, foreign economic aid remained throughout the Johnson administration under congressional attack, and, while its opponents complained that it did not seem to be doing any good, the opposition included not only skeptics about foreign aid who wanted foreign programs to work, but also congressmen who were not interested in foreign aid in the first place.

Keynesian expansionism was an important factor in this experience of avoiding resource trade-off questions. Keynesian expansionism was the idea that the U.S. economy, at any given time in the postwar era (until stagflation took over during the Johnson administration) could, with proper management, be pushed to higher productivity levels by demand-side government policies, among which were military programs. Needless to say, this view, which was largely correct until Kennedy and Johnson squeezed most of the slack out of the economy with demand-expanding full-employment fiscal policies, usually served the advocates of American power by justifying government spending for international security. They often coupled advocacy of expanded foreign aid or military or other security-related programs with the claim that the economy could not only carry the burden, but that the economic effect would be beneficial. In the short run, the economy would expand toward its capacity (toward full employment) and in the long run it would grow more rapidly than otherwise. Americans would have more guns and more butter, all at the same time.

A notable case of Keynesian expansionism coupled with the advocacy of expanded national security programs was NSC-68, a long-range national security planning document written in the Department of State shortly before the beginning of the Korean War. NSC-68 made a case for increasing the defense budget by a factor of three to four. It answered the question of whether the economy could carry the added economic burden with the logic of Keynesian economics. At the time (1950), Keynesian economics, at least as it was applied in these terms, was generally accepted by the (overlapping) internationalist and progressive wings of the Republican Party but not by conservative Republicans. Liberal Democrats were particular enthusiasts of Keynesian expansionism. President Eisenhower, although a Republican internationalist, was a skeptic about expansionist fiscal policies, but by the end of his administration, the prevailing view among Republicans as well as Democrats supported the Keynesian concept of expanding the economy through demand-side fiscal measures up to a postulated full-employment limit. As long as there was unemployment, on the assumption that there were no structural impediments to achieving full employment, the GNP could be raised with expansionary fiscal policies—which, again, included expanding defense budgets.

Keynesian expansionism had come to be accepted by the mainstream leaders of both political parties by the end of the Eisenhower administration and remained in favor long after the Johnson administration. It was not seriously challenged until the arrival on the national political scene of Ronald Reagan.

Public indifference or hostility to foreign commitments, what was often labeled isolationism, remained a persistent constraint on expenditures for national security. President Eisenhower, in the midfifties, defied the logic of Keynesian expansionism in favor of a more static calculus, what he called the "Great Equation," which was a statement about national resource questions that presented choices as clear trade-offs. He claimed that economic constraints should govern in connection with his efforts to cut the defense budget after the Korean War. More than any other modern president, Eisenhower was willing to force the military budget down. But by the end of his second term his view no longer prevailed. Mainstream Republicans as well as Democrats talked of an expanded military effort which would be keyed to the threat and not limited by economic factors. Since they also talked of neglected domestic problems, the logic of demand-driven economic expansion was particularly appealing at the beginning of the sixties. For prudent politicians like the two presidential candidates in 1960, John F. Kennedy and Richard Nixon, the lesson from the Eisenhower years was that, particularly when it came to national security, economic constraints were not the problem. Once elected, the Kennedy administration cut taxes under conditions that generated a net increase in demand. It was an audacious application of Keynesian expansionism, and it worked as predicted.

To a surprising degree, then, the circumstances that prevailed during the two decades after World War II, until the mid-sixties, contrived to relieve American political leaders of the need to weigh national security goals against the material costs of military preparations and military operations. This situation began to change in the spring and summer of 1965, when Lyndon Johnson had to cope with the demands of his military commander in Vietnam for a heavier commitment. Until then, American internationalists had, broadly speaking, not confronted the economic costs of war. During the most recent war, in Korea, the United States had actually experienced an expansion not only of the GNP, but of per capita incomes and personal consumption. Starting from a mild recession, it was guns *and* butter, somewhat like the American experience with World War II. In this respect, Vietnam was a quite different experience. Starting from a full employment-limited GNP, there was, so to speak, no slack in the economy. Since Johnson decided against financing the war out of current consumption with current tax increases, the increased government spending on the war effort generated a particularly troublesome combination of slow economic growth and inflation, or stagflation. This economic malady became a highly pertinent backdrop to the popular U.S. reaction to the Vietnam War.

But in Johnson's postwar experience, and in that of the internationalist, bipartisan Republicans and Democrats who were Johnson's foreign policy assistants and advisors, foreign policy was more often depicted as a politically constrained than a resource constrained choice. Johnson himself was no alien to this viewpoint.

Truman, the first (as was Johnson the last) of three postwar Democratic presidents who tried to copy Franklin D. Roosevelt's politically successful New Deal domestic program, abandoned the more ambitious objectives of his Fair Deal program as he adopted a foreign policy style of dramatic responses to foreign policy challenges, beginning with the Truman Doctrine as a response to Soviet-supported threats to Greece and Turkey and going on to the Marshall Plan and to military aid to and alliance with Western Europe. Truman's presidential style had the effect of winning additional political attention to foreign policy issues when it was expected that the public would mainly attend to domestic issues. This was a shift in the attention of national political leaders and a lesser shift in public attention. It was an act of political leadership, not a calculated choice to solve international problems with resources that otherwise would have been spent solving domestic problems. This emphasis was confirmed by Truman's decision to use the occasion of the Korean War for a general expansion of military expenditures to strengthen the conventional military forces of the United States and of American allies and client states on the premise that the United States could readily carry a much heavier military burden than it was carrying at the beginning of the Korean War. The premise reflected a Keynesian expansionist viewpoint. It held that the national economy could be managed into a much higher rate of general production. It was confirmed for liberal Democrats in the fact that the increased military expenditures associated with the Korean War expansion were accompanied by increased domestic consumption and a rising per capita standard of living as the GNP surged. The resource costs of the war were never a serious issue. It was the human costs—the casualties suffered by American military personnel in Korea—that ultimately sapped American support for the war. The optimistic lesson of this period, when United States economic power was at its postwar zenith in comparison with other national economies, was that political leadership, not resource limits, was the more serious constraint on the realization of American foreign policy objectives. The pessimistic lesson was that the American public would not sustain its initial support of a foreign war.

Eisenhower took a quite different approach to both domestic and foreign policy. He objected to Truman's crisis-oriented style of political leadership, and he confronted what he considered to be the proper limits of government action and its demand on resources, particularly with respect to the demands of national security. His views were congruent with an American professional military viewpoint which had emerged on the eve of World War I among an influential group of U.S. Army reformers and which had come to maturity during the interwar period. Eisenhower would have been exposed to it in a particularly intense form at the Army Command and General Staff School, where he was the star pupil, and the Army War College, both of which he attended in the late twenties. It held that sound military strategy (and therefore foreign policy) must be a steady commitment to measures that are sustainable over the long term, and it was premised on a view, which reflected a creditable sense of the subordinate role of the military in the United States, that strategists must limit their expectations about the resources available to them to reflect the proper scope of government, which was limited by the perspectives of the 1920s. Eisenhower's reconstruction of strategy and military posture in the mid-fifties, popularly known as the "New Look," conformed to this viewpoint. In the fifties, as president, he reflected this sense of resource limits in the phrase "the Great Equation," which he used to express the idea that political leaders must make hard choices about public expenditures in order not to exceed the burden-carrying capacity of the economy, because exceeding it would weaken national power.

Eisenhower's conception of self-limiting political leadership, which recognized finite limits to the resources available for defense and foreign policy, had the effect of reducing reliance on popular political support for the measures required to achieve national security goals. Eisenhower's critics were inclined to see this effect as inadvertent, the by-product of a conservative, midwestern viewpoint about government. His performance in resisting pressure to become involved in the "first Vietnam war," which ended with France's defeat in 1954 and the division of Vietnam into two provisional states, indicates otherwise. Eisenhower insisted on a show of congressional support before acting. Critics interpreted this position as an excessive concern with constitutional formalities, but his concern with political support can scarcely be dismissed on that basis.

Johnson, as the Democrats' leader in the Senate during the Eisenhower presidency, was relatively cooperative with the Republican president and attentive to his viewpoints on national security policy, although he did not associate himself with Eisenhower's fiscal conservatism, particularly with respect to domestic programs. Kennedy, moreover, acting on the recommendation of Keynesians, who saw the national economy in a special situation in 1961, by cutting taxes, set off an economic surge toward full employment that produced a growing stream of public revenues,[75] as well as private benefits. This was taken as a distinct "proof" of Keynesian expansionism. Kennedy's successful tax cut repudiated Eisenhower's tenet of a fixed-sum "Great Equation" and served to confirm the validity of Keynesian expansionism. But Keynesian expansionism had in fact assumed that national economic choices took place in a slack economy, a condition which the confirming experiment, as it were, Kennedy's tax cut, eliminated. Johnson inherited from the Kennedy administration an economy running at full employment, with virtually no slack in it.

Kennedy's tax cut had confirmed Keynesian expansionism, and therefore the claim that the economy could carry whatever military and economic burdens it needed to carry to achieve national security. Yet it had eliminated the slack in the economy which had made it possible for previous major military expansions to take place without adverse economic effects. Under these circumstances, from the beginning, and throughout the Johnson administration, Vietnam should have posed the resource-constrained question that Eisenhower's concern about "the Great Equation" was intended to pose, the question that would have led Johnson and his advisors to confront the limits to their resolve which they did not confront until tragically late: How important to the United States was the survival of South Vietnam, and how much should the United States devote in terms of material and human resources to ensuring its survival?

Johnson himself, and his advisors, were concerned from the beginning with the trade-off between domestic and foreign programs, but it was a trade-off more in the assets and scarcities of his own political leadership than in the fungible resources that were allocated through the federal budget. It is quite clear that they were aware of the latter. The decision-forcing efforts of Bundy and McNamara in 1964 and 1965, for instance, were directed at facing up to choices about taxing and spending as well as about the political management of war, but the viewpoint of Keynesian expansionism softened choice and underwrote *hubris*.

Berman's and the other studies of Johnson's advisory process make possible a comparison of Johnson's decision making and oversight procedures with respect to Vietnam with Kennedy's procedures in handling the Cuban missile crisis. This missile crisis was essentially a week-long confrontation with the Soviet Union during October 1962, which was conducted largely in secret, before the American public became aware of it. The comparison is useful because of the prevailing judgment, in almost every quarter, that the missile crisis procedures, as well as their outcomes, were superior to Johnson's Vietnam decisions. The trouble is that two of the main complaints about Johnson's employment of advisors, that he restricted executive search and limited his own exposure to the information and analysis that resulted from the search process, apply with equal or superior force to the missile crisis. Quite apart from the high stakes at risk in the missile crisis, the first applies because of quite different time constraints.

Johnson's major Vietnam decisions, when the time for them arrived, were urgent, but their urgency was of a different order from the urgency encountered in the action deadlines of the missile crisis. The second constraint applies also in the missile crisis because Kennedy *chose* to apply it. He chose to limit his exposure to the discussions in the so-called ExCom, his ad hoc Cabinet subcommittee which he formed to advise him during the crisis in order to generate candor in those discussions.[76] With respect to Johnson's handling of executive searching in general and with respect to Vietnam in particular, one rarely finds any reference to the possible advantages, as distinct from the drawbacks, attendant on Johnson's practice of demanding that his advisors reach agreement among themselves before reporting to him.

Urgency, priority, and normality are all critical factors in deciding how to decide. With respect to the matter of priorities, maybe there were more important things for Kennedy and his chief advisors to be doing during those two weeks in October 1962, when they devoted themselves almost exclusively to the missile crisis, but they did not think so, and no one has seriously challenged since then the near-absolute priority they accorded the missile crisis. As it unfolded, Robert McNamara questioned the strategic importance of Soviet missiles in Cuba.[77] In doing so, he opened up an interesting line of inquiry, but it was immediately abandoned. The missile crisis deliberations, to the extent that they deserve to be emulated, serve as a model only for decisions undisputedly entitled to the very highest priority.

The missile crisis model is of little use to the executive faced with less serious decisions, or who thinks he or she faces less serious decisions, or who must cope with others who doubt the seriousness of the business at hand, or who must consider, in order to prioritize, such pre-decision questions concerning the process of searching for answers as these: How important is this decision? How much attention should I give it? How much of my organization's resources should I invest in deliberating over it? What opportunity costs (i.e., what else should I be doing, should my advisors be doing?) would be incurred if I set high deliberative standards and which of them are justified? What negative side effects, such as arming my critics, will these deliberations generate? If the answers to these questions are in doubt, very likely the missile crisis model is of little use; very likely the executive finds himself or herself in a situation in which the issue of priority that put the missile crisis "off the charts" remains open and must dominate in the choice of deliberative procedures. Reflecting such considerations as these "how much" questions raise, decision makers, presidents among them normally, limit their search for knowledge and options in an effort to render the burden of choosing manageable and to assure that they continue to pay attention to other important matters.

Johnson has been much criticized by measuring him against standards of deliberation that exceed the normal behavior of presidents. Alexander L. George, long interested in rationality in the White House,[78] developed a set of standards that illuminates the whole problem of the president's advisory process.[79] Had Johnson followed George's prescriptions fully, it is likely that the major decisions of his presidency would have been more rational. One can scarcely fault the efforts to invent better procedures for presidential deliberation, or defend a position that the president, and the country, should settle for less than the best. Yet applying the highest standards to a few decisions, or a partial set of them, without reference to the whole set that burden the president, or to the other tasks that he must perform, is to hide the costs of achieving rationality in general for a few moments of rational behavior. This situation was the starting point of Cyert and March's descriptive conception of rational decision making in the firm, called executive search and "satisficing," which produces decisions much more cheaply and quickly than does the scientific search for truth, and does not require the total devotion of the leader and his advisors to the problem at hand on the assumption that it is *the one big problem* such as the missiles in Cuba.[80]

I hasten to say that these criticisms of the attack on Johnson's deliberations are not intended to put him beyond criticism, which would in any case be impossible, but to clear the way to see better how to describe and evaluate important foreign policy decisions. The essence of executive judgment, once a decision must be made, lies in deciding what mode of deliberation to follow and what standard of deliberation to meet.[81] Johnson was not conspicuously inferior in exercising such judgments, judging by his *methods* and many of their products, his *decisions*.

Given what happened in Vietnam, it is easy to make the case that more should have been invested in the deliberative process: more information gathered, with more of an investment in expertise and procedures to assure its accuracy and its careful assessment; a more open, adversarial process followed; and more involvement of the Congress. To say, as I do, that Johnson employed normally open procedures does not vitiate such criticism. It was a judgment call about what the trade-offs were as well as about how to make them—which forks in the road to take, so to speak. Berman, in assessing Johnson's July 1965 decision, faulted the procedures, but much more clearly the decision, which he described in terms of trade-offs, thus: "He chose between short- and long-run risks [i.e., in favor of the short-run], and his fatal mistake occurred in that choice. In holding back from total commitment Johnson was juggling the Great Society, the war in Vietnam, and his hopes for the future. He *chose* to avoid a national debate on the war, to keep the Reserves home, and to buy time for a domestic record meriting nothing less than Mount Rushmore (he would later settle for the Johnson library). . . . Lyndon Johnson's greatest fault as a political leader was that *he chose* not to choose between the Great Society and the war in Vietnam."[82]

7. Johnson's Foreign Policy Leadership in Larger Perspective

Introduction

ONLY BAD LUCK could have brought Lyndon Johnson to the White House in November 1963, just after the assassination of South Vietnam's president, Ngo Dinh Diem. The circumstances of Johnson's succession, his personal style as a politician, and the general conditions that he faced combined to make his task as foreign policy leader extraordinarily difficult and the prospects of his success unlikely. In succeeding Kennedy, who had been assassinated in Johnson's own state, Johnson faced the question which lay beyond the issue of constitutional succession, his political legitimacy. It was much like the situation Harry S. Truman faced when Franklin D. Roosevelt died in 1945, but Truman's political weakness became, it appears, an asset in foreign relations. It forced the establishment of bipartisanship, with profound consequences. Johnson's self-perceived political weakness passed with his landslide election in 1964, but other vulnerabilities came to plague him in his efforts to keep Vietnam a secondary issue in his administration.

Both Truman and Johnson emphasized continuity with their predecessors' policies as they took control of the executive branch. But Johnson, a consensus politician, was peculiarly concerned about legitimacy. Each was deferential to his predecessor's foreign policies. But at the end of World War II Truman had to make changes in his foreign policy crew. He even fired his own appointed Secretary of State, James F. Byrnes, for what amounted to political disloyalty.

Johnson, a more masterful politician than Truman, did not act as quickly—indeed, ever—to become master of his foreign policy house. A more demanding personality, Johnson never came to have Truman's confidence that he controlled his foreign policy advisors. Johnson had problems working with his inherited domestic staff, and he turned it over. He clung to Kennedy's foreign policy staff; to Kennedy's Secretary of State, until the end.

Johnson made no changes of consequence in his foreign policy crew after the 1964 election, when he had a free hand. It is difficult to imagine whom he would have chosen to replace Kennedy's men: Men of sufficient stature from the Senate—Mike Mansfield, William J. Fulbright, George D. Aiken, and others—became more troublesome to him while remaining in the Senate than Kennedy's men who remained with him in the Cabinet, the subcabinet, and the White House—McNamara, Rusk, Bundy, even George Ball, General Maxwell D. Taylor, and Henry Cabot Lodge. Personally domineering, even intimidating, Johnson, in foreign relations, was also deferential. Skillfully distrustful in handling all his staff, he remained distrustful of his national security advisors, yet deferential to them as well.

One can go far in explaining Johnson's conduct of foreign policy, at least his handling of Vietnam, in terms of the general difficulties of his situation. One can likewise look to wider, impersonal factors to which Johnson was peculiarly vulnerable: American hegemonic decline, we now know, began in the mid-sixties. America's share of the world product began to decline more rapidly than in the first two postwar decades. The trade balance, which earlier had turned negative, began, in its accumulating effects, to narrow U.S. foreign policy options, as was demonstrated by an offset payments problem with the Germans. It plagued the Johnson administration's relations with Bonn. The Erhard government fell largely as a result of Johnson's pressures upon it. Military base rights became more difficult to gain and keep. Military clients became less cooperative. America's allies in Western Europe and elsewhere became less confident of America's nuclear guarantees. Vietnam doubtless contributed to these trends but was scarcely their sole cause.[1] Johnson, when he finally faced up to the limits of American power through the demands of his Vietnam policies, was dealing with more than a self-generated problem. He was dealing with an historic watershed which reversed the course of expanding resources—of Keynesian expansionism—upon which his presidential agenda depended.

While largely succeeding with his legislative agenda, with gaining the statutes and funding for a massive program of domestic reform, Johnson had to cope with the limitations of American power internationally. As noted in Chapter 2 he had cut back on Kennedy's goals in Latin America to reflect the sobering failure of Kennedy's Alliance for Progress. Kennedy, to induce Latin America's ruling elites, in the interest of democratic development, to share power with otherwise weak domestic groups, had relied upon persuasion, through the influence of both his own prestige and the nation's hegemonic power, or what Susan Strange has called "structural power,"[2] the capacity to influence by setting the rules of the regional order.

Structural or hegemonic power can accomplish many things. Rarely does it induce power sharing within states in the absence of strong incentives for sharing. In the short run it is more inclined to protect the political order than to alter it. At best, it can be used to change economic and social conditions which may, in turn, induce political changes: This is to work internal political change indirectly. Kennedy had appealed to the empowered groups which ruled in Latin America to share power, but he had done little to induce them to do so. Johnson, lacking Kennedy's ambitions in Latin America, or his prestige, cut back on general political reform as a goal and returned to the more prudent goals of the Eisenhower administration: trade-induced economic development, supplemented with a literal-minded anti-communism that disillusioned American liberals.

Johnson, in the course of adjusting his foreign policies to the growing commitment in Vietnam, adapted to a Western Europe growing stronger and more independent of the United States. Perhaps Kennedy's goals in Western Europe had reflected an early sensing of the limits of American power there, a clearer recognition of what was feasible in Europe than his policies in Latin America showed with respect to that region. The MLF was an attempt either to rescue the credibility of the American nuclear guarantee or to displace that guarantee with a European nuclear force. Whichever it was, if one took seriously the viewpoint and power of the Joint Committee on Atomic Energy, which was unwilling to permit Europeans to gain custody over American nuclear weapons, there was something fishy about the MLF. It was designed to fool either the Joint Committee or the Europeans about nuclear custody. Given the severe constraint on American nuclear options with respect to NATO imposed by the Joint Committee's strict rules about custody, the challenge to European NATO regarding the MLF, which Kennedy issued and Johnson renewed, ostensibly relied on structural power, or at least on the authoritative persuasiveness of American leadership in NATO as voiced by SACEUR and from Washington by the president himself. Kennedy's challenge sought to build a backfire of European support against the Joint Committee's custody rules. But Kennedy and Johnson failed to induce the Europeans to act.

In Chapter 3 we employed the Indian short tether case to examine the relationship between presidential initiatives and routine technical relations with other governments. We used it also to examine the political limits of coercive influence under conditions favoring coercion, for Johnson did, indeed, employ the leverage he had with India to its limits. Employing the short tether might have proved to be a demonstration for future American policy of the uses of economic leverage to achieve internal reform. It did not become a precedent or threaten like dependencies with the prospect of similar coercive behavior. The Indian conditions were uniquely favorable to Johnson's coercive diplomacy, or what Theodore Geiger has called relational power,[3] and to its application, because it involved the president directly and intensively and it did not suggest that similar treatment might be meted out to other governments. The short tether remained therefore mainly a demonstration of Johnson's particular skills and resolve.

There is considerable merit in comparing how presidents deliberate, because comparisons provide alternatives that are rooted in reality. Comparisons that establish structural normalities can be particularly helpful. An important element of such normalities is the distribution between White House staffs and Cabinet departments of the main tasks of foreign policymaking. Graham Allison and Peter Szanton, for instance, drawing upon the distinguished and extensive work of the Murphy Commission's supporting studies, which Szanton directed, came to focus on this issue.[4] Answers to this critical question vary from issue to issue and from president to president. General answers are dominated by a much larger question about how foreign relations works. This larger question centers upon the importance of presidential initiative and leadership. It is not about the division of labor between the president and the Secretary of State, and therefore, it is not the issue that has focused Washington gossip on occasion about whether the president's Special Assistant for National Security Affairs is getting along with the Secretary of State or the Secretary of Defense. It is a more profound question about the nature of the international order and therefore of foreign relations; about the role of the U.S. government in the international order and therefore, about the appropriate kinds of foreign policy to reconcile that role, and to reconcile American interests, with the international order; about the president's role in making and implementing those foreign policies; and finally, about the advisory and administrative structure most likely to support him in performing these tasks.

The vision of limited presidential leadership might have been associated in the pre–World War II era with an international order based on international law. Were it possible to handle political, military, and economic issues through the International Court of Justice in the Hague—an ancient dream—then the burdens of national foreign policy, especially for the United States as the Superpower, would be considerably lightened and the burden on the president comparably lightened. The president could look to the Secretary of State to supervise the lawyers who would practice before the Hague Court and be done with it.

After World War II, hope for a somewhat comparable development was first expressed by the functionalists. They held out the hope of uniting Europe and then other regions through an evolutionary, integrative process which lost its utopianism in more practical-minded ideas about economic and technical integration.[5]

The pursuit of international peace and harmony through means that compete with dependence on national foreign policies, and therefore with reliance on strong presidential foreign policy leadership, is not confined to theory-minded academics. The MLF promoters were called "true believers" in part because their agenda included, in addition to the specifics of a mixed-manned nuclear force, a politically integrated Western Europe. They were one of the most effective foreign policy factions of the postwar era within the U.S. government. The trouble was that they remained a small faction. A more mundane force resisting presidential leadership appeared in Chapter 3 in the guise of practical bureaucratic links between India and the United States in connection with administering economic assistance programs. We will return to this shortly.

Power realism became an appealing way to speak about foreign relations in the United States after World War II largely because it served to screen foreign policy from populist sentimentality—from neglecting external relations and claiming they served either noble or venal interests. Quite apart from its scientific merit, which has been the main (and misguided) focus of academic interest, power realism has underpinned most public discussion of foreign policy, facilitating the business of government in both the executive and legislative branches. It has largely been employed as a rhetorical framework to explain and justify the American role as hegemon and Soviet rival. In performing this role it has served to explain and doubtless to influence the exercise of presidential power.

Power realism justifies the greater role for presidential leadership because it sees the unitary state, with a relatively powerful foreign policy leadership, as the main unit of the international system. It fits or seems to fit when state-to-state relations and diplomatic and programmatic initiatives are important. By doing so, it validates a strong presidential role in U.S. foreign policy and supplies, as it were, outside as well as inside support for the heroic conception of the presidency.

Professors Lloyd I. and Susanne Hoeber Rudolph, both eminent authorities on Indian politics, were close observers and strong critics of Lyndon Johnson's response to the Indian famine of 1965–1967. They also directed a study of American relations with South Asia for the Murphy Commission during 1974–1975. In an illuminating essay for the Murphy Commission they describe conflict between what they call "imperative coordination," which they associate with the president and with other foreign policy generalists, and the "deliberative coordination of complexity." They associate deliberative coordination with regional specialists who are knowledgeable professionals. They extend this dialectic on both sides.

On the side of the president and other foreign policy generalists, the Rudolphs place Richard Neustadt's conception of the president who must, in order to exercise leadership, "seek to amplify his influence, enhance and tighten his control," and be able to cope with "resistance and sabotage." The result, "imperative coordination," sets aside a pluralism that leaves "the public interest in the hands of congressional committees, bureaucracies and private interests" and employs "the mystique of high office, hierarchy in organizational and personal relationships, and will as the source of policy and of compliance." On the other side are the regional specialists whose work proceeds through a process they call deliberative coordination which they describe as involving "the knowledge and judgment of officials, collegiality in formal and informal relationships and reasoned argument and bargaining as the source of policy and compliance."[6] Imperative coordination, in its employment of directive means, tends to be arbitrary and it simplifies in order to coordinate. But regional foreign policy interests are highly complex. They should be handled by means that can cope with complexity. Deliberative coordination can do so; imperative coordination cannot. The Rudolphs' description of what they mean by "deliberative coordination" bears a striking resemblance to the standards of static rationalism discussed in Chapter 6. It means organizational arrangements and procedures that are characterized by thorough consideration of the matter at hand, a concern for consequences, and attention to the reasons offered for and against proposed measures.[7]

The Rudolphs acknowledge that deliberative coordination must take place within the foreign policy machinery of government. In this context, collegiality becomes a constructive use of governmental pluralism. It is related to the interest group pluralism which prevails in domestic policy formation, but it differs from interest group pluralism in the "relatively greater importance" it places on "professional knowledge, judgment and accountability for foreign policy formulation, choice and management."[8]

The Rudolphs' treatment of Johnson's India policy during the food crisis places Johnson and imperative coordination on the wrong side. In their view, this was a case of a willful president overreacting. In this respect they agree with Chester Bowles, who was ambassador to India at the time.[9] They conclude that Johnson's pressure was counterproductive because it "weakened the influence of those Indians who advocated a more liberal economic strategy," and that a more routine handling of food aid policy for India would have avoided such costs while securing most of the same benefits that Johnson's tougher policy gained.[10] They use the food case to make the point that foreign relations are more often better handled by deliberative coordination.

Imperative and deliberative coordination are terms that describe differences in the way policy is made *within* the U.S. government, but it is clear from the Rudolphs' use of these terms that they mean them to connote also how the U.S. government deals with *other* governments. The Rudolphs argue that it would have been better to permit Ambassador Bowles and other American officials who held the trust and confidence of Indian officials to persuade them to alter India's agricultural policies. They claim that Indian officials were altering that policy anyway and would have accomplished as much change as was necessary, at less cost to American interests and to America's friends in India, without the harsher method of coercive influence that Lyndon Johnson employed. It was a mistake in their view for Johnson to have forced the pace and extent of India's agricultural policy reforms by holding back shipments of American grain.

The Rudolphs caution that their two models "simplify and exaggerate in order to generate concepts for analysis."[11] Their dialectic does in fact enable them to put the issue of their study, and an important issue of the present one, extraordinarily well: "The problem is how to reconcile . . . a presidency of energy and initiative with a presidency that is constrained by forms of representation, debate and advice."[12] The first model they call Hamiltonian, the second, Madisonian, and they attempt, as they state it, to reconcile the two. But, acknowledging that in 1975 they are "[w]riting at a different historical moment," they reject Richard Neustadt's 1960 version of the Hamiltonian president.[13] The present study has not.

It is an argument of this book that we must look beyond the rejection at an "historic moment" of a Hamiltonian or (to employ a related concept explained earlier in this study) *heroic* presidency in foreign relations and come to terms once again with the dangers and opportunities that it entails. Reflecting the coverage that has occurred in earlier chapters of foreign policy influence and the president's role in applying it, it is appropriate to ask now—at a different time and with a different presumptive answer—the question that the Rudolphs asked: How to reconcile a "presidency of energy and initiative" with the more deliberative, professional, and what I would call institutional elements of foreign relations.

Reflecting the discussion of the Indian case in Chapter 3, we can, in the interest of penetrating to the ends of foreign policy, track the links of those internal workings of government policymaking, which the Rudolphs call deliberative coordination, to other governments and nongovernmental entities. Deliberative coordination can be associated particularly with the linkages that are nonexceptional, repeated, normal. They implement established policies and smooth their adaptation. They deal routinely with administratively technical matters—the stuff of functional integration. Where a foreign policy is well established, where it is embodied in routines of adaptation and implementation that run to outside groups, these links are part of the foreign policy infrastructure that conserves and sustains policy.

Having drawn this connection, we can place imperative and deliberative coordination in a framework which was developed in previous chapters. This framework acknowledges the value of directive presidential action. It also recognizes the utility of policy infrastructures that constrain and support such action and that achieve influence as much as possible by friendly means, discreetly. Friendly, discreet influence accomplishes more over time with fewer undesirable side effects than imperative influence or splendid coercion. It is also more discriminating and therefore can sometimes be employed when directive influence cannot. But it has drawbacks. It is more subject to reverse influence, as the Indian case illustrated at its beginning, when routine transfers of grain demonstrated an American dependence on India for disposing of U.S. grain as well as India's dependence on the United States as a grain supplier. Furthermore, imperative political leadership can set the underlying conditions which make friendly, discreet influence productive.

The Rudolphs pose in a constructive way the question about presidential leadership in foreign relations which has proved so troublesome since the late sixties. They do not deny the relevance of initiative in foreign relations (although their preferred answer accepts weakened initiative) or propose disengagement from other regions and other countries as a result of their disillusionment with the Hamiltonian presidential style. Their answer relies heavily upon permanent, professional foreign policy staffs, as opposed to the political appointees of any given administration, the "regulars," as opposed to the "irregulars."[14] This is the conventional solution of professional reformers who seek to reduce or eliminate politics in foreign relations, and in the real world it often means that policy becomes aimless, as it had in India. But they go much further. They want to rely also on the knowledgeable nonprofessionals such as Kennedy's and Johnson's ambassador to India, Chester Bowles. This stand of theirs associates them with a quite different mode of internal deliberation and external linkage, a mode characterized in both internal procedures and external relations by its collegiality, its professionalism, its knowledge and appreciation of the complexity of the political and economic forces with which regional powers must come to terms, its mode of influence. Their proposal puts a high value on the assets of expertise and bilateral access to be found among government officials who deal with a given region. The import of this view of foreign relations, which takes on new relevance now that the ending of the Cold War weakens the case for global policies and strengthens the importance of regional foreign policies, can be understood by comparing it with power realism and other theories about influence and control.

The Postwar Hegemonic Order

As noted earlier, realism, with its emphasis on the interstate system, became a convenient framework for rationalizing American foreign policy after World War II. Even George Kennan, who was more interested in state-level politics than international system politics, employed it to explain himself. American policy was actually aimed more at states than at the system, at changing the behavior of states and people—at building their confidence and their economies, at stabilizing their politics, sometimes at making them more democratic. Kennan's own expectations were always modest regarding change, but for him the locus of change was quite clearly within states.[15] This put him at odds with power realism, although he himself employed it to advantage in explaining his views in his first book.[16] Kenneth Waltz, more recently the authoritative voice of neorealism, has insisted that its logic excludes change based on forces internal to the state.[17] In the course of this effort, the United States established itself as the hegemonic leader of a postwar trade and security system. With the collapse of the Soviet bloc this development has become all the more significant.

The realists had postulated an international system of anarchy, covered with a thin layer of cooperation based largely on bargains struck for mutual advantage. NATO, for instance, was the "Trans-Atlantic Bargain."[18] The trouble was that to justify the international system these bargains had to be fair, and fair bargaining implies a certain equality among bargainers, leading to a mutual adherence to pertinent rules. One might go further and say that fairness in bargains presupposes a fair system. But the United States is generally more powerful than its individual partners and often makes the rules which govern bargaining. Realism was an asset in explaining why the United States should strengthen trading partners and military clients, which became its main function in the first fifteen years of the postwar era. But with confidence in government and the presidency fallen over Vietnam, realism seemed hypocritical and dangerous, hypocritical in its ignoring of power inequality, and therefore the injustices of the postwar international order, and dangerous in its seemingly unconstrained pursuit of power and security.

Strictly speaking, realism, or at least neorealism as a scientific theory, is not interested in the role of the president. But in its public applications it became a liability because of its association with strong presidential action. Power realism was a convenient way to locate the president at the "vital center of action," to employ Arthur Schlesinger's term. Yet during the Johnson administration it lost much of its value as a rhetorical framework for deliberating over and explaining policy. Its shortcomings can be overcome, however, by joining it with pluralist and integrationist concepts of order and mutual benefit. That is what the concept of policy infrastructures as employed in this study has served to do.

While the United States was building a postwar order based on the superiority of its economic, military, and political power, the integrationists first looked for ways to generate and assure cooperation and then turned from this normative quest to ask the more empirical question, how to account for and predict integration. At first, after World War II, they tried to bypass the state, or at least severely constrain and control it. It was states that had reverted to dictatorship and states that had fought wars. But their vision clouded. Political integrationists such as Ernst Haas soon limited their expectations to technical and economic integration and demanded answers to the empirical questions.[19]

Those who are interested in making foreign policy work better now must deal with national governments and the foreign policy infrastructures that states have in place. The most helpful developments for figuring out how to do this have come out of inquiries about economic cooperation and integration, and particularly about the relationship between economic and political power, or international political economy (IPE). IPE has roots in power realism as well as in a political pluralism which rejected the exclusive attention to states as actors in the international system, in a revolt against formalism more than out of suspicion about their association with war and with interwar and postwar totalitarianism.

Of central importance here is hegemonic stability theory, for one particular reason. It provides us with an explanation of the postwar international order led by the United States, but it starts from different premises and has different purposes from those of power realism. Politics addresses interests. Realism is one approach to politics. Hegemonic stability theory is a special alternative to it. Realism identifies and differentiates political interests. It uncovers or diagnoses interest conflicts. As noted, it sees bargains as deals cut in the pursuit of national self-interest. The hegemonists seek, in common with the integrationists, to explain and usually to nurture cooperation, and they do it in a surprising way. Where the integrationists usually look for some sort of reciprocity in approximately equal relationships, the hegemonists seek unequal partnerships and find value in what the strongest can do as leader. They find that establishing the postwar order depended upon unequal power, on the United States's exercise of its hegemony, or paramount power. They explain cooperation as a product of that order, and therefore of the unequal distribution of power among states.

For power realists, unequal power can be dangerous because the strong tend to exploit their advantage over the weak. The hegemonists, seeking the basis for cooperation, find inequality in power the basis for the stability and prosperity of the postwar international system because these features of the postwar order depended upon the order-creating and order-keeping behavior of the superior political and economic power. In the postwar era, this superior power outside the Soviet bloc has been the United States. Superior political and economic power benefitted the United States as the hegemon, but the order and stability it produced also benefitted other states— not, to be sure, equally, but also not negligibly.

The hegemonists explain cooperation by noting that both large and small powers benefit from participation in the hegemonic order. Cooperation is further explained as depending upon political leadership asserted by the hegemon, who will initially have employed superior power. Traditional integrationists, in contrast, usually explained cooperation as the outgrowth of working-level, technical initiatives that did not begin with the employment of superior power. The MLF promoters, whose activities were described in Chapters 4 and 5, were in certain respects functional integrationists trying to take advantage of America's hegemony. They were, by the standards of bureaucratic politics, risk-taking initiators. But they lacked the power to be serious leaders.

The hegemonists' viewpoint allows for leaders and followers, for regime builders and regime users, for large and small powers, for system maintainers, for free riders. These characteristics of the hegemonic order account for presidential leadership as a necessary if not a sufficient condition of effectively asserted hegemonic power. They also account for the policy choices that confront hegemonic states in seeking to achieve a beneficial international order. They are comparable to the choices which states make about their own internal economies and polities. Few informed observers would claim that even in democracies we can expect economic and political power to be distributed equally, at least as a practical matter. This accounting for the unequal distribution of power gives a comfortable place to the dialectic between presidential leadership and infrastructural stability. Presidential initiative is employed to build alliances into international institutions, and therefore, from the standpoint of one's own government, into national policy infrastructures. These infrastructures implement national policies, but also constrain national action.

The hegemonists, by showing us that states which are unequal in power and wealth benefit from cooperating with one another, provide an explanation for the sorts of continuing relationships with other states that embody American foreign policies and that conserve the application of raw power. Policy infrastructures can be viewed as cross-sections of a general hegemonic order, sliced, as it were, to reveal the policy intentions and goals of the state.

For the purposes of the present study, these concepts are a convenient way to look at presidential leadership and management of foreign policy. Within the context of an international order created during a period of American hegemony, policy infrastructures usually have included some degree of cross-national integration: In the MLF case it was manifest in the NATO alliance and more broadly in the Atlantic alliance, which was (and is) composed of a rich set of political, military, and economic connections. In India, as with other third world countries where fewer connections exist and the network is thinner, it occurred more narrowly, in the working linkage between the two governments which handled foreign commodity and economic aid. In South Vietnam, it occurred through the sheer size of the American presence in that country. These are quite different types of commonality, but with reference to American influence, all three were composed of linkages that stabilized and reassured and served to permit but also constrain influence. The latter linkages were working relationships that, in the interest of maintaining trust and confidence, constrained the United States from exploiting the interdependency that the linkage supported.

Bringing Presidential Leadership Back In

Hegemonic state leadership is a critical factor in the hegemonists' interpretation of the postwar order. Since the United States has been the order-creating hegemonic power, and since the president is the central figure in American foreign relations, one should expect hegemonic order theory to devote a considerable amount of attention to the American presidency. In fact, it has not. The hegemonists have virtually ignored this subject. One suspects that this neglect is because they are skeptical of the formalities of state sovereignty and intent upon accounting for nongovernmental actors in foreign relations. But the effect, oddly enough, is to make them look like realists, intent upon dealing with the state as though it were unitary, rather than as a complex polyarchy in which presidential leadership is a source of order. Despite this impression, hegemonic order theory offers, in its conception of the postwar order and the function of hegemonic leadership in creating that order, strong tools for extending the analysis of the internal presidency into the tasks of the external presidency. Employing them would bring presidential leadership back into the analysis of foreign relations where it is much needed whether one likes it or not.

A convenient way to put the president back is to assess the benefits and risks of three conceptions of the presidency, a Hamiltonian, a Madisonian, and a Jayist conception. In foreign relations, do we want a Hamiltonian leader, building policy infrastructures through which the president manages and maintains the wider hegemonic order within which they are built; an energetic, risk-taking manager who employs directive methods of administration and applying power and influence? Or, do we want a Madisonian leader who moves more cautiously, working mainly to integrate American interests and American policies with the configurations of interest found in geographic regions and regional power systems, employing discreet methods of influence? Or do we want a president whose style John Jay anticipated in the *Federalist Papers*, one who emphasizes diplomatic maneuver, who plays the interests of other states against one another, perhaps a weak but venturesome Hamiltonian leader, one without strongly institutionalized policies, or policy infrastructures, perhaps avoiding such institutionalization in order to maintain freedom of action; a president who avoids entangling alliances?

There is something to be said for the Jay option, but only in order to assure that the United States does not become an Atlas, a giant with no options because of the burden it carries, a victim of "imperial overstretch," quite possibly as a result of a role maintained and in part imposed by smaller powers. There is more to be said for the Madisonian model because it takes into account the peculiar, pluralistic genius of American politics, a characteristic that is needed as the United States adapts itself from the dominating hegemon to a more responsive and flexible hegemon, perhaps a more collegial one, sharing power by choice and necessity, relying on the skills that come from operating its own big, diverse, pluralistic governmental system to share the burdens as well. But the Madisonian model, at least as it is often applied, gives too little heed to the presidency as a major asset of foreign policy. Its appeal, as the Rudolphs show us, comes these days in part by default, from a lack of confidence in presidents as directive foreign policy leaders, as well as from the attractions of knowledge-based, deliberative openness—the tribute which democratic theorists pay to science.

The promise of presidential leadership in foreign relations lies largely in the Hamiltonian model. It is there that the presidency can take advantage of the very infrastructures which embody and sustain foreign policies, working through them, managing them. But this is a Hamiltonian role, the presidency as viewed from underneath, the way the Rudolphs view it, against the bright sky of politics, where it has a strong policy profile as well as an administrative function, not as viewed from above, against the dark background of the bureaucracy, where its role is to reduce the politics of foreign policy to administrative routines. The infrastructures of foreign policy not only support the hegemonic order itself, but provide supporting frames for the president's political role in foreign relations. Against the sky of trans-national politics, the routines of foreign policy provide both stability and the points of departure for policy innovation. It is the function of foreign policy leadership, accordingly, not only to sustain foreign policy infrastructures, but also to transform and on occasion abandon them, but not to permit them, in their propensity to maintain the status quo, or through their momentum, to reduce foreign policy to a technical process. To say this, of course, is to turn against the functional integrationists, to charge that a foreign policy composed of technical processes devoid of political aims will be dangerous.

Presidential leadership in foreign relations should be policy-laden. It should employ the assets of government, defined in the inclusive terms of policy infrastructures, as a source of momentum and counter-momentum, innovation, and directive rationality, shaping and managing these assets to achieve common and, where necessary, exclusive interests.

Structure and Infrastructure

This study has reflected a skepticism about the conventional approach to governmental structure and about conventional process norms in dealing with foreign policy. But it has resisted the propensity to treat presidential initiative as the major source of foreign policy error. The result has been to offer the beginnings of a theory of foreign policy process which rejects the conventional practice of isolating that process from the external linkages which are included in foreign policy infrastructures.[20] This alternative theory should define as primary concerns of foreign relations (1) self-management (i.e., managing the pertinent behavior of one's own government) and (2) influencing the behavior of other governments. It should include two corrective factors which have been described in preceding chapters. The first addresses a bias in foreign policy studies, paralleling the attention span, as it were, of foreign policy leaders in the government, to focus on critical issues to the neglect of secondary and lesser issues, particularly when those issues are handled by routine or normal means. By neglecting the "default mode" of foreign relations, as it were, analysts and policymakers miss the connections between ordinary and exceptional elements of foreign relations. Yet if the default mode is a strong policy infrastructure, this strength enables policymakers and their advisors to concentrate on adaptation and on generating new initiatives. If the infrastructure is weak they will be required to spend their time and resources on maintaining the status quo.

In this respect, two closely connected worlds can be identified with respect to the management and administration of foreign relations. One is the world of conspicuous issues, issues that draw the attention of the highest levels of government. The other is the normal functioning of foreign relations. There are aspects of each revealed in the three cases discussed in Chapters 3 through 6. Perhaps the starkest distinction appeared in the handling of the Indian grain shortage. Routine procedures were underway to maintain the flow of grain, and to raise the volume of that flow, all of it handled routinely, or normally. President Johnson intervened to make these activities, and the situation in India that they addressed, exceptional rather than routine for the U.S. government. Having a routine made it possible for Johnson to choose to intervene.

The second correction factor is a concept that has already been explained at some length and referred to often. We return to it now to show its relationship to executive, that is presidential, initiative. It is *infrastructure*. The term, in this use of it, encompasses both the internal networks of government and clienteles that compose the governmental process and the external networks of foreign relations that the implementation of foreign policies entails. It amounts to a state-centered, policy-structured "regime." By the time Johnson became president, a relatively extensive set of patterned relationships had long existed with Western Europe and in the way the United States dealt with third areas, and in dealings with the Soviet Union, the Soviet bloc, and China. I have in earlier chapters referred to these patterned relationships as infrastructure.

Foreign policies that are implemented through measures with sizeable material components and that therefore have relatively large budgets, such as foreign economic and military aid programs, have obvious parallels to domestic programs like public housing policies or farm subsidies which perform distributive functions. Policy in all of these cases becomes a political institution supported by constituencies when networks of governmental and private groups develop relationships which are stable and effective enough to sustain and defend it over time, whether these relationships are tight little "iron triangles," as some observers have claimed them to be, or messy hexagonals.[21] They lose their status as institutions and become mere policies when the political alliances that sustain them can be described as traces in the sand.[22]

The foreign policy infrastructures[23] referred to in this study depend upon multiple-sided relationships that are usually dominated by their governmental sides. They also extend the meaning of clientele relationships in recognition of the fact that foreign policy has, compared with domestic policy, an additional class of important clienteles or player groups which are foreign. These groups consist of foreign governments, elements of foreign governments, and nongovernmental groups and organizations, national and multinational—or internal and external. There is plenty of room here for pluralism, but not for ignoring the state. Whether one speaks of U.S. policy toward NATO or U.S. commitments to Western Europe, the policies involved have little meaning without explaining them in terms of this phenomenon of extended clientele relationships of the U.S. government and its pertinent components.

The three cases dealt with in the four preceding chapters showed the vital importance of relating the routines and momentum of policy infrastructures properly to presidential initiative if both the resilience and continuity of policy, on the one hand, and the phenomenon of policy innovations and the role of policy leadership, on the other, are to be accounted for. The Indian grain case details strong presidential action in a secondary theater of foreign policy. The MLF case describes constrained presidential action in what is usually recognized as the primary theater of American foreign policy, Europe. The action involved took advantage of the resilience of the North Atlantic alliance structure. The Vietnam case discusses presidential action in what began as a secondary, and became a central, issue of foreign policy, and what also came to involve enormously powerful momentum in the policy infrastructure involved in fighting a war.

All three are in some respects limiting cases. Each marks the outer limits of an important dimension in the presidential management of foreign policy. The Indian case deals with an extreme example of the personal assertion of the president's role in the implementation of foreign policy and constitutes an extreme version of exercising influence on another government. Johnson's Vietnam policy is extreme in several dimensions: extreme in the escalation of American involvement in a secondary theater of American interests, extreme in the involvement of the president in the details of military action, extreme in that it tested his administration's very political limits—its capacity to maintain its public mandate and accomplish its goals. The MLF case marks the outer limits of a quite different kind of initiative, a prominent but limited, hedged attempt at a major policy innovation in a policy domain that was central to American hegemony, yet highly constrained by reciprocal commitments.

Bureaucratic analysis seeks to observe discrete actions. In doing so, it tends to associate itself with static rationalism as a norm because it is the stock-in-trade of the policy analyst. Static rationalism holds that rational choice is choosing among arrayed options, or horizontal choices. It exaggerates the role of individual choices. It pays particular attention to decision confrontations, to lion-like rather than fox-like behavior, to employ the metaphor that James

MacGregor Burns applied to Franklin D. Roosevelt's complexities.[24] It focuses on the decision as the climax and triumph of executive behavior, ignoring the utility of executive craft as it is applied to avoiding detectable decisions, to building roads that do not have forks. It misses the point that having to make a decision can itself be a disaster, and that when decisions are not required, or not possible, that may be a triumph of policy engineering. Static rationalism's definition of rational choice, by defining choice as separate from the infrastructures of implementation, has also generated a separate cottage industry of academics whose analysis is dedicated to implementation.[25]

As noted earlier, Johnson's main foreign policy choices in the three cases dealt with were not horizontally arrayed, they were "vertical." With respect to India, he first decided to become involved, then to interrupt the routine rollover of the annual surplus grain agreement, then to stop grain shipments, then to insist on a deal between Orville Freeman, his Secretary of Agriculture, and Chidambaram Subramaniam, Freeman's opposite number in the Indian government, then to control grain shipments, then to continue to control them in the face of criticism that he was doing it in the first place. In the MLF case the choice was at first whether or not to go along with Kennedy's policy, or with what Johnson supposed it to be. Eventually it became a question of when or whether to back away from the MLF proposal. Along the way, there was a prospect that, somehow, Europeans would actually take up the proposal enthusiastically. Had that occurred, the Johnson administration would then have faced the embarrassment of having been seen to sell Europeans on an idea that it could not sell to the powerful congressional Joint Committee on Atomic Energy.

With respect to Vietnam, choice was a series of decisions over time about going along or getting out. There certainly were optional decisions along the way. Johnson's critics are entitled to their point that he ought to have arrayed his choices. But to have arrayed them accurately presupposes an accurate diagnosis of the situation, and the needed accuracy came only incrementally. It was plain enough from the beginning that, with respect to North Vietnam, he had to contend with a small power in a remote place in the world. It remained unclear to Johnson and his principal advisors, with certain notable exceptions, that Hanoi was resolved to stay the course for many years if necessary, that it was a regime shaped by and wholly committed to the mission of uniting and ruling Vietnam as a single country, and that it would receive the needed material and technical support from China and the Soviet Union to carry through with this resolve. Johnson's first decision about Vietnam was to give it second place to his domestic program. Hanoi made a quite different choice.

Vertical choice can be linked to certain configurations of policy infrastructure as the preferred norm. Infrastructure can be a force against innovation, but also a force for continuity and stability, for political durability and operational effectiveness. Even more to the point, by providing a status quo that is more acceptable and resilient, and by supplying the supporting mechanisms for implementing change, the infrastructure defines the fundamental vertical option: How bad is the status quo? How much are you willing to do to change it? On this score, Vietnam was, from the beginning, a bad status quo. At no time during Johnson's presidency was the status quo in South Vietnam acceptable to Washington. Presidential decisions almost always dealt with what actions had to be taken to make it acceptable. Usually they dealt with how to keep it from getting worse. Johnson was always playing catch-up.

If one is looking for ways to avoid the errors of Vietnam, here is a good place to start: One ought to find ways to avoid entrapping the president into close identification with bad situations that are getting worse, to facilitate the president's own efforts to avoid entrapment from below, as it were, through bureaucratic momentum reinforced with political expectations.

The American experience in Vietnam was a test of American hegemony. In earlier chapters our inquiry led to questions about the limits of American interest relative to American power. The Indian and MLF cases involved the management of relations clearly within the reach of American power. The Indian case posed the value of hegemonic control in the interest of major national economic policy reforms. To exercise that control required cutting through impediments both sides had constructed to prevent such hegemonic power being exercised.

The MLF case involved the reach of American power in Europe, where American hegemony had much diminished relative to Soviet military power and Western European political and economic power. But it involved those relations with Western Europe with respect to which American hegemony remained strongest, yet most constrained in its exercise: nuclear military power. For this reason, American diplomacy was employed cautiously. It came as an invitation, a challenge, following the model of the Marshall Plan. By the time Johnson became president, Europeans had registered their indifference through delay, and American convictions had narrowed to a group of "true believers." The implications of Western Europe's adopting and the United States' following along to implement the MLF proposal could have been far-reaching. Its American promoters saw it as a way to move Western Europe into a degree of political as well as military integration that most of them had supported for a decade or more.

These American efforts to keep the MLF alive—incautious in particulars, but cautious in their scale—moved within an infrastructure which integrated normal U.S. government actions with multilateral military cooperation in NATO and which maintained U.S. commitments and policies through routine force deployments and force posture and routine multilateral military planning at NATO's main integrated military command headquarters, SHAPE (Supreme Headquarters Allied Powers Europe). Johnson, as we know, inherited the MLF proposal and its proponents, both of which he left in place until they became an embarrassment. We can observe that this cautious approach to change in NATO was consistent with his crediting what he would have heard from his assistants and would have observed from his Senate experience, that the U.S. had more stakes across the Atlantic, more ties to Western Europe, by far more hostages to its fortune beyond (but also including) the troops that we kept there, than in any other region.

NATO, from the standpoint of U.S. policy, was an elaborate network of interests which could have been jeopardized by a heavy-handed promotion of the MLF. Had the Americans pushed the MLF proposal hard, they would have put at stake their credibility as nuclear guarantor of Western Europe, because Europeans would have seen the Americans as saying that the MLF was needed to maintain that guarantee. As this happened, European allies would have sought to distance themselves from the United States in other respects.

I argued in Chapter 6 that Johnson and his advisors were overly committed to the idea that the United States could, if necessary, raise its stakes in the Vietnam War in order to achieve its objectives there. I called this *hubris*, as others have, and associated it with Keynesian expansionism. It is *hubris* because it was an inability to recognize that U.S. objectives in Vietnam might not be achievable by committing more and more American resources. I called it Keynesian expansionism because Keynesian macroeconomics had come to represent a view that one could spend more on foreign affairs *and* have at the same time more for domestic consumption and investment, a claim that, as implausible as it seems, proved to be true for the United States in the peculiar circumstances of both World War II and the Korean War. No such *hubris* can be found in Kennedy's or Johnson's handling of the MLF proposal. On the contrary, that handling was a discriminate, although not always controlled, employment of American hegemonic power.

The Interrupted Inquiry

How much should the United States rely upon energetic presidential leadership in foreign relations? It was to be expected that the president would figure heavily in American efforts to build the new postwar order after World War II, an order in which the United States would be assured of its own security. Once it was built, however, one might expect that the United States would seek to base its security on something more stable and less dangerous than presidential leadership. President Eisenhower actually anticipated this question, even virtually asked it, because his view of the presidency reflected a professional military attitude that national security plans and other important national policies should depend minimally on presidential leadership. It is an intriguing speculation that the revisionist appreciation of Eisenhower, when it is applied to national security and foreign policy, is a validation of the long-run appeal of this attitude.

More than any other president since World War II, with the possible exception of Richard Nixon, Lyndon Johnson poisoned the well of public trust of the presidency in foreign relations. As a result of the poisoning, little attention has been paid in recent years to analyzing the utilities of presidential power in foreign relations. I noted in the Preface that the inquiry about presidential power as it applied to foreign relations started by Richard Neustadt virtually stopped. That inquiry needs to be revived.

Neustadt dealt mainly with the domestic dimensions of presidential power, with how the president should handle himself in the competitive struggle for power within the American governmental system. It was an important premise of Neustadt's account that this competitive struggle assured that presidential actions would be scrutinized and challenged and that, given the difficulties that presidents have in getting and using power, its abuse and misuse would not be a major problem. Neustadt's metaphor of "the president in sneakers" evoked conditions which would be likely to induce deliberate prudence in the exercise of power and which required careful attention to its application.

This nurturing and protecting of presidential influence seemed in the early and mid-sixties less relevant to external relations than to domestic politics. The president's prerogatives in foreign relations had not been seriously challenged since the defeat of the Bricker

Amendment in 1954. American hegemonic power was at its zenith. The president relied heavily on the general advantages that it provided in foreign relations.

The postwar hegemonic order which the United States built was for American and therefore presidential power in foreign relations the equivalent of Neustadt's presidential reputation in domestic politics. By building "situations of strength," in Dean Acheson's phrase, and establishing political, commercial, monetary, and security relationships generally favorable to U.S. interests, particular issues in foreign relations could be handled without the relentless pursuit of narrow national interest such as so often characterized French foreign policy, for example, during the fifties and sixties. The United States could exercise power with less regard for its application in specific cases—for its *terminal* application—than was often necessary in domestic affairs. In this respect, from the standpoint of presidential power, the postwar hegemonic order served the same purpose externally as the president's reputation for success served him in his domestic venue.

One could argue that presidential power is no longer needed in the way it used to be when the task was to build the postwar hegemonic order,[26] that the postwar order survives, and that presidential leadership is even dangerous. That presidential leadership is dangerous seems to be the viewpoint of influential theorists, especially the anti-realist pluralists. Joseph Nye is one of them. His book *Bound to Lead*, which is an imaginative and vigorous defense of the United States against the charge that it is a declining great power, illustrates this position. Nye defines broadly and acknowledges generously the assets which the United States brings to its international leadership position, with the notable exception of the presidency. He has nothing to say about presidential leadership as an asset! He mentions the presidency only as a source of self-inflicted wounds, such as "budget deficits, protectionist measures, or curtailment of foreign aid."[27]

Nye is not alone in this view of the presidency. Strong intellectual forces have minimized claims about the presidential role in foreign relations, but with no great effect on how presidents have actually performed in their foreign relations role. Presidential leadership has continued to be an important factor there. President Bush's diplomatic successes in building a military coalition to deal with Iraq's conquest of Kuwait is a recent, and stunning, example of its importance.

We may fear the consequences of the exercise of presidential power in foreign relations. We may be disappointed by presidential behavior in Vietnam or Irangate or the liberation of Kuwait, yet presidential leadership is unavoidably necessary to generate the political support required for most major foreign policy moves, including such opportunities as the transformation of relations with the Soviet Union. Indeed, Nye's own examples in *Bound To Lead* are all actions which could never be accomplished without the commitment and efforts of a relatively assertive president. Nye's account illustrates a pluralist viewpoint about foreign relations which avoids or greatly diminishes the requirement for presidential leadership. It contradicts a common view that is held across a fairly wide political spectrum, that when it comes down to the making and implementing of foreign policy, presidential leadership is essential.

A second group, the static rationalists, as noted, have tried to develop norms for decision making that would reduce the dangers of presidential leadership in foreign relations noted with respect to Vietnam. From George through Berman, VanDeMark, Greenstein, and Burke, all of whose views have been discussed previously in this book, the static rationalists aim to fix a manifestly faulted presidential behavior. They want presidents to face a wide array of choices and to see that those choices are seriously presented in explicit deliberative procedures. They assume or assert that presidents, advised by such means, are more likely to make sound decisions. At least they claim that when presidents do not follow such procedures, their decision failures can be explained in part by the procedural shortfall. Despite a careful qualifying and limiting of these claims, the argument of the static rationalists expands to make much broader claims: Fix the options; fix the decision maker; fix the decision.

The purpose is worthy enough, the rational standard, useful, but the effort, misplaced. Johnson, it turns out, despite claims to the contrary, was not conspicuously more prone to limit his consideration of foreign policy options or his circle of foreign policy advisors than other presidents have been. To put it more generally, better foreign policy decisions (sometimes defined with respect to Vietnam as decisions not to intervene), when compared with worse decisions, do not strongly correlate with more options and more advisors.

It would be helpful if we could fix the performance of presidents by fixing their behavior at the point of explicit, observable decision making, but we cannot hope to do very much to modify the deliberative process at the point of critical decisions. To begin with, that process at that particular point is usually heavily constrained by its role as a legitimizer. Observed decisions will always be to some extent a performance because they are supposed to be a performance. Second, whichever decisions are observed and evaluated are likely to be only a few of many turning points in the process of policy determination. This second criticism should actually be stated much more broadly, for more is involved in executive strategies than what appears and what does not appear as a decision. A president or other executive who seeks advice, whether from inside advisors or outsiders, or from both, not only is able to control the agenda for his advisors, of necessity he also makes other decisions—usually prior decisions—which place the advisory task within a larger context of his administration's goals and interests. As I have argued in Chapter 6, Johnson's placement of Vietnam in a secondary position on his agenda, while recognizing that he would have to work at keeping it there, set conditions that degraded the quality of his deliberations with respect to Vietnam.

Neither the general distrust of presidential power nor the rigorous analysis of the static rationalists can save us from confronting the questions about it that Richard Neustadt raised in the 1950s. These questions are particularly difficult to answer when they pertain to foreign relations: How much leeway should the president have in foreign relations? How much should he be trusted? We need to be sorting out the puzzles regarding presidential power that set its exercise in foreign relations apart from its exercise domestically. These puzzles have to do mainly with two special, though not unique, conditions that pertain to foreign policy: the greater discretion the president is often permitted and the fact that foreign policy actions usually impact the most on interests that lie outside American politics.

If Neustadt's analysis is still valid, it is because two premises which he employed are also still valid. The first concerns the limited nature of presidential power and the claim that, since he must share it, he must compete with other power sharers. It is the competitive struggle for power in which the president is always engaged that insures that when he exercises power he will do so safely. The other is that there is value in presidential initiative, in the president's exercise of leadership. The Rudolphs concluded that the first premise was wrong and attacked the second. They offered instead their Madisonian view of executive deliberation.

The good news for those who acknowledge the need for presidential power in foreign relations but worry about the risks of its use is demonstrated by the MLF case. Important foreign policies are often pursued within the context of a highly constraining policy infrastructure. The assets of this infrastructure may be ill-defined and the trade-off costs with reference to it, poorly stated. At the same time, as in the case of the MLF, effective officials must have a considerable amount of practical skill and insight in order to work within such an infrastructural order. The puzzle here is how to take account of such behavior, how at once to appreciate such a policy setting with all its complexities and to make better use of it.

When it comes to fundamental foreign policy issues, such as trade-off choices between domestic policy and foreign policy priorities, and questions about the general magnitude of the commitment to American goals in foreign relations, it is evident that the presidential advisory process, including formal and informal NSC procedures, rarely addresses them seriously, even captures them for addressing. These are matters the president often handles privately. Congress, to its credit, often addresses them, but not often in good time. This sort of top-down decision making seems to be unavoidable. We see it as dangerous with reference to Lyndon Johnson. He gave first priority to his domestic program and handled Vietnam so that it would not interfere with his first priority. Giving first priority to his domestic program by itself did not prove to be dangerous, but the way he went about protecting it in his handling of Vietnam was dangerous. Dwight Eisenhower employed priority-setting decisions to guide his advisors about his foreign policy, and he has been commended for his performance with respect to his advisors, at least since Eisenhower revisionism took hold in the early eighties. We can expect that the large-scale changes in foreign policy that confront the U.S. government at the beginning of the 1990s will require, or at least induce, the answering, by directive presidential action, of more of these fundamental priority-setting questions.

Imperative or coercive influence often competes with deliberative persuasion in dealing with established foreign partners and clients, as the Indian grain case illustrates. The relationship between coercion and persuasion is highly complex. It is rarely to be understood outside of particular contexts. Yet if it is not understood, influence is wasted. In a period when the relative power of the United States is declining, the value of influence rises and wasting it is less and less excusable. Managing regional relations such as the Indian case illustrated is thus an increasingly important matter for American foreign policy management.

We can scarcely deny, for the single superpower in the 1990s, the value of presidential leadership in foreign relations. The wrong question is how, in the interest of minimizing the dangers of presidential action, to minimize the president's powers and role. The right question is how to use the presidency to advantage, taking account of the dangers of its use. To deny or even diminish the presidency's utility in foreign relations is to be irrelevant. To be pre-occupied with its dangers is to miss its necessity. How, then, can it be put to advantage and its dangers minimized? This is the work that Neustadt began in the late fifties and that has faltered. It is a work that needs resuming.

Notes

Preface

1. Richard E. Neustadt, *Presidential Power: The Politics of Leadership* (1960).

2. Clinton E. Rossiter, in *The American Presidency*, had dealt with the presidency by decomposing it into several roles.

3. Richard E. Neustadt, *Presidential Power: The Politics of Leadership from FDR to Carter* (1980); Neustadt, *Presidential Power: The Politics of Leadership from Roosevelt to Reagan* (1990).

4. Conveniently available in Henry M. Jackson (ed.), *The National Security Council*, pp. 281–288.

5. Henry Brandon, "Skybolt," *London Sunday Times*, 3 December 1963, reprinted in Morton H. Halperin and Arnold Kanter (eds.), *Readings in American Foreign Policy: A Bureaucratic Perspective*, pp. 403 ff.

6. Richard E. Neustadt, *Alliance Politics*, pp. 139–145.

7. Neustadt, *Alliance Politics*, p. 151.

8. John P. Burke and Fred I. Greenstein, *How Presidents Test Reality: Decisions on Vietnam, 1954–1965.* See Chapters 7 and 8 for further discussion of the Eisenhower revisionist literature.

9. Aaron Wildavsky and Jeffrey Pressman, *Implementation: How Great Expectations in Washington Are Dashed in Oakland.*

10. John D. Steinbruner, *The Cybernetic Theory of Decision: New Dimensions of Political Analysis.*

1. Johnson's Foreign Relations: Toward a Broader Inquiry

1. *Public Papers of the Presidents of the United States: Lyndon B. Johnson, 1963–65*, pp. 27–29.

2. A colorful account of Johnson's work with constituents and bureaucrats during his early years in the House can be found in Robert A. Caro, *The Years of Lyndon Johnson*, vol. 1, *The Path to Power*, and vol. 2, *The Means of Ascent*, pp. 531 ff.

3. Interview with Dean Rusk, 28 January 1986.

4. Richard L. Schott and Dagmar S. Hamilton, *People, Positions, and*

Power: The Political Appointments of Lyndon B. Johnson, p. 39.

5. U.S. Congress, Senate Committee on Government Operations, Subcommittee on National Policy Machinery, *Organizing for National Security*, vol. 1, 87th Cong., 1st sess., pp. 1337–1338; I. M. Destler, *Presidents, Bureaucrats and Foreign Policy*, p. 98.

6. Arthur M. Schlesinger, Jr., *A Thousand Days: John F. Kennedy in the White House*, p. 133.

7. Schlesinger, *A Thousand Days*, Ch. 16; Theodore C. Sorenson, *Kennedy*, pp. 287–290. These complaints were not common among the NSC staffers, Bundy, and his associates.

8. Schott and Hamilton, *People, Positions, and Power*, p. 39.

9. Schlesinger, *A Thousand Days*, p. 435. Schlesinger discusses Rusk's initiation with the White House staff on p. 436.

10. *In Re Neagle*, 135 U.S. 1 (1890).

11. Emmette S. Redford and Richard T. McCulley, *White House Operations: The Johnson Presidency*, pp. 66, 100–108, 110–112, 190–192.

12. Richard F. Fenno, *The President's Cabinet: An Analysis in the Period from Wilson to Eisenhower*, pp. 100–103, 107–113.

13. Paul Y. Hammond, "The National Security Council as a Device for Interdepartmental Coordination: An Interpretation and Appraisal," *The American Political Science Review* 54:4 (December 1960): 899–910; Douglas Kinnard, *President Eisenhower and Strategy Management: A Study in Defense Politics*, pp. 16, 64–65, 121–122, 133–134; Fred I. Greenstein, *The Hidden-Hand Presidency: Eisenhower as Leader*, pp. 124–138.

14. W. W. Rostow, *The Diffusion of Power*, pp. 363–364.

15. Hammond, "The National Security Council," pp. 899–910.

16. Greenstein, *The Hidden-Hand Presidency*, pp. 132–134.

17. Stephen Hess, *Organizing the Presidency*, p. 102.

18. Faced with a frantic demand for intervention from the American ambassador there, and confronted at the same time with detailed intelligence information, including FBI reports about communists in Santo Domingo, Johnson evidently acted without benefit of advice from regional experts, who would have told him, if nothing else, that intervention even under these circumstances would be much more politically costly than he anticipated.

19. David C. Humphrey, "Tuesday Lunch at the Johnson White House: A Preliminary Assessment," *Diplomatic History* 8:1 (Winter 1984): 81–101; Burke and Greenstein, *How Presidents Test Reality*, p. 99.

20. Humphrey, "Tuesday Lunch"; Burke and Greenstein, *How Presidents Test Reality*, pp. 118–134, 179–186, 190–191, 200, 257–259.

21. Rostow, *The Diffusion of Power*, pp. 359–360.

22. Humphrey, "Tuesday Lunch," pp. 92–93; William P. Bundy, transcript of oral history interview, 2 June 1969, Tape 5, p. 12, Oral History Interviews, LBJ Library.

23. Doris Kearns, *Lyndon Johnson and the American Dream*, pp. 319–320; Edward A. Kolodziej, "The National Security Council: Innovations

and Implications," *Public Administration Review* 29:6 (November/December 1969): 573–585.

24. Brian VanDeMark, *Into the Quagmire: Lyndon Johnson and the Escalation of the Vietnam War*, pp. 40–41, 64–65, 104–105, 140–141, 157–158; William Conrad Gibbons, *The U.S. Government and the Vietnam War: Executive and Legislative Roles and Relationships*, part 3, details Johnson's contacts with his Senate colleagues (see, e.g., index entries for Ernest Gruening, Jacob K. Javits, Russell Long, Mike Mansfield, Richard Russell); Rostow, *The Diffusion of Power*, Ch. 33.

25. George defines the "custodian-manager" role as embracing a "number of subtasks and functions," which he lists as follows:

1. balancing actor resources within the policymaking system;
2. strengthening weaker advocates;
3. bringing in new advisers to argue for unpopular options;
4. setting up new channels of information so that the president and other advisers are not dependent upon a single channel;
5. arranging for independent evaluation of decisional promises and options, when necessary;
6. monitoring the workings of the policymaking process to identify possible dangerous malfunctions and instituting appropriate corrective action.

Alexander L. George, *Presidential Decisionmaking in Foreign Policy: The Effective Use of Information and Advice*, pp. 195–196.

26. Walt W. Rostow, *The Diffusion of Power*, p. 363.

27. Arthur M. Schlesinger, Jr., *The Age of Roosevelt*, vol. 2, *The Coming of the New Deal*, pp. 522–523; Neustadt, *Presidential Politics*, esp. pp. 153–161; Schlesinger, *A Thousand Days*, p. 120.

28. Greenstein, *The Hidden-Hand Presidency*, esp. Ch. 4.

29. David K. Hall, "The 'Custodian-Manager' of the Policymaking Process," Ch. 12 in vol. 2, Murphy Commission *Appendices*, esp. p. 108 [pp. 100–119]. John F. Bowman II expands on Hall in "The Role of the Special Assistant to the President for National Security Affairs in the Formulation and Implementation of National Security Policy: An Evaluation." See also George, *Presidential Decisionmaking in Foreign Policy*, pp. 196–197, 200.

30. Interview with Francis M. Bator, 17 November 1983; Testimony, Bator before U.S. Congress, House Committee on Foreign Affairs, Subcommittee on Foreign Economic Policy, *U.S. Foreign Economic Policy: Implications for the Organization of the Executive Branch*, Hearings, 25 July 1972, 92d Cong., 2d sess., 1972, pp. 107–121, 126–137.

31. Raymond A. Bauer, Ithiel de Sola Pool, and Lewis Anthony Dexter, *American Business and Public Policy: The Politics of Foreign Trade*, pp. 75–78.

32. Other volumes in this series have employed the concept of the subpresidency, which has special reference to the economic decisional process of the Johnson presidency. Redford and Blissett (Emmette S. Redford and

Marlan Blissett, *Organizing the Executive Branch: The Johnson Presidency,*
p. 11) defined the subpresidency as "all those who served the president—
continuously or ad hoc, in an institutional capacity or otherwise—in the
exercise of his responsibilities. This included, on occasion, individuals in
departments or independent agencies who had separate official responsibilities but whose loyalties to the president led them to look at problems from
a presidential perspective."

Johnson used the economic subpresidency as an ad hoc group to handle
issues of immediate concern to him to circumvent the Cabinet and avoid
established departmental positions on those issues. James E. Anderson and
Jared E. Hazleton, *Managing Macroeconomic Policy: The Johnson Subpresidency,* p. 13.

33. Henry Kissinger, *White House Years,* pp. 25–32. Kissinger goes into
great detail on how Nixon and Rogers did not get along.

34. Zbigniew Brzezinski, *Power and Principle: Memoirs of the National
Security Adviser, 1977–1981,* pp. 29–30 and 36–44; Cyrus Vance, *Hard
Choices,* pp. 35–37.

35. Bator's description. See interview with Bator; Testimony, Bator before
U.S. Congress, *U.S. Foreign Economic Policy,* pp. 107–121, 126–137.

36. Schott and Hamilton, *People, Positions, and Power,* provide an excellent example of Johnson's testing-but-deferential style in Ch. 3, pp. 45–46.
"Katzenbach remembered one incident clearly. He had gone to the White
House with an executive order putting Hubert Humphrey in charge of a
number of civil rights matters and presented the order to Johnson for signature. Johnson 'stuck his face right in my face and said "this doesn't make
any sense whatsoever"; "it's a terrible idea"; "it's not going to work"; "you
can't give me any good reasons why you should do this!" And I said, "yes I
can. I can give you three good reasons why I should do it." When I told him
the three reasons, he turned around, went over and signed the executive
order, and handed it back to me. He did that on two or three occasions.'"

37. Johnson's interest in the Mekong Delta project was initiated during a
meeting with George Woods, president of the World Bank during the first
weeks of Johnson's presidency. See Vaughn Davis Bornet, *The Presidency of
Lyndon B. Johnson,* p. 24.

38. Luigi Einaudi. *Peruvian Military Relations with the United States,*
P4389, pp. 34–35; Charles T. Goodsell, "The Politics of Direct Investment,"
in Luigi Einaudi, ed., *Latin America in the 1970's.*

39. Alfred Stepan, *The Military in Politics: Changing Patterns in Brazil.*

40. Joyce Carol Townsend, *Bureaucratic Politics in American Decision
Making: Impact on Brazil,* claims to prove American encouragement and
connivance, but does not. See Stepan, *The Military in Politics,* for a different view.

41. Vernon A. Walters, *Silent Missions.* In particular pp. 378 and 385 address Walters's recollection of the events preceding the coup.

42. This was George Ball's impression. George W. Ball, *The Past Has Another Pattern: Memoirs,* pp. 326–331. The declassified NSC files on the

Dominican intervention contain several FBI reports on the presence and movement of persons identified by the FBI as communists. The FBI's assigned task in Santo Domingo, it appears, was to identify, track, and report on communists. The reports lack any political analysis.

43. William B. Quandt, *Decade of Decisions: American Policy Towards the Arab-Israeli Conflict 1967–1976*, p. 53.

44. *Department of State Bulletin*, 30 May 1966, p. 855.

45. *Department of State Bulletin*, 24 October 1966, p. 824.

46. Dan Caldwell, *American-Soviet Relations from 1947 to the Nixon-Kissinger Grand Design*, pp. 65–66.

47. Karen Dawisha, *Eastern Europe, Gorbachev and Reform: The Great Challenge*, p. 25.

48. George McT. Kahin, *Intervention: How America Became Involved in Vietnam*, p. 431.

49. McGeorge Bundy to President, 27 January 1965, "Basic Policy in Vietnam," NSC History—Troop Deployment, NSF, LBJ Library. Unless otherwise stated, Bundy is McGeorge Bundy.

50. Rowland T. Berthoff, "Taft and MacArthur, 1900–1901: A Study in Civil-Military Relations," *World Politics* 5:2 (January 1953): 196–213.

51. VanDeMark, *Into the Quagmire*, pp. 205, 207.

52. Quoting Taylor, "The Senior Interdepartmental Group," *State Department Administrative History*, vol. 1, Ch. 2, pt. B, LBJ Library.

53. John W. Evans, *The Kennedy Round in American Trade Policy: The Twilight of the GATT?*, p. 156.

54. Ibid.

55. Interview with Bator; Testimony, Bator before U.S. Congress, *U.S. Foreign Economic Policy*, pp. 107–121; Anderson and Hazleton, *Managing Macroeconomic Policy*, especially Chs. 2, 6, and 7.

56. Humphrey, "Tuesday Lunch," p. 90.

2. The Larger Vision of Foreign Policy Management

1. Dorwin Cartwright, "Influence, Leadership, Control," Ch. 1 in James G. March (ed.), *Handbook of Organizations*, pp. 19–20.

2. Robert O. Keohane, *After Hegemony: Cooperation and Discord in the World Political Economy*.

3. Committee on Foreign Affairs Personnel (Herter Committee), *Personnel for the New Diplomacy*.

4. For a thorough examination of considerations that went into this law, see Harold Stein's standard-setting case study: "The Foreign Service Act of 1946," CPAC #9.

5. I. M. Destler's fine study is still a handy critique of this phenomenon. Destler, *Presidents, Bureaucrats and Foreign Policy*, esp. Chs. 1 and 2.

6. For a definition of SOPs see Graham T. Allison, *Essence of Decision: Explaining the Cuban Missile Crisis*, p. 83; and Richard M. Cyert and James G. March, *A Behavioral Theory of the Firm*, pp. 101–112.

7. Keohane, *After Hegemony*, Ch. 4.

8. Nelson Polsby's life histories of policy innovations in *Political Innovation in America: the Politics of Policy Initiation* go far to dispel the illusion of the single inventor.

9. Kennan himself has acknowledged that the prominence accorded his "telegraphic dissertation from Moscow" was due in part to timing. With much exaggeration, he has written: "Six months earlier this message would probably have been received in the Department of State with raised eyebrows and lips pursed in disapproval. Six months later, it would probably have sounded redundant, a sort of preaching to the convinced." See his book, *Memoirs 1925–1950*, p. 295.

10. Mr. X, "The Sources of Soviet Conduct," *Foreign Affairs* 25:4 (July 1947): 566–582. Excerpts from the telegrams Kennan has published in his *Memoirs*, pp. 547–559.

11. Kennan, *Memoirs*, p. 364.

12. Ibid., pp. 359–364.

13. Ibid., pp. 408–409.

14. Ibid., pp. 410ff.

15. George F. Kennan, "America's Administrative Response to Its World Problems," *Daedalus* 87:1 (Spring 1958): 13.

16. Hans J. Morgenthau's views during this period about the importance of diplomacy in the maintenance of power fit well Kennan's view of political containment. See Morgenthau's *In Defense of the National Interest: A Critical Examination of American Foreign Policy*, pp. 232–237. Morgenthau had been skeptical of the Marshall Plan and all that followed, preferring to rely on diplomacy—and therefore on strong diplomatic leadership. Kennan had supported the Marshall Plan (indeed, helped to invent it), but became a skeptic of the immediate next step in Europe, the Mutual Defense Assistance Program and NATO.

17. As quoted in John Lewis Gaddis, *Strategies of Containment: A Critical Appraisal of Postwar American National Security Policy*, p. 28.

18. Paul Y. Hammond, "NSC-68: Prologue to Rearmament," in Warner R. Schilling, Paul Y. Hammond, and Glenn H. Snyder, *Strategy, Politics, and Defense Budgets*, pp. 333–336; Gaddis, *Strategies*, pp. 93–94.

19. *Public Papers of the Presidents: Lyndon B. Johnson, 1963–1964*, p. 875; Gaddis, *Strategies*, pp. 204, 227.

20. Kennan, *Memoirs*, pp. 413–414. [Emphasis added.] In another context, Kennan opposed summit diplomacy. Negotiations between heads of state could be dangerous. In his view, negotiations should be insulated from politics and conducted by skilled professionals who could be expected to set reasonable objectives and produce agreements that were not subject to misunderstanding. "Below the Summit," Letter to the Editor, *Time*, 23 June 1958, pp. 2–4.

21. Graham Allison and Peter Szanton, *Remaking Foreign Policy: The Organizational Connection*, p. 471. For earlier statements to this effect, see H. Bradford Westerfield, *Foreign Policy and Party Politics: From Pearl Har-*

bor to Korea, pp. 8 ff.; Holbert N. Carroll, *The House of Representatives and Foreign Affairs*, pp. v, 1–24.

22. Kennan's preference for statesmen did not include presidents. He had been appalled with Roosevelt's cavalier approach to wartime diplomacy. Paul Y. Hammond, "Directives for the Occupation of Germany: The Washington Story," in Harold Stein (ed.), *American Civil-Military Decisions*, p. 338. For a full treatment of Kennan see David Mayers, *George Kennan and the Dilemmas of US Foreign Policy*.

23. Essay No. 63, *The Federalist*, p. 420.

24. The constancies of military programs have been a subject of extensive, mostly hostile, comment. They are not demonstrable by annual budgets, which are, in terms of military capabilities, only statements about annual purchases of hardware, annual investments, and annual operating costs. Counting weapons overcomes some of these problems, but introduces others. The Commission on Integrated Long-Term Strategy, *Discriminate Deterrence*, drew comparisons between Soviet and U.S. force capabilities by describing weapons in terms of inventories, i.e., in terms which take account of age, modernity, and useful life.

25. Aaron Wildavsky, "The Two Presidencies," Ch. 19 of Wildavsky (ed.), *Perspectives on the Presidency*, p. 449.

26. Donald A. Peppers has summarized these developments in "The Two Presidencies: Eight Years Later," Ch. 20 in Wildavsky, *Perspectives*.

27. Richard E. Neustadt, "The Constraining of the President," *The New York Times Magazine* (14 October 1973), reprinted as Ch. 18 in Wildavsky (ed.), *Perspectives*.

28. Eisenhower averaged a 64 percent approval rating from 1953 to 1961, better than any postwar president except Kennedy (who did not live to suffer an end-of-term slump), and Reagan, who left office with an extraordinary 68 percent approval rating. Greenstein, *The Hidden-Hand Presidency*, p. 4. A convenient compilation of Eisenhower popularity data can be found in George H. Gallup, *The Gallup Poll: Public Opinion, 1935–1971*, vols. 2 and 3. I have discussed the decline of public confidence in the Eisenhower administration after *Sputnik* (4 October 1957), in my *Cold War and Detente*, pp. 109–117.

29. In a January 1957 Gallup Poll, Eisenhower received a 79 percent approval rating. In the first poll after *Sputnik* (October 1957), his approval rating was 57 percent. American Institute of Public Opinion, as compiled in *Public Opinion Quarterly* 25 : 1 (Spring 1961): 136; Hammond, *Cold War and Detente*, pp. 110–116. Several factors would suggest that this judgment about Eisenhower was wrong, or at least much exaggerated. The most obvious was the groundless charge that the Eisenhower administration permitted an adverse "missile gap" to develop.

30. I have summarized this phenomenon in my *Cold War and Detente*, pp. 110–117.

31. Neustadt, *Presidential Power: The Politics of Leadership* (1960), pp. 33–34.

32. Ronald Reagan's Congress-bashing, which was a skilled political tactic, exploited cases where the president lost to the Congress. It is difficult to fathom Reagan—how much he calculated his actions, his Congress-bashing in particular. One might hazard the guess that he, more than any other modern president, wanted to lose.

33. The best demonstration of this point is Congress's record of failing to challenge the president under the War Powers Resolution of 1973. President Ford's *Mayaguez* rescue operation in 1975, President Carter's attempt to rescue the hostages in Iran in 1980, President Reagan's invasion of Grenada in 1983, his attack of Libya in 1986, and his deployment of U.S. warships to protect shipping in the Persian Gulf in 1987 all involved military actions which were not accompanied by all the required consultations with the Congress provided by the act. See Gordon L. Crovitz and Jeremy A. Rabkin (eds.), *The Fettered Presidency: Legal Constraints on the Executive Branch;* Gordon S. Jones and John A. Marini (eds.), *The Imperial Congress: Crisis in the Separation of Powers.* "Although Presidents have rivals for power in foreign affairs, the rivals do not usually succeed. Presidents prevail not only because they may have superior resources but because their potential opponents are weak, divided, or believe that they should not control foreign policy." Wildavsky, "The Two Presidencies," reprinted in Wildavsky (ed.), *Perspectives,* p. 234.

34. Kennan was concerned at times about the reckless use of American power but had little enthusiasm for either vision. The political president, the first vision, was too much inclined to play the political hero, mobilizing public support for his foreign policy commitments by simplifying the international situation, usually at the expense of the Soviet Union, generating interest and expectations that were bound to be troublesome. The second vision, the internationalist vision of America entangled, could be taken as a consequence of the first, of steering public support into programs that Kennan did not approve of. He worried, rightly, that the vision of American power constrained by entanglement was intended to become American strength augmented by alliance and by political and military mobilization.

35. Robert E. Osgood, *NATO: The Entangling Alliance,* p. 347.

36. See Allison, *Essence of Decision,* p. 170.

37. The normal may be quite dynamic—in part because of the effects of outside forces. John Zysman, in his *Political Strategies for Industrial Order: State, Market, and Industry in France,* p. 170, states it thus: "Since many of the conflicts inside an organization will be settled in the political arena outside, and the rules imposed on the organization by the state, *the institutionalization of the political struggles of the past, the establishment of particular values in the forms of rules and procedures in organizations, can contribute to the formation of the typical behaviors of a culture.* Thus, routine behavior in an organization can be seen in part as political process outside the organization as well as inside it, and thus it may be considered both as a product of the members' active manipulation of their environment and a result of their passive accommodation to it."

38. One might define presidential power as the range of the president's choice, but the definition avoids one of the main issues explored in this study, what might be called the Atlas dilemma. Atlas was powerful, by one account, but powerless to choose another course, once he was burdened with carrying the world. There will be a particular concern in the chapters that follow with the problem of a powerful nation losing its options, and therefore, in a certain way, its power. An important subsidiary problem concerns delegation, on the one hand, and my special use of the term *heroic,* on the other. Presidential power may be well or badly exercised by delegating. It may also be well or badly exercised by the president's playing the executive hero and not delegating.

Attempts to define effective power lead quickly to complications. The range of choice in a given decision task may exclude option X because to choose it—maybe even to be seen considering it—would weaken another official whose performance one counts on, or undermine the confidence of a client or ally. Some of these issues are explored in Alexander L. George, "The Case for Multiple Advocacy in Making Foreign Policy," *The American Political Science Review* 66:3 (September 1972): 751–785; I. M. Destler, "Comment: Multiple Advocacy: Some 'Limits and Costs,'" pp. 786–790; and George, "Rejoinder to 'Comment' by I. M. Destler," pp. 791–795.

39. According to Stephen D. Krasner in Krasner (ed.), *International Regimes,* p. 2: "Regimes can be defined as sets of implicit or explicit principles, norms, rules, and decision-making procedures around which actors' expectations converge in a given area of international relations. Principles are beliefs of fact, causation, and rectitude. Norms are standards of behavior defined in terms of rights and obligations. Rules are specific prescriptions or proscriptions for action. Decision-making procedures are prevailing practices for making and implementing collective choice."

". . . Keohane and Nye [Robert O. Keohane and Joseph S. Nye, *Power and Interdependence,* p. 19.] . . . define regimes as a 'set of governing arrangements' that include 'networks of rules, norms, and procedures that regularize behavior and control its effects.'"

40. The congressional side of that burden is described in Westerfield, *Foreign Policy and Party Politics,* Chs. 13 and 14. See also Bauer, Pool, and Dexter, *American Business and Public Policy.* An early reference to the constituency problem—to concessions made in Congress to gain support for foreign economic aid programs—can be found in William A. Brown, Jr., and Redvers Opie, *American Foreign Assistance,* pp. 563–569.

41. For the observation of the British ambassador to Washington concerning British reactions at the time of the Skybolt cancellation in 1962 to American governmental processes, see Lord Harlech, "Suez SNAFU, Skybolt SABU," *Foreign Policy* 2 (Spring 1971), especially p. 50.

42. Sen. Mansfield, judging by his behavior, as demonstrated in Phil Williams's excellent account, *The Senate and US Troops in Europe.* He understood very well the difference between his role as a senator sponsoring threats against NATO and the role of the president were he to do the same.

Johnson did not demonstrate the same regard for this role differentiation. At least in the records available to this author, he never made the point that Mansfield's toughness made it easier for him to be more conciliatory.

Sen. Sam Nunn opposed the Mansfield amendments in the seventies. In the early 1980s, "with Mansfield gone, he took over the tough role, sponsoring Nunn amendments." It was the 1984 Amendment to the FY '85 DOD Authorization Bill. It provided for the withdrawal of U.S. troops stationed in Europe if European NATO members did not make a sufficient (but unspecified) commitment to NATO themselves. Nunn's staff has indicated that Nunn did not want the Nunn amendment to pass the Senate and had to take steps—needless to say, unpublicized steps—to assure that it did not.

43. Destler, "Comment: Multiple Advocacy: Some 'Limits and Costs,'" p. 788. Italics in original.

44. Ibid.; Kennan, "America's Administrative Response to Its World Problems," as reprinted in Jackson Subcommittee, U.S. Senate, *Organizing for National Security*, vol. 2, p. 233; Allison, *Essence of Decision*, p. 146.

45. David Braybrooke and Charles E. Lindblom, *A Strategy of Decision: Policy Evaluation as a Social Process.*

3. The Indian Famine and Presidential Leverage

1. Interview with Orville L. Freeman, 10 May 1990.

2. James W. Bjorkman, "Public Law 480 and the Policies of Self-Help and Short-Tether: Indo-American Relations, 1965–68," in Commission on the Organization of the Government for the Conduct of Foreign Policy, *Appendices*, vol. 7, p. 203. Hereafter these volumes will be called Murphy Commission *Appendices.*

3. Freeman interview.

4. Robert A. Packenham, *Liberal America and the Third World: Political Development Ideas in Foreign Aid and Social Science*, esp. Ch. 3.

5. M. F. Millikan and W. W. Rostow et al., *Foreign Aid: A Proposal*, illustrates the significance of long-range, performance-contingent aid.

6. Bjorkman, in Murphy Commission *Appendices*, p. 203; Schott and Hamilton, *People, Positions, and Power*, pp. 54–57.

7. Bjorkman, in Murphy Commission *Appendices*, p. 203.

8. Orville Freeman, *World without Hunger.*

9. Randall B. Ripley, "Interagency Committees and Incrementalism: The Case of Aid to India," *Midwest Journal of Political Science* 8:2 (May 1964): 152.

10. Bjorkman, in Murphy Commission *Appendices*, p. 199. See also Schott and Hamilton, *People, Positions, and Power*, pp. 54–57, for further discussion of Freeman's relationship with Johnson.

11. Bjorkman, in Murphy Commission *Appendices*, pp. 198–200.

12. Ibid., p. 199.

13. Ibid., p. 200.

14. Ibid., p. 203.

15. Bowles reported that he introduced Freeman to the idea and implied that the two agreed on what it meant. Chester Bowles, *Promises to Keep: My Years in Public Life, 1941–1969,* p. 527. They probably did. But the circumstances in which they worked, their "bureaucratic location," moved them in quite different directions, at least until the end of 1966, when Freeman lost interest in Johnson's short leash.

16. Millikan and Rostow et al., *Foreign Aid.*

17. This is a major thesis of Packenham, *Liberal America,* esp. Chs. 1 and 2.

18. Memo, Komer to president, 22 March 1965, Box 2, Memos to the President.

19. Myron Weiner, "Assessing the Political Impact of Foreign Assistance," Ch. 3 in John W. Mellor (ed.), *India: The Rising Middle Power,* p. 59.

20. John P. Lewis, *Quiet Crisis in India: Economic Development and American Policy,* p. 263.

21. Ibid., p. 264.

22. Ibid., p. 321.

23. Ibid.

24. Stanley A. Kochanek, *The Congress Party of India: The Dynamics of One-Party Democracy,* Ch. 16; Krishan Bhatia, "India Adrift," *Foreign Affairs* 45 : 4 (July 1967): 652–662; Norman D. Palmer, "India's Fourth General Election," *Asian Survey* 7 : 5 (May 1967): 275–291; Francine Frankel, *India's Political Economy, 1947–1977,* Ch. 8.

25. A reliable if brief account can be found in Nandan Deviki Presad, *Food for Peace: The Story of the U.S. Food Assistance to India,* pp. 88–89.

26. Bjorkman, in Murphy Commission *Appendices,* p. 204.

27. Presad, *Food for Peace,* p. 89n, cites Bowles's 21 July 1964 letter to Freeman in Bowles papers, Sterling Library, Yale.

28. Bjorkman, in Murphy Commission *Appendices,* p. 204.

29. Johnson's marginalia on the Memo, Komer to president, 23 April 1965.

30. Memo, Bundy to president, 30 March 1965, Box 2, Memos to the President.

31. Interview with McGeorge Bundy, 1 November 1984.

32. See, e.g., Memo, Bundy to president, 30 March 1965, and Memo, Komer to president, 25 May 1965, Memos to the President.

33. Ibid.

34. They made almost daily inquiries at State and AID, for instance. See Memo, "Chronology of Major Indian Approaches on the P.L. 480 Agreement," 21 April 1965, National Security Files (NSF), LBJ Library.

35. Memo, Komer to Cook, 3 July 1965, "Indian Famine Background: Tabs 1-1B," National Security Council (NSC) History.

36. Memo, Bundy and Komer to president, subject: India and Pakistan, 5 October 1965, "Indian Famine Background," NSC History.

37. Memo, Bundy to president, 22 October 1965, "The Indian Food Pipeline," NSC History.

38. Lloyd I. Rudolph and Susanne H. Rudolph, "Summary Report," in Murphy Commission *Appendices*, vol. 7, p. 112 ff. This valuable study has also been published as Rudolph, Rudolph, et al., *The Regional Imperative: The Administration of U.S. Foreign Policy towards South Asian States under Presidents Johnson and Nixon*, p. 31 ff.

39. Letter, Komer to Cook, 3 June 1965. Italics added.

40. The following account about the World Bank is based on I. P. M. Cargill, "Efforts to Influence Performance: Case Study of India," Ch. 5 in John P. Lewis and Ishan Kapur (eds.), *The World Bank Group, Multilateral Aid, and the 1970s*, pp. 89–109, and on confidential interviews conducted by members of the Murphy Commission staff.

41. George Rosen, *Democracy and Economic Change in India*, p. 290. See also James G. March and Herbert A. Simon, *Organizations*, on distinction between persuading on merits and persuading by authoritative or political means.

42. e.g., see Fenno, *The President's Cabinet*.

43. Interview with Bundy.

44. Memo, Freeman to president, "India—Food and Agriculture," 1 December 1965, Indian Famine File.

45. Ibid.

46. Ibid.

47. Department of State (DOS) telegram no. 976 to American Embassy, New Delhi, 2 December 1965, Indian Famine File.

48. Embassy New Delhi telegram 1430 to DOS, 6 December 1965, Indian Famine File.

49. Memo, Freeman to president, "Talks with the Indian Minister of Food and Agriculture," 23 December 1965, Indian Famine File.

50. Ibid.

51. Ibid.

52. Comparable State Department documentation had at that time envisaged no significant role for the president and likewise did not state one for Shastri. Consistent with normal handling of economic and security assistance, relations between the two governments, even on the occasion of a state visit, were to be kept in working channels where they had become routinized. It was a position that accepted and reinforced the status quo in Indo-American relations, one that depended on the mutual accommodation between career officials of the U.S. government and their counterparts in India with the expectation that relations between the two governments would continue much as before.

53. "Visit of Prime Minister Indira Gandhi . . . Background Paper, Indian Food Situation," 16 March 1966, Indian Famine File.

54. Ibid.

55. Ibid.

56. Memo, Freeman to president, 4 January 1966, "Indian Famine, Background: Tab 2," NSC History.

57. Ibid.

58. "Visit of Prime Minister Indira Gandhi . . . Strategy Paper," undated, pp. 5–6 (underlining in original), Indian Famine File.

59. "Strategy Paper," p. 7, underlining in original.

60. Ibid.

61. "Background Paper, Indian Food Situation," 16 March 1966, p. 3.

62. "Emergency Food Aid Program to India," Message to Congress, 30 March 1966, in *Public Papers of the Presidents of the United States: Lyndon B. Johnson, 1966*, p. 367.

63. Freeman to president, 4 January 1966: "In the absence of further action there will be a gap in arrivals during April until whatever amount of grain the President sees fit to make available following Shastri's visit has been dispatched and reached India."

64. Memo, Rusk to president, "The Economic Bargain with Mrs. Gandhi," 23 March 1966, Country File, NSF, LBJ Library.

65. Mitchell B. Wallerstein, *Food for War—Food for Peace: United States Aid in a Global Context*, p. 192.

66. Interview with Harold Saunders, 26 November 1984.

67. Memo, Bromley Smith to president, 24 August 1966 [attached to Aug. 22 recommendation on PL 480 allotments for India and Pakistan, 22 August 1966], Indian Famine File.

68. W. W. Rostow, "Memorandum of Conversation . . . World Bank Assessment of Indian Agricultural Performance," 14 November 1966, LBJ Library.

69. Bhatia, "India Adrift," pp. 652–667; Palmer, "India's Fourth General Election," pp. 275–291; Frankel, *India's Political Economy, 1947–1977*; R. S. Chavan, *Nationalism in Asia*.

70. e.g., see Susanne Hoeber Rudolph, "The Writ from Delhi: The Indian Government's Capabilities after the 1971 Election," *Asian Survey* 11:10 (October 1971): 958–969.

71. Rudolph, Rudolph, et al., *Regional Imperative*, pp. 13–18.

72. I have examined this phenomenon at some length in two technical reports and a book. Paul Y. Hammond, *Foreign Military Access and Advice: Some MAAG and Milgroup Options*, R-485-PR/ISA, Rand Corporation, April, 1970; Hammond, *Military Aid and Influence in Pakistan: 1954–1963*, RM-5505/1-ISA, Rand Corporation, June, 1971; Hammond, David J. Louscher, Michael D. Salomone, and Norman A. Graham, *The Reluctant Supplier: U.S. Decisionmaking for Arms Sales*, Ch. 8.

73. See March and Simon, *Organizations*, pp. 129–134, for a general description of this characteristic form of organizational behavior.

74. Woodrow Wilson, "The Study of Administration," reprinted in *Political Science Quarterly* 56:4 (December 1941): 481–506.

75. Jawaharlal Nehru was also first in a ruling dynasty. India's third and fourth premiers were, respectively, his daughter and grandson.

76. John W. Mellor, "The Indian Economy," in Mellor (ed.), *India: A Rising Middle Power*, p. 94.

77. Arnold L. Wolfers and Lawrence I. Martin, *The Anglo-American Tradition in Foreign Affairs*, pp. xx–xxiii.

78. Mellor (ed.), *India: A Rising Middle Power*, pp. 92, 94.

79. Myron Weiner, "Assessing the Political Impact of Foreign Assistance," Ch. 3 of Mellor (ed.), *India: A Rising Middle Power*, p. 50.

80. They were scarcely the sorts of choices that were used in China and the Soviet Union in the twenties, China in the late 1940s, or Ethiopia or the Sudan in the 1980s, when famine was used as a means of political coercion. The author is unaware of any evidence that Indian policy approached such use of food shortages, or that American officials suspected this to be the case.

81. Eric von Hipple, *The Sources of Innovation*, esp. Chs. 1 and 2.

82. Memo, Charles J. Zwick to Walt Rostow, "Effect of P. L. 480 Sales on Domestic Wheat Prices," 1 September 1966, "Indian Famine," NSC History.

83. Mellor, "The Indian Economy," in Mellor (ed.), *India: A Rising Middle Power*, pp. 92, 102.

84. Mellor (ed.), *India: A Rising Middle Power*, p. 104.

85. Rudolphs, "Summary Report," in Murphy Commission *Appendices*.

86. Herbert A. Simon, *Models of Man: Social and Rational*, pp. 204 ff. and 263 ff.; March and Simon, *Organizations*, pp. 48 ff. and 140 ff.

87. Morgenthau, *In Defense of the National Interest*, pp. 232–237.

88. Neustadt, *Alliance Politics*, pp. 133–135.

89. Memo, Wriggens to Bowles, 12 November 1966, Indian Famine File.

90. Ibid.

91. Interview with Howard Wriggens, 31 October 1984.

92. Memo, Wriggins and Saunders to Rostow, 26 September 1966, and Memo, Rostow to the president, "New Indian PL 480 Agreement," 26 September 1966, Indian Famine File.

93. "Terms of Reference," 12 November 1966, Indian Famine File.

94. Cyert and March, *A Behavioral Theory of the Firm*, pp. 120–122.

4. Johnson and Europe: The MLF and Alliance Politics

1. Memo, Bundy to president, 11 February 1964, Document 28+, "5/1–27/64" folder, Memos to the President.

2. Memo, Bundy to president, 14 July 1964, "7/1–9/30, 1964" folder, Memos to the President.

3. Ibid.

4. Memo, Bundy to president, 6 December 1963, "McGeorge Bundy, 11/63–2/64" folder, Box 1, Memos to the President.

5. Steinbruner identifies them as Robert Bowie, Admiral John Lee, Livingston Merchant, Henry Owen, Robert Schaetzel, and Gerard Smith, with Walt Rostow and Under Secretary George Ball lending support. Steinbruner, *Cybernetic Theory*, pp. 223, 249–255. One could add to this list at least Thomas K. Finletter, the U.S. ambassador to NATO.

6. Memo, Bundy to president, 6 December 1963, "11/63–2/64" folder, Memos to the President.

7. *New York Times*, 30 December 1963.

8. John F. Kennedy, "Memorandum for the Members of the MLF Negotiating Delegation," 21 February 1963, Multilateral Force, General, NSF Subject File, LBJ Library.

9. Memo, Bundy to president, 15 June 1963, Document 58n, "10/1–12/31/64" folder, Memos to the President.

10. Ibid.

11. Ibid.

12. Interview with Bundy.

13. Memo, Bundy to the president, 6 December 1964, Document 58, "10/1–12/31/64" folder, Memos to the President.

14. I depart from Steinbruner (*Cybernetic Theory*, pp. 279–282) here. He attributes a more positive position to Kennedy and then, following Geyelin and his own interview material, dates the Bundy memorandum after the trip. (It was not available when Steinbruner wrote.)

15. Steinbruner, *Cybernetic Theory*, p. 281.

16. Ibid., pp. 281–282.

17. Ibid., p. 281.

18. Memo, "The Coming Crisis on the MLF," by Alastair Buchan, 23 June 1964, "Multilateral Force, General—Vol. 2" folder, Subject File, National Security Files (NSF), LBJ Library.

19. *New York Times*, 27 November 1964.

20. Steinbruner, *Cybernetic Theory*, p. 288. This account depends heavily on Steinbruner, to a lesser extent on Philip Geyelin, *Lyndon B. Johnson and the World*, esp. p. 160.

21. Catherine McA. Kelleher, *Germany and the Politics of Nuclear Weapons*, pp. 237–238. For the German side of the MLF story I have relied heavily on Chapters 9 and 10 of this work.

22. *Public Papers of the Presidents of the United States: Lyndon B. Johnson, 1963–64*, p. 772.

23. Memo, "The Coming Crisis on the MLF," 23 June 1964, "Multilateral Force, General—Vol. 2" folder, Subject File, NSF, LBJ Library.

24. Memo, "The British Labour Party and the MLF," prepared by Richard E. Neustadt, 6 July 1964, "Multilateral Force, General—Vol. 2" folder, Subject File, NSF, LBJ Library. This document leaked to the press. For the general reader it is most readily available in Halperin and Kanter (eds.), *Readings in American Foreign Policy*, pp. 419–430. "Cabal," according to Neustadt, was a term used by the British to identify Rostow, Owen, Schaetzel, and Bowie. Their positions "were identified and classified in London." He did not mention Merchant, or Gerard Smith, who meanwhile had replaced Merchant as head of the special MLF office.

25. Neustadt memo, "The British Labour Party."

26. Memo, Thomas L. Hughes to Rusk, 7 October 1964, "Multilateral Force, General—Vol. 2" folder, Subject File, NSF, LBJ Library. Steinbruner's

interviews, at least as he reports on the Grewe mission, discussed below, missed these preparations. Steinbruner, *Cybernetic Theory*, pp. 289–291.

27. David N. Schwartz, *NATO's Nuclear Dilemmas*, p. 117; see also Kelleher, *Germany and the Politics of Nuclear Weapons*, pp. 248–251.

28. Letter, Schroeder to Rusk, 30 September 1964, "Multilateral Force, General—Vol. 2" folder, Subject File, NSF, LBJ Library.

29. Memo, Hughes to Rusk, 7 October 1964, "Multilateral Force, General—Vol. 2" folder, Subject File, NSF, LBJ Library.

30. Steinbruner's account is slightly different. *Cybernetic Theory*, pp. 290–291; *New York Times*, 9 October 1964.

31. Steinbruner and Kelleher, who both drew on private sources—interviews and correspondence—substantially agree in claiming that Erhard's disclosure of the purpose of the Grewe mission was premature and unintentional—a slip. Steinbruner, *Cybernetic Theory*, p. 290; Kelleher, *Germany and the Politics of Nuclear Weapons*, pp. 248–249.

32. It was not the first time that Finletter had sent an ill-informed European to the White House to talk about the MLF. He pressed the Secretary General of NATO, Dirk U. Stikker, into similar service. Robert S. Jordan, *Political Leadership in NATO: A Study in Multinational Diplomacy*, pp. 149–150.

33. There is suggestive but not definitive evidence that no major players at this juncture worried, as they should have, about how German Gaullists, including Erhard's own Christian Democratic colleagues, would take an American rejection of a German-American MLF. White House files examined by the author, which document Bundy's engineering of the withdrawal of support by Johnson fairly well, in part on an assessment that Erhard's own party was divided over the MLF, disclose no concern over this point. Rusk, in repudiating a two-power MLF, made no effort publicly to cope with Erhard's exposure to Gaullist criticism. Indirect evidence further indicates that Erhard's vulnerability to nationalist attacks over the Grewe mission was not taken seriously in Bonn either. Even Steinbruner, who refers to the Gaullist-Atlanticist split, and Kelleher, who deals with it authoritatively, fail to mention this consideration. Evidently it was a matter of remarkably little concern in Washington or Bonn at the time.

34. Kelleher, *Germany and the Politics of Nuclear Weapons*, p. 248.

35. Evidently Finletter talked about the bilateral option with British and Italian diplomats under circumstances that suggest this to have been the intent. Memo, "MLF," David Klein to Bundy, 20 October 1964, in "Multilateral Force, General—Vol. 2" folder, Subject File, NSF, LBJ Library.

36. Klein informed Bundy on October 20: ". . . a German correspondent, Hans Meyer, called me this morning to say that the Washington correspondent of *Die Welt*—having first written the story about the "fiasco" of the Grewe visit—was called in by Henry Owen and told the U.S. intends to move ahead with the MLF on the agreed schedule with or without the British. The British have no choice—they must either knuckle under or watch the MLF go on without them." Ibid.

37. Ibid. Also, Schwartz, *NATO's Nuclear Dilemmas*, pp. 119–120; Kelleher, *Germany and the Politics of Nuclear Weapons*, pp. 250–254.

38. Steinbruner, *Cybernetic Theory*, p. 292.

39. Memo, David Klein to Bundy, 10 October 1964, "Multilateral Force, General—Vol. 2" folder, Subject File, NSF, LBJ Library.

40. Neustadt memo, "The British Labour Party."

41. Memo, George W. Ball to president, 5 December 1964, "McGeorge Bundy, 10/1–12/31/64" folder, Box 2, Memos to the President.

42. Steinbruner, *Cybernetic Theory*, p. 293.

43. George, *Presidential Decisionmaking in Foreign Policy*, pp. 122–127, 192–193, 196–200; Hall, "The 'Custodian-Manager' of the Policymaking Process" in Murphy Commission *Appendices*, vol. 2, pp. 109–110.

44. Steinbruner, *Cybernetic Theory*, pp. 292–294.

45. "Summary of Discussion on MLF, Atlantic Defense and Related Matters," 31 October 1964, MLF General File, vol. 2, NSF, LBJ Library. The rapporteur was Benjamin H. Read, Executive Secretary of the Department of State.

46. Ibid.

47. NSAM 318, 14 November 1964, Document 87, "10/1–12/31/64" folder, Memos to the President.

48. Howard Margolis, "Notes on the MLF," *Bulletin of the Atomic Scientists*, November 1964, p. 30.

49. Memo, Klein to Bundy, 10 October 1964, "Multilateral Force," p. 4.

50. The document, in addition to being classified top secret, was marked "Sensitive—Personal—Literally Eyes Only."

51. Memo, Bundy to Rusk, McNamara, and Ball, 25 November 1964, "McGeorge Bundy, 10/1–12/31/64" folder, Box 2, Memos to the President.

52. Memo, Bundy to president, 27 November 1964, "McGeorge Bundy, 10/1–12/31/64" folder, Box 2, Memos to the President.

53. "Remarks at the 175th Anniversary Convocation of Georgetown University" (3 December 1964), in *Public Papers of the Presidents of the United States: Lyndon B. Johnson, 1963–64*, pp. 1632–1635.

54. Memo, Bundy to president, 3 December 1964, "McGeorge Bundy, 10/1–12/31/64" folder, Box 2, Memos to the President.

55. Ibid.

56. Cable, Ball to Bundy, 10 December 1964, "McGeorge Bundy, 10/1–12/31/64" folder, Box 2, Memos to the President.

57. Steinbruner, *Cybernetic Theory*, p. 297.

58. Memo, Ball to president, 5 December 1964, "McGeorge Bundy, 10/1–12/31/64" folder, Box 2, Memos to the President. The MLF office had drafted an elaborate new proposal that failed to surface. Steinbruner, *Cybernetic Theory*, pp. 301–302. Neustadt assured Bundy that he had a definite hand in the preparation of the Ball report. Memo, Richard Neustadt to Bundy, 7 November 1964, "Multilateral Force, General—Vol. 2" folder, Subject File, NSF, LBJ Library.

59. Steinbruner, who had the benefit of extensive interviewing with un-

named officials in the early 1970s, plus assurance from these interviewees that Geyelin's account, based on contemporary interviews, was accurate, parallels Bundy's memorandum: He noted the vehement opposition of the French, the embarrassment of the Italians, the cross-pressure on Erhard, and concluded that "he could not present the proposal to Congress as a necessary response to European pressure." Steinbruner, *Cybernetic Theory,* pp. 305, 305 n.

60. Ibid., pp. 304–306.

61. Memo, Klein to Bundy, 30 November 1964, probably in Multilateral Force, NSF Subject File, LBJ Library.

62. Memo, Bundy to president, 6 December 1964, "McGeorge Bundy, 10/1–12/31/64" folder, Box 2, Memos to the President.

63. At least one other group was listed, but it has been deleted from this version of the document.

64. Memo, Bundy to president, 6 December 1964, "McGeorge Bundy, 10/1–12/31/64" folder, Box 2, Memos to the President.

65. Steinbruner, *Cybernetic Theory,* p. 306.

66. Memo, Klein to Bundy, 10 October 1964, "Multilateral Force, General—Vol. 2" folder, Subject File, NSF, LBJ Library.

67. Very likely they had examined these costs when they met the previous weekend to consider Bundy's "sink out of sight" memorandum. Steinbruner relates that "American prestige and alliance leadership had been placed on the line, they argued, and the President could not back down without suffering consequences. Wilson was expecting to have to concede on the surface ships and would be surprised if he were let off the hook. They warned that there would be a resurgence of support for a land-based MRBM system to meet the officially established NATO requirement." Steinbruner, *Cybernetic Theory,* p. 307. It may be that Steinbruner's account reflects Johnson's moving more abruptly toward the exit than either Bundy, McNamara, or Rusk had anticipated. The nonpromoters to whom Bundy listened, at least his staffer David Klein, and Neustadt, and possibly moderates like Tyler in the State Department, were more revisionists than rejectionists. While Bundy's closely-held memorandum to McNamara and Rusk of November 25, for instance, took a back-away position, it is doubtful that he considered this position as entirely rejecting the MLF.

68. Steinbruner, *Cybernetic Theory,* p. 307.

69. Geyelin, *Lyndon B. Johnson and the World,* p. 162.

70. Steinbruner, *Cybernetic Theory,* p. 308.

71. Memo, Richard M. Moose to Rusk, 14 December 1964, and "U.S. Comments on the UK Proposal of a Project for an Atlantic Nuclear Force," 8 December 1964, "Multilateral Force, General—Vol. 3" folder, Subject File, NSF, LBJ Library.

72. Steinbruner, *Cybernetic Theory,* p. 309.

73. Geyelin, *Lyndon B. Johnson and the World,* pp. 174–175.

74. Memo, Bundy to president, 2 February 1965, "1/1–2/28/1965" folder, Memos to the President.

75. Memo, "Review of Possible Modifications in the MLF to Take Account of West European Problems Revealed during the MLF Negotiations," 28 October 1964, "Multilateral Force, General—Vol. 2" folder, Subject File, NSF, LBJ Library. The polarization within the Department of State by this time was so extreme that any conclusion of this ilk could be suspect. While hard-core promoters were closing for the kill, Hughes (Ibid., p. v) proposed a delay of six to nine months beyond the Johnson-Erhard communique deadline of the end of 1964.

76. Telegram, Bonn Embassy to State Department, January 1965, "Multilateral Force, General—Vol. 3" folder, Subject File, NSF, LBJ Library.

77. Steinbruner, *Cybernetic Theory,* pp. 320–326.

78. Kelleher, *Germany and the Politics of Nuclear Weapons,* p. 254.

79. Harlan Cleveland, *NATO: The Trans-Atlantic Bargain,* p. 52.

80. For example, see Robert Jordan, *Political Leadership in NATO,* p. 49 and *passim.*

81. Edward L. Morse, *Foreign Policy and Interdependence in Gaullist France,* p. 108.

82. Telegram, Bohlen to Rusk, 14 December 1964, "Multinational Force, General—Vol. 2" folder, Subject File, NSF, LBJ Library.

83. Edgar S. Furniss, Jr., *De Gaulle and the French Army: A Crisis in Civil-Military Relations,* p. 301.

84. Morse, *Foreign Policy and Interdependence in Gaullist France,* pp. 174–178, 315–322; Wilford L. Kohl, *French Nuclear Diplomacy,* Ch. 9.

5. Influence, Strategy, and Western Europe

1. *Documents on American Foreign Relations, 1965,* no. 1, pp. 3–4.

2. Pierre Hassner, "Change and Security in Europe; Part I: The Background." *Adelphi Papers* 45 (February 1968): 2.

3. Ibid., p. 3.

4. Osgood, *NATO: The Entangling Alliance.*

5. Abraham Chayes, "Bureaucratic Politics and Arms Control: An Inquiry into the Workings of Arms Control Agreements," *Harvard Law Review* 85 (1972): 905–969, has developed a similar thesis in an extraordinarily one-sided application to assure an American audience that it would take Russians a great deal of detectable effort to change their arms control policies, ignoring the fact that, by the same token, it could take a great deal of effort for the United States to overcome bureaucratic inertia to respond to such a Soviet policy change.

6. John W. Kingdon, *Agendas, Alternatives, and Public Politics,* esp. pp. 17–19; Hugh Heclo, "Issue Networks and the Executive Establishment," Ch. 3 of Anthony King (ed.), *The New American Political System;* R. W. Cobb and C. D. Elder, *Participation in American Politics: The Dynamics of Agenda-Building;* Charles Levine, "Where Policy Comes from: Ideas, Innovations, and Agenda Choices," *Public Administration Review* 45:1 (January/February 1985): 255–258; Charles O. Jones, *An Introduction*

to the Study of Public Policy, 3d ed., pp. 63–74; Polsby, *Political Innovation in America,* esp. Ch. 5; Paul Charles Light, *The President's Agenda: Domestic Policy Choice from Kennedy to Carter.*

7. e.g., Thurman Arnold, *The Symbols of Government;* Murray Edelman, *The Symbolic Uses of Politics.*

8. Wilson, "The Study of Administration," *Political Science Quarterly* (June 1887).

9. P. Bachrach and M. S. Baratz, "Decisions and Non-Decisions: An Analytical Framework," *The American Political Science Review* 57:3 (September 1963): 632–642; M. A. Crenson, *The Un-Politics of Air Pollution;* Raymond E. Wolfinger, "Nondecisions and the Study of Local Politics," *American Political Science Review* 65:4 (December 1971): 1063–1080.

10. Westerfield, *Foreign Policy and Party Politics,* esp. p. 16.

11. Gen. T. R. Milton, U.S. Air Force, Ret., "Helmut Schmidt's Extreme Idea," *Air Force Magazine,* February 1986, p. 126.

12. Karl Kaiser, "Public Support for NATO—A German View," in Joseph Godson (ed.), *35 Years of NATO: A Transatlantic Symposium on the Changing Political, Economic and Military Setting,* p. 92.

13. Kaiser, "Public Support for NATO," pp. 92–93.

14. Gregory F. Treverton, *Making the Alliance Work: The United States and Western Europe,* Ch. 1.

15. Political leaders in opposition in Europe tend to advocate disengagement, then abandon it when they come to power. David S. Yost, "Alternative Structures of European Security," *International Security Studies Program, Working Papers.*

16. Aaron Wildavsky, *The Politics of the Budgetary Process,* 2d ed., pp. 15–18.

17. For a contrary view see Yost, "Alternative Structures of European Security."

18. See Keohane and Nye, *Power and Interdependence,* for the authoritative synthesis of this concept.

19. Keohane and Nye, "Transgovernmental Relations and International Organization," *World Politics* 27:1 (October 1974): 43.

20. Michael Howard, "Reassurance and Deterrence: Western Defense in the 1980s," *Foreign Affairs* 61:2 (Winter 1982/83): 310–311.

21. Yost, "Alternative Structures of European Security." Henry Kissinger provided the most striking example of this in his statement to a conference in Brussels in 1979 on the occasion of NATO's thirtieth anniversary. Kenneth Meyers, "The Future of NATO," Ch. 1 in Meyers (ed.), *NATO the Next Thirty Years: The Changing Political, Economic, and Military Setting,* p. 7.

22. For example, Meyers, "The Future of NATO," Ch. 1 in Meyers (ed.), *NATO the Next Thirty Years,* p. 7.

23. Steinbruner, *Cybernetic Theory,* p. 332.

24. Albert O. Hirschman, *Development Projects Observed;* Hirschman, "The Principle of the Hiding Hand," *The Public Interest* 6 (Winter 1967): 10–23.

25. It was Rusk's practice to withhold his advice to Johnson, as he had with Kennedy, until he could talk with the president privately. This arrangement had worked badly with Kennedy but worked well with Johnson.

26. For an accurate description of McNamara's outlook, see William W. Kaufmann, *The McNamara Strategy*, esp. Chs. 2 and 3.

27. In Washington, the flexible response viewpoint was dominated by a concern with assuring that the president had options. William Kaufmann, who presents Robert McNamara's views authoritatively, wrote: "While McNamara no doubt saw the creation of multiple options as the answer to the President's demand for a choice between humiliation and holocaust," McNamara "also regarded it as the only appropriate method of dealing with the uncertainties of the future." Kaufmann, *The McNamara Strategy*, p. 87.

28. Neustadt, *Presidential Power: The Politics of Leadership* (1960), pp. 39–46.

29. Fred C. Ikle, who played a major role in demonstrating the need for PALs, later turned his attention to war termination. See especially his *Every War Must End.*

30. Graham Allison makes this point well in *Essence of Decision*, pp. 32–33.

6. Vietnam: Normality and Innovation

1. David M. Barrett, "The Mythology Surrounding Lyndon Johnson, His Advisors, and the 1965 Decision to Escalate the Vietnam War," *Political Science Quarterly* 103:4 (Winter 1988–1989): 637.

2. Leslie H. Gelb and Richard K. Betts, *The Irony of Vietnam: The System Worked*, p. 1.

3. Johns Hopkins University address, "Peace without Conquest," 7 April 1965, in *Public Papers of the Presidents of the United States: Lyndon B. Johnson, 1965*, p. 395.

4. Rusk memorandum, 1 July 1965, contained in *The Pentagon Papers: The Defense Department History of United States Decisionmaking on Vietnam*, ("The Senator Gravel Edition") vol. 4, p. 23.

5. Alexander L. George set the most general standard of rational norms against postulates about how to protect rational deliberation against group pressures first with his article, "The Case for Multiple Advocacy in Making Foreign Policy," *American Political Science Review* 66:3 (September 1972): 751–785. The fullest development of George's attempt to develop rational standards can be found in his *Presidential Decisionmaking in Foreign Policy*. Irving Janis, *Groupthink*, 2d ed., was less successful because it failed to take as much account as George's work did of the organizational setting as an asset for rational behavior and because, in applying its standards to Johnson's Vietnam decision making, it relied too heavily on hindsight. Kahin, *Intervention*, is the first of the recent historical studies referred to here. His was followed, in order, by Larry Berman, *Planning a Tragedy: The Ameri-*

canization of the War in Vietnam; Gibbons, *The U.S. Government and the Vietnam War;* Larry Berman, *Lyndon Johnson's War: The Road to Stalemate in Vietnam;* Burke and Greenstein, *How Presidents Test Reality;* VanDeMark, *Into the Quagmire.*

6. Both are needed to account for the extent to which Robert McNamara assisted him.

7. Berman, *Lyndon Johnson's War.*

8. Berman, *Planning a Tragedy,* p. 152. Richard E. Neustadt and Ernest R. May, *Thinking in Time,* pp. 79–80, agree with Berman.

9. Greenstein, *The Hidden-Hand Presidency.*

10. For the original description of problemistic search, see Cyert and March, *A Behavioral Theory of the Firm,* pp. 120–122. For a careful effort to demonstrate that Johnson engaged Cabinet officers in problemistic search after he had already made up his mind, see Berman, *Planning a Tragedy,* Ch. 4.

11. Chester L. Cooper, *Oral History Interview,* 5 January 1971 and William P. Bundy, *OHI,* 2 June 1969, LBJ Library; Cooper, *The Lost Crusade: America in Vietnam,* p. 223.

12. Johnson succeeded with his efforts to underplay his Vietnam decisions at this time, and earlier. But the result was that, when the press began to catch up, they came to exaggerated conclusions about how much he had misrepresented himself. For example, Tom Wicker, *JFK and LBJ: The Influence of Personality upon Politics,* argues that Johnson had decided before the election that he was going to escalate in Vietnam.

13. A rigorously critical account of ROLLING THUNDER is James Clay Thompson's *Rolling Thunder: Understanding Policy and Program Failure.*

14. VanDeMark, *Into the Quagmire,* pp. 27–31; the report is excerpted in *The Pentagon Papers,* vol. 3, pp. 216–217, 622–628.

15. VanDeMark, *Into the Quagmire,* p. 31.

16. Ibid., p. 31.

17. "Instructions from the President to Ambassador Taylor as approved by the President, December 3, 1964," 12-3-64, McGeorge Bundy Files, Memos to the President.

18. Bundy, "Memorandum for the President: Basic Policy on Vietnam," 1-27-65, McGeorge Bundy Files, Memos to the President.

19. Ibid.

20. Quoted in Berman, *Planning a Tragedy,* p. 43.

21. "When you were out of the room yesterday, Bob McNamara repeatedly stated that he simply has to know what the policy is so that he can make his military plans and give his military orders." Bundy, "Memorandum to the President; Subject: Vietnam Decisions," 2-16-65, McGeorge Bundy Files, Memos to the President.

22. Berman, *Planning a Tragedy,* pp. 65–66.

23. Berman, *Planning a Tragedy,* pp. 56–67.

24. As quoted in Berman, *Planning a Tragedy,* p. 61.

25. William C. Westmoreland, *A Soldier Reports,* p. 139.

26. Jack Valenti, *A Very Human President*, p. 358; George Ball, *The Past Has Another Pattern: Memoirs*, p. 399. See also Kahin, *Intervention*, p. 527; Berman, *Planning a Tragedy*, p. 125; VanDeMark, *Into the Quagmire*, p. 204; and especially Burke and Greenstein, *How Presidents Test Reality*, pp. 213–230. Burke and Greenstein draw upon Greenstein's correspondence with participants, Cyrus Vance in particular. Neustadt and May, *Thinking in Time*, p. 79.

27. Neustadt and May, *Thinking in Time*, p. 80.

28. As quoted in Berman, *Planning a Tragedy*, p. 125.

29. Berman, *Planning a Tragedy*, makes this point with judicious care. See especially Chs. 4 and 5.

30. Schlesinger, *The Coming of the New Deal*, Chs. 32–34; Neustadt, *Presidential Power: The Politics of Leadership* (1960).

31. Greenstein's *The Hidden-Hand Presidency* reassesses Eisenhower primarily with respect to domestic affairs. McGeorge Bundy, *Danger and Survival: Choices About the Bomb in the First Fifty Years*, adds much to refurbish Eisenhower's reputation with respect to foreign relations. See also John P. Burke and Fred I. Greenstein, "Presidential Personality and National Security Leadership: A Comparative Analysis of Vietnam Decisionmaking," *International Political Science Review* 10:1 (January 1989): 73–92.

32. Louis Gerson, *John Foster Dulles*, vol. 17, *The American Secretaries of State and Their Diplomacy*, pp. 283–290, alluded to this fact, but was largely ignored because he was unable to cite the documents on which his observations were based.

33. Eisenhower's employment of an Oval Office caucus where he could discuss issues more freely than he could in NSC meetings was first revealed in Kinnard, *President Eisenhower and Strategy Management*, pp. 16, 64–65, 121–122, 133–134. Greenstein, *The Hidden-Hand Presidency*, deals at length with Eisenhower's skillful use of formal deliberative (or advisory) procedures. Burke and Greenstein, *How Presidents Test Reality*, goes too far with this theme, yet is a superb study of both Eisenhower and Johnson.

34. There are two main versions of this position. One is the multiple advocacy model, which George designed to offset psychological factors working against the optimal rationality of the deliberative group. George, "The Case for Multiple Advocacy in Making Foreign Policy," and *Presidential Decisionmaking in Foreign Policy*, Ch. 11. The second is the arrayed choice version. In theory, an arrayed choice model ought to define an adequate array of options. In fact, at least in its application to Johnson's Vietnam deliberations, in the absence of a definition of adequacy, the adequacy test for the arrayed option model has usually been whether some particular option(s) were considered. The most common test has been whether Johnson considered withdrawal.

35. Cyert and March, *A Behavioral Theory of the Firm*, pp. 120–122.

36. This is an aspect of Eisenhower's leadership that has been too much neglected. For a brief coverage of it see Hammond, *Cold War and Detente*, Ch. 5.

37. Burke and Greenstein, *How Presidents Test Reality,* p. 239.

38. Richard E. Neustadt, *Alliance Politics;* Richard Gould-Adams, *The Time of Power: A Reappraisal of John Foster Dulles;* Hugh Thomas, *The Suez Affair;* Anthony Eden, *Full Circle;* Dwight D. Eisenhower, *Waging Peace;* Herman Finer, *Dulles over Suez;* Leon Epstein, *British Politics in the Suez Crisis.*

39. Quoted in Berman, *Planning a Tragedy,* p. 74.

40. "We cannot be sure how far the cancer has infected the whole body politic of South Vietnam and whether we can do more than administer a cobalt treatment to a terminal case." Berman, *Planning a Tragedy,* p. 74.

41. Gelb and Betts, *The Irony of Vietnam.*

42. Barrett, "The Mythology Surrounding Lyndon Johnson," p. 638. Barrett declares that "the myths that a pathological advisory process or a tremendously egotistical personality prevented Johnson from considering alternatives to (and the drawbacks of) escalation in Vietnam should be laid to rest. In retrospect, it is clear that Lyndon Johnson made a tragically bad decision when he committed ground troops to a land war in Southeast Asia. But unlike the picture drawn in many accounts, the President certainly heard and seems to have agonized over the different options facing him before making the decision."

43. Gibbons, *The U.S. Government and the Vietnam War,* part 3, *passim.*

44. Clark M. Clifford, *Counsel to the President: A Memoir,* Chs. 24, 25, 26.

45. Burke and Greenstein, *How Presidents Test Reality,* p. 119n.

46. Lyndon B. Johnson, *The Vantage Point,* p. 43.

47. Stanley Karnow, *Vietnam: A History,* p. 251.

48. D. Michael Shafer, *Deadly Paradigms: The Failure of U.S. Counterinsurgency Policy,* p. 240.

49. Gaddis, *Strategies of Containment,* pp. 240–243.

50. Westmoreland, *A Soldier Reports,* Ch. 6; the BDM Corporation, *A Study of Strategic Lessons Learned in Vietnam* (hereinafter cited as *BDM Study*), vol. 6, pp. 2/24–2/27.

51. Westmoreland, *A Soldier Reports,* p. 57.

52. "I thought we had been mistaken in our failure to support Diem. But all that, I said, was behind us. Now we had to concentrate on accomplishing our goals. We had to help the new government get on its feet and perform effectively." Johnson, *Vantage Point,* p. 44.

53. R. W. Komer, *Bureaucracy at War: U.S. Performance in the Vietnam Conflict,* esp. pp. 4, 12–13, and 41–44.

54. Ibid., p. 82.

55. Ibid., p. 90.

56. Ibid., p. 91.

57. Herbert Y. Schandler, *The Unmaking of a President: Lyndon Johnson and Vietnam,* p. 122.

58. The best account of the Camp David meeting is in VanDeMark, *Into the Quagmire,* pp. 204–208.

59. Kissinger, *White House Years,* p. 292.

60. The group varied slightly. This time it consisted of Dean Acheson, George Ball, McGeorge Bundy, Arthur Dean, Douglas Dillon, Henry Cabot Lodge, Robert Murphy, General Matthew Ridgway, General Maxwell Taylor, and Cyrus Vance.

61. Schandler, *The Unmaking of a President*, p. 328.

62. Berman published a revealing statement to this effect in a letter he received from Bundy. Bundy, who was attempting to help Berman interpret a document from the LBJ Library, wrote that by the time the document in question was under consideration, "my own role had become that of a staff officer who knows the big decision is made and is working to help in its execution." *Planning a Tragedy*, p. 123.

63. Schandler, *The Unmaking of a President*, p. 313. As the source for these statements, Schandler cites [his] personal interview with Clark Clifford, 15 February 1973.

64. Johnson, *Vantage Point*, p. 63.

65. e.g., David Halberstam's *The Making of a Quagmire*; Neil Sheehan, *A Bright Shining Lie: John Paul Vann and America in Vietnam*.

66. Berman, *Lyndon Johnson's War*, p. 13.

67. The inaccuracy of the quagmire thesis was discovered by Daniel Ellsberg and Leslie Gelb. Ellsberg and Gelb were, respectively, an author of the study and the project leader. They presented their initial findings at a panel of the American Political Science Association annual meeting in Los Angeles in September 1970. Ellsberg later published his paper as "The Quagmire Myth and the Stalemate Machine," in *Public Policy* 19:2 (Spring 1971): 217–274, in shortened form. In extended form it appears in Ellsberg, *Papers on the War*, pp. 42–135. Gelb published his as "Vietnam: The System Worked," in *Foreign Policy* 3 (Summer 1971): 140–167.

68. While Gelb's and Ellsberg's articles were the initiators of this thesis, the most extended treatment of it now available is Gelb and Betts, *The Irony of Vietnam*. See also Berman's two excellent studies *Planning a Tragedy* and *Lyndon Johnson's War*.

69. Townsend Hoopes attributes this quotation in his *The Limits of Intervention*, p. 204.

70. Examples of such documents are in Thompson, *Rolling Thunder*; Gelb and Betts, *The Irony of Vietnam*; and the *Pentagon Papers*.

71. Komer, *Bureaucracy at War*, proves a persuasive overview of the issue and focuses on the U.S. and GVN bureaucracies; Shafer, *Deadly Paradigms*, Ch. 3, makes the sobering argument that Vietnam could be a precursor for other failures in the Third World due to U.S. policymakers' misunderstanding of the problems involved.

72. See Kinnard, *President Eisenhower and Strategy Management*; Greenstein, *The Hidden-Hand Presidency*; Burke and Greenstein, "Presidential Personality and National Security Leadership." A more critical account of NSC formalities under Eisenhower is presented in Hammond, "The National Security Council as a Device for Interdepartmental Coordination."

73. This concept is well developed in Barbara Tuchman, *The March of Folly: From Troy to Vietnam.*

74. Bruce Russett, "The Mysterious Case of Vanishing Hegemony: Or, Is Mark Twain Really Dead?" *International Organization* 39:2 (Spring 1985): 207–231. See especially Russett's excellent table at p. 212.

75. Walter W. Heller, *New Dimensions of Political Economy,* esp. Ch. 2.

76. Robert Kennedy, *Thirteen Days,* pp. 30–31; Allison, *Essence of Decision,* p. 57; James G. Blight, Joseph S. Nye, Jr., and David A. Welch, "The Cuban Missile Crisis Revisited," *Foreign Affairs* 66:1 (Fall 1987): 170–188.

77. Allison, *Essence of Decision,* pp. 195–196; Raymond L. Garthoff, *Reflections on the Cuban Missile Crisis,* rev. ed., p. 44.

78. See Alexander L. George and Juliette L. George, *Woodrow Wilson and Colonel House: A Personality Study.*

79. George, *Presidential Decisionmaking in Foreign Policy,* esp. Chs. 8–12.

80. Cyert and March, *A Behavioral Theory of the Firm,* pp. 120–122.

81. Paul A. Anderson, "Deciding How to Decide in Foreign Affairs: Decision-Making Strategies as Solutions to Presidential Problems," in George C. Edwards III, et al., *The Presidency and Public Policy Making.*

82. Barrett, "The Mythology Surrounding Lyndon Johnson," p. 637; Gelb and Betts, *The Irony of Vietnam,* p. 1.

7. Johnson's Foreign Policy Leadership in Larger Perspective

1. Theodore Geiger, *The Future of the International System: The United States and the World Political Economy,* pp. 35–38; Henry Kissinger, *Years of Upheaval,* p. 238; Richard K. Betts, "Elusive Equivalence: The Political and Military Meaning of the Nuclear Balance," in Samuel P. Huntington (ed.), *The Strategic Imperative: New Policies for American Security,* p. 118; Samuel P. Huntington, "The U.S.—Decline or Renewal?" *Foreign Affairs* 67:2 (Winter 1988/1989): 81–82; Joseph Lepgold, *The Declining Hegemon: The United States and European Defense, 1960–1990,* p. 17.

2. Susan Strange, "The Persistent Myth of Lost Hegemony," *International Organization* 41:4 (Autumn 1987): 565–571.

3. Geiger, *The Future of the International System,* pp. 35–39. See also Lepgold's *The Declining Hegemon,* Ch. 1.

4. Allison and Szanton, *Remaking Foreign Policy,* pp. 66–85.

5. This literature is vast. Exemplary works are Ernst Haas, *The Uniting of Europe: Political, Social, and Economic Forces, 1950–1957;* and Karl W. Deutsch, et al., *Political Community in the North Atlantic Area: International Organization in the Light of Historical Experience.*

6. Rudolph, Rudolph, et al., *The Regional Imperative,* p. 10. Other quotes from pp. 6–10.

7. Ibid., p. 13.

8. Ibid., p. 16.

9. Bowles, *Promises to Keep,* p. 525.

10. Rudolph, Rudolph, et al., *The Regional Imperative*, pp. 40, 41.

11. Ibid., p. 10.

12. Ibid., p. 7.

13. Ibid., p. 7.

14. Bert A. Rockman, "America's Departments of States: Irregular and Regular Syndromes of Policy Making," *American Political Science Review* 75:4 (December 1981): 911–927.

15. Gaddis, *Strategies of Containment*, pp. 18–25.

16. George Kennan, *American Diplomacy, 1900–1950*, pp. 93–99.

17. Kenneth Waltz, *Theory of International Politics*, pp. 93–99; Robert Keohane (ed.), *Neorealism and Its Critics*, Ch. 3.

18. Cleveland, *NATO: The Trans-Atlantic Bargain*. This insightful book employs the bargain metaphor to demonstrate the mutual advantage of NATO to its members.

19. Ernst B. Haas, "Regionalism, Functionalism, and Universal International Organization," *World Politics* 8:2 (January 1956): 238–263; Haas, *The Uniting of Europe*; Haas, "Persistent Themes in Atlantic and European Unity," *World Politics* 10:4 (July 1958): 615–628; Haas, *The Obsolescence of Regional Integration Theory*.

20. cf. James N. Rosenau (ed.), *Linkage Politics: Essays on the Convergence of National and International Systems*.

21. Iron triangles is a metaphor of criticism and reform. See Milton Friedman and Rose Friedman, *Tyranny of the Status Quo*, pp. 42–51, 77–79, 154–155, 165–168. Two early works that deal with stable governmental processes are Philip Selznik, *TVA at the Grassroots*, and Paul H. Appleby, *Big Democracy*. For a more recent, balanced view see Charles O. Jones, "American Politics and the Organization of Energy Decision Making," *Annual Review of Energy* 4 (1959): 99–121. For a related discussion of the institutionalization of policy see Paul Y. Hammond, "Strategic Supply Security Policy: Always a Bridesmaid?" Occasional Papers, Institute for Strategic Economics and Industrial Vulnerability.

22. Anthony King, "The American Policy in the Late 1970s: Building Coalitions in the Sand," Ch. 10 of King (ed.), *The New American Political System*, p. 392.

23. The term has been used to refer to the general phenomenon and to specific foreign policy sectors, but always in terms of the extended scope described here.

24. James MacGregor Burns, *Roosevelt: The Lion and the Fox*.

25. While scarcely the first work on this subject, Wildavsky's and Pressman's *Implementation* started this cottage industry.

26. Keohane, *After Hegemony*.

27. Joseph Nye, *Bound to Lead: The Changing Nature of American Power*.

Bibliography

Allison, Graham. *Essence of Decision: Explaining the Cuban Missile Crisis.* Boston: Little, Brown, 1971.

———, and Peter Szanton. *Remaking Foreign Policy: The Organizational Connection.* New York: Basic Books, 1976.

Anderson, James E., and Jared E. Hazleton. *Managing Macroeconomic Policy: The Johnson Subpresidency.* Austin: University of Texas Press, 1986.

Anderson, Paul A. "Deciding How to Decide in Foreign Affairs: Decision-Making Strategies as Solutions to Presidential Problems." In George C. Edwards III, et al., *The Presidency and Public Policy Making.* Pittsburgh: University of Pittsburgh Press, 1985.

Appleby, Paul H. *Big Democracy.* New York: Alfred A. Knopf, 1945.

Arnold, Thurman. *The Symbols of Government.* New Haven, Conn.: Yale University Press, 1935.

Bachrach, P., and M. S. Baratz. "Decisions and Non-Decisions: An Analytical Framework." *The American Political Science Review* 57:3 (September 1963): 632–642.

Ball, George W. *The Past Has Another Pattern: Memoirs.* New York: Norton, 1982.

Barrett, David M. "The Mythology Surrounding Lyndon Johnson, His Advisors, and the 1965 Decision to Escalate the Vietnam War." *Political Science Quarterly* 103:4 (Winter 1988–1989): 637–664.

Bauer, Raymond A., Ithiel de Sola Pool, and Lewis Anthony Dexter. *American Business and Public Policy: The Politics of Foreign Trade.* New York: Atherton Press, 1963.

BDM Corporation. *A Study of Strategic Lessons Learned in Vietnam,* vol.6, *Conduct of the War,* BDM/W-78-128-TR. McLean, Va.: BDM Corp., 1980.

Berman, Larry. *Lyndon Johnson's War: The Road to Stalemate in Vietnam.* New York: Norton, 1989.

———. *Planning a Tragedy: The Americanization of the War in Vietnam.* New York: Norton, 1982.

Berthoff, Rowland T. "Taft and MacArthur, 1900–1901: A Study in Civil-Military Relations." *World Politics* 5:2 (January 1953): 196–213.

Betts, Richard K. "Elusive Equivalence: The Political and Military Meaning of the Nuclear Balance." In Samuel P. Huntington (ed.), *The Strategic Imperative: New Policies for American Security.* Cambridge, Mass.: Ballinger, 1982.

Bhatia, Krishan. "India Adrift." *Foreign Affairs* 45:4 (July 1967): 652–662.

Bjorkman, James W. "Public Law 480 and the Policies of Self-Help and Short-Tether: Indo-American Relations, 1965–68." In Commission on the Organization of the Government for the Conduct of Foreign Policy, *Appendices,* vol. 7. Washington, D.C.: Government Printing Office, May 1975.

Blight, James G., Joseph S. Nye, Jr., and David A. Welch. "The Cuban Missile Crisis Revisited." *Foreign Affairs* 66:1 (Fall 1987): 170–188.

Bohlen, Charles E. *Witness to History, 1929–1969.* New York: Norton, 1973.

Bornet, Vaughn Davis. *The Presidency of Lyndon B. Johnson.* Lawrence: University Press of Kansas, 1983.

Bowles, Chester. *Promises to Keep: My Years in Public Life, 1941–1969.* New York: Harper & Row, 1971.

Bowman, John F., II. "The Role of the Special Assistant to the President for National Security Affairs in the Formulation and Implementation of National Security Policy: An Evaluation." Ph.D. Dissertation, University of Pittsburgh, Graduate School of Public and International Affairs, 1986.

Brandon, Henry. "Skybolt." *London Sunday Times,* 3 December 1963. Reprinted in Morton H. Halperin and Arnold Kanter (eds.), *Readings in American Foreign Policy: A Bureaucratic Perspective.* Boston: Little, Brown, 1973.

Braybrooke, David, and Charles E. Lindblom. *A Strategy of Decision: Policy Evaluation as a Social Process.* New York: Free Press of Glencoe, 1963.

Brown, William Adams, Jr., and Redvers Opie. *American Foreign Assistance.* Washington, D.C.: Brookings, 1953.

Brzezinski, Zbigniew. *Power and Principle: Memoirs of the National Security Adviser, 1977–1981.* New York: Farrar, Straus & Giroux, 1983.

Bundy, McGeorge. *Danger and Survival: Choices about the Bomb in the First Fifty Years.* New York: Random House, 1988.

Burke, John P., and Fred I. Greenstein. *How Presidents Test Reality: Decisions on Vietnam, 1954–1965.* New York: Russell Sage Foundation, 1989.

————, and ————. "Presidential Personality and National Security Leadership: A Comparative Analysis of Vietnam Decisionmaking." *International Political Science Review* 10:1 (January 1989): 73–92.

Burns, James MacGregor. *Roosevelt: The Lion and the Fox.* New York: Harcourt, Brace, 1956.

Caldwell, Dan. *American-Soviet Relations from 1947 to the Nixon-Kissinger Grand Design.* Westport, Conn.: Greenwood Press, 1981.

Cargill, I. P. M. "Efforts to Influence Performance: Case Study of India." Chapter 5 in John P. Lewis and Ishan Kapur (eds.), *The World Bank Group, Multilateral Aid, and the 1970s.* Lexington, Mass.: Lexington Books, 1973.

Caro, Robert A. *The Years of Lyndon Johnson*, vol. 1, *The Path to Power*; vol. 2, *The Means of Ascent*. New York: Alfred A. Knopf, 1982, 1990.

Carroll, Holbert N. *The House of Representatives and Foreign Affairs*. Boston: Little, Brown, 1966.

Cartwright, Dorwin. "Influence, Leadership, Control." Chapter 1 in James G. March (ed.), *Handbook of Organizations*. Chicago: Rand-McNally, 1965.

Chavan, R. S. *Nationalism in Asia*. New Delhi: Sterling Publishers, 1973.

Chayes, Abraham. "Bureaucratic Politics and Arms Control: An Inquiry into the Workings of Arms Control Agreements." *Harvard Law Review* 85 (1972): 905–969.

Cleveland, Harlan. *NATO: The Trans-Atlantic Bargain*. New York: Harper & Row, 1970.

Clifford, Clark M. *Counsel to the President: A Memoir*. New York: Random House, 1991.

Cobb, R. W., and C. D. Elder. *Participation in American Politics: The Dynamics of Agenda-Building*. Boston: Allyn & Bacon, 1972.

Commission on Integrated Long-Term Strategy. *Discriminate Deterrence*. Washington, D.C.: Government Printing Office, January 1988.

Committee on Foreign Affairs Personnel (Herter Committee). *Personnel for the New Diplomacy*. New York: Carnegie Endowment for International Peace, 1962.

Cooper, Chester L. *The Lost Crusade: America in Vietnam*. (New York: Dodd, Mead, 1970.

Crenson, M. A. *The Un-Politics of Air Pollution*. Baltimore: The Johns Hopkins Press, 1971.

Crovitz, Gordon L., and Jeremy A. Rabkin (eds.). *The Fettered Presidency: Legal Constraints on the Executive Branch*. Washington, D.C.: American Enterprise Institute for Public Policy, 1989.

Cyert, Richard M., and James G. March. *A Behavioral Theory of the Firm*. Englewood Cliffs, N.J.: Prentice-Hall, 1963.

Dawisha, Karen. *Eastern Europe, Gorbachev and Reform: The Great Challenge*. Cambridge, England: Cambridge University Press, 1988.

Destler, I. M. "Comment: Multiple Advocacy: Some 'Limits and Costs,'" *American Political Science Review* 66:3 (September 1972): 786–790.

———. *Presidents, Bureaucrats and Foreign Policy: The Politics of Organizational Reform*. Princeton, N.J.: Princeton University Press, 1972.

Deutsch, Karl W., et al. *Political Community in the North Atlantic Area: International Organization in the Light of Historical Experience*. Princeton, N.J.: Princeton University Press, 1957.

Documents on American Foreign Relations, 1965, no. 1. New York: Harper & Row, 1966.

Edelman, Murray. *The Symbolic Uses of Politics*. Urbana: University of Illinois Press, 1964.

Eden, Anthony. *Full Circle*. London: Cassell, 1960.

Einaudi, Luigi. *Peruvian Military Relations with the United States*, P4389. Santa Monica, Calif.: Rand Corp., 1970.

Eisenhower, Dwight D. *Waging Peace.* New York: Doubleday, 1965.
Ellsberg, Daniel. *Papers on the War.* New York: Simon and Schuster, 1975.
———. "The Quagmire Myth and the Stalemate Machine." *Public Policy* 19:2 (Spring 1971): 217–274.
Epstein, Leon. *British Politics in the Suez Crisis.* Urbana: University of Illinois Press, 1964.
Evans, John W. *The Kennedy Round in American Trade Policy: The Twilight of the GATT?* Cambridge, Mass.: Harvard University Press, 1971.
The Federalist Papers. New York: Random House, The Modern Library, 1941.
Fenno, Richard F. *The President's Cabinet: An Analysis in the Period from Wilson to Eisenhower.* Cambridge, Mass.: Harvard University Press, 1959.
Finer, Herman. *Dulles over Suez.* Chicago: Quadrangle, 1964.
Frankel, Francine. *India's Political Economy, 1947–1977.* Princeton, N.J.: Princeton University Press, 1977.
Freeman, Orville. *World without Hunger.* New York: Frederick A. Praeger, 1968.
Friedman, Milton, and Rose Friedman. *Tyranny of the Status Quo.* New York: Harcourt Brace Jovanovich, 1984.
Furniss, Edgar S., Jr. *De Gaulle and the French Army: A Crisis in Civil-Military Relations.* New York: Twentieth Century Fund, 1964.
Gaddis, John Lewis. *Strategies of Containment: A Critical Appraisal of Postwar American National Security Policy.* New York: Oxford University Press, 1982.
Gallup, George H. *The Gallup Poll: Public Opinion, 1935–1971,* vols. 2 and 3. New York: Random House and American Institute of Public Opinion, 1972.
Garthoff, Raymond L. *Reflections on the Cuban Missile Crisis,* rev. ed. Washington, D.C.: Brookings, 1989.
Geiger, Theodore. *The Future of the International System: The United States and the World Political Economy.* Boston: Unwin Hyman, 1988.
Gelb, Leslie H. "Vietnam: The System Worked." *Foreign Policy* 3 (Summer 1971): 140–167.
———, and Richard K. Betts. *The Irony of Vietnam: The System Worked.* Washington, D.C.: Brookings, 1979.
George, Alexander L. "The Case for Multiple Advocacy in Making Foreign Policy," *The American Political Science Review* 66:3 (September 1972): 751–785.
———. *Presidential Decisionmaking in Foreign Policy: The Effective Use of Information and Advice.* Boulder, Colo.: Westview Press, 1980.
———. "Rejoinder to 'Comment' by I. M. Destler." *The American Political Science Review* 66:3 (September 1972): 791–795.
———, and Juliette L. George. *Woodrow Wilson and Colonel House: A Personality Study.* New York: J. Day Co., 1956.
Gerson, Louis. *John Foster Dulles,* vol. 17, *The American Secretaries of State and Their Diplomacy.* New York: Cooper Square Publishers, 1967.

Geyelin, Philip. *Lyndon B. Johnson and the World.* New York: Frederick A. Praeger, 1966.

Gibbons, William Conrad. *The U.S. Government and the Vietnam War: Executive and Legislative Roles and Relationships,* parts 1, 2, and 3. Princeton, N.J.: Princeton University Press, 1986, 1989 (first published as a U.S. Senate document in 1985).

Godson, Joseph. "Public Support for NATO—A German View." In Joseph Godson (ed.), *35 years of NATO: A Transatlantic Symposium on the Changing Political, Economic and Military Setting.* New York: Dodd, Mead, 1984.

Goodsell, Charles T. "The Politics of Direct Investment." *Latin America in the 1970's.* Santa Monica, Calif.: Rand, 1972.

Gould-Adams, Richard. *The Time of Power: A Reappraisal of John Foster Dulles.* London: Weindenfelt & Nicolson, 1962.

Greenstein, Fred I. *The Hidden-Hand Presidency: Eisenhower as Leader.* New York: Basic Books, 1982.

Haas, Ernst B. *The Obsolescence of Regional Integration Theory.* Berkeley: Institute of International Studies, University of California, 1975.

———. "Persistent Themes in Atlantic and European Unity." *World Politics* 10:4 (July 1958): 615–628.

———. "Regionalism, Functionalism, and Universal International Organization," *World Politics* 8:2 (January 1956): 238–263.

———. *The Uniting of Europe: Political, Social, and Economic Forces, 1950–1957.* Stanford, Calif.: Stanford University, 1958.

Halberstam, David. *The Making of a Quagmire.* New York: Random House, 1965.

Hall, David K. "The 'Custodian-Manager' of the Policymaking Process." In Commission on the Organization of the Government for the Conduct of Foreign Policy, Murphy Commission *Appendices,* vol. 2. Washington, D.C.: Government Printing Office, May 1975.

Halperin, Morton H., and Arnold Kanter (eds.). *Readings in American Foreign Policy: A Bureaucratic Perspective.* Boston: Little, Brown, 1973.

Hammond, Paul Y. *Cold War and Detente.* New York: Harcourt Brace Jovanovich, 1975.

———. "Directives for the Occupation of Germany: The Washington Story." In Harold Stein (ed.), *American Civil-Military Decisions.* Maxwell: University of Alabama Press, 1963.

———. "The National Security Council as a Device for Interdepartmental Coordination: An Interpretation and Appraisal." *American Political Science Review* 54:4 (December 1960): 899–910.

———. "NSC-68: Prologue to Rearmament." In Warner R. Schilling, Paul Y. Hammond, and Glenn H. Snyder, *Strategy, Politics, and Defense Budgets.* New York: Columbia University Press, 1962.

———. "Strategic Supply Security Policy: Always a Bridesmaid?" Occasional Papers, Institute for Strategic Economics and Industrial Vulnerability. Pittsburgh: University Center for International Studies, 1987.

———, David J. Louscher, Michael D. Salomone, and Norman A. Graham. *The Reluctant Supplier: U.S. Decisionmaking for Arms Sales.* Cambridge, Mass.: Oelegslager, Gunn & Hain, 1983.

Harlech, Lord. "Suez SNAFU, Skybolt SABU." *Foreign Policy* 2 (Spring 1971): 38–50.

Hassner, Pierre. "Change and Security in Europe; Part I: The Background." *Adelphi Papers* 45 (February 1968): 2.

Heller, Walter W. *New Dimensions of Political Economy.* Cambridge, Mass.: Harvard University Press, 1967.

Heclo, Hugh. "Issue Networks and the Executive Establishment." Chapter 3 of Anthony King (ed.), *The New American Political System.* Washington, D.C.: American Enterprise Institute, 1978.

Hess, Stephen. *Organizing the Presidency.* Washington, D.C.: Brookings, 1976.

Hipple, Eric von. *The Sources of Innovation.* New York: Oxford University Press, 1988.

Hirschman, Albert O. *Development Projects Observed.* Washington, D.C.: Brookings, 1967.

———. "The Principle of the Hiding Hand." *The Public Interest* 6 (Winter 1967): pp. 10–23.

Hoopes, Townsend. *The Limits of Intervention.* New York: David McKay, 1969.

Howard, Michael. "Reassurance and Deterrence: Western Defense in the 1980s." *Foreign Affairs* 61:2 (Winter 1982/1983): 309–324.

Humphrey, David C. "Tuesday Lunch at the Johnson White House: A Preliminary Assessment." *Diplomatic History* 8:1 (Winter 1984): 81–101.

Huntington, Samuel P. "The U.S.—Decline or Renewal?" *Foreign Affairs* 67:2 (Winter 1988/1989), 76–96.

Ikle, Fred C. *Every War Must End.* New York: Columbia University Press, 1971.

In Re Neagle, 135 U.S. 1 (1890).

Jackson, Henry M. (ed.). *The National Security Council.* New York: Frederick A. Praeger, 1965.

Janis, Irving. *Groupthink,* 2d ed. Boston: Houghton Mifflin, 1983.

Johnson, Lyndon B. *The Vantage Point.* New York: Holt, Rinehart, 1971.

Jones, Charles O. "American Politics and the Organization of Energy Decision Making." *Annual Review of Energy* 4 (1959): 99–121.

———. *An Introduction to the Study of Public Policy,* 3d ed. Monterey, Calif.: Brooks/Cole, 1984.

Jones, Gordon S., and John A. Marini (eds.). *The Imperial Congress: Crisis in the Separation of Powers.* Washington, D.C.: The Heritage Foundation and Claremont Institute, 1989.

Jordon, Robert S. *Political Leadership in NATO: A Study in Multinational Diplomacy.* Boulder, Colo.: Westview Press, 1979.

Kahin, George McT. *Intervention: How America Became Involved in Vietnam.* New York: Alfred A. Knopf, 1986.

Kaiser, Karl. "Public Support for NATO—A German View." In Joseph Godson (ed.), *35 Years of NATO: A Transatlantic Symposium on the Changing Political, Economic and Military Setting*, New York: Dodd, Mead, 1984.

Karnow, Stanley. *Vietnam: A History*. New York: Penguin, 1983.

Kaufmann, William W. *The McNamara Strategy*. New York: Harper & Row, 1964.

Kearns, Doris. *Lyndon Johnson and the American Dream*. New York: Harper & Row, 1976.

Kelleher, Catherine McA. *Germany and the Politics of Nuclear Weapons*. New York: Columbia University Press, 1975.

Kennan, George. *American Diplomacy, 1900–1950*. Chicago: University of Chicago Press, 1951.

———. "America's Administrative Response to Its World Problems." *Daedalus* 87:1 (Spring 1958), as reprinted in Jackson Subcommittee, U.S. Senate, *Organizing for National Security*, vol. 2, 1961.

———. *Memoirs 1925–1950*. Boston: Little, Brown, 1967.

Kennedy, Robert. *Thirteen Days*. New York: Norton, 1968.

Keohane, Robert O. *After Hegemony: Cooperation and Discord in the World Political Economy*. Princeton, N.J.: Princeton University Press, 1984.

——— (ed.). *Neorealism and Its Critics*. New York: Columbia University Press, 1984.

———, and Joseph S. Nye. *Power and Interdependence*. Boston: Little, Brown, 1977.

———, and ———. "Transgovernmental Relations and International Organization." *World Politics* 27:1 (October 1974): 39–62.

King, Anthony. "The American Policy in the Late 1970s: Building Coalitions in the Sand." Chapter 10 of Anthony King (ed.), *The New American Political System*. Washington, D.C.: American Enterprise Institute, 1978.

Kingdon, John W. *Agendas, Alternatives, and Public Politics*. Boston: Little, Brown, 1984.

Kinnard, Douglas. *President Eisenhower and Strategy Management: A Study in Defense Politics*. Lexington: University Press of Kentucky, 1977.

Kissinger, Henry. *White House Years*. Boston: Little, Brown, 1979.

———. *Years of Upheaval*. Boston: Little, Brown, 1982.

Kochanek, Stanley A. *The Congress Party of India: The Dynamics of One-Party Democracy*. Princeton, N.J.: Princeton University Press, 1968.

Kohl, Wilford L. *French Nuclear Diplomacy*. Princeton, N.J.: Princeton University Press, 1971.

Kolodziej, Edward A. "The National Security Council: Innovations and Implications." *Public Administration Review* 29:6 (November/December 1969): 573–585.

Komer, R. W. *Bureaucracy at War: U.S. Performance in the Vietnam Conflict*. Boulder, Colo.: Westview Press, 1986.

Krasner, Stephen D. "According to Regimes." In Stephen D. Krasner (ed.), *International Regimes*. Ithaca, N.Y.: Cornell University Press, 1983.

Lepgold, Joseph. *The Declining Hegemon: The United States and European Defense, 1960–1990*. New York: Frederick A. Praeger, 1990.

Levine, Charles. "Where Policy Comes from: Ideas, Innovations, and Agenda Choices." *Public Administration Review* 45:1 (January/February 1985): 255–258.

Lewis, John P. *Quiet Crisis in India: Economic Development and American Policy*. Washington, D.C.: Brookings, 1962.

Light, Paul Charles. *The President's Agenda: Domestic Policy Choice from Kennedy to Carter*. Baltimore: The Johns Hopkins University Press, 1982.

"Making Europe Whole: An Unfinished Task," address by President Johnson. *Department of State Bulletin* 55:1426 (24 October 1966): 822–825.

March, James G., and Herbert A. Simon. *Organizations*. New York: John Wiley, 1958.

Margolis, Howard. "Notes on the MLF." *Bulletin of the Atomic Scientists*, November 1964, pp. 28–30.

Mayers, David. *George Kennan and the Dilemmas of US Foreign Policy*. New York: Oxford University Press, 1988.

Mellor, John W. (ed.). *India: A Rising Middle Power*. Boulder, Colo.: Westview Press, 1979.

Meyers, Kenneth. "The Future of NATO." Chapter 1 in Kenneth Meyers (ed.), *NATO the Next Thirty Years: The Changing Political, Economic, and Military Setting*. Boulder, Colo.: Westview Press, 1980.

Millikan, M. F., W. W. Rostow, et al. *Foreign Aid: A Proposal*. New York: Harper & Row, 1957.

Milton, General T. R., U.S. Air Force, Ret. "Helmut Schmidt's Extreme Idea." *Air Force Magazine*, February 1986, p. 126.

Mr. X (George Kennan). "The Sources of Soviet Conduct." *Foreign Affairs* 25:4 (July 1947): 566–582.

Morgenthau, Hans J. *In Defense of the National Interest: A Critical Examination of American Foreign Policy*. Lanham, Md.: University Press of America, 1983.

Morse, Edward L. *Foreign Policy and Interdependence in Gaullist France*. Princeton, N.J.: Princeton University Press, 1973.

Neustadt, Richard E. *Alliance Politics*. New York: Columbia University Press, 1970.

———. "The Constraining of the President." *The New York Times Magazine*, 14 October 1973, reprinted as Chapter 18 in Aaron Wildavsky (ed.), *Perspectives on the Presidency*. Boston: Little, Brown, 1975.

———. *Presidential Power: The Politics of Leadership*. New York: John Wiley, 1960.

———. *Presidential Power: The Politics of Leadership from FDR to Carter*. New York: John Wiley, 1980.

———. *Presidential Power: The Politics of Leadership from Roosevelt to Reagan*. Boulder, Colo.: Westview Press, 1990.

———, and Ernest R. May. *Thinking in Time.* New York: The Free Press, 1986.

Nye, Joseph. *Bound to Lead: The Changing Nature of American Power.* New York: Basic Books, 1990.

Osgood, Robert E. *NATO: The Entangling Alliance.* Chicago: University of Chicago Press, 1962.

O'Toole, Edward. "Brussels Preparing Troop Withdrawal." *New York Times,* 27 November 1964.

Packenham, Robert A. *Liberal America and the Third World: Political Development Ideas in Foreign Aid and Social Science.* Princeton, N.J.: Princeton University Press, 1973.

Palmer, Norman D. "India's Fourth General Election." *Asian Survey* 7:5 (May 1967): 275–291.

The Pentagon Papers: The Defense Department History of United States Decisionmaking on Vietnam (Boston: Beacon Press, 1971), 5 vols. ["The Senator Gravel Edition"].

Peppers, Donald A. "The Two Presidencies: Eight Years Later." Chapter 20 in Aaron Wildavsky, *Perspectives on the Presidency.* Boston: Little, Brown, 1975.

Polsby, Nelson W. *Political Innovation in America: The Politics of Policy Initiation.* New Haven, Conn.: Yale University Press, 1984.

Presad, Nandan Deviki. *Food for Peace: The Story of the U.S. Food Assistance to India.* New York: Asia Publishing House, 1980.

Public Papers of the Presidents of the United States: Lyndon B. Johnson, 1963–65. Washington, D.C.: Government Printing Office, 1965.

Public Papers of the Presidents of the United States: Lyndon B. Johnson, 1966. Washington, D.C.: Government Printing Office, 1967.

Quant, William B. *Decade of Decisions: American Policy Towards the Arab-Israeli Conflict 1967–1976.* Berkeley: University of California Press, 1977.

Raymond, Jack. "Bonn A-Fleet Bid Finds Rusk Wary." *New York Times,* 9 October 1964.

Redford, Emmette S., and Richard T. McCulley. *White House Operations: The Johnson Presidency.* Austin: University of Texas Press, 1986.

———, and Marlan Blissett. *Organizing the Executive Branch: The Johnson Presidency.* Chicago and London: University of Chicago Press, 1981.

"Report of the Special Committee on U.S. Trade with Eastern European Countries and the Soviet Union." *Department of State Bulletin* 54:1405 (30 May 1966): 845–855.

Ripley, Randall B. "Interagency Committees and Incrementalism: The Case of Aid to India." *Midwest Journal of Political Science* 8:2 (May 1964): 143–165.

Rockman, Bert A. "America's Departments of States: Irregular and Regular Syndromes of Policy Making." *American Political Science Review* 75:4 (December 1981): 911–927.

Rosen, George. *Democracy and Economic Change in India.* Berkeley and Los Angeles: University of California Press, 1967.

Rosenau, James N. (ed.). *Linkage Politics: Essays on the Convergence of National and International Systems.* New York: Free Press, 1969.

Rossiter, Clinton E. *The American Presidency.* New York: Harcourt Brace, 1956.

Rostow, W. W. *The Diffusion of Power.* New York: Macmillan, 1972.

Rudolph, Lloyd I., Susanne H. Rudolph, et al. *The Regional Imperative: The Administration of U.S. Foreign Policy Towards South Asian States Under Presidents Johnson and Nixon.* Atlantic Highland, N.J.: Humanities Press, 1980.

———, and ———. "Summary Report." In Murphy Commission *Appendices,* vol. 7, pp. 112 ff.

Rudolph, Susanne Hoeber. "The Writ from Delhi: The Indian Government's Capabilities after the 1971 Election." *Asian Survey* 11 : 10 (October 1971): 958–969.

Russett, Bruce. "The Mysterious Case of Vanishing Hegemony: Or, Is Mark Twain Really Dead?" *International Organization* 39 : 2 (Spring 1985), 207–231.

Schandler, Herbert Y. *The Unmaking of a President: Lyndon Johnson and Vietnam.* Princeton, N.J.: Princeton University Press, 1977.

Schlesinger, Arthur M., Jr. *The Age of Roosevelt,* vol. 2, *The Coming of the New Deal.* Boston: Houghton Mifflin, 1959.

———. *A Thousand Days: John F. Kennedy in the White House.* Boston: Houghton Mifflin, 1965.

Schott, Richard L., and Dagmar S. Hamilton. *People, Positions, and Power: The Political Appointments of Lyndon B. Johnson.* Chicago: University of Chicago Press, 1983.

Schwartz, David N. *NATO's Nuclear Dilemmas.* Washington, D.C.: Brookings, 1983.

Selznik, Philip. *TVA at the Grassroots.* Berkeley: University of California Press, 1949.

Shafer, D. Michael. *Deadly Paradigms: The Failure of U.S. Counterinsurgency Policy.* Princeton, N.J.: Princeton University Press, 1988.

Sheehan, Neil. *A Bright Shining Lie: John Paul Vann and America in Vietnam.* New York: Random House, 1988.

Simon, Herbert A. *Models of Man: Social and Rational.* New York: John Wiley, 1957.

Sorenson, Theodore C. *Kennedy.* New York: Harper and Row, 1965.

Stein, Harold. "The Foreign Service Act of 1946," CPAC #9. Syracuse, N.Y.: Inter-University Case Program, 1949.

Steinbruner, John D. *The Cybernetic Theory of Decision: New Dimensions of Political Analysis.* Princeton, N.J.: Princeton University Press, 1974.

Stepan, Alfred. *The Military in Politics: Changing Patterns in Brazil.* Princeton, N.J.: Princeton University Press, 1971.

Strange, Susan. "The Persistent Myth of Lost Hegemony," *International Organization* 41:4 (Autumn 1987): 565–571.

"Text of Joint Communique by Johnson and Erhard," *New York Times*, 30 December 1963.

Thomas, Hugh. *The Suez Affair*. London: Weidenfeld, 1966.

Thompson, James Clay. *Rolling Thunder: Understanding Policy and Program Failure*. Chapel Hill: University of North Carolina Press, 1980.

Townsend, Joyce Carol. *Bureaucratic Politics in American Decision Making: Impact on Brazil*. Washington, D.C.: University Press of America, 1982.

Treverton, Gregory F. *Making the Alliance Work: The United States and Western Europe*. Ithaca, N.Y.: Cornell University Press, 1985.

Tuchman, Barbara. *The March of Folly: From Troy to Vietnam*. New York: Random House, 1984.

U.S. Congress, House Committee on Foreign Affairs, Subcommittee on Foreign Economic Policy. *U.S. Foreign Economic Policy: Implications for the Organization of the Executive Branch*. Hearings, 25 July 1972, 92d Cong., 2d session, 1972.

U.S. Congress, Senate Committee on Government Operations, Subcommittee on National Policy Machinery. *Organizing for National Security*, vol. 1. 87th Cong., 1st session.

Valenti, Jack. *A Very Human President*. New York: Norton, 1975.

Vance, Cyrus. *Hard Choices*. New York: Simon and Schuster, 1983.

VanDeMark, Brian. *Into the Quagmire: Lyndon Johnson and the Escalation of the Vietnam War*. New York: Oxford University Press, 1991.

Wallerstein, Mitchell B. *Food for War—Food for Peace: United States Aid in a Global Context*. Cambridge, Mass.: MIT Press, 1980.

Walters, Vernon A. *Silent Missions*. Garden City, N.Y.: Doubleday, 1978.

Waltz, Kenneth. *Theory of International Politics*. Reading, Mass.: Addison-Wesley, 1979.

Weiner, Myron. "Assessing the Political Impact of Foreign Assistance." Chapter 3 in John W. Mellor (ed.), *India: The Rising Middle Power*. Boulder, Colo.: Westview Press, 1979.

Westerfield, H. Bradford. *Foreign Policy and Party Politics: From Pearl Harbor to Korea*. New Haven, Conn.: Yale University Press, 1955.

Westmoreland, William C. *A Soldier Reports*. Garden City, N.Y.: Doubleday, 1976.

Wicker, Tom. *JFK and LBJ: The Influence of Personality upon Politics*. New York: Penguin, 1968.

Wildavsky, Aaron. *The Politics of the Budgetary Process*, 2d ed. Boston: Little, Brown, 1974.

———. "The Two Presidencies." Chapter 19 of Aaron Wildavsky (ed.), *Perspectives on the Presidency*. Boston: Little, Brown, 1975.

———. "The Two Presidencies." Reprinted in Aaron Wildavsky (ed.), *The Presidency*. Boston: Little, Brown, 1969.

———, and Jeffrey Pressman. *Implementation: How Great Expectations in*

Washington Are Dashed in Oakland. Berkeley: University of California Press, 1971.

Williams, Phil. *The Senate and US Troops in Europe.* London: Macmillan, 1985.

Wilson, Woodrow. "Study of Administration." *Political Science Quarterly,* June 1887, reprinted in *Political Science Quarterly,* 56:4 (December 1941): 481–506.

Wolfers, Arnold L., and Lawrence I. Martin. *The Anglo-American Tradition in Foreign Affairs.* New Haven, Conn.: Yale University Press, 1956.

Wolfinger, Raymond E. "Nondecisions and the Study of Local Politics." *American Political Science Review* 65:4 (December 1971): 1063–1080.

Yost, David S. "Alternative Structures of European Security." *International Security Studies Program, Working Papers,* No. 81. Washington, D.C.: The Wilson Center, 1987.

Zysman, John. *Political Strategies for Industrial Order: State, Market, and Industry in France.* Berkeley: University of California Press, 1977.

Personal Interviews

Francis M. Bator, 17 November 1983.
Howard Wriggens, 31 October 1984.
McGeorge Bundy, 1 November 1984.
Harold Saunders, 26 November 1984.
Dean Rusk, 28 January 1986.
Orville L. Freeman, 10 May 1990.

Document Collections

Indian Famine File. National Security Files, LBJ Library.
Memos to the President. National Security Files, LBJ Library.
National Security Council (NSC) History. National Security Files, LBJ Library.

Index

DATE DUE		
PUBLIC AFFAIRS		
3·1	2:15	JUN 7 2002
3-1	4 10	
3·1	6:00	
3/2	9:00	JUN 2 7 2002
3-5	12:30	
MAR 7 1995		
OCT 1 4 1995		
FEB 1 1 1999		
MAR 2 0 2001		
2/9/02		
GAYLORD		PRINTED IN U.S.A.